RETROMANIA

by the same author

Blissed Out: The Raptures of Rock
The Sex Revolts: Gender, Rebellion and Rock 'n' Roll (with Joy Press)
Energy Flash: A Journey Through Rave Music and Dance Culture
Rip It Up and Start Again: Post-Punk 1978–84
Bring the Noise: 20 Years of Writing About Hip Rock and Hip Hop
Totally Wired: Post-Punk Interviews and Overviews

SIMON REYNOLDS

RETROMANIA

Pop Culture's Addiction to Its Own Past

faber and faber

First published in 2011
by Faber and Faber Ltd
Bloomsbury House
74–77 Great Russell Street
London WC1B 3DA

Typeset by Ian Bahrami
Printed in England by CPI Mackays, Chatham

A CIP record for this book is available from the British Library

ISBN 978–0–571–23208–6

10 9 8 7 6 5 4 3 2 1

In memory of my brother Tim.
And with love to my surviving brothers Jez and Hugo.

Contents

INTRODUCTION: The 'Re' Decade/The Retroscape ix
PROLOGUE: Don't Look Back: Nostalgia and Retro xxv

Part One: 'Now'

1 POP WILL REPEAT ITSELF: Museums, Reunions, Rock Docs, Re-enactments 3
2 TOTAL RECALL: Music and Memory in the Time of YouTube 55
3 LOST IN THE SHUFFLE: Record Collecting and the Twilight of Music as an Object 86
4 GOOD CITATIONS: The Rise of the Rock Curator 129
5 TURNING JAPANESE: The Empire of Retro and the Hipster International 162

Part Two: 'Then'

6 STRANGE CHANGES: Fashion, Retro and Vintage 183
7 TURN BACK TIME: Revival Cults and Time-Warp Tribes 202
8 NO FUTURE: Punk's Reactionary Roots and Retro Aftermath 240
9 ROCK ON (AND ON) (AND ON): The Never-Ending Fifties Revival 276

Part Three: 'Tomorrow'

10 GHOSTS OF FUTURES PAST: Sampling, Hauntology and Mash-Ups 311

11 OUT OF SPACE: Nostalgia for Giant Steps and Final Frontiers 362

The Retroscape (Slight Return) 399

12 THE SHOCK OF THE OLD: Past, Present and Future in the First Decade of the Twenty-First Century 403

Acknowledgements 429
Bibliography 431
Index 441

For footnotes and additional material related to the book, go to the blog Retromania – The Footnotes at http://retromaniafootnotes.blogspot.com/

INTRODUCTION

The 'Re' Decade

We live in a pop age gone loco for retro and crazy for commemoration. Band reformations and reunion tours, tribute albums and box sets, anniversary festivals and live performances of classic albums: each new year is better than the last one for music from yesteryear.

Could it be that the greatest danger to the future of our music culture is . . . *its past*?

Maybe that sounds unnecessarily apocalyptic. But the scenario I'm imagining isn't a cataclysm so much as a gradual winddown. This is the way that pop ends, not with a BANG but with a box set whose fourth disc you never get around to playing and

---

THE RETROSCAPE

2000/April: The Smithsonian Institution's Memphis Rock 'n' Soul Museum opens >>>>>>> 2000/May: Julien Temple's Sex Pistols doc *The Filth and the Fury* is released, kicking off a decade-spanning trilogy of punk documentaries by the director of *The Great Rock'n'Roll Swindle* >>>>>>> 2000/June: The Experience Music Project, a huge rock'n'pop museum founded by billionaire infotech mogul Paul Allen, opens in Seattle >>>>>>> 2001/July: Garage-rock revivalists The White Stripes release their commercial breakthrough album *White Blood Cells* to huge acclaim >>>>>>> 2001/November: Here and Now, a nostalgia revue offering 'The Very Best of the 80s', tours the UK, with reanimated stars Paul Young, Kim Wilde, Curiosity Killed the Cat, Heaven 17, Go West, T'Pau and Nick Heyward performing to 60,000 across seven arenas >>>>>>> 2002/February: *Spring Term*, a compilation spinning off the seventies/eighties nostalgia club School Disco, hits no. 1 in the UK

an overpriced ticket to the track-by-track restaging of the Pixies or Pavement album you played to death in your first year at university.

Once upon a time, pop's metabolism buzzed with dynamic energy, creating the surging-into-the-future feel of periods like the psychedelic sixties, the post-punk seventies, the hip-hop eighties and the rave nineties. The 2000s felt different. *Pitchfork* critic Tim Finney noted 'the curious slowness with which this decade marches forward'. He was specifically monitoring electronic dance music, which all through the nineties had been pop culture's vanguard, hurling forth a new Next Big Thing every season. But Finney's observation can be applied not just to dance music but to popular music in its entirety. The sensation of moving forward grew fainter as the decade unfurled. Time itself seemed to become sluggish, like a river that starts to meander and form oxbow lakes.

If the pulse of NOW felt weaker with each passing year, that's because in the 2000s the pop present became ever more crowded out by the past, whether in the form of archived memories of yesteryear or retro-rock leeching off ancient styles. Instead of being about itself, the 2000s has been about every other previous decade happening again all at once: a simultaneity of pop time

>>>>>>> 2002/April: Release of *24 Hour Party People*, a sort of 'collective biopic' focused on Factory Records boss Tony Wilson but including Joy Division, Martin Hannett, Happy Mondays and the Hacienda >>>>>>> 2002/May: Mash-up craze reaches the mainstream as Sugababes' 'Freak Like Me' hits no. 1 – it's their 'cover' of Richard X aka Girls On Top's 'We Don't Give a Damn About Our Friends', a mash-up of Gary Numan's 'Are "Friends" Electric?' and Adina Howard's 'Freak Like Me' >>>>>>> 2002/July: School Disco's nostalgia festival *School Fields* on Clapham Common draws 40,000-strong crowd, many wearing school-uniform-style ties and pleated skirts >>>>>>> 2003/March: Young British artists Iain Forsyth and Jane Pollard's *File Under Sacred Music*, an event at London's ICA, is a re-enactment of a 1978 show by The Cramps at the Napa State Mental Institute, California >>>>>>> 2003/March: 251 Menlove Avenue, John Lennon's childhood home in Liverpool, is opened to the public, having been acquired by Yoko Ono, donated to the National Trust and painstakingly restored to fifties style >>>>>>> 2003 November: *Let It Be . . . Naked*, a version of the final Beatles album stripped of Phil Spector's added-on-after-the-fact or-

that abolishes history while nibbling away at the present's own sense of itself as an era with a distinct identity and feel.

Instead of being the threshold to the future, the first ten years of the twenty-first century turned out to be the 'Re' Decade. The 2000s were dominated by the 're-' prefix: *revivals, reissues, remakes, re-enactments*. Endless *re*trospection: every year brought a fresh spate of anniversaries, with their attendant glut of biographies, memoirs, rockumentaries, biopics and commemorative issues of magazines. Then there were the band *re*formations, whether it was groups *re*uniting for nostalgia tours in order to *re*plenish (or to bloat still further) the members' bank balances (Police, Led Zeppelin, Pixies . . . the list is endless) or as a prequel to *re*turning to the studio to *re*launch their careers as recording artists (Stooges, Throbbing Gristle, Devo, Fleetwood Mac, My Bloody Valentine et al.).

If only it was just the old music and old musicians coming back, in archived form or as reanimated performers. But the 2000s was also the decade of rampant *re*cycling: bygone genres *re*vived and *re*novated, vintage sonic material *re*processed and *re*combined. Too often with new young bands, beneath their taut skin and rosy cheeks you could detect the sagging grey flesh of old ideas.

---

chestral overdubs and embellishments, is released >>>>>>> 2003/December: The Doors of the 21st Century – Ray Manzarek and Robbie Krieger plus The Cult's Ian Astbury as ersatz Jim Morrison – play Wembley Arena, the climax to a year of touring and legend-milking. Original drummer John Densmore and the Morrison estate are not happy and eventually win an injunction against the use of The Doors' name >>>>>>> 2004/spring–summer: The Pixies re-form for a tour that takes in the US, Europe, Brazil and Japan, an emotionally fraught reunion documented in the rock doc *loudQUIETloud* >>>>>>> 2004/September: Brian Wilson releases SMiLE, his attempt (with Van Dyke Parks) to complete the legendarily unfinished Beach Boys album *Smile*, which was started in 1966 >>>>>>> 2004/October: *Chronicles, Volume 1*, the first instalment of Bob Dylan's memoirs, is published to much acclaim >>>>>>> 2005/February to November: Mötley Crüe's reunion tour grosses almost $40 million and becomes the eleventh most lucrative US tour of the year >>>>>>> 2005/March: Queen embark on a massive world concert tour, with deceased frontman Freddie Mercury replaced by Paul Rodgers of Free/Bad Company >>>>>>> 2005/July: *No*

As the 2000s proceeded, the interval between something happening and its being *re*visited seemed to shrink insidiously. The *I Love the [Decade]* TV series created by the BBC and adapted by VH1 for America hurtled through the seventies, eighties and nineties, and then – with *I Love the New Millennium*, which aired in the summer of 2008 – wrapped up the 2000s before the decade was even over. Meanwhile, the *re*issue industry's tentacles have already reached the late nineties, with box sets and remastered/ expanded versions of German minimal techno, Britpop and even Morrissey's lamest run of solo albums. The rising tide of the historical past is lapping at our ankles. As for *re*vivals, the music scene mostly abided by the Twenty-Year Rule of Revivalism: the eighties were 'in' for much of the 2000s, in the form of the post-punk, electropop and most recently Goth resurgences. But you also had precocious glimpses of nineties revivalism, with the nu-rave fad and the rise of shoegaze, grunge and Britpop as reference points for new indie bands.

The word 'retro' has a quite specific meaning: it refers to a self-conscious fetish for period stylisation (in music, clothes, design) expressed creatively through pastiche and citation. Retro in its strict sense tends to be the preserve of aesthetes, connoisseurs and collectors, people who possess a near-scholarly depth

---

Direction Home: Bob Dylan, Martin Scorsese's two-part rock-doc mini-series about Dylan in the sixties, is a global event >>>>>>> 2005/August–September: The first 'Don't Look Back' season of classic albums played in their original order includes The Stooges doing *Funhouse*, Gang of Four performing *Entertainment!* and Dinosaur Jr playing *You're Living All Over Me* >>>>>>> 2005/October: Cream play three shows at Madison Square Garden and gross $10.6 million >>>>>>> 2005/December: Coldplay release the single 'Talk', which recycles the chord sequence from Kraftwerk's 1980 'Computer Love', with the German synth-pioneers' permission and blessing >>>>>>> 2006/January: *Rock of Ages*, a musical that does for eighties Sunset Strip hair metal what *Grease* did for fifties rock'n'roll and *Mama Mia!* did for ABBA, premieres at The Vanguard, Los Angeles. MTV smashes by Journey, Bon Jovi, Twisted Sister, Poison, Whitesnake et al. soundtrack the story of a 'legendary Hollywood rock club facing its demise at the hands of eager developers'. What the *Los Angeles Times* hails as 'a burst of retro adrenaline' then moves to Las Vegas for a sell-out run at the Flamingo Las Vegas Hotel and Casino, and then on to New York and Broadway

of knowledge combined with a sharp sense of irony. But the word has come to be used in a much more vague way to describe pretty much anything that relates to the relatively recent past of popular culture. Following this looser common usage of the word, *Retromania* investigates the entire range of contemporary uses and abuses of the pop past. This includes phenomena such as the vastly increased presence in our lives of old pop culture: from the availability of back-catalogue records to YouTube's gigantic collective archive and the massive changes in music consumption engendered by playback devices like the iPod (which often functions as a personal 'oldies' radio station). Another major area is the natural greying of rock music some fifty years into its existence: performers from the past who stick around, continuing to tour and record, as well as artists who mount comebacks after a long period of retirement. Finally, there's 'new old' music made by young musicians who draw heavily on the past, often in a clearly signposted and arty way.

Earlier eras had their own obsessions with antiquity, of course, from the Renaissance's veneration of Roman and Greek classicism to the Gothic movement's invocations of the medieval. But there has never been a society in human history so obsessed with the cultural artifacts of *its own immediate past*. That is what

---

>>>>>>> 2006/March: Having already re-formed to play concerts, the surviving members of the original line-up of The Stooges release their first studio album in over twenty years, *The Weirdness* >>>>>>> 2006/March: VH1 Classic sponsor a joint tour by Blondie and The New Cars (featuring Todd Rundgren on vocals as a prosthesis for the unwilling Ric Ocasek). Blondie's latest greatest-hits package is promoted by the single 'Rapture Riders', a mash-up of their disco-rap hit 'Rapture' with The Doors' 'Riders on the Storm' >>>>>>> 2006/June: Cirque du Soleil's Beatles extravaganza *Love* opens in Las Vegas >>>>>>> 2006/July: VH1 Classic airs a documentary on Platinum Weird, a legendary lost soft-rock group who paved the way for Fleetwood Mac. The doc features Mick Jagger, Elton John and Ringo Starr, but the band is fictitious, a concoction of Dave 'Eurythmics' Stewart and Kara DioGuardi's launched earlier in the year with fake fan sites on the Web. The album *Make Believe*, ten recordings 'from 1974', is released in the autumn >>>>>>> 2006/August: MTV celebrates its twenty-fifth birthday by re-broadcasting the entirety of its first twenty-four hours output from 1 August 1981 >>>>>>> 2006/September: Elton John and Bernie

distinguishes retro from antiquarianism or history: the fascination for fashions, fads, sounds and stars that occurred within living memory. Increasingly, that means pop culture that you already experienced the first time around (as a *conscious*, pop-aware person, as opposed to stuff that you lived through unaware as a small child).

This kind of retromania has become a dominant force in our culture, to the point where it feels like we've reached some kind of tipping point. Is nostalgia stopping our culture's ability to surge forward, or are we nostalgic precisely because our culture has stopped moving forward and so we inevitably look back to more momentous and dynamic times? But what happens when we run out of past? Are we heading towards a sort of cultural–ecological catastrophe, when the seam of pop history is exhausted? And out of all the things that happened this past decade, what could possibly fuel tomorrow's nostalgia crazes and retro fads?

I'm not alone in feeling perplexed by these prospects. I've lost count of the number of hand-wringing newspaper columns and blog posts that worry about what happened to innovation and upheaval in music. Where are the major new genres and sub-cultures of the twenty-first century? Sometimes it's the musicians themselves who sound a note of weary déjà vu. In a 2007

Taupin release a sequel to the 1975 semi-autobiographical concept album *Captain Fantastic & the Brown Dirt Cowboy*. It's titled *The Captain & the Kid*, and although the title track warns 'and you can't go back, and if you try it fails', its sales figures are nearly twice those of its immediate precursor, 2004's *Peachtree Road*, described by Elton as 'probably one of my lowest-selling albums of all time' >>>>>>> 2006/November: *Love*, a collection of re-mixed and mashed-up Beatles classics, wrought by George Martin and his son Giles as the soundtrack to Cirque du Soleil's Las Vegas stage show of the same name, debuts at no. 4 in *Billboard* and no. 3 in the UK charts >>>>>>> 2006/winter: Lou Reed performs his classic *Berlin* album in its entirety for the first time; Martin Stephenson and the Daintees also perform their 'classic' *Boat to Bolivia* album in its entirety for the first time >>>>>>> 2006/2007/2008: Having re-formed once already in 1996 for the Filthy Lucre tour, The Sex Pistols reunite again for five UK gigs and several European festivals >>>>>>> 2007/February: Young British artist Jo Mitchell stages a re-enactment at London's ICA of *Concerto for Voice and Machinery*, a notorious 1984 performance-cum-riot involving members of Ger-

interview, Sufjan Stevens declared: 'Rock and roll is a museum piece. . . . There are great rock bands today – I love the White Stripes, I love the Raconteurs. But it's a museum piece. You're watching the History Channel when you go to these clubs. They're just reenacting an old sentiment. They're channeling the ghosts of that era – the Who, punk rock, the Sex Pistols, whatever. It's been done. The rebellion's over.'

This malaise is not restricted to pop music, of course. Look at the Hollywood mania for remaking blockbuster movies from a couple of decades earlier: *Alfie, Ocean's Eleven, Bad News Bears, Casino Royale, The Pink Panther, Hairspray, Journey to the Center of the Earth, Fame, Tron, True Grit* . . . The near future promises remakes of *The Fly* (yes, it's being made for the third time), *The Incredible Shrinking Man, The Dirty Dozen* . . ., while Russell Brand is due to star in remakes of *Arthur* and *Drop Dead Fred*. When they're not revamping proven box-office successes of the past, the movie industry is adapting much-loved 'iconic' TV series for the big screen, like *The Dukes of Hazzard, Charlie's Angels* and *Get Smart*, along with bygone kiddy cartoons like *Yogi Bear* and *The Smurfs*. Somewhere between the two is the *Star Trek* that hit cinema screens in mid-2009: not strictly a remake but a prequel (the ad slogan drips with unintentional irony: 'The Future

man metal-bashing ensemble Einstürzende Neubauten which also took place at the ICA >>>>>>> 2007/March: Retro-rap outfit The Cool Kids release their debut EP *Totally Flossed Out*. Their big anthem is '88', a celebration of hip hop's wonder year – which also happens to be the year that the younger half of the duo, Mikey Rocks, was born. The *New York Times* reveals they are part of a back-to-the-golden-age-of-rap, lo-fi-sounding movement alongside Kidz in the Hall and The Knux, whose Krispy Kream says, 'We recorded songs in the worst way possible so you get a certain feel from it, like an old hip-hop record from 1990 or whenever' >>>>>>> 2007/April: Rage Against the Machine reunite to headline the final night of the Coachella Valley Music and Arts Festival in California >>>>>>> 2007/April: Theatre of Hate's *Westworld* twenty-fifth anniversary tour >>>>>>> 2007/June: Paul McCartney releases his twenty-first album, *Memory Almost Full*, full of elegiac songs like 'Ever Present Past', 'Vintage Clothes', 'That Was Me' and 'The End of the End'. 'All you've got is the past, really,' he tells one interviewer. 2007/September: Held at a Scottish castle, Retrofest is the UK's first eighties-themed music festival. Promising 'the Biggest 80s Line-

Begins') featuring the young Spock and Kirk. This movie trades off the generation-spanning cumulative affection created by the original sixties TV series, the eighties film versions and the subsequent *Star Trek: The Next Generation* TV series.

Theatre has a long tradition of reviving canonic plays and much-loved musicals, but here too you can see the remake and the spin-off catching on with productions like *Spamalot* (based on the movie *Monty Python and the Holy Grail*) and 'jukebox musicals' written around golden oldies by legendary bands or drawn from vintage genres: *We Will Rock You* (Queen), *Good Vibrations* (Beach Boys), *The Times They Are A-Changin'* (Bob Dylan) and *Rock of Ages* (eighties hair metal). There's even 'jukebox TV' with shows like *Glee* and *Pop Idol/American Idol* (with its Beatles nights, Stones nights et al.), which fold rock and soul back into the non-threatening tradition of showbiz/light entertainment/variety. Television has even got in on the remake action, albeit with generally less success than Hollywood. People in the industry describe the contemporised version of the classic TV series as 'a presold concept', but so far the attempts – glitzy remakes of *The Prisoner*, *The Survivors*, *The Rockford Files*, *Charlie's Angels*, *Dragnet*, *The Twilight Zone*, *The Fugitive*, *Kojak*, *Bionic Woman*, *Hawaii Five-O*, *Beverly Hills 90210*, *Dallas*, plus Britcom favourites like *Minder*,

---

up since Live Aid', it features The Human League, Spandau Ballet's Tony Hadley, ABC, Howard Jones, Kajagoogoo and Bananarama, among many others. 2007/September: *Control*, Anton Corbijn's biopic of Joy Division's Ian Curtis, is released >>>>>> 2007/winter: Treading the UK boards again are Madness, Happy Mondays, Hugh Cornwell and band, The Stranglers (Not Featuring Hugh Cornwell), Ian Hunter, New Model Army, The Men They Couldn't Hang and the movie-fictional Irish soul band The Commitments. There's also The Pogues doing their twenty-fifth anniversary tour and The Wedding Present doing The *George Best* 20th Anniversary Tour, while tribute band The Other Smiths embark on a Strangeways Tour devoted to The Smiths' last album *Strangeways Here We Come* plus 'Best of Most of 1984–2006'. In a competitive season, though, the Pure Sadness Prize goes to the twenty-two-date tour by From the Jam, which is Bruce Foxton and Rick Buckler but not Paul Weller >>>>>> 2007/2008: The Police Reunion Tour plays 159 arena-size concerts across the world between 28 May 2007 and 7 August 2008, grossing over $340 million and becoming the third most lucrative tour of all time >>>>>> 2007/2008: Sonic Youth

Reggie Perrin and *The Likely Lads* – have not 'sold' especially well in terms of ratings (indeed, in America these remakes often get cancelled before the season is through). Still, people keep trying: the logic of renovating the tried-and-true, of milking the cult status of the original, seems an irresistible pitch.

Then there's fashion, where rummaging through yesterday's wardrobe closet has been integral to the industry for some time, but whose recycling of old ideas nonetheless seemed to reach a frenzied rate of rotation this last decade. Designers like Marc Jacobs and Anna Sui ransacked the styles of previous epochs almost as soon as they ended. The market for vintage clothing boomed ('vintage' now meaning as recently as the eighties, with designers like Azzedine Alaia in huge demand), and this was paralleled by the 'antique-isation' of furniture and artifacts from the second half of the twentieth century, as the shelter magazines went nuts for mid-century modern furniture.

Those are just some of the most visibly fevered zones of retromania. But there's also retro toys (crazes for everything from the View-Master to the Blythe doll of the early seventies) and retrogaming (playing and collecting old-school computer, video and arcade games from the eighties). There's retro food (sandwich chain Pret A Manger offers 'Retro Prawn on Artisan', a sort

---

perform their hallucinatory, epoch-defining 1988 album *Daydream Nation* at twenty-four concerts in the US, Spain, Germany, France, Italy, the UK, Australia and New Zealand >>>>>>> 2008/February: Tribute bands The Clone Roses and The Smiths Indeed team up for a double bill that never happened in historical reality (The Smiths played their last UK concert on 12 December 1986, when the Roses were unknowns). Keeping the theme Mancunian is the night's DJ, Clint Boon of Inspiral Carpets, who are actually embarking on their own Return of the Cow tour the following month >>>>>>> 2008/February–March: Bettye Swann-abe Duffy is number one in the UK for five weeks with 'Mercy', a slice of retro-soul whose intro samples the opening bars of Ben E. King's 'Stand By Me' and which ends up the third-best selling single of the year >>>>>>> 2008/February–March: The Mission play a four-date concert series at London's Shepherd's Bush Empire, performing 'an entire album' per night 'plus all B sides from the singles of that time' >>>>>>> 2008/April: Mudcrutch, Tom Petty's not-actually-fake 'lost group' from his pre-Heartbreakers early-seventies period, re-form, tour and record an album of their vintage material. Petty: 'We left

xvii

of poshed-up sandwich version of that seventies fave the Prawn Cocktail), and there's also retro interior design, retro candy, retro ring-tones, retro travel and retro architecture. You even get retro-style commercials on television now and then, like the one for Heinz Baked Beans that mega-mixes snippets from vintage UK ads from the sixties, seventies and eighties, capped off with the imperishable slogan 'Beanz Meanz Heinz'. But strangest of all is the demand for retro porn: collectors who specialise in erot-ica and skin mags from particular periods; websites with scores of specialist categories such as 'retro face-sitting', 'retro big tits,' 'natural' (breasts from before boob jobs became widespread) and 'vintage hairy' (porn from before the era of the Brazilian wax). Phone-line ads on cable-TV porn stations are punctuated every so often with interludes from black-and-white stag movies and nudie reels from the fifties (or even earlier), inviting the mel-ancholy thought that the lascivious ladies cavorting in them are now either in assisted-living facilities or – gulp – food for worms.

For all its ubiquity across culture, retro-consciousness nonethe-less seems most chronically prevalent in music. That may well be because it somehow feels especially *wrong* there. Pop ought to be all about the present tense, surely? It is still considered the domain of the young, and young people aren't supposed to be nostalgic;

some music back there and it was time to go get it' >>>>>>> 2008/May: Public Enemy per-form their incendiary, epoch-defining 1988 album *It Takes a Nation of Millions to Hold Us Back* at London's Brixton Academy, Glasgow's ABC1 and the Manchester Academy >>>>>>> 2008/May: Sparks trump everybody else in the play-your-classic-LP-in-the-right-order stakes by performing all twenty of their albums over twenty nights at the Islington Academy, London, climaxing on the twenty-first night with the unveiling of their new and twenty-first album at the Shepherd's Bush Empire >>>>>>> 2008/summer: A decade after disintegrating My Bloody Valentine re-form for a worldwide tour, playing to a legion of *Loveless* lovers who never saw them the first time plus long-term fans back for punish-ment after being deafened in 1992 >>>>>>> 2008/September: Late-eighties/early-nineties retro infiltrates prime-time TV: *Gossip Girl*'s middle-aged alt-rocker dad Rufus Humphrey re-forms his one-hit-wonder grunge-lite band Lincoln Hawk for a support-slot tour. 'Oh my god, I just got the call. We're opening for The Breeders. I guess the Luscious Jackson re-union didn't work out' >>>>>>> 2008/September: Echo and the Bunnymen perform their

they haven't been around long enough to build up a backlog of precious memories. Likewise, the essence of pop is the exhortation to 'be here now', meaning both 'live like there's no tomorrow' *and* 'shed the shackles of yesterday'. Popular music's connection to the new and the now explains its unparalleled capacity to distil the atmosphere of a historical era. In period-drama movies and TV shows nothing conjures the vibe of an epoch more effectively than pop songs from that time. Nothing – except maybe fashion, which, intriguingly, is the other area of popular culture that's utterly rife with retro. In both cases, this very topicality, this date-stamped quality is what causes it to become quickly dated and then, after a decent interval, so potently epoch-evoking, so *revivable*.

In terms of mainstream pop music, many of the 2000s' most commercially prominent trends involved recycling: the garage-punk resurgence of The White Stripes, The Hives, The Vines, Jet et al.; the vintage-soul style of Amy Winehouse, Duffy, Adele and other young white Brit females who pass for black American lady singers from the sixties; eighties synth-pop-inspired femmes like La Roux, Little Boots and Lady Gaga. But where retro truly reigns as the dominant sensibility and creative paradigm is in hipster-land, pop's equivalent to highbrow. The very people who you would once have expected to produce (as artists) or champion (as

fourth album, *Ocean Rain*, in its entirety and in its original sequence at the Royal Albert Hall >>>>>>> 2008/autumn: Conde Nast's/*Vogue*'s Fashion Rocks supplement: Dhani Harrison dressed and moustached as father George *c.*1968, with blonde model Sasha Pivovarova playing the Patti Boyd role in luxe-bohemian look of wide-brimmed hat and furs >>>>>>> 2008/December: The Rock and Roll Hall of Fame Annex opens in downtown Manhattan, a New York-focused branch of the Cleveland-based Rock and Roll Hall of Fame and Museum >>>>>>> 2009/February: In synch with Black History Month, VH1 Classic launches a four-part series called *Black to the Future*, a celebration of African-American pop-cult ephemera in the kitschadelic vein of their *I Love the '70s/'80s/'90s* series >>>>>>> 2009/February: ArtCore – an exhibition of the 'visual culture' of acid house and rave – launches at Selfridges Ultralounge in London, to be followed by an auction of the work, which includes flyers for clubs and raves like Hacienda, Spectrum, Raindance, Tribal Gathering >>>>>>> 2009/February: Van Morrison releases an album with one of the least appetising titles of all time: *Astral Weeks Live at the Hollywood Bowl*. It's the document of his 'Don't

consumers) the non-traditional and the groundbreaking – *that's* the group who are most addicted to the past. In demographic terms, it's the exact same cutting-edge class, but instead of being pioneers and innovators, they've switched roles to become curators and archivists. The avant-garde is now an arrière-garde.

At a certain point the sheer mass of past accumulating behind the music began to exert a kind of gravitational pull. The sensation of movement, of going somewhere, could be satisfied as easily (in fact, *more* easily) by going backwards within that vast past than by going forwards. It was still an exploratory impulse, but now it took the form of archaeology.

You could see this syndrome starting to emerge as far back as the eighties, but it's really escalated in the last decade. The young musicians who've come of age during the last ten years or so have grown up in a climate where the musical past is accessible to an unprecedentedly inundating degree. The result is a recombinant approach to music-making that typically leads to a meticulously organised constellation of reference points and allusions, sonic lattices of exquisite and often surprising taste that span the decades and the oceans. I used to call this approach 'record-collection rock', but nowadays you don't even need to collect records any more, just harvest MP3s and cruise through YouTube. All the

---

Look Back'-style performance of his classic 1968 LP >>>>>>> 2009/March: A state-of-the-art, hi-tech rock'n'pop museum, the British Music Experience, opens at the O2 in London >>>>>>> 2009/April: A reissue programme for Nick Cave's entire discography kicks off. Every deluxe repackaging includes the CD plus a DVD containing a film about each album made by re-enactment artists Iain Forsyth and Jane Pollard >>>>>>> 2009/April–May: The Specials' original line-up (albeit with the singular exception of leader/founder Jerry Dammers) re-form for a thirtieth-anniversary reunion tour >>>>>>> 2009/May: The Breeders, who haven't technically re-formed because they just went very quiet for a very long time but never actually split, curate the All Tomorrow's Parties festival, featuring reactivated post-punkers Gang of Four, X and Wire, plus late-eighties/early-nineties alt-rock warhorses Shellac, Throwing Muses, Teenage Fanclub, Giant Sand and Th' Faith Healers >>>>>>> 2009/May: Great Gig in the Sea, the first Pink Floyd-themed cruise to the Bahamas, sets sail, promising two full shows by tribute band Think Floyd USA, including a track-by-track rendition of *Dark Side of the Moon* >>>>>>> 2009/June: Neil Young releases

sound and imagery and information that used to cost money and physical effort to obtain is available for free, just a few key and mouse clicks away.

It's not that nothing happened in the music of the 2000s. In many ways, there was a manic bustle of micro-trends, subgenres and recombinant styles. But by far the most momentous transformations related to our modes of consumption and distribution, and these have encouraged the escalation of retromania. We've become victims of our ever-increasing capacity to store, organise, instantly access, and share vast amounts of cultural data. Not only has there never before been a society so obsessed with the cultural artifacts of its immediate past, but there has never before been a society that is *able* to access the immediate past so easily and so copiously.

Yet *Retromania* is not a straightforward denunciation of retro as a manifestation of cultural regression or decadence. How could it be, when I'm complicit myself? As much as I've written as a journalist about 'brave new frontier' musics like rave and electronica, and as much as I've celebrated at book length movements like post-punk that were all about futurism, I'm also an avid participant in the retro culture: as a historian, as a reviewer of reissues, as a talking head in rock documentaries and as a sleeve-note writer.

---

the first volume of his long-awaited *Archives* project. The ten-disc box *Archives, Vol. 1: 1963–1972* is just the first of four such sets and contains unreleased music plus twenty hours of video, the 1974 Young doc *Journey Through the Past*, photos, lyrics, letters, memorabilia, a replica journal and audio of interviews, radio spots and concert raps >>>>>>> 2009/July: Release of *Horehound* by The Dead Weather, a retro-rock supergroup featuring Jack White of The White Stripes and The Kills singer Alison Mosshart (whose image/voice channels Patti Smith). Meanwhile, Kills guitarist Jamie Hince (whose playing channels Dr Feelgood's Wilko Johnson) starts thinking about forming a group with his girlfriend Kate Moss >>>>>>> 2009/August: Forty years to the minute after The Beatles crossed Abbey Road on 8 August 1969 for the front-cover photograph of the *Abbey Road* LP, the owner of The Beatles Coffee Shop, Richard Porter, conducts a special Beatles tour across the road >>>>>>> 2009/August: Ang Lee's movie *Taking Woodstock* is released on the fortieth anniversary of the 1969 rock festival >>>>>>> 2009/September: Richard Hell, the man whose haircut and ripped T-shirt Malcolm McLaren ripped off for The Sex Pistols,

xxi

But it goes beyond professional involvement. As a music fan, I'm as addicted to *retro*spection as anybody: trawling the second-hand record stores, poring over rock books, glued to VH1 Classic and YouTube, ogling rock docs. I pine for the future that's gone AWOL on us, but I also feel the lure of the past.

Sifting through old articles of mine when researching this book, I was surprised to see the extent to which retro-related issues have been a long-running preoccupation. Amid all the wide-eyed burbling about the next big thing in music, its polar opposite – the peculiar burden upon rock of its own mounting history – has persistently cropped up as a cause for concern. Retro has haunted me, the ghostly inverse of 'the future' I'm better known for banging on (and on) about. Looking back, I can see that I've often been mustering all my resources of belief and optimism in an unconscious drive to cast aside that feeling of belatedness common to my generation: the negative birthright of all those who missed, as a conscious participant, the sixties or punk. As much as they catalysed belief, nineties movements like grunge and rave also triggered *relief* – finally, something on a par with the storied glory of the past was actually happening in our own time, in real time.

I've had plenty of time and love for bands who could easily be dismissed as mere retro pastiche. It's caused me to resort to ingenious arguments and tortured metaphors to explain why a particular adored band is not just another grave-robbing necrophile. The most recent example is Ariel Pink, who is probably

releases a re-recorded version of The Voidoids' second album, *Destiny Street*, entitled *Destiny Street Repaired* >>>>>>> 2009/September: The Beatles' long-awaited remastered albums, plus two highly priced deluxe box sets of their discography in both stereo and mono versions, top the LP charts worldwide. In the video-game charts, *The Beatles: Rock Band* outsells *Guitar Hero 5* >>>>>>> 2009/September: Disney and Apple Corps strike a deal for Robert Zemeckis's 3D motion-capture adaptation of the 1968 Beatles-inspired animation movie *Yellow Submarine* >>>>>>> 2009/October: The Pixies tour the in-sequence entirety of *Doolittle* to celebrate its twentieth anniversary, and there is talk of them actually making a brand-new album, their sixth, in the studio >>>>>>> 2009/November: Kraftwerk

my favourite musician of the 2000s, and whose *Before Today* was widely acclaimed as one of 2010's best albums. Without a trace of embarrassment, Ariel describes his sound, woven out of blurry echoes of halcyon radio pop from the sixties, seventies and eighties, as 'retrolicious'. And it is! Nostalgia is, after all, one of *the* great pop emotions. And sometimes that nostalgia can be the bittersweet longing pop feels for its own lost golden age. To put that another way: some of the great artists of our time are making music whose primary emotion is towards *other* music, *earlier* music. But then again, isn't there something profoundly wrong about the fact that so much of the greatest music made during the last decade sounds like it could have been made twenty, thirty, even forty years earlier?

Up until now, the introduction to a book has always been the last thing I've written. This time I'm starting at the beginning. I don't have that much sense of what I'm going to discover before I set off. This book is very much an investigation – not just of the hows and whys of retro as a culture and an industry but also of the larger issues to do with living *in*, living *off* and living *with* the past. Given that I enjoy many aspects of retro, why do I still feel deep down that it is lame and shameful? How new is this retromania phenomenon, and how far back in pop's history can its roots be traced? Is retromania here to stay or will it one day get left behind, revealed to have been just a historical phase? If so, what lies beyond it?

---

release *12345678: The Catalogue*, which is their entire discography (bar three early experimental efforts) remastered and repackaged >>>>>>> 2009/November: Sonic Youth make a cameo appearance in *Gossip Girl* as the wedding band for Rufus Humphrey's nuptials, playing an acoustic version of 1986's 'Starpower' >>>>>>> 2009/December: John 'I have never, ever been interested in repeating myself' Lydon re-forms Public Image Ltd for a series of gigs to celebrate the thirtieth anniversary of *Metal Box*, albeit not with the line-up that made the album (which included Keith Levene and Jah Wobble) but with the late-eighties incarnation. A US tour follows in spring 2010 >>>>>>> 2009/December: The Flaming Lips release a cover version of Pink Floyd's *Dark Side of the Moon* >>>>>>>

Prologue
Don't Look Back
Nostalgia and Retro

Nostalgia as both word and concept was invented in the seventeenth century by the physician Johannes Hofer to describe a condition afflicting Swiss mercenaries on long tours of military duty. Nostalgia was literally homesickness, a debilitating craving to return to the native land. Symptoms included melancholy, anorexia, even suicide. Up until the later years of the nineteenth century, this malady (in retrospect, obviously psychosomatic) remained the concern of military doctors, because maintaining morale was crucial to successful warfare.

So nostalgia originally referred to a longing to return through space, rather than across time; it was the ache of displacement. Gradually it shed these geographical associations and became a temporal condition: no longer an anguished yearning for the lost motherland but a wistful pining for a halcyon lost time in one's life. As it became de-medicalised, nostalgia also began to be seen not just as an individual emotion but as a collective longing for a happier, simpler, more innocent age. The original nostalgia had been a *plausible* emotion in the sense that there was a remedy (catching the first warship or merchant vessel back home and returning to the warm hearth of kith and kin, a world that was *familiar*). Nostalgia in the modern sense is an impossible emotion, or at least an incurable one: the only remedy would involve time travel.

This change of meaning doubtless came about because mobility became more commonplace and unremarkable, thanks to mass immigration to the New World and the movement of settlers and pioneers within the Americas; to colonial or military service by Europeans in their various empires; and to the increases in the number of individuals who relocated for migrant work opportunities or to advance their careers. Nostalgia for the past also intensified because the world was changing faster. Economic transformations, technological innovations and sociocultural shifts all meant that for the first time there were increasingly stark differences between the world that you grew up in and the world in which you grew old. From landscapes dramatically altered through development ('It were all fields round here when I were a lad') to new technologies affecting the feel and rhythm of everyday life, the world in which you had felt at home gradually disappeared. The present became a foreign country.

By the middle of the twentieth century, nostalgia was not considered a pathology any more but a universal emotion. It could apply to individuals (a morbid harking back to the past) or to society at large. Often the latter has taken the form of a reactionary longing for an old social order considered more stable owing to its clearly defined class structure, where 'everybody knew their place'. But nostalgia hasn't always served the forces of conservatism. Radical movements throughout history have often envisioned their goals not as revolutionary but resurrectionary: restoring things to how they used to be, a golden age of social equilibrium and justice that had been interrupted by historical trauma or by ruling-class machinations. In the build up to the English Civil War, for instance, the parliamentarians saw themselves as conservatives and King Charles I as the innovator expanding the powers of the Crown. Even the Levellers, one of the most radical factions active during Oliver Cromwell's interregnum following the king's execution, believed they were just upholding the Magna Carta and 'natural rights'.

Revolutionary movements have often constructed narratives based around 'paradise lost and paradise regained' scenarios. The Situationists, theorists of 1968's Paris riots, wrote of 'the lost totality': an Edenic state of social unity and individual non-alienation, which they believed existed before the era of industrial capitalism and the fragmented consciousness caused by class division, specialisation in the workplace and labour sold by the hour. The Situationists thought that automation would free humankind of the need to work, enabling it to recover the 'totality'. Similarly, some feminists believe in a lost primordial matriarchy that had once upon a time flourished free of domination and exploitation, with humankind placidly at one with itself and with Mother Nature.

What reactionary and radical nostalgias share is dissatisfaction with the present, which generally means the world created by the Industrial Revolution, urbanisation and capitalism. As this

---

NOSTALGIA AS REVERIE VERSUS NOSTALGIA AS RESTORATION

Theorist Svetlana Boym distinguishes between the personal and political manifestations of nostalgia with her dichotomy: reflective nostalgia versus restorative nostalgia. The latter ranges from curmudgeonly intransigence towards all things newfangled and progressive, to full-bore militant efforts to turn back the clock and restore an older order (ranging from recent American eruptions like the Tea Party movement and Glenn Beck's 2010 'Restoring Honor' rally to various flavours of theocratic fundamentalism, royalism, nativism, neo-fascist campaigns for an ethnically cleansed homeland, etc.). Restorative nostalgia tends to be big on pageantry (think of the Orange parades in Ulster), folklore and Romantic nationalism. These bolster the collective ego with tales of past glory, but also nurse ancient injuries and insults (think of the centuries-old grievances festering in the nations of the former Yugoslavia).

Reflective nostalgia, in contrast, is personal, eschewing the political arena

new era was ushered in, time itself became increasingly organised around the schedules of the factory and the office (and also school, which trained children for those workplaces) rather than natural cycles like dawn and dusk or the seasons. A component of nostalgia can actually be a hankering for a time before time: the perpetual present of childhood. That notion can also extend to entire past epochs (as with the Victorian fascination for the Medieval era) that are seen as History's equivalent to childhood. Svetlana Boym, author of *The Future of Nostalgia*, talks about how it's even possible to be 'nostalgic for a prenostalgic state of being'. And it's true that when I think wistfully about golden periods in my life, they all share this quality of total immersion in the now: childhood, or falling in love, or phases of total involvement in current music (post-punk when I was a teenager, the early rave scene during my late twenties).

Where pop nostalgia gets interesting is in that peculiar

---

altogether in favour of reverie, or sublimating itself through art, literature and music. Far from wanting to resurrect a lost golden age, reflective nostalgia takes pleasure in the misty remoteness of the past and cultivates the bittersweet pangs of poignancy. The danger of restorative nostalgia lies in its belief that the mutilated 'wholeness' of the body politic can be repaired. But the reflective nostalgic understands deep down that loss is irrecoverable: Time wounds all wholes. To exist in Time is to suffer through an endless exile, a successive severing from those precious few moments of feeling at home in the world.

In pop terms, Morrissey is the supreme poet of reflective nostalgia (although Ray Davies closely rivals him with 'Waterloo Sunset' and that autumnal almanac of English wistfulness, *The Kinks Are the Village Green Preservation Society*). Throughout The Smiths and his solo career, Morrissey mourns a place and a time (Manchester of the sixties and seventies) where he never stole a happy hour. Now and then, though, Morrissey has crossed over into the restorative nostalgia danger zone, with controversial public gestures (wrapping himself in the Union Jack at a rock festival), ambiguous songs ('The National Front Disco') and unguarded interview comments (observing to the *NME* in 2007 that today's England is barely recognisable as the country of his youth and attributing that partly to immigration).

nostalgia you can feel for the glory days of 'living in the now' that you didn't . . . actually . . . *live* through. Punk and the rock'n'roll fifties both stir feelings of this kind, but the Swinging Sixties beats all comers when it comes to triggering vicarious nostalgia. Ironically, it's the absence of revivalism and nostalgia during the sixties itself that partly accounts for why there have been endless sixties revivals ever since. Part of the period's attraction is its spirit of total immersion in the present. This was the decade that coined the slogan 'be here now', after all.

In the second half of the twentieth century, nostalgia became steadily more and more bound up with popular culture. It expressed itself *through* pop culture (revivals, golden-oldie shows on the radio, reissues et al.), but it would also be triggered *by* the pop culture of one's youth: artifacts of mass entertainment such as bygone celebrities and vintage TV shows, quaint commercials and dance crazes, ancient hit songs and dated slang. As Fred Davis argued in his 1979 study *Yearning for Yesterday: A Sociology of Nostalgia*, bygone mass culture increasingly superseded political events like wars and elections as the warp-and-weft of generational memory. So for those who grew up in the thirties, wistful memories are aroused by radio comedies and live musical broadcasts, whereas for those who grew up in the sixties and seventies, the markers are TV pop shows like *American Bandstand* and *Soul Train*, *Ready Steady Go* and *Top of the Pops*. And for a later generation still (many of them now making music and making waves) the nostalgia triggers are various aspects of the eighties' garish modernity: the gauche early stabs at video-as-art-form aired on MTV and the once-futuristic, now laughably primitive computer and arcade games of the day, along with the robotically jaunty melodies and day-glo synth tones of games music.

Nostalgia is now thoroughly entwined with the consumer-entertainment complex: we feel pangs for the products of yesteryear, the novelties and distractions that filled up our youth.

xxix

Eclipsing individual pursuits (like hobbies) or participatory local activities (like amateur sports), the mass media and pop culture take up an ever-increasing proportion of our mental lives. Which is why those *I Love the '70s/'80s/*etc. shows are so effective: the passage of our time has become indexed to the procession of rapidly obsolescing fads, fashions, celebrity careers et al.

The intersection between mass culture and personal memory is the zone that spawned retro. Time, perhaps, for a provisional definition distinguishing retro from other modes of relating to the past:

(1) Retro is always about the relatively immediate past, about stuff that happened in living memory.

(2) Retro involves an element of exact recall: the ready availability of archived documentation (photographic, video, music recordings, the Internet) allows for precision replication of the old style, whether it's a period genre of music, graphics or fashion. As a result, the scope for imaginative misrecognition of the past – the distortions and mutations that characterised earlier cults of antiquity like the Gothic Revival, for instance – is reduced.

(3) Retro also generally involves the artifacts of popular culture. This differentiates it from earlier revivals, which, as the historian Raphael Samuel points out, were based around high culture and originated from the higher echelons of society – aristocratic aesthetes and antiquarians with a rarified taste for exquisite collectables. Retro's stomping ground isn't the auction house or antique dealer but the flea market, charity shop, jumble sale and junk shop.

(4) A final characteristic of the retro sensibility is that it tends neither to idealise nor sentimentalise the past, but seeks to be amused and charmed by it. By and large, the approach is not

scholarly and purist but ironic and eclectic. As Samuel puts it, 'retrochic makes a plaything of the past'. This playfulness is related to the fact that retro is actually more about the present than the past it appears to revere and revive. It uses the past as an archive of materials from which to extract subcultural capital (hipness, in other words) through recycling and recombining: the bricolage of cultural bric-a-brac.

Where does the word 'retro' come from? According to the design historian Elizabeth Guffey, the term entered common parlance in the early sixties as a linguistic spin-off of the Space Age. Retro rockets provided reverse thrust and slowed a spaceship's propulsion. The connection of 'retro' to the era of sputnik and the space race lends itself to an appealing analogy: retro as the cultural counterpart to 'reverse thrust', with nostalgia and revivalism emerging in the seventies as a reaction against the sixties' full-tilt surge into the 'out there'.

As attractive as this notion is, though, it seems more likely that 'retro' came into use as a detached prefix that had gotten unstuck from 'retrospection', 'retrograde', 'retrogressive' and similar words. Terms starting with 'retro' tend to have a negative connotation, whereas 'pro' is attached to words like 'progress'. Retro itself is something of a dirty word. Few people like to be associated with it. The most bizarre example of this is the tragic story of Birmingham pub landlord Donald Cameron, who committed suicide in 1998 when owner Bass Breweries decided to convert his establishment into a retro theme pub called Flares. At the inquest, his ex-wife Carol talked about how the humiliating prospect of 'wearing a seventies outfit and a wig' plunged Cameron into despair. 'He felt he could not deal with any trouble in the pub. People would laugh at him because he looked ludicrous.' A few days after being reprimanded by his Bass bosses for obstinately turning up for work in his sharp nineties suit and tie, the thirty-nine-year-old father of two asphyxiated himself in his car.

That's an extreme reaction. But I did notice that people I approached for interviews were keen to stress that they had *nothing* to do with retro. These would often be people whose entire lives were dedicated to a particular bygone era of music or subculture. But retro? *Oh no* . . . It's not that people dislike the image of being obsessed with musty, mouldering old stuff, or of being a curmudgeon who thinks the present can't compare with the past. In fact, many proudly dismiss all modern pop culture. What makes them recoil from retro are the associations with camp, irony and mere trendiness. Retro, as far as they're concerned, signifies a shallow, surface-oriented attunement to style, as opposed to a deep, passionate love of a music's essence.

In many people's minds, retro is twinned with hipster, another identity that almost nobody embraces voluntarily, even when they outwardly appear to fit the profile completely. The last few years of the 2000s witnessed a spasm of hipster-hate, with a spate of magazine critiques of hipsterdom as pseudo-bohemia. These articles were then followed by meta-critiques examining the phenomenon of hipster-phobia itself, invariably pointing out that nobody would ever voluntarily describe themselves as a hipster, and that hipster-haters themselves usually fit the profile of the hipster rather closely. This orgy of hipster-inspired debate has paralleled – without quite overlapping – the journalistic subgenre that asks, 'Whatever happened to innovation?' Here retro tended to be used in a vague, all-encompassing way to refer to anything old-fashioned or derivative, with some futurist zealots (myself included sometimes) going so far as to use retro as a stick to bash any artist who is blatant about their influences and debts to specific ancestors.

Obviously, having influences is not retro per se. I don't totally agree with Norman Blake of Teenage Fanclub, who suggested to me once that 'Any music that *doesn't* sound like anything else in rock history always sounds *terrible*.' But how do you make music without a starting point? Most musicians, artists, writers learn how to do what they do by copying, to begin with at least. Similarly, being a musical traditionalist does not automatically make you retro. A good way to illustrate this is to consider the British folk scene. The movement began at the very end of the nineteenth century as a form of antiquarian ethnomusicology: song collectors like Cecil Sharp traipsed up and down the British Isles making cylinder recordings of old men and women who were typically the last surviving people in their village to remember ancient folk ballads. But this preservationist project – documenting Britain's traditional music and, later, attempting to perform it as faithfully as possible – was nothing like retro in the modern sense. It was a deadly earnest business, freighted with political idealism (folk was deemed the People's Music and thus intrinsically left-wing). Gradually, as the British traditional scene developed, a schism grew between the purists and those who felt that keeping the music *vital* meant bringing contemporary elements into play. The latter took liberties with folk forms, changing the instrumentation or going electric, blending in non-indigenous influences and writing original songs with increasingly bohemian and countercultural lyrics.

Of today's younger generation of British folk singers, Eliza Carthy is considered a leading figure. What she does is on the surface conservative: she literally carries on the family business (the renovation of British traditional music) by following in the footsteps of her parents, Norma Waterson and Martin Carthy. But she might feature synthesizers in her music alongside acoustic instruments such as her own fiddle, or work in influences from trip hop or jazz. She happily records using state-of-the-art digital techniques. Closer to retro in the more precise sense is the American free-folk movement (sometimes known as freak folk or wyrd folk). These young minstrels – performers like Joanna Newsom,

Devendra Banhart, MV & EE, Wooden Wand, Espers – venerate the same late-sixties and early-seventies heyday of British folk during which Martin Carthy and Norma Waterson made their name, but they fixate on the more kooky figures from that time such as The Incredible String Band and Comus, or obscure artists like Vashti Bunyan. The free-folk outfits fetishise the acoustic and the analogue: they take great pains to get a vintage sound and use the right period instrumentation. The differences also come across in self-presentation and packaging. Eliza Carthy onstage and on album covers has been known to sport a nose ring and punky-style purple or crimson hair dye. In contrast, the free-folk troubadours signpost their allegiances to the lost golden age through their raggle-taggle clothing, long maiden-like tresses and beards. Their record artwork is often reverential and referential. Publicity photos of Espers evoke the woodland tableaux favoured by The Incredible String Band on their classic sixties albums; the cover of Wooden Wand and the Sky High Band's *Second Attention* recreates the lovers-snuggling-on-a-hilltop cover photograph of John and Beverley Martyn's 1970 album *Stormbringer*.

Where Eliza Carthy wants to update folk music and make it appeal to contemporary audiences, the freak-folk outfits want to bring the past *into* the present, like time travel. Folk is literally in Carthy's blood, it's something she grew up with; in contrast, the freak-folk artists' relationship with their sources is almost entirely mediated through recordings from a much earlier era, and is given further distance by being largely focused on British folk rather than the American counterparts of the same era. They have *zero interest* in contemporary practitioners like Carthy or even in the current activities of veterans of the original late-sixties/early-seventies Britfolk era like Richard Thompson.

'It's record collector music,' Byron Coley, one of the free-folk scene's journalistic champions and a record dealer himself, told music critic Amanda Petrusich. Rather than folk as a tradition

passed from generation to generation and learned through teaching or watching the music performed, free folk is 'a fabulous
simulation' based around listening to records. Coley: 'It was
largely guys, sitting alone in their rooms, at night, looking at liner
notes.' One of the genre's patron saints, the guitarist John Fahey,
was an obsessive record collector, and in his later years founded
the archival reissue label Revenant (it means a visible ghost or
reanimated corpse that returns after death to persecute the living)
through which to release the obscure primitivist folk, blues and
gospel he'd disinterred.

Developed in the nineteenth century but defining the twentieth, recording in all its forms is what ultimately created the conditions of possibility for retro. Audio recordings and other types
of documentation (photographic, video) not only provide retro
with its raw materials, they also create the sensibility, based as it is
on obsessive repeat-play of particular artifacts and focused listening that zooms in on minute stylistic details. 'It's a total paradigm
shift, it's completely screwed with our brains,' says Ariel Pink of
the shift between music sold as scores and music sold as records.
'The recording medium actually crystallises an event and makes
it more than the sum of the score. The feel of the moment is captured. That has changed everything – people being able to revisit
memories like that.' Poring over records allows sound-fiends like
Pink to isolate and replicate the specific qualities of bygone production styles and vocal modes. So on *Before Today*'s 'Can't Hear
My Eyes', for instance, there's a tom-tom roll where the drum
timbre, the feel of the pattern, is like a portal through time to the
end-of-the-seventies era of Gerry Rafferty's 'Baker Street' and
Fleetwood Mac's *Tusk*. Pink describes his music's relationship
to pop's past as 'preserving something that has died. Something
that's going extinct. And just saying, "No!!!" That's all it is for me,
as a music lover. I like to do things that I *like*. And what I like is
something that I don't *hear*.'

Pop's impact was dependent on records. Its qualities of now-ness and the way it penetrated deep into everyday life came about through records being played on the radio or being bought from stores by masses of people all within the same approximate time span, and then taken home and played over and over and over again. Musicians could reach many more people across the world, in a much more intimate and more pervasive way than they ever could by performing live to audiences. But records created a kind of feedback loop: there was now the possibility of getting stuck on a particular record or performer. Eventually, after pop built up enough history, it became possible to fixate on an earlier period you preferred to your own pop time. Ariel Pink: 'When people like sixties music, they live there for ever. They live in a moment when the person they are listening to was growing their hair long for the first time. They look at the pictures and they feel like they can actually live there. For my generation, we weren't even there' – he means biologically alive in the sixties; he was born in 1978 – 'so we really live "there". We have no concept of time.'

The phonographic recording is something of a philosophical scandal in that it takes a moment and makes it perpetual; it drives in the wrong direction down the one-way street that is Time. In another sense, one of the problems for pop music is that its essence is the Event – epoch-defining moments like Elvis Presley's appearance on *Ed Sullivan* or The Beatles arriving at JFK airport, Hendrix immolating 'The Star-Spangled Banner' at Woodstock or The Sex Pistols firing off expletives on the Bill Grundy show. But the very media it is dependent on and disseminated through – records and television – enable the Event to become permanent, subject to endless repetition. The moment becomes a monument.

i: 'NOW'

1

POP WILL REPEAT ITSELF

Museums, Reunions, Rock Docs, Re-enactments

At the outset I should make a confession: my gut feeling is that pop and the museum just don't go together. Actually, I'm not sure music of any kind really works in a museum, a place of hush and decorum. Museums are primarily visual, oriented around display, designed for the contemplative gaze. The crucial element of sound has either to be absent or suppressed. Unlike paintings or sculptures, you can't have sonic exhibits side by side; they interfere with each other. So music museums contain the ancillary stuff (instruments and stage costumes, posters and packaging) but not the main thing itself. Ephemera, not what's essential.

But it's also true that a museum – a becalmed resting place for works of art considered to have passed the test of time – is opposed to the vital energies of pop and rock. I'm with Nik Cohn here: writing at the end of the sixties, anxious about the art aspirations and respectability of recent rock, which boded a future of seated audiences 'applauding politely', his book *Awopbopaloobopalopbamboom* was an elegiac celebration of 'Superpop, the noise machine, and the image, hype and beautiful flash of rock'n'roll music'. Pop is about the momentary thrill; it can't be a permanent exhibit.

Walking towards the British Music Experience, the UK's big

3

new rock museum, on a weekday morning in August 2009, for a moment I think maybe, just maybe they've got the right idea. The museum is housed inside London's gigantic O2 entertainment complex, and the route across the plaza towards the silver bubble-dome takes you past gigantic blown-up photographs from the key stages of pop history: frozen moments of frenzy and delirium from Beatlemania and Bay City Rollermania, through snarling punks, shrieking Durannies to metal monsters and Madchester ravers.

My big worry, with rock museums, is always punk: that rift in rock time that consigned the Old Wave to History's dustbin. Can such an apocalyptic rupture be contained within the filing system of an archive and still retain its essence, the truth of its ruthlessness? Passing a roller-disco busy with pubescent girls whizzing around in glee and a pair of giant-size cutouts of Jarvis Cocker and Dizzee Rascal pointing me in the right direction, I reach the British Music Experience itself. To maintain a steady flow of visitors, punters are admitted at intervals, so we loiter in an anteroom which doubles as a gift shop. Just as we're about to be let in, 'Anarchy in the UK' comes over the sound system, right on cue to renew my uneasiness.

Before you get to the main exhibition area, you watch a short introductory film about how to get the most out of your Experience experience. 'Like rock'n'roll, there are no rules' but there is a timeline you can refer to 'in case you get lost in music'. Finally inside the Experience proper, my first impression is that it's been designed to mimic netspace. Instead of the high ceilings and empty spaces of a traditional museum, the British Music Experience is dim and intimate, with every corner flickering with LED activity. There's a central hub area surrounded by Edge Zones, rooms that each represent a chunk of British pop time (1966–70, or 1976–85, or . . .). So you can proceed through them in chronological sequence (in a clockwise circle) or criss-cross the

4

central concourse randomly, putting History into shuffle mode. In another Web 2.0 attempt to update and pep up the museum experience, the far interior wall of each room features a projected gallery of icons indicating specific performers, albums, events, trends, which you can scroll through and click on to find out more.

A subdued clamour fills the hub zone, mingling leakage of music from the seven chambers with the sound from various interactive displays in the central area. So you feel like you're immersed not just in electronic light but in a trans-temporal mush of music: 'Relax' + 'Rock Island Line' + 'West End Girls' + 'What Do I Get' + _____. Each pop-period room features Table Talk: four chairs with video screens on the backrest arrayed around a table, with each screen displaying an interview segment. So in the first Edge Zone you can eavesdrop on a sort of virtual dinner party attended by veterans of the early days of British rock'n'roll – Vince Eager, Joe Brown, Cliff Richard, Marty Wilde – where the main topic of conversation is the impact of Elvis in the UK.

Still, if you subtract the flashy state-of-the-art stuff, most of the Experience is fundamentally identical to what you get at an old-fashioned museum. Instead of cabinets of ethnological curiosities or stuffed animals, behind the glass you have relics from the world of UK pop and rock: instruments, stage clothes, concert posters, sheet music and record covers. In the fifties room that means things like a handbill for a musical boat cruise (the Floating Festival of Jazz) that went from London to Margate and back in 1958, or Johnny Kidd of the Pirates' black eyepatch. In the sixties room you get the Beatles frock worn by usherettes at the premiere of *A Hard Day's Night*, or the sitar played by Justin Hayward on The Moody Blues' *In Search of the Lost Chord*. After glam (Bowie's Thin White Duke outfit complete with Gitanes in the waistcoat pocket, etc.) punk is next. The introductory plaque informs the viewer, sensibly, that punk was 'shocking, novel and subversive'. Naturally none of this insurrectionary energy is transmitted by the lifeless objects on display: Pete Shelley's broken-in-twain Starway guitar, a Stranglers set list, and so forth.

Scrolling through the scores of punk-related topics projected onto the wall, I click on one icon that does gesture at the earth-shaking impact of 1977: 'Music Press Struggle to Nail the Essence of Punk'. Apparently the British rock papers couldn't 'quite create a satisfactory new language and scale of values to assess punk, so still employ their old values', resulting in The Clash being dubbed 'the new Beatles', The Jam as 'the new Who', The Stranglers as 'the new Doors', and so forth. These specific examples may be true, but it's odd that this is the only place where the museum acknowledges the music papers' existence, and not only does it downplay their role as a cultural agent, it argues that the British music press got punk *wrong*. Actually, it would be closer to historical truth to say that the UK weeklies – *NME*, *Sounds*, *Melody Maker* – were the prime arena in which punk could dramatise itself, given that many gigs were banned and radio play was minimal. So the music press was actually the forum in which the meaning of punk was thrashed out, fought over and disseminated across the country and around the world. The rock media not only documented history in real time (they were newspapers, whereas museums can only be about 'the olds'), they actually helped to make that history, to be a real creative force within it.

The jibe at the music papers reminded me of a famous singles-review column by the *NME*'s punk-era firebrand Julie Burchill. Written in October 1980, when diehard believer Burchill was embittered and disillusioned, the column starts with the declaration: 'There are two ways to view music. One is with tunnel vision, what I've got. If a record isn't by the Sex Pistols or Tamla Motown . . . it's just pointless. But how unhealthy! I'm just a cranky old punk past its prime. But the alternative is hideous, and it is the only alternative. It is to believe in ROCK'S RICH TAPESTRY.' Alluding to a TV series called *History of Rock* that left out the Pistols, Burchill accused: 'There can only be one reason . . . *fear*. Everyone just wants to forget the whole nasty thing and get back to leading a normal life . . . So many smug saps think they're rebels, but anything that can fit into ROCK'S RICH TAPESTRY is dead at heart.'

Rock (and rock writing) was always energised and focused by being *against*. But animosity, the sort of polarised vision that fuelled Burchill's snarling, strident rhetoric, has gone now, everywhere. Rock museums like the British Music Experience represent the triumph of the Tapestry, with even the most troubling threads, like The Sex Pistols, neatly woven into its fabric. The Old Wave/New Wave war is distant history, and that's the point of the rock museum: it presents music with the battle lines erased, everything wrapped up in a warm blanket of acceptance and appreciation. So Johnny Rotten, middle-aged and mellow now, admits that despite the 'I Hate Pink Floyd' T-shirt that got him the job as Sex Pistols singer, he always liked the Floyd (not just the Syd Barrett-era stuff but *Dark Side of the Moon*). And Elvis Costello, the nasty New Waver who once said abhorrent things just to wind up decrepit American hippies Stephen Stills and Bonnie Bramlett, can be found on TV hosting his show *Spectacle*, where he interviews the likes of James Taylor and Elton John and finds amiable common ground in a shared love of American roots music and singer-songwriter balladry.

Next I plunge into the eighties room, which contains indie (The Smiths et al.), metal (Iron Maiden, Def Leppard, etc.) and Hacienda-era Manchester. The final Edge Zone contains most of the nineties and all of the 2000s, which means that Britpop and the Brit female boom (Amy Winehouse, Kate Nash, Adele, Duffy et al.) are crammed together with The Spice Girls and the Brit Awards (both of which get a glass case each). British 'urban' music

7

(mostly meaning grime) is dealt with as Table Talk: MCs Dizzee Rascal, Kano and D Double E & Footsie chat about the 'recently evolved genre' and tease the other guest at the table, the BBC's veteran rap DJ Tim Westwood, for 'sleeping on grime'. It's striking that this last room, which feels cursory and rushed, covers a sixteen-year period, whereas the four-year stretches of 1962–6 and 1966–70 get a whole chamber each. The covert argument of the museum's structure would appear to be that any single year in the sixties was approximately four times more exciting than any year in the last decade and a half. Not that I disagree. And that bias probably mirrors the outlook of the average BME visitor, who leans towards middle age rather than youth.

Museums, by definition, can't have that much room for the present. But the Experience website had actually promised a final Edge Zone, a whole space dedicated to the future and the question of where music might go next. I must have missed it, though, because after the 1993–Present room I find myself back in the gift shop. On the way out, I notice a giant cut-out pop-star figure directing visitors to the museum that I didn't see on the way in: Johnny Rotten in all his safety-pinned glory. In my head I hear him singing, '*No future, no future/ No future for you.*'

LIBRARIANS OF ROCK

A few days later I visit what's meant to be a punk-rock response to the British Music Experience: the Rock'n'Roll Public Library. For five weeks in the late summer of 2009, former Clash guitarist Mick Jones is throwing open to the general public his personal archive of memorabilia, which is kept in a suite of Ladbroke Grove offices tucked directly under the Westway dual carriageway. Access is free (although for £10 you can buy a memory stick and scan in pages from the magazines, books and other printed material on display). The press release for the Rock'n'Roll Public

Library trumpets Jones's generosity as a 'direct artistic challenge to the likes of the corporate O2 British Music Experience' and advises visitors that despite the exhibition's sedate name, they should not 'expect peace and quiet'.

Actually, it is pretty quiet in there when I drop by at noontime on Saturday, the Portobello vintage-clothing market in full swing directly below. And it doesn't feel like a challenge to anything in particular, this cosy clutter of souvenirs and keepsakes, the detritus of a life spent rocking and rolling. Clash/punk-related artifacts (dusty amps, a Watkins Copicat effects box, a hand-drawn tour map from 1982 titled Rat Patrol Over South East Asia & Australia) jostle alongside bric-a-brac of the kind you'd find at the flea market on the other side of the road: vintage cameras, radios and Super-8 equipment, a Spike Milligan annual, a Diana Dors gatefold. In tune with The Clash's fascination with military glory, the walls are decorated with nineteenth-century watercolours of battle scenes and images from World War II, such as a print of US marines raising the Stars and Stripes on Iwo Jima.

Give or take the odd youngster, the visitors are mostly veterans of the punk wars. There's a middle-aged couple, the woman plump and with a purple streak in her hair, the guy wearing a Pistols T-shirt and a bedraggled Mohawk. And there's an endless supply of guys who all seem to wear the cowboy-like hats that The Clash and Big Audio Dynamite favoured. One of these stupid-hat diehards – a Mancunian Clash fan – sits down beside me and, already quite drunk even though it's not lunchtime yet, regales me with stories of climbing onstage at a Clash gig and being invited to play the A, E and G chords. Eventually I make my excuses and slope off into a side-room that's like a cavern of pop periodicals: issues of *Crawdaddy!* and *Trouser Press*, *CREEM* and *ZigZag*, squeezed into see-through bags and pinned neatly to the walls.

Pumping at moderate volume out of speakers all through the

office space there's a Radio Clash-style stream of Mick Jones's favourite tunes. 'Memo from Turner', a Mick Jagger song from the soundtrack to *Performance*, comes on. I flash on The Clash's the-time-is-NOW anthem '1977', with its iconoclastic chorus 'No Elvis, Beatles or the Rolling Stones in 1977', then notice the signed poster for the Beatles Royal Command Performance at the London Palladium in 1963, the framed photo of the young Jagger and Richards. But The Clash long ago stitched themselves into a corner of Rock's Rich Tapestry – as early as *London Calling*, which re-rooted punk in the riches of rock'n'roll and Americana, and was duly anointed Greatest Album of the Eighties by *Rolling Stone*.

Browsing the Rock'n'Roll Public Library, I think back to seeing Mick Jones on TV in 2003, when The Clash were getting inducted into the Rock and Roll Hall of Fame. The latter, co-founded by *Rolling Stone*'s Jann Wenner, is not just an awards ceremony but the world's first rock museum: the Rock and Roll Hall of Fame and Museum, which opened in 1995 and is based in Cleveland. At the 2003 ceremony, Mick Jones – balding, clad in black suit and tie – didn't look like a rock'n'roll soldier getting a medal so much as a stoop-shouldered clerk shuffling to the podium to receive his retirement gift for forty-five years' loyal service to the firm. The Clash's meek compliance with their incorporation into the rock pantheon contrasts pleasingly with the intransigence of The Sex Pistols, who threw their invitation to the 2006 ceremony back in the institution's face. (This didn't stop the Hall of Fame inducting them anyway, of course.) The accompanying rude and crudely scrawled note brought a smile to the wrinkled faces of ageing punks everywhere:

Next to the Sex Pistols, rock and roll and that hall of fame is a piss stain. Your museum. Urine in wine. We're not coming. We're not your monkeys. If you voted for us, hope you noted your reasons. Your anonymous as judges but your still music industry people. We're not coming. Your not paying attention. Outside the shit-stream is a real Sex Pistol.

On one level, it was a curious gesture of defiance. After all, the group had already thrown in their lot with retro culture by re-forming for 1996's six-month Filthy Lucre Tour, and only a year after middle-fingering the Hall of Fame they would monetise the legend once again with a series of shows in 2007–8. Still, these reunions – *Never Mind the Bollocks* as travelling museum exhibit – could be seen as bracingly cynical, even an extension of the Pistols' original demystification of the music industry: not 'cash from chaos' but cash from *nostalgia* for chaos. Turning up to the Rock and Roll Hall of Fame induction, though, really would have meant the blunting of any residual edge the group had. In an interview for National Public Radio, Pistols guitarist Steve Jones claimed that 'once you want to be put into a museum, rock and roll's over'.

Induction into the Rock and Roll Hall of Fame, which bands become eligible for twenty-five years after they formed, is a last rite of passage into the rock afterlife. In some cases, the artist is literally dead; in almost all other instances, the creative life of the performer expired a good way back. Theodor Adorno was the first to point out the similarity of the words 'museum' and 'mausoleum'. Beyond the phonetic resemblance is a deeper proximity: museums are the final resting place of 'objects to which the observer no longer has a vital relationship and which are in the process of dying'. The Hard Rock chain (who started using rock memorabilia such as signed guitars as decor way back in the seventies) came up with the name of the Vault for its own museum in Orlando, Florida. And Wolfgang's Vault is the slightly creepy name of one of the world's largest music-memorabilia companies, derived from the massive underground storage centre in which famed San Francisco promoter Bill Graham (whose real name was Wolfgang Grajonca) kept his archive of audio and video concert recordings, posters and assorted rock relics. Creepy because Graham/Grajonca died in 1991, and Wolfgang's Vault suggests the idea of the burial mound, the king interred with all his treasures.

Before visitors are admitted into the Rock and Roll Hall of Fame and Museum Annex in New York, they wait in a little room that actually resembles a mausoleum. From top to bottom, the walls are covered with small rectangular plaques, each commemorating – and bearing the signature of – an artist who's been inducted into the Hall of Fame. It starts, near the entrance, with the first inductees from back in the mid-eighties – your Carl Perkins's and Clyde McPhatters – and works around to more recent ones like The Pretenders (anointed in 2005), located by the door that leads to the museum proper. The plaques are redolent of the small 'niches' you find in some burial vaults that are made for cremated ashes. Music plays, and in a touch that's both kitsch and eerie, when a particular song comes on, the silver-engraved signature of the artist glows orange or purple.

The parent museum in Cleveland goes one better, though. Fusing museum and mausoleum, it displays the earthly remains of Alan Freed, the DJ who popularised the term 'rock'n'roll' and organised the music's first major concert with 1952's Moondog Coronation Ball in Cleveland. Jim Henke, the museum's chief curator, explained that 'we'd been working with Freed's kids on putting an exhibit together and then one day they said, "Listen, our dad is buried in upstate New York, and that doesn't make any sense. If we brought the ashes, would you guys accept it?" So we said OK, and in the section of the Alan Freed exhibit we have a little glass part of the wall where his ashes are.'

The Rock and Roll Hall of Fame is intended to edify and enlighten, though, not to trigger superstitious feelings of ancestor worship. Henke describes the original process of curating the museum's contents as an extension of the work he'd done as editor of *Rolling Stone*'s *Illustrated History of Rock'n'Roll*: 'I put together an outline as if I was doing a book on the history of rock.' He's proud of the major library and archive that they've recently opened, which is intended to be the world's pre-eminent research centre for popular music. Still, there is an aspect to many of the exhibits in Cleveland and at the New York Annex that's close to medieval sacred relics such as splinters from the cross, the bones of a saint or vials of Christ's blood: they elicit morbid awe rather than scholarly respect. For instance, Cleveland has one of Bob Marley's dreadlocks on display. 'That came from his family,' says Henke. 'I guess when he had his cancer, some of his hair started falling out, and they had saved one of the dreadlocks.' In New York, the special exhibit documenting John Lennon's New York years climaxes with a large paper bag containing the clothes Lennon was wearing on the day he was shot, which were returned to Yoko Ono by the hospital. While you can't actually see dried blood, it does mean that visitors are just inches away from physical traces of the slain singer, as close to a saviour as rock has produced.

Other museum exhibits cast their spell through metonymy rather than being part of the idol's body: irradiated with 'aura', and in some cases stained with sweat, these are the actual clothes the stars wore, the instruments the musicians held. The New York Annex features two *pièces de résistance*. First is the 1957 Chevrolet Bel Air convertible that was Bruce Springsteen's first car and which he actually drove during the recording of *Born to Run* in 1975. The second is the diorama reconstruction of CBGB's interior that incorporates actual things from the legendary punk club: the old-fashioned cash register, the vintage phone box that dates back to the twenties, when the venue was a flophouse. There are some nice touches – empty beer bottles, graffiti and band stickers everywhere – but there are no ashtrays (a crucial period touch, given that this is meant to be CBGB's prime, the era of The Ramones). Nor is there any dried-out chewing gum under the tables. I'm also wondering where CBGB's infamously squalid toilet is, only to find it when I'm about to leave the museum and dart downstairs for a quick visit to the gents. Lo and behold, in a glass case just before the door to the gents, there's the CBGB urinal, with band stickers speckling the white ceramic outer surfaces. 'The bathroom at CBGB had a notorious reputation,' notes the plaque on the display, soberly but accurately. Marcel Duchamp meets retro culture! I reckon they should have kept it in service, inside the men's room, but I guess it's an antique, this piss-pot, and besides it would have meant that only one gender could take a gander at it. (Incidentally, while wrapping up this chapter, I learned that during the summer of 2010 artist Justin Lowe recreated the graffiti-daubed CBGB lavatory at the Wadsworth Atheneum in Connecticut – a homage not just to the punk venue but also the museum's history of supporting surrealist art – while that August the porcelain commode from John Lennon's 1969–72 English country estate sold for fifteen thousand bucks at a Beatles memorabilia auction.)

'We are a museum with attitude,' asserted the Rock and Roll Hall of Fame and Museum's director Dennis Barrie, optimistically, on its launch in September 1995. The Cleveland institution's big rival, the Experience Music Project – which opened in the year 2000 and was built by billionaire Paul Allen using the fortune he acquired as co-founder of Microsoft – attempted to outdo its predecessor with an emphasis on interactive exhibits and the avant-kitsch flashiness and kookiness of its building (designed by Frank Gehry and often compared to a smashed guitar). 'Experience', the same buzzword resorted to by the British Music Experience, seems to be an attempt to ward off the dour, didactic aura of the word 'museum', to promise something more sensorily overloaded and visceral. It's also a nod to Jimi 'Are You Experienced' Hendrix, Seattle rock's most famous scion.

The EMP made a big splash initially. But over the course of the past decade, it struggled to meet what were probably unrealistic expectations (a million visitors a year). Allen, a sci-fi buff as well as a rock fan, added the Science Fiction Museum and Hall of Fame to the building to bump up its appeal. Still, when you consider the continued existence of these two major rock museums in Seattle and Cleveland and the numerous smaller genre- or city-focused ones elsewhere in America (the Grammy Museum in Los Angeles, the Smithsonian Rock 'n' Soul Museum in Memphis, Detroit's Motown Historical Museum, etc.), and then factor in the recent opening of the British Music Experience and the imminent launch of Hall of Fame/Experience-style institutions in Barcelona and in the Norwegian city of Trondheim, it's clear that rock is now old enough and established enough as an art form to support its own museum industry. These institutions are competing for artifacts and funding as well as for visitors. Keith Richards may once have jeered, on being introduced to Jim Henke, 'A rock and roll curator?! That's the silliest thing I've ever heard!', but pop-culture curatorship is gradually becoming a field, a career option. In addition to people employed by the museums, working in academia or for auction houses, there are also freelance curators and dealer-collectors: people like Johan Kugelberg and Jeff Gold, who work closely with Jim Henke at the R&RHoF&M and his EMP counterpart Jasen Emmons, helping them to locate materials for particular exhibitions.

All these people involved in the museum-ification of rock share a common ideology, based around the twinned concepts of posterity and historicity. Posterity is self-explanatory: it's on whose behalf all these materials are carefully preserved and tidily presented. 'Sometimes you'll see something and think, "This belongs in a museum,"' says Jeff Gold, who is regarded as one of the top five collector-dealers in the world. 'Sometimes somebody has a collection that includes a lot of personal papers or sixties press clippings, and you think, "I *could* sell this, but this is really going to be useful to somebody writing a book somewhere down the line." If you donate stuff like that to the Rock and Roll Hall of Fame, you know it's going to be in an institution where it can be studied for generations to come.'

As for historicity, that's something like 'aura of era'. To a large degree, historicity entails a leap of faith: it's an intangible quality that depends on an element of trust and projection on the part of the museum visitor or collector. In the text for his book *Vintage T-Shirts*, Johan Kugelberg notes the huge difference in price between an original tour T-shirt and a reproduction, which may actually look indistinguishable from the real thing, given that

---

JOHAN KUGELBERG

Swedish-born but New York-based Johan Kugelberg leads a charmed life dedicated to collecting and writing about his discoveries for the retrozine *Ugly Things* and the deluxe photo-books he edits, alternating with bouts of organising exhibitions and compiling reissue anthologies. Some canny 'investment venture capitalist type' activity has placed him in the enviable position of being able to follow his wife's motto, 'Why pay less?' In other words, instead of doing what your typical cash-strapped collector (like, say, me) does, i.e. scour through thrift stores and bargain basements, he goes straight to collector-dealers who've done all the hard graft. Or he'll be a pre-emptively high bidder in auctions online and offline alike.

After spending the nineties working at various record labels, around the turn of the millennium Kugelberg fell into a modus operandi: focusing in on a specific area of the past and scooping everything up – not just records but fanzines, flyers and every kind of memorabilia related to the period. Obscure punk (as compiled on his *Killed by Death* compilations) and post-punk DIY were stabs in this direction, but it was when he got interested in the earliest days of hip hop that he first went about things more strategically.

'The agenda for the hip-hop immersion was always to create a substantial archive to place at an academic institution, to do a great book, and to do some

not only period stylisation but ageing and distressing of fabric can be faked. Historicity is paradoxical in the sense that it pertains to something only after it has been left behind by History, when it's become a remnant. During the time period when they actually have currency, tour T-shirts have no extra value; they derive their later lustre by harkening back to a time when they were unremarkable, just used. Archly echoing the Romantic poets and their obsession with medieval abbeys, Kugelberg describes the vintage T-shirt as a 'ruin', but warns that these ruins can themselves be ruined, in terms of collectability, by 'the dreaded pit stains'.

Jeff Gold uses a funkier synonym for historicity: mojo. This belief that the life force of an idolised musician can still cling to objects he or she owned explains why, every so often, he'll make a potentially lucrative acquisition but then decide not to put it on

---

really good reissues,' Kugelberg explains. The materials he gathered for the *Born in the Bronx* exhibition and book – 500 flyers, unreleased 'battle tapes' from the late seventies, photographs by Joe Conzo Jr, magazines, posters – were ultimately donated to Cornell University's Division of Rare and Manuscript Collections, where they serve as a resource to students of a hip-hop history course launched in spring 2009. 'The hope is to build this out to other satellite campuses around the world. Get some critical mass and start putting some pride in this aspect of minority history.'

Like many collector-curator types, Kugelberg is obsessed with loss, the unstaunchable wound that is Time's passage. 'My fear is that things get lost. In the past I have immersed myself in early jazz and blues, and I have heard the stories about stuff that got thrown out into dumpsters in the fifties and sixties. Important photography archives that went into the great toilet of time.' Projects like his involvement in Christie's November 2008 auction of punk memorabilia (everything from Vivienne Westwood bondage pants to Buzzcocks badges to Max's Kansas City flyers) are done with one eye towards posterity. 'When it comes to punk I think it is important for the future scholarly endeavours in that field to gain critical mass, so you need establishment people like Christie's. Also, if things are catalogued in printed form, there's a record of what they were. I'm probably shooting myself in the foot saying this, but all this stuff is *way* underpriced compared to how important it is.'

the auction block. For instance, he's hanging onto 'some Hendrix records – not records by Jimi but other people's records actually owned by him. There's about twenty-five of them, and they were auctioned off by a woman who'd lived with Hendrix in London. Blues records, *Sgt Pepper*, Roland Kirk stuff, Dylan.' Record collectors are normally looking for as close to mint condition as they can find, but in this case added value was conferred by the fact that the platters were 'beat to shit. Because that meant they'd been used by Hendrix.' Gold says he was all set 'to clean them as they were so screwed-up, but then I thought, "Well, it's got Hendrix's gook on them, his fingerprints. That would be the wrong thing to do."' The scratches and stains actually made the records 'more precious to me, because they were obviously things he'd played like crazy. It gave a view into the mind of Hendrix and his musical taste. Owning his records was like owning a little bit of his mojo.'

Gold's interest in rock memorabilia goes back to the trade's beginnings in the late sixties. The very first things to become collectable were posters, specifically the famous San Francisco psychedelic posters for shows at the Fillmore and Avalon, plus the similar-looking posters that came out of Detroit in the late sixties. Gold mentions a 1968 copy of a Bay Area fanzine he owns that contains a reference to wanting a particular Fillmore poster. 'So you had guys already collecting San Francisco posters and trying to get a whole set only a year after they started making them.'

Historicity, that paradoxical property, is a prime concern for psychedelic poster collectors: they want the first printing because these were the ones that were actually in circulation. When Bill Graham realised that the posters were desirable, that people were ripping them down and putting them up on the walls of their homes, he started doing second or third printings purely to sell as souvenirs. But the first edition, the run of posters that was done to promote the show and was 'stuck up around town on telephone poles and in store windows', Gold explains, that was the printing

18

that had actual cultural currency. And those promotional first-run posters are 'much more valuable than the ones printed after the show to be sold as souvenirs'. He tells me about the foremost authority on this area, collector-dealer Eric King, 'who literally wrote the book on this subject, a 650-page, Xeroxed and single-spaced guide'. Over the years, King has got the art of authentication down to a science. 'He and a couple of other specialists in this field did unbelievably exhaustive research to figure out which were the first-run posters. So there might be a Jefferson Airplane poster where some of the first run featured a stamp on it saying "Associated Students of UC Berkeley", and that meant that if you were putting up posters on the Berkeley campus you had to get it stamped by the Student Council as an approved event. In other cases, you can only tell which is first edition by the thickness of the paper used. So Eric gets his calipers out and measures the paper thickness and will actually certify your poster for you, for $20.'

The sixties and early seventies dominate the wares on offer at Gold's website, where you can find things like a Led Zeppelin inflatable promotional blimp or a batch of eight unsigned contracts pertaining to the Monterey Pop Festival. Punk is creeping in there (the original screenplay for *Who Killed Bambi?*, the aborted Sex Pistols movie written by Roger Ebert and directed by Russ Meyer, is on sale for $800), but for the most part the classic-rock era seems to be where the action remains. According to Peter Doggett, a former editor of *Record Collector* currently dividing his energy between writing music histories and working with Christie's to authenticate rock memorabilia, 'The market hasn't actually changed that much since the first major auctions, which were in the early eighties. Back then it was anything to do with Elvis Presley, The Beatles and the Stones. Those were the really big-selling artists in auction terms, and almost the only names to have been added to that premier league in the last twenty years are The Sex Pistols and – on a good day – Madonna. Christie's sold some Blur- and Oasis-related stuff, but it generated nowhere near the same excitement as there would be for anything to do with The Beatles. It's almost impossible for anybody after that era to acquire that status.'

Johan Kugelberg attempted to get the bandwagon rolling for early hip hop in terms of collector and curator interest with his 2007 exhibition *Born in the Bronx*. Just over a year later, the UK auction house Dreweatts made an even more audacious move with the exhibition/sale *ArtCore*: a precocious and possibly premature attempt to open up a market for rave-culture artifacts. The brainchild of Dreweatts curator Mary McCarthy, who had been a raver while studying art history in the nineties, *ArtCore* opened in February 2009 in an exhibition space in the basement of Selfridges department store in central London. Even though I'd been involved in rave culture, I didn't find this development disconcerting so much as pleasantly disorienting. The era being nostalgised was only fifteen to twenty years ago. Wandering around the exhibition on the eve of its launch, I also wondered who would really want to buy these large-canvas versions of flyers, whose garish cyberdelic imagery, already kitschy in its own time, had aged badly. You might want to have the flyer itself, to peek at occasionally for a pleasant trip down memory lane. But to actually have it dominate your living room?

I had assumed that the paintings were the flyer-art originals, but it turned out to be more complex than that. Because mass-produced items like flyers, T-shirts and so forth do not have the singularity that produces either market value or 'aura' in the Walter Benjamin sense, McCarthy had to come up with an ingenious ruse to create collectability. There wasn't even necessarily an original artwork behind the flyer: many of the flyers started as sketches that were then put together on a computer using what would now be considered risibly clumsy and primitive graphic-design programs. So the solution was to ask the design-ers to create one-off paintings based on their original flyers, in effect creating a singular work of art where one had never existed. This led to some peculiarities of dating – a flyer that came out in 1988 had to be dated 2008, because that's when the reproduction was painted – but according to McCarthy, 'It's the only way that I could get this work into the art market.'

Personally, I'd rather own the mass-produced copy that was originally in circulation, rather than the retro-actively created pseudo-original. The flyer has a real connection to history. And in fact there is a fan-collector trade for old-skool rave flyers. But for an auction house like Dreweatts, 'selling original flyers would be quite difficult', says McCarthy. 'They're so *small.*' Collectors want visual bang for their buck, something they can display. One of the few originals on show at *ArtCore* – a framed flyer for legend-ary acid-house club Shoom, pamphlet-size and with rudimentary black-and-white graphics – does look rather unimposing, I have to admit.

A PAST GONE MAD

Punk seems hostile to museum-ification on account of its icono-clastic contempt for the past. With rave, it's the movement's orien-tation towards the future that should really repel the dustiness of the archive's embrace. The punishing minimalism of early techno especially – music stripped to rhythm and texture, a true art of noises – recalls the spirit of the Italian Futurists circa 1909–15. As much as I love history and poring over the past, there's a part of me that will always thrill to, and agree with, the Futurist manifes-tos, which showered scalding scorn over 'the passéists': antiquar-ians, curators, tradition-loving art critics. Italian Futurism was a response to the spiritual oppression of growing up in a country that pioneered tourism as time travel (for it is nearly always the past of a country you visit on vacation, at least in the Old World), a land covered with magisterial ruins, venerable cathedrals, grand squares and palaces, the monumental residues not just of one golden age (the Roman Empire) but of two (the Renaissance).

Futurist leader F. T. Marinetti's founding manifesto proclaimed, 'We want to free this land from its smelly gangrene of professors, archaeologists, *ciceroni* and antiquarians. For too long has Italy been a dealer in second-hand clothes. We mean to free her from the numberless museums that cover her like so many graveyards . . . Museums: cemeteries! . . . Identical, surely, in the sinister promiscuity of so many bodies unknown to one another.' Continuing the sexual imagery, he ranted about how 'admiring an old picture is the same as pouring our sensibility into a funerary urn instead of hurtling it far off, in violent spasms of action and creation'. To venerate artworks from the past was like wasting one's *élan vital* on something inert and decayed; like fucking a corpse.

Marinetti imagined setting fire 'to the library shelves' and redirecting 'the canals to flood the museums' so that 'the glorious old canvases' bobbed 'adrift on those waters'. What would he, writing in 1909, have made of the state of Western culture a hundred years later? The last decades of the twentieth century saw what Andreas Huyssen has called a 'memory boom', with a surge in the foundation of museums and archives being just one facet of a culture-wide obsession with commemoration, documentation and preservation. Examples include the trends for restoring old urban centres and for creating museum villages where people in period costume practise traditional crafts; the popularity of reproduction furniture and retro decor; the widespread obsession with self-documentation using video recorders (and, since Huyssen wrote his essay in 2000, mobile-phone camera, blogging, YouTube, etc.); the rise of documentaries and history programmes on TV; and the frequency of commemorative articles or special magazine issues (celebrating the fortieth anniversary of the Summer of Love, the moon landings, and even the magazine having reached its twenty-year mark or hundredth issue).

Borrowing Hermann Lübbe's concept of 'musealisation' – the archival mindset no longer confined within the institution of the museum but seeping out to infect every zone of culture and everyday life – Huyssen contrasted the attitudes of the second half of the twentieth century with the first half as a shift from a concern with 'present futures' to 'present pasts'. For the greater part of the last century, modernism and modernisation were the watchwords: the emphasis was on harking forward, an intent focus on everything in the present that seemed to represent 'tomorrow's world today'. That changed, gradually but with increasing momentum from the early seventies, towards a preoccupation with the residues of the past in the present, a massive cultural shift that encompassed the rise of the nostalgia industry with its retro fashions and revivals, postmodernism's pastiche and renovation of historical styles, and the spectacular growth of heritage.

The concept of heritage can be traced back to the end of the nineteenth century. That was when the National Trust was founded in Britain in order to protect 'places of historic interest or natural beauty'. After World War II, the conservationist impulse began to spread beyond its antiquarian and aristocratic hardcore, with campaigns to preserve the steam engine and stately homes, the growth of traction-engine clubs and rallies, and the cult of canal and barge restoration. As a mass movement, though, heritage really took off in the eighties. The 1983 National Heritage Act established the Historic Buildings and Ancient Monuments Commission, or as it's more generally known, English Heritage. Antique collecting was no longer a posh activity but a middle-class pastime, helped by the expanded definition of antique beyond the hand-crafted to include mundane, often machine-made artifacts such as quaint old bottles, enamel signs, tea chests, and so forth. Along with mass-produced objects, the places where these things were actually produced soon began to seem quaint and charming: hence the rise of industrial museums (working mines, kilns, pumping stations, even Victorian sewage works). In a classic example of this syndrome of aestheticising things only after they've shed their association with production, canal barges became picturesque when they lost their original function of lugging coal or industrial materials to manufacturing towns (a role taken over by trucks on the new post-war motorways). What had once been a floating slum that grimly combined workplace and home became an inland-waterways version of the converted terrace house, its blend of bygone charm and footloose eccentricity appealing to mildly nonconformist members of the bourgeoisie.

By the end of the nineties, heritage had become such a dominant force in the UK that Julian Barnes could write a satirical novel about it, *England, England*, that imagined a theme-park version of the country taking over the entirety of the Isle of Wight, based around the most touristic clichés of Britishness (thatched cottages, bowler hats, double-decker buses, cricket, etc.). In the UK, almost the only people who remain immune to the romance of the antiquated are the 'chavs', a derogatory term for working-class whites who identify with black American style and music at its most flashy and materialistic. Although chav-haters complain about their lack of taste and vulgarity – the blingy jewellery, shiny sportswear, spaceship trainers – the subtext of the animosity is the chav's un-English lack of interest in old stuff: antiques, heritage, costume drama. This abhorrence of the vintage, the worn-and-faded-looking, the previously owned, is something that ethnic minorities on both sides of the Atlantic share with the traditional white working class.

In Britain, chavs are a kind of ethnic minority in themselves.

24

The vast sprawling middle class of middle England has succumbed to the middlebrow appeal of the old-fashioned. A shift in attitudes took hold in the eighties, doubtless connected to the same social and cultural forces that led to the 1983 National Heritage Act. As architectural blogger Charles Holland has shown, well into the seventies interior-design and DIY books advocated covering over panelling, ripping out iron-grate fireplaces, painting over exterior brickwork and hiding high ceilings with false ones. The modern-look household originally came into fashion in the fifties, the golden age of design showcases, World's Fairs and exhibitions with titles like *This Is Tomorrow*. Formica and chrome, fluorescent light tubes and the streamlined elimination of decorative clutter like cornices and mouldings were de rigueur in every middle-class home. But by the eighties, it had all gone into reverse: suspended ceilings were stripped away, fireplaces were exposed once more, plastic doorknobs were replaced by original-style brass ones. Tiling and wooden floorboards came back into style and all kinds of quaintnesses were treated as desirable 'original features' by estate agents and prospective buyers. This was followed by a boom for trades like restoration and architectural salvage (old-fashioned enamel baths and other fittings pulled out of soon-to-be-demolished houses, schools and hotels) and the rise of a range of 'archaizing fads' (Samuel Raphael's term) such as the artificial distressing of furniture or building materials (artificially aged bricks that look soot-stained or pockmarked).

Given this culture-wide dominance of preservationist attitudes, it's hardly surprising that a rock-heritage industry should emerge. In this context, things like the Abbey Road studio in North London being granted protected status by the Ministry of Culture or the walking tour of Macclesfield landmarks offered to commemorate the thirtieth anniversary of Ian Curtis's death seem perfectly logical, even inevitable. 'Rock now belongs to the past as much as to the future,' James Miller argued in his book *Flowers in the Dustbin*, which derives its title from a Sex Pistols song and argues that rock had run through all the fundamental moves, archetypes and avenues of self-reinvention available to it by 1977, such that everything since has been either recycling or tweaking of established templates. I wouldn't go that far. But I do wonder, when Huyssen asks rhetorically, 'Why are we building museums as if there were no tomorrow?', if the answer is that we can no longer imagine tomorrow.

ARCHIVE FEVER

The title of a book by Jacques Derrida, 'archive fever' is a good term for today's delirium of documentation, which extends beyond institutions and professional historians to the Web's explosion of amateur archive creation. There is a feeling of frenzy to all this activity; it's like people are *slinging* stuff 'up there' – information, images, testimonials – in a mad-dash hurry before some mass shutdown causes all our brains to burn out simultaneously. Nothing is too trivial, too insignificant, to be discarded; every pop-culture scrap, every trend and fad, every forgotten-by-most performer or TV programme is being annotated and

---

DERRIDA, FREUD AND THE ARCHIVE

It sounds almost like a genuine illness, 'archive fever': the occupational ailment of librarians who spend too long in the stacks, a derangement afflicting academics and antiquarians as they test the limits of the human brain to digest information. But actually – and as you'd expect with Jacques Derrida – the concept turns out to be much more complicated, subtle and paradoxical.

In *Archive Fever: A Freudian Impression*, Derrida traces 'archive' all the way back to *archeion*, the ancient Greek word for the residence of superior magistrates (the *archons*). At the root of the word 'archive' is a double meaning of 'commencement' and 'commandment'. The concept of the archive is thus deeply entangled with ideas of origin and order, authenticity and authority. 'Arch' is the same 'arch' that is in words like 'archaic', 'archetype' and

26

auteur-ised. The result, visible above all on the Internet, is that the archive degenerates into the *anarchive*: a barely navigable disorder of data-debris and memory-trash. For the archive to maintain any kind of integrity, it must sift and reject, consign some memories to oblivion. History must have a dustbin, or History will *be* a dustbin, a gigantic, sprawling garbage heap.

One mainstream manifestation of the anarchive is the *I Love the [Decade]* series that was massively popular all through the 2000s. Originating in Britain as the BBC2 brainchild of the producer Alan Brown, the show was franchised and adapted for America by VH1, and also inspired imitators like Channel 4's *Top 10* shows. Frothy and fast-moving, the *I Love . . .* programmes featured an array of second-division comedians and minor celebrities quipping facetiously about the mass-cultural fads and follies of a particular decade: TV soap operas, hit movies, pop songs, hairstyles and fashions, toys and games, scandals, slogans and catchphrases. In the US, the series started in 2002 with the eighties, doubled back to do *I Love the '70s*, then got back in sequence with *I Love the '90s* and spun-off variants like *I Love Toys* and *I Love the Holidays*. The convulsive logic of archive fever accelerated the series' metabolism such that the US version

---

'archaeology', but it is also the 'arch' that's in words like 'monarchy'. Archive is also related to the word 'ark', as in Noah's Ark (the vessel in which, at God's command, the animals were preserved and classified) and the Ark of the Covenant (a different kind of vessel, one in which the tablets of the Ten Commandments were stored).

In French, '*mal d'archive*' contains the concept of both illness and evil. For Derrida, there is something morbid and sinister at the core of the archival impulse. 'It is to have a compulsive, repetitive, and nostalgic desire . . . to return to the origin . . . the most archaic place of absolute commencement.' Derrida relates this compulsion to the Freudian death drive. Freud argued that 'the task' of the death drive was 'to lead organic life back into the inanimate state'. One of its manifestations in human behaviour (and by extension, culture) is 'a compulsion to repeat'. Freud saw this regressive impulse as 'more primitive,

began summing up the noughties in the summer of 2008, with the series *I Love the New Millennium*.

'Those programmes were played to *death*,' says Mark Cooper, who as BBC Television's Creative Head of Music Entertainment has been the driving force behind the past decade's boom of high-quality rock documentaries on BBC2 and especially BBC4. 'What was nice about them initially was that it was driven by a desire to create a sense of nostalgia, but they didn't want to interrogate it or understand it; they just wanted to give a taste of it, a smell of it, in that biscuit sense. It was very much, "Remember that haircut?" But after a while it became a form of blanket programming. They were seen by the production teams as more like shows than documentaries, seeing the past not as history but as pure nostalgia.'

History is a form of editing reality; for a historical account to work it requires a filter, otherwise the sheer sludge of information silts up the narrative flow. The kind of documentaries that Cooper shepherds into existence at the BBC, and in particular BBC4's 'Britannia' series (*Folk Britannia*, *Blues Britannia*, *Prog Britannia*, *Synth Britannia* et al.), are the opposite of all the list shows. 'They are about looking at music genres from the fifties to the present and attempting to tell the story of British music in terms of our search for an identity,' says Cooper. 'All the ways that things like jazz and blues and soul have helped to liberate us from who we were in the fifties.' In some cases, the narratives might break with or challenge the official histories. For instance, Cooper

---

more elementary' than the pleasure principle, which is why Thanatos can often 'over-ride' Eros.

'*En mal d'archive*' also means to be 'in need of archives', a desperate hunger comparable to addiction. As Derrida writes, 'It is to burn with a passion. It is never to rest, interminably, from searching for the archive right where it slips away. It is to run after the archive, even if there's too much of it . . .' Impelled by a mixture of hubris and mania, the drive to accumulate and store knowledge escalates out of control, threatening to collapse the entire edifice of the archive.

says that the *Prog Britannia* documentary came from his being 'bored with the punk cliché that everything before 1976 was shit, that "official" view of the first half of the seventies as a wasteland. *Prog Britannia* attempted to understand that post-*Sgt Pepper's* territory, that more expansive sense they had that music could go further than the three-minute pop song. Maybe it ultimately went wrong, but there's a lot that was laudable about that sense of ambition.' The key point is that these revisionist documentaries are trying to tell a *story*, as opposed to presenting a shuffle-mode miscellany of collective memory: they offer a counter-narrative, rather than an encyclopedic accumulation.

The 'Britannia' series and the many other BBC documentaries that Cooper instigated have contributed to a veritable noughties rock-doc boom, ranging from Julien Temple's punk trilogy (docs on The Sex Pistols, Joe Strummer and Dr Feelgood) to the hugely successful and award-winning tale of a no-hoper metal band, *Anvil! The Story of Anvil.* One reason for the boom is economics. With their small crews and low budgets (no scripts, actors, costumes, props or effects), these films are cheap to make. For many rock documentaries archival footage is one of the largest costs. Cooper says that his documentary budgets are in the region of £120–140,000, and typically a quarter of that goes on archival material. 'We have two people here who specialise in sourcing and procuring archival material,' he says, explaining that this often involves working with commercial archives and with companies that acquire and license footage. According to Cooper, 'The industry is realising the importance of archivists. They've just started to do an award for archivists working in TV called the Focal Awards.' He points out that the BBC itself makes a lot of money off licensing old footage and is currently exploring the possibility of putting its entire archive on the Web. The big internal debate is, he says, whether the archive should be a commercial enterprise or a public service. The BBC could 'charge people to download stuff' or they could make it free in the manner of the British Library Sound Archive (which recently put swathes of its collection online).

Another reason for the rise of music documentaries is that there are ever-expanding opportunities for them to get shown and seen. This is not so much in movie theatres (although some of the most high-profile rock docs, like *Anvil!* or the Metallica documentary *Some Kind of Monster*, have had successful runs on the big screen), but is thanks to the increase in the number of cable and digital television channels. Although they often serve as cheap schedule filler, rock docs also provide channels like the UK's BBC4 and Channel 4 and the US's Sundance and VH1-Classic with a means of attracting both baby boomers and the youth audience. The former enjoy seeing the classic-rock era they lived through endlessly chewed over; the latter enjoy seeing the classic-rock era they *didn't* live through endlessly chewed over.

The greying of the baby-boomer generation (and its immediate descendant/extension, the punk generation) is another explanation for the boom. The bulk of the rock docs are still concerned with the sixties and seventies, an era with a seemingly limitless scope for being rehashed. 'I think it's because we haven't had enough wars,' laughs Mark Cooper. He suggests that the golden age of rock – from Dylan and The Beatles to glam and punk – offered the closest thing to the collective sense of purpose that World War II created for the previous demographic cohort. It's an idea given credence by nostalgia scholar Fred Davis, who wrote about 'present tense' periods of great drama and urgency, when people were fully engaged in struggle. Those who lived through the Depression or World War II often look back to that time with paradoxical affection as 'the best years of my life', despite the danger, hardship, self-sacrifice, loss of loved ones and other trials. 'People always said their parents never talked about the war,' muses Cooper. 'Well, we talk about our own "war" experiences over and over and over. Particularly the sixties generation, because the sixties were such a turbulent time, there was so much change. It's such an *alive* decade, politically and socially and culturally. So I really think pop culture has become the new "What did you do in the war, Daddy?"'

REUNITED AND IT PAYS SO GOOD

While it's true that the sixties and seventies exert a vice-like grip on our imaginations, it seems as though the museum-isation of music is likely to keep extending itself as each passing decade slips into pop history. The British Music Experience might deal with the nineties and 2000s rather cursorily, and the memorabilia auctions might only just be monetising punk and early hip hop, but as documentaries like *Live Forever* (on Britpop) and exhibitions like *ArtCore* demonstrate, every generation as it ages will want to see its musical youth mythologised and memorialised.

Nineties nostalgia is already showing up in one area: rock reunions and nostalgia tours. Rage Against the Machine's reformation, after a seven-year furlough, to headline the 2007 Coachella Valley Music and Arts Festival in South California helped the promoters shift their pricey tickets ($249 for a three-day pass) in record speed. Blur, The Pixies, Dinosaur Jr, My Bloody Valentine, Pavement and Smashing Pumpkins are just some of the bigger alternative rock and shoegaze names to start treading the boards again (although in the case of the Pumpkins and Dinosaur, those groups are making all-new records and can be said to have picked up where they left off, as opposed to pandering to college rock/grunge nostalgia).

When alt-rock bands like these reunite and go on the road, there is a mutually beneficial arrangement between the musicians and their audience. The ageing audience gets dependability (they know what the music is going to be) and a chance to relive their youth. The band gets to bask in their legend and reconnect with their fans. They also make more money than they did as on-the-rise legends-to-be (tickets can be priced much higher without scaring off their audience, no longer college students or slackers but middle-aged professionals) and they can tour in greater comfort than in the old days of get-in-the-van.

Re-formed alt-rock bands from the late eighties and nineties have become such a common feature of rock-festival line-ups that critic Anwyn Crawford has dubbed it the Indie Rock Heritage Circuit. But it extends even further than indie with the emergence of a nineties techno-rave circuit, the return (not necessarily after splitting up but certainly after a long period of having faded from public prominence) of those vaguely rock-ish dance acts (think Orbital, Leftfield, Underworld, The Orb, Chemical Brothers) who could actually play live and put on a good show.

The pioneers of Indie Rock Heritage are ATP, the promoters responsible for the successful All Tomorrow's Parties festivals, which began in the UK and soon spread to the US and beyond. Right from the start, these have been curated by renowned musicians (Portishead, Stephen Malkmus, Sonic Youth) and occasionally famous non-musicians (*Simpsons*' creator Matt Groening, Jim Jarmusch). And from quite early on, the line-ups featured old bands brought out of retirement. So, as Crawford pointed out, when Nick Cave made his selections for the first ATP in Australia, he scheduled a large number of 'acts drawn from the years of his disreputable youth: Laughing Clowns, The Saints, Robert Forster, Primitive Calculators and the late, lamented Rowland S. Howard [Cave's bandmate in The Birthday Party]'.

I met with ATP founder Barry Hogan when he was in New York to organise the sequel to their 2008 extravaganza at the Kutsher's Country Club (a family-style resort in the Catskills similar to the Camber Sands and Minehead holiday camps where

ATP had staged some of their UK festivals). That first upstate New York event had been curated by My Bloody Valentine, who also performed at it, kicking off a hugely successful reunion tour of America that basically replayed their last US tour, in early 1992 (same songs and the same twenty-minute deafening, dizzying, noise-blitz set-closer of 'You Made Me Realise'). Hogan told me that 'putting on the MBV reunion tour was lucrative for everyone involved'. When I asked him if reunion tours had become a crucial part of the promotion industry's business, Hogan said he had no hard figures but thought it was 'significant. It seems to me that for every promoter, as part of their annual run of shows they'll always have some comeback tour in there.'

According to the *Wall Street Journal*, one reason that the concert industry turns to old legends is that the record business hasn't established enough big-level artists during the 2000s. At the same time, the former members of these disbanded legends rarely approach comparable success in their solo careers, and so have a financial incentive for reconciling and going on the road. But even bands no one ever gave a shit about are re-forming. Take Mudcrutch, Tom Petty's first group, who only ever released two singles and then split in 1975. They reunited to tour and recorded a debut album, 2008's *Mudcrutch*, featuring a mixture of old and new songs.

The swarm of elderly rockers playing oldies sets, from superstars (The Police, The Eagles) to cult figures (The Pixies, Swervedriver), has caused consternation among those for whom pop and youth culture are synonymous. John Strausbaugh wrote a whole book, *Rock 'Til You Drop: The Decline from Rebellion to Nostalgia*, railing against the wrinkling of rock. For others the problem is not the advancing years of the artists but the fact that the nostalgia market doesn't allow bands to advance beyond the music of their youth. Musician/critic Momus railed against the 'museumification' of pop, comparing it to the way that classical music has

33

a repertory of 'venerated masterpieces' that are endlessly reinterpreted. But others have used precisely this analogy to defend this canonisation of rock. When PBS schedules music programmes designed to appeal to its baby-boomer audience as part of its fundraising activities (Blind Faith performing live in Hyde Park in 1969, a tribute concert to Roy Orbison featuring admirers such as Elvis Costello, Tom Waits, Bruce Springsteen and k. d. lang), the presenter Laura Sevigny can enthuse confidently, 'We want to make sure we're able to continue being an archive of American culture . . . This is the new classical music . . . for our generation. It's rock'n'roll, and we want to make sure on public television it's preserved.' Similarly, in 2007 the *New York Times* music critic Ben Ratliff defended rock's reunion boom by comparing it to the way jazz had gracefully aged: starting around the mid-seventies, it became a 'culture of incessant re-experience, endless tributes', in which 'actual reunions are barely noticed' while 'a huge percentage of the music refers to great moments of the past'. He argued that this hadn't stopped jazz from continuing to be 'fantastic, even transformative'. He claimed that rock bands often get better at what they do with age, and benefit from the far superior sound systems at their disposal today.

The 'whole album' phenomenon was what specifically made Momus think of the analogy with the classical repertory: a band performing its most famous album in its original sequence, from beginning to end. Nobody knows who first resorted to this fan-pleasing ploy. It might have been Cheap Trick, who promoted the 1998 reissues of their first four albums with a tour organised around four-night stands in particular cities, where they'd perform an album per night. With their most celebrated album, 1979's *Live at Budokan*, singer Robin Zander even reproduced his stage patter, because the deliberately stilted way he spoke (slow and clear so that the Japanese audience could understand it) had became a feature that fans adored.

What Cheap Trick did as a one-off promotional gimmick became a small industry in the second half of the 2000s, spearheaded by All Tomorrow's Parties with their 'Don't Look Back' franchise. It started as a season of concerts in 2005, with groups like Belle & Sebastian, The Stooges and Mudhoney, to name just a few, performing their most famous albums. These whole-album renditions became a regular fixture of All Tomorrow's Parties' festivals but also branched out to become ATP/'Don't Look Back'-branded stages at other promoters' events, like the Pitchfork Music Festival in Chicago (where Public Enemy performed *It Takes a Nation of Millions to Hold Us Back*, Sebadoh did *Bubble & Scrape* and Mission of Burma played *Vs.* . . .).

ATP's Barry Hogan describes the concept as a 'rebellion' against the culture of iPod shuffle and a defence of the album as an integral artwork. 'Nowadays it's all about convenience and iTunes. But MP3s sound like shit. "Don't Look Back", it's trying to say, "Remember when you used to buy records, and you'd get the gatefold sleeve and look at it, and you'd put the record on and it sounded great."'

Just about everybody in the world seems to have copied the 'Don't Look Back' template, from Liz Phair with *Exile in Guyville* to Jay-Z with *Reasonable Doubt* to Van Morrison, who in November 2008 performed his most famous album, resulting in a new album with the hideous title *Astral Weeks: Live at the Hollywood Bowl*. Sparks took the concept to the dizzy limit by performing all twenty-one of their albums in sequence over twenty-one nights in London during May 2008 (the final night being the debut unveiling of their new album). That same month they opened the Sparks Museum at the Bodhi Gallery in Brick Lane, East London, an exhibition of record covers, photographs, videos and other memorabilia from their long career as art-pop geek-freaks.

For the bands, Hogan says, it can literally be like reanimation.

'My Bloody Valentine, that was like the movie *Awakenings*, where the person's life just stops, and then it gets restarted,' he says, adding that 'They are talking about recording and writing new songs.' Reigniting the creative spark is a potential side-benefit of the reunion, but at the end of the day nobody would do this if it didn't make them money. And it can make bands lots and lots of money. For when a band hasn't played for a long time, Hogan explains, it builds up a kind of pent-up consumer demand.

Even bands who've kept active, touring and making records tirelessly, like Sonic Youth, find it hard to resist the opportunities presented by a quick flick through their back pages. During 2007 and early 2008, Sonic Youth performed their 1988 masterpiece *Daydream Nation* on twenty-four separate occasions, with large-venue gigs in the major American cities and in the UK (where they played London's Roundhouse three nights in succession), concerts and festival appearances in Spain, Germany, France and Italy, and the Daydream Nation Down Under tour of New Zealand and Australia. In an interview with *Spin*, Thurston Moore seemed aware of the contradictions inherent in the band that wrote 'Kill Your Idols' – and that called itself Sonic Youth – caving in to alternative nostalgia. He admitted, 'I didn't really want to do it at first . . . I thought it would be taking up too much time from us doing something new and progressive.' But once Hogan, who had got both Sonic Youth and Thurston Moore separately to curate some ATPs, persuaded them to do *Daydream Nation* in London, the band's European booking agent started trying to persuade them to repeat it at festivals on the Continent, saying those promoters would pay 'an extra few thousand bucks'. According to *Billboard*, the 2007 *Daydream Nation* performances in America grossed substantially more per show than the group's tour of the US the previous year, when they were promoting the new LP *Rather Ripped*. When a band has been around long enough, there is always going to be more demand from the fan base for a career-peak classic than for the latest musical effort.

Paul Smith, a veteran of the left-field music industry and the man who originally put out *Daydream Nation* in the UK via his label Blast First, currently specialises in helping underground legends like Suicide and Throbbing Gristle return to action without losing integrity and dignity. He thinks there is a silly stigma about the rock reunion that doesn't apply to other art forms. 'Painters, poets, classical composers – age isn't a factor there. But in rock and pop, there's this idea you are supposed to die of an overdose or a car crash. At least with blues musicians they get old and people respect them even more.'

For Smith, reunions are valid both in terms of doing justice to a band's importance in the history of music, and as a reward for an artist who most likely laboured hard for minimal financial payback. He feels that reformations can be done well or done badly. As an example of the latter, he cites the eternal returns of The Buzzcocks. 'They've run the brand into the ground,' Smith says, through endless touring. 'Playing to balding punks at festivals in Margate, it's throwing out of the window all the things that made them great art, reducing it to the level of Gerry and the Pacemakers trudging on the cabaret circuit. But the guys in Buzzcocks are happy that they still don't have day jobs, that they can make a living as working musicians.'

Instead, Smith prefers to instigate reunions with a finite end in sight. As he says, for 'a definite length of time, and a fairly specific set of goals: put them back onto a more generalised rock map and make a bit of money.' The nostalgia aspect is minimised, because 'it's presented to a predominantly younger audience'. There are psychological benefits too, he says, for the group. 'It's coming to terms with what your life has amounted to, and the fact that it was an achievement, wanting to own that, and claim whatever you deserve out of it.' Smith says he told Wire guitarist Bruce

Gilbert, 'Look, it's going to say Wire on your gravestone anyway, so you might as well do the tour.'

Throbbing Gristle's re-formation was the byproduct of the December 2002 exhibition at London's Cabinet Gallery based around the *24 Hours of TG* box set of the group's live cassette releases from the late seventies and early eighties. 'It was the first time all four of them were in one room in twenty years,' Smith recalls. At dinner with the band (and Daniel Miller of Mute Records, who maintain TG's back catalogue), Smith seized the opportunity and popped the question: 'So . . . are you going to play again?' Genesis P-Orridge initially demurred, insisting, 'I'm not that person any more.' Smith argued that true TG fans understood that they wouldn't get a time-travel trip to 1979, a reproduction of the classic TG sound; they respected the fact that they were artists in a constant state of evolution. 'I told them, "As far as I'm concerned the four of you can stand on stage and play finger cymbals if you want, it will still be TG."' His patter was persuasive and the group re-formed in 2004, initially intending to stage their own All Tomorrow's Parties-style weekend festival at a British seaside holiday camp. That didn't pan out, but (like Wire and Suicide) they started recording new albums and then played a series of shows, including one inside the massive Turbine Hall of the Tate Modern art museum, and followed it up with a 2009 tour of the US. Although all four members are involved in other bands, Throbbing Gristle is an ongoing entity, with a whole-album cover of Nico's *Desertshore* in the pipeline.

Coming originally out of the performance-art world, TG always placed an emphasis on self-documentation (resulting in an endless stream of live tapes and records, videos of performances, etc.). So it's appropriate that the Tate museum has been in conversation with the group and with Genesis P-Orridge about acquiring their archive. 'There's a whole new wave of curators in the art world,' Smith says. 'They're in their mid-twenties and slightly older than that, and they are starting to look at punk and mid-eighties stuff and say, "This is important.'"

Generally speaking, I avoid reunions, especially when I saw the band in their original prime. My Bloody Valentine's comeback tour, on which they played a set drawn entirely from their *Isn't Anything/Loveless* heyday, seemed to be a recipe for disappointment. This music was draped with very personal memories associated with the hormonal electricity of falling in love, the kind of reveries that can still flush memory's cheek. Basically, I didn't want me and the missus to be in a room full of other middle-aged couples relighting those sparks.

The exceptions to my 'no reunions' policy are a few bands that I loved as a youth but never managed to see live. Like Gang of Four. At New York's Irving Plaza in May 2005 they were so good I made the mistake of going again a few months later. This second gig was at the Hard Rock Cafe, just off Times Square. This time, the vibe was just wrong: post-punk's most rocking anti-rockists playing amid framed pictures of Janis and Jimi, autographed guitars and sundry rock memorabilia. The band seemed to know it but attempted to push through the oppressively reverential yet tacky-as-hell surroundings by being even more stern than usual. No opening pleasantries or 'Hello, New York': guitarist Andy Gill pursed his lips and pout-scowled like the actor Alan Rickman, singer Jon King looked both haughty and harried like a teacher with an out-of-control classroom, and drummer Hugo Burnham just stared ahead with a grim, dead-eyed look of disdain. Despite the incongruity, Gang of Four would go on to play further gigs that autumn at House of Blues venues (the sister chain to the Hard Rock Cafe) on a tour promoting their comeback album *Return the Gift*.

The record itself was one of the most conceptually intriguing band resurrections ever: a kind of tribute album to themselves,

auto-karaoke. Plenty of groups had done whole albums covering a particular artist's songs, or even covered an entire album.
Gang of Four made a brand-new album of re-recorded versions
of songs from their first three albums. Named after a tune on
Entertainment! they didn't actually remake, the title *Return the
Gift* suggested that the whole project was an oblique commentary on retro culture's 'eternal returns'. The album placed in plain,
unavoidable sight the redundancy and reconsumption involved
in rock's nostalgia market. When fans buy new albums by re-
formed favourites of their youth, at heart they're not really interested in what the band might have to say now, or where the band
members' separate musical journeys have taken them in subsequent decades; they want the band to create 'new' songs in their
vintage style. *Return* seemed to be saying: 'You want a Gang of
Four resurrection? Here you are, then, exactly what you secretly
crave: the old songs, again.'

But there was also a mundanely pragmatic side to this consistent with the group's demystification of capitalism in their lyrics. 'Covering' their own songs was Gang of Four's canny way of
honouring the legacy while profiting from it. A straightforward
repackaging of the old recordings – a standard compilation or box
set – would only have served to enrich EMI, their original record
company in the UK. 'We have never made any money at all from
record sales with EMI and still have unrecouped advances,' Jon
King told me. 'We didn't want them to benefit as they did nothing
to support us.' Re-recording the songs – something which contracts typically allow artists to do after twenty years – put Gang
of Four in a strong bargaining position in terms of negotiating
a new deal with superior royalty rates (in this case, a one-off
licensing deal, rather than an outright sale of the material). 'It will
mean that whatever we make will go to us.'

Listening to *Return the Gift* was a curious experience for this
ultra-fan. I couldn't help wondering what it must have *felt* like for

the band members, re-recording songs they'd laid down definitively long ago. On the new version of 'Love Like Anthrax' – a song which in its original form juxtaposed an agonised lyric of heartbreak sung by King with a dourly intoned text from Andy Gill critiquing the institution of the love song in pop – Gill added some different lines that, in Brechtian style, addressed Gang of Four's re-formation. He talks in the song about *Return the Gift* as 'an exercise in archaeology', an attempt to find out where their heads were at in those heady post-punk days. When I asked Jon King and bassist Dave Allen about the project, they both referred to the original recordings as 'Dead Sea Scrolls' they could refer to when memory failed.

Another curious, even eerie thing about listening to *Return the Gift* for me was that on some level the new versions of the songs were stronger than the originals (better recorded, with a big modern drum sound, and generally benefiting from Gill's experience as a record producer in the years after the group disbanded), but they didn't have the specific sonic aura of the original recorded versions I'd known for years. This was especially apparent with the songs from *Entertainment!*, widely criticised by reviewers on its release in 1979 for having a dry, clinical sound that wasn't as exciting as the group live. But it was precisely that airless *Entertainment!* sound that I and other fans were attached to. As a result, the new versions of the songs seemed to exist neither in 1979 nor 2005 but in a peculiar limbo of non-time.

The only other legendary band I've seen in re-formation mode is one I was never really a fan of, The New York Dolls. Partly what made me curious enough to go was that the show was taking place at 315 Bowery – the very space that had once been CBGB. Now it was a clothes boutique for designer John Varvatos, a big fan of punk rock who had tried to retain something of the scuzzy, rock'n'roll ambience. So on 5 May 2009 I walked the six blocks from my apartment to watch the Dolls perform tracks from their

41

new album *'Cause I Sez So*, very much an attempt to recapture their lost glory (they'd even hooked up with producer Todd Rundgren, who'd recorded their debut album back in 1973). The full time-travel experience was going to be hard to pull off, given that so many members of the original group had passed away, with David Johansen and Syl Sylvain the sole survivors.

Most of the audience looked like they'd once been regulars at CBGB in its seventies heyday: greying rebels, balding famous rock photographers, faces that seemed vaguely familiar from rock documentaries, and quite a lot of remarkably well-preserved women in their fifties enjoying the opportunity to dress up as the rock chicks they'd been a couple of decades ago. On the wall, there were framed posters of The Ramones and The Plasmatics. When a clutch of pretty young things sauntered in, there was a discernible ripple of surprise and tension: these stylish twenty-somethings looked as out of place as old-age pensioners at a rave.

After a long wait The New York Dolls 2.0 sidled onstage: Johansen, looking dapper as ever in a navy velvet jacket, ruffly white shirt and leopard-skin scarf, and Sylvain, resembling some kind of fruity hybrid of Pierrot and goblin. The new recruits to the band were a generation younger than the Dolls but still pretty old, and with that 'rock'n'roll' look spawned somewhere between the Sunset Strip and Soho, all scarves and wide-brimmed hats and skin-tight pants. It was quickly obvious we weren't going to be magically transported to the Mercer Theater circa 1972, though: not only were the band not dressed in women's clothing and high heels and wigs, but they didn't play a single classic Dolls tune. Instead they doggedly stuck to the new album, the sound not of the sloppy, rambunctious Dolls of punk mythology but a tight, lean hard-rock band.

Listening to them in 2009 it struck me how small the gap appeared in retrospect between the Dolls and other blues-derived rock of the seventies, groups like The Faces and Grand Funk Railroad and ZZ

Top, who filled arenas and sold millions. The gap was real, of course, based on the Dolls' relative deficiency as players, plus their attitude-blend of snarling snottiness and over-the-top camp. In that small but significant difference, a space opened up for the emergence of punk rock. Decades after the fact, that difference, so significant once, had shrivelled to the point of seeming unrecoverable. Where it lingered still was in Johansen's arch wisecracks: 'I would venture to say we are as good as The Seeds,' he teased, or 'Someday this'll all be just a memory.' But the humour turned sour as the band gradually realised that the audience didn't dig the new material and only wanted to hear the old tunes. Johansen started to get waspish at the muted response: 'You're not dead, are you?' Sylvain actually looked like he was trying not to cry. But after exiting the stage the Dolls came back on for an encore anyway – Johansen bitterly muttering, 'Don't know why we're out here again, you're not even cheering' – and did a note-perfect rendition of 'Trash'. Unfortunately it wasn't the 'Trash' that appeared on the debut album, but the new album's comically misguided reggae version of it. It was one of the saddest spectacles I've ever witnessed.

Yet the Dolls' refusal to pander to their ageing home crowd, their stubborn insistence on playing only their brand-new songs, was probably an expression of pride. They were defying the fate that befalls nearly all bands once their prime has passed, something ex-Strangler Hugh Cornwell described well when he declared ,'We're all tribute bands now. If you play the old catalogue you're a tribute band. I would include myself in that . . . I can't imagine what it's like being a young person trying to get a start in the music business – it must be a nightmare. Because none of the old fuckers like myself are giving up.' Cornwell is actually in competition with another 'tribute band' playing old *Rattus Norvegicus* and *No More Heroes* tunes: his estranged former bandmates, still gigging under the name The Stranglers, but with a new frontman.

HISTORY REPEATS

Tribute bands originally inspired one of the strangest trends in the whole 'pop will repeat itself' culture: the art-world fad for re-enactments. Iain Forsyth and Jane Pollard, the duo who pioneered this largely British phenomenon, were already doing work influenced by their passion for music when in the late nineties they saw a poster advertising a Smiths tribute act called The Still Ills. At this point the tribute-band craze largely consisted of big theatre tours by outfits like ABBA copyists Bjorn Again or The Bootleg Beatles. But something about the idea of a tribute to The Smiths, a band they both loved, intrigued Forsyth and Pollard and they went to see The Still Ills play at a venue in New Cross, South London. 'We saw this really peculiar collapsing of the distance between performer and audience,' recalls Pollard. 'When you compared the guy onstage fronting the band and the guys in the front row, some of the audience looked more like Morrissey than he did. They knew the words.'

Treating The Still Ills 'as a ready-made, in the Marcel Duchamp sense', they staged an event involving the band, with mixed results; they were then invited to restage it at the ICA by curator Vivienne Gaskin, who would soon become the principal art-world impresario behind Britain's re-enactment boom. This second event involving The Still Ills was much more developed and conceptually resonant. It was timed for the ten-year anniversary of The Smiths splitting up in 1987. Forsyth and Pollard persuaded The Still Ills to split up as well. 'They were quite jaded and thinking of jacking it in anyway, becoming a Pulp tribute act as there was more money in that. We also knew from a publicity point of view we would get the coverage we needed, and people would come to it. That sense of something happening on that haunted day.'

Forsyth and Pollard developed a bunch of 'visual devices' to intensify the time-travel experience. They installed a phalanx

44

of televisions along the hallway to the ICA performance area, all playing alternative-music videos from the year leading up to The Smiths' break-up, and 'absolutely nothing from after they split. So there was this sense of being in this time warp.' Forsyth and Pollard took The Still Ills' frontman out to a derelict greyhound track in his home town of Litchfield and took hundreds of Morrissey-esque photographs to be slide-projected onto the walls of the venue. 'And we laid tons of flowers out on the front of the stage, hoping the audience would grab them and wave them like at the early Smiths gigs.' They describe the atmosphere as feverish, a bizarrely intense catharsis of mourning for The Smiths. 'It was absolutely mental – six hundred people, so much sweat that the camera we brought to film it on broke through condensation. The audience took it to a different level altogether: they ripped the singer's shirt off when he leaned in to the audience, there was a stage invasion with about forty people on stage.' Afterwards Vivienne Gaskin saw a girl on the ICA steps, doubled up and sobbing her heart out. 'I think it was the sense of loss,' Pollard says. Yet The Smiths had split a decade ago.

Sticking to the theme of orgiastic grief, Forsyth and Pollard's next major work, 1998's *A Rock 'N' Roll Suicide*, restaged the 'farewell' Ziggy Stardust concerts of July 1973 – in which David Bowie killed off his alter ego – exactly twenty-five years to the day after they occurred. The multiple levels of fakeness – getting an actor to pretend to be the cracked actor Bowie performing his own meta-rockstar persona Ziggy – were irresistible. This time Forsyth and Pollard assembled their own tribute band. Unlike the Still Ills show, this was an actual recreation of a historical event, so they could draw on documentary footage of the concert: principally D. A. Pennebaker's *Ziggy Stardust and the Spiders from Mars*, but also Super-8 films made by fans.

'Pennebaker's film makes the gig look red,' says Forsyth. 'It turned out to be something to do with the 16-mm film that he

45

used. But we decided to have the lighting make the gig look red, because even people who had gone to the original gig, through watching the movie over and over, it had distorted their memory.' Another distortion from the Ziggy movie was that flashes from the photographers taking pictures of the show looked much bigger on celluloid than they would have done to people actually at the concert. 'We set up a strobe to create the same effect.' As with the Still Ills/Smiths event at the ICA, the audience 'let themselves be totally swept away', says Pollard. 'They completely played what they perceived to be their part. They were there with their seventies Bowie scarves and were right there on every cue, clapping, shouting, gasping.'

Completing a sort of trilogy of rock re-enactments, 2003's *File Under Sacred Music* took as its source a show played by The Cramps in 1978 at the Napa State Mental Institute, to an audience of genuinely crazy people rocking out dementedly to the group's 'psychobilly' sound. Guitarist Poison Ivy recalled the gig as 'like playing for children. People had no sense of space boundaries . . . people dry humping on the ground . . . There was very little supervision from the staff. It was insane.' How the free concert came about is lost to the mists of time, but the performance was captured on film and circulated for years as a fan bootleg video. 'It was this mythologised, underground thing,' says Pollard. 'Only twenty minutes long, but really powerful.'

File Under Sacred Music differed from *A Rock 'N' Roll Suicide* in a fundamental way: the goal was not to re-enact the performance but to recreate the video itself. The restaged gig, which took place at the ICA, was just a means to an end; the actual art object would be the simulacrum of the specific bootleg copy that had come into Pollard and Forsyth's hands, complete with its unique glitches and copy-of-a-copy defects. This meant that *File Under Sacred Music* could reach a much bigger audience, touring as a film to museums and galleries around the world, in comparison with *A*

Rock 'N' Roll Suicide, which took a huge amount of preparation but resulted in only two unrepeatable performances. Recreating the Cramps gig itself was a huge undertaking, involving the recruitment of genuinely mentally ill people to play the role of the Napa psychiatric hospital's audience. Having filmed the event (which developed 'its own weird, chaotic energy – one guy threw up, another threw beer on someone's face who was asleep', says Pollard), the next set of challenges involved converting their footage into an exact replica of the bootleg they owned. 'That had been transferred from NTSC to PAL somewhere along its history, and then it had been re-filmed off a television. The bootlegger had played their copy on a VHS machine and they pointed a camera at the TV screen – you can see the edge of the television, and the lines of the screen.' Pollard and Forsyth painstakingly retraced all the steps taken by the original bootlegger and then explored various digital methods to get the tape glitches, before settling on old-fashioned analogue techniques like crumpling the tapes up or getting water on them and drying them out.

The project's title was taken from the spine of The Cramps' debut LP, *Songs the Lord Taught Us*. Its combination of archival anal retentiveness ('file under') and spiritual ecstasy ('sacred music') captures the contradiction of The Cramps themselves: a group who believed in rock'n'roll's primal frenzy, but who were too knowledgeable and too knowing, as record-collector scholars of rockabilly, to get 'real gone' for real. At the Napa gig, their stylised version of Dionysian madness confronts the real thing; psychobilly meets psychosis. Like *A Rock 'N' Roll Suicide*, *File Under Sacred Music* is a simulation of a simulation, a replica of a replica.

For their next project, Pollard and Forsyth toyed with the idea of other rock re-enactments (including a New York Dolls piece) but decided that the idea was played out. So the duo moved from re-enactments to reworkings: adaptations or reinterpretations of pioneering works of video performance art from the seventies by figures like Bruce Nauman and Vito Acconci. Nauman's *Art Make Up* became *Kiss My Nauman*, performed by a member of the world's longest-running Kiss tribute band, who is filmed applying his cosmetics.

The shift to reworkings was also a response to the duo's sense that re-enactments had become a bit too trendy in the art world. Jeremy Deller's famous 2001 recreation of the Battle of Orgreave, the critical clash between picketing miners and riot police at a South Yorkshire coking plant in June 1984, had received a lot of attention and contributed heavily to Deller winning the 2004 Turner Prize. Another key figure in the emerging field, Rod Dickinson, founded a collective called The Jonestown Re-enactment. At the ICA in May 2000, they staged the 'reconstruction' of an anti-capitalist sermon delivered by cult leader Jim Jones to his People's Temple flock. Dickinson would go on to re-enact Dr Stanley Milgram's 1961 social-psychology experiment 'Obedience to Authority' and recreate the audio portion of the Waco siege (the FBI's use of monstrously amplified music and 'irritating sounds' as a weapon). Soon, artists from outside the UK started getting in on the re-enactment action, like Slater Bradley with his work based around Kurt Cobain, or Marina Abramović's *Seven Easy Pieces*, which re-performed seminal performance art from the sixties and seventies (including works by Nauman and Acconci). There were exhibitions and seminars with titles like *A Little Bit of History Repeated* and *Once More . . . with Feeling*. There was even a novel, Tom McCarthy's *Remainder*, published in 2005 to great acclaim. In it, an accident victim whose memory has been impaired uses his unexpectedly huge compensation payment to restage ultra-vivid but opaque scenes from his own life: for instance, buying a building and altering its decor, hiring re-enactors to play the occupants, and recreating every last sense impression, from the smell of liver cooked by a downstairs neighbour to the faltering sound of a practising pianist on another floor.

At the height of the buzz about re-enactment, the ICA's Vivienne Gaskin sent out a call for proposals. One of the pieces she commissioned was British artist Jo Mitchell's recreation of *Concerto for Voice & Machinery*, a legendary January 1984 performance at the ICA by members of the infamous German metal-bashing outfit Einstürzende Neubauten which had escalated into an audience riot. The idea of restaging the event, complete with the disorder, in the very same auditorium at the ICA had a conceptual neatness that was irresistible.

Concerto for Voice & Machinery II was a meticulous attempt to recreate the original event, which primarily involved members of Einstürzende Neubauten playing their usual unconventional musical instruments (power drill, angle grinder, cement mixer, and so forth), with contributions from various industrial-music fellow travellers such as Genesis P-Orridge. Accounts vary widely, but the performance appears to have gotten out of hand, with someone – a member of the ensemble or an audience member – attempting to drill through the auditorium floor. The audience then got the impression, possibly mistaken, that the ICA officials were attempting to shut the show down, resulting in altercations, shouting and some low-level destruction.

The notion of a planned riot obviously courts absurdity; as does the attempt to meticulously replicate chaotic events that have been exaggerated and distorted in their telling over the years. When Mitchell wrote her proposal, she was unaware of the dearth of documentation. 'I really did think I would find film footage of it. I thought the ICA would have recorded it.' But the ICA archives had nothing; after all, this was not an era in which everything was automatically filmed or sound-recorded (today, the most minor gig is likely to be saved for posterity by a band member or put onto YouTube as unofficial cellphone footage before the gig is even finished). All Mitchell had to draw on were live reviews in the three music papers that covered the event, pictures taken by

49

those papers' photographers and an assortment of wildly contradictory accounts from eye witnesses.

During the year-long process of researching and preparing for the event, Mitchell did eventually get hold of a bootleg
audio recording of the 1984 event, and Neubauten member Mark
Chung provided her with the score for the *Concerto*. 'It has three
movements, basically: an intro, and then road drills come in
and chords and voices, and it climaxes with this big finale called
"Down to the Queen". The idea was that as a climax the group
would drill through the floor in the vague direction of the tunnels rumoured to exist deep underneath the ICA which allegedly
connected Buckingham Palace to underground bunkers built as
shelters for the royal family and members of the government in
the event of a nuclear attack.

Through the photographers, who supplied her with contact-
sheet images that had never been printed, Mitchell was able to get
a sense of who had been the ringleaders and troublemakers in the
audience, and to cast and costume actors appropriately (one particularly proactive rioter sported a Mohican, for instance). The
re-enactment involved actors playing the musicians, crowd members and ICA security people and officials; this meant that the
performance on 20 February 2007 had a real audience mingled
with the actor audience, and two sets of ICA employees, one fake
and the other real. These real-deal ICA officials had a somewhat
sanitising effect on the re-enactment, stepping in to prevent over-
enthused members of the actual audience from joining in with
the staged destruction. There were also tighter health-and-safety
regulations: 'There couldn't be as much dust or smoke as there
was in 1984, and ICA people even handed out earplugs to the
audience. There was a limit on the amount of decibels we were
allowed to go to and restrictions on the sparks generated by the
angle grinder.'

Another aspect oddly dissonant to the original spirit of the event was the fact that Mitchell secured the sponsorship of the equipment-rental company HSS Tool Hire. Re-enactments are very expensive, she explains, what with all the rehearsals and cast members. 'In the photographs I could see all the cement mixers, and they were from HSS, one of the biggest tool-hire companies. I needed the machinery for the three weeks of rehearsals, and so they covered that, which would have otherwise cost £10,000.'

Blixa Bargeld, Neubaten's chief conceptualist and frontman, had given Mitchell his blessing and found the whole idea of recreating the *Concerto* to be 'charming'. Although he'd participated in the later stages of mayhem in the original performance, he decided not to attend as a spectator for fear of being a distraction (and perhaps compromising the temporal integrity of the re-enactment). But while today's mellow, urbane Bargeld was tickled pink, I can't help suspecting that the young, amphetamine-wired Blixa would have seen red. For Einstürzende Neubauten were even more fundamentally opposed to the idea of heritage culture than punk. Steeped in Artaud, Nietzsche and Bataille, their whole artistic project was fuelled by an apocalyptic lust for collapse (their name translates as 'collapsing new buildings'), a hunger to hasten the end of history. *Concerto for Voice & Machinery* was also Neubauten's small-scale version of The Sex Pistols' boat trip on the Thames – the moment when rock collides with authority. But what does it mean to make that clash happen 'again', this time with the permission of the authority in question?

I've never really seen the point of historical re-enactments: all that meticulous attention to getting the uniforms right, the cannon smoke. It seems obvious that the simulation of 'being there' fails on every level: you know there's no real danger of death; you know what the outcome is going to be. It's an exercise in pageantry. Nothing is really in jeopardy. In history-as-lived, the participants at Gettysburg didn't know that the Confederates were not going to win. Likewise, the audience who turned up for the

51

original *Concerto for Voice & Machinery* didn't know that the event would descend into chaos.

Doubtless these contradictions are integral to the restaging by Mitchell. 'In a way, the impossibility of recreating the event was part of it,' she says. Similar sentiments have been voiced by other prominent re-enactment artists: Rod Dickinson, for instance, has described his work as 'constructing a series of paradoxes . . . high-lighting the contradictions that arise through trying to do some-thing like that, the impossibility of it'. Forsyth and Pollard often talk in interviews about how 'failure is hugely important to us . . . Copying anything, the copy never reproduces the original com-pletely. And this shortfall is where the Real emerges . . . Good art always, at some level, fails.'

Chatting with Mitchell and with Forsyth and Pollard, I noticed how animated they became when they talked about the challenges of the projects, the strenuous research, the obsessive attention to getting the period details as precise as possible. For *Rock 'N' Roll Suicide*, Iain and Jane located one of Bowie's original costume designers. Mitchell enthused about getting 'really sucked into just utter immersion . . . it's probably the geekiest I have ever felt. I had hundreds of still images, most of them rephotographed from contact sheets supplied by the three original photographers and printed up as pictures, and I'd strewn them across the floor, try-ing to put them into some sort of narrative.'

Mitchell and Forsyth and Pollard were forthcoming and engaged about all these 'how' aspects of their re-enactment proj-ects. But somehow the 'why' kept eluding us in our conversations. The same thing happened when I checked out art criticism on this subject, which left me with little more than a vague impres-sion that the work was timely and resonant.

What *is* it about the present that makes this kind of art not just conceivable and desirable but even inevitable? As this chap-ter indicates, re-enactment is indebted to and at some level is a response to the rise of heritage: museums, spectacles of 'living history' such as working villages or restaged battles, preservation as a cultural ideal. Re-enactment art is also enmeshed in a wider culture of the copy, encompassing everything from karaoke, TV shows like *Stars in Their Eyes*, which involve ordinary people impersonating famous performers, the huge (but off the media radar) live-music economy of tribute bands, the online subcultures of fan fiction and YouTube parody, to monstrously successful music video games like *Rock Band* and *Guitar Hero*. At a more highbrow level, there have been conceptual remakes such as the artist Pierre Huyghe's *Fenêtre sur cour* (a recreation of Hitchcock's *Rear Window*, reset in a Parisian housing estate) and Gus Van Sant's shot-by-shot recreation of *Psycho*. Hollywood's endless stream of remakes contribute heavily to the culture of replication and redundancy. In a rock-specific way, so do movies like *School of Rock* and *The Rocker*: comically presenting rock'n'roll as a highly formularised style of rebellion, they simultaneously satirise and perpetuate the syndrome. In the former, Jack Black's teacher trains the children in all the orthodox, time-honoured gestures that signify freedom, excess and 'sticking it to the Man'. It's a copy of a copy of a copy, but his regimented notion of true rock'n'roll, as implemented through his pupils, is not so different from what can be seen on stages all across the developed world. Johan Kugelberg uses the analogy of the historical battle re-enactment to describe modern-day punk bands who effectively recreate 'thirty-year-old gigs' that originally took place at legendary dives like CBGB, the Masque in LA, the Mabuhay in San Francisco and London's 100 Club (not forgetting the numerous actual surviving punk bands from that era still arthritically treading the boards).

Although they've emerged out of the art world rather than from rock culture itself, rock re-enactments resonate with a buried hunger within the music scene for a spasm like punk or rave

53

that would turn the world upside down. On the face of it, re-enactments seem just to feed into a backwards-looking culture that's taking us ever further from the conditions in which such total transformations and singular disruptions were possible. But perhaps the artists are onto something when they talk about failure as the goal: a *goad* to the audience, simultaneously stirring up and frustrating the longing for the Event. The latter is the philosopher Alain Badiou's term for a dramatic historical break, a rupture that is also an irruption of newness. It can take political form (various revolutions, May 1968) or be a scientific or cultural breakthrough (Schoenberg's twelve-tone scale), but the Event divides up time into Before and After, opening towards a future that promises to be absolutely different from the past.

Re-enactment art is at once an extension of and an inversion of performance art, which is event-based by definition. Performance is all about the here and now. Its components include the bodily presence of the artists, a physical location and its duration: it is an experience that you have to sit through. Performance art's power is bound up with its ephemerality: it can't be reproduced, collected or enter the art market, and any incidental documentation it leaves behind is no substitute for having seen it in the flesh. Re-enactment is like a spectral form of performance art: what the viewer witnesses never quite achieves full presence or present-ness.

The defining quality of performance art is that it happens in real time, but with re-enactments time is out of joint. As Tom McCarthy puts it, 'Re-enactment brings about a kind of split within the act itself . . . on the one hand it's something you do, and on the other it's not something you're actually "doing": it's a citation, a marker for another event that this one isn't.' No matter how much research and preparation goes into a re-enactment, it is doomed to be an absurd ghost, a travesty of the original. Yet the re-enactment may still have the power to remind the audience that Events are possible, because they've happened before.

2

TOTAL RECALL

Music and Memory in the Time of YouTube

Sometimes I think our culture has succumbed to Chris Farley Syndrome. That's the name of both a character in a regular sketch they used to do on *Saturday Night Live* and the now deceased comedian who played the role. A young man who presents a cable TV talk show out of his own living room, 'Chris Farley' has bizarrely good luck getting interviews with really famous stars (i.e. the weekly guest hosts on *SNL*). In a typical sketch, a celebrity such as Paul McCartney would sit politely on Farley's sofa, while the bumbling amateur interviewer, flustered and visibly dripping sweat, stammered his way through a series of inane questions, invariably starting with: 'D'ya remember . . .'. So in Macca's case, this took the form of 'D'ya remember, Paul . . . d'ya remember . . . "Eleanor Rigby"?' To which Macca would reply, with just the faintest hint of bemusement, 'Why yes, Chris, I *do* remember "Eleanor Rigby".' Farley then would blurt, ''Cos that was . . . that was . . . so . . . *cool*.' Then, suddenly realising his own vacuity, he'd start slapping his own forehead and berating himself: 'Idiot, IDIOT.' Only to do it again. And again.

All those *I Love the [Decade]* programmes were chronic cases of Chris Farley Syndrome. Most of the guest commentators did barely more than parrot the catchphrase/song lyric/advertising

slogan under consideration or emit some variant of 'That was . . .
so . . . *cool.*' But the true metastasis of Chris Farley Syndrome must
be YouTube's indiscriminate chaos of amateur cultural salvage.

YouTube's ever-proliferating labyrinth of collective recollection is a prime example of the crisis of overdocumentation triggered by digital technology. When cultural data is dematerialised,
our capacity to store, sort and access it is vastly increased and
enhanced. The compression of text, images and audio means that
issues of space and cost no longer deter us from keeping anything and everything that seems remotely interesting or amusing.
Advances in user-friendly technology (the scanner, the domestic
video recorder, the mobile-phone camera) make it irresistibly
quick and convenient to share stuff: photographs, songs and mix-
tapes, excerpts from television, vintage magazines, book illustrations and covers, period graphics, you name it. And once it's up
on the Web, a lot of it stays out there, for ever.

A profound shift has taken place in which YouTube serves as
both major player and potent symbol: the astronomic expansion
of humanity's resources of memory. We have available to us, as
individuals, but also at the level of civilisation, immensely more
'space' to fill with memorabilia, documentation, recordings, every
kind of archival trace of our existence. And naturally, we are
busily filling that space, even as its capacity continues to balloon.
Yet there is no evidence that we have significantly increased our
ability to process or make good use of all that memory.

Writing about the 'memory epidemic' that's gripped the developed world in the last couple of decades, Andreas Huyssen asked
plaintively, 'Total recall seems to be the goal. Is this an archivist's
fantasy gone mad?' But what's really significant isn't so much the
'total recall' as the instant access that the Web's cultural databases
make possible. In the pre-Internet era, there was already way
more information and culture than any individual could digest.
But most of this culture data and culture matter was stashed

out of our everyday reach, in libraries, museums and galleries. Nowadays search engines have obliterated the delays involved in searching through a library's murky, maze-like stacks.

What this means is that the presence of the past in our lives has increased immeasurably and insidiously. Old stuff either directly permeates the present, or lurks just beneath the surface of the current, in the form of on-screen windows to other times. We've become so used to this convenient access that it is a struggle to recall that life wasn't always like this; that relatively recently, one lived most of the time in a cultural present tense, with the past confined to specific zones, trapped in particular objects and locations.

The easiest way to convey how things have changed is to compare the present with conditions when I was a lad back in the late seventies. Let's look at music first. Record companies deleted records from their catalogues in those days; I dare say you could find out-of-print releases in second-hand stores or obtain them from specialist mail-order companies, but the whole record-collector culture was in its infancy. I can distinctly remember the first few times I noticed reissues getting reviewed in the music papers – Tim Buckley's *Greetings from LA*, a pair of Faust albums – because it was a really unusual occurrence. Box sets and deluxe repackagings of classic artists were virtually unheard of in the late seventies. Listening to old music was limited to what you could find in shops, what you could afford on a limited budget. You could also tape music from the collections of your friends, or from public libraries, but this was limited by what was available and the cost of blank cassettes. Today, any young person has access to virtually anything that's ever been recorded, free of charge, and anyone can easily bone up on all the history and context of the music through Wikipedia and a thousand music blogs and fan sites.

The situation was similar in other areas of popular culture. TV repeats were few and far between, rarely dating back further than a few years. There were no channels devoted entirely to vintage TV, no DVD collections of classic series, no Netflix or even video stores. Classic movies and cineaste obscurities would flicker onto TV schedules, but if you missed them, they were gone, utterly inaccessible (apart from fleeting, unpredictable appearances at 'midnight movie'-type cinemas that screened esoteric repertory).

Our relationship to time and space in this YouTubeWikipedia-RapidshareiTunesSpotify era has been utterly transformed. Distance and delay have been eroded to nearly nothing. To give you just one example, close at hand: while I was writing the preceding paragraph, I was listening to a parody version of Beethoven's Symphony No. 6 (the Pastoral Symphony) on a compilation of 'comic' avant-garde music called *Smiling Through My Teeth*. This made me want to hear the real thing in un-mangled form. I could easily have strolled across the apartment to the walk-in closet where most of my record collection is stashed, but rather than break my workflow I stayed in front of the computer and headed for YouTube, where I found dozens of versions performed by various orchestras. (I could equally have listened to it without pictures, via the sound files embedded at the Wikipedia entry on Beethoven's Sixth, or downloaded it in a trice, legally or illegally). I marvelled at how swiftly I could scratch this particular musical itch – though of course I got sucked into comparing the many alternate versions of the Pastoral juxtaposed on YouTube's scroll-down sidebar: proof, if any were needed, that there's a downside to access and choice.

YouTube is not the only online video upload site, of course. But as the pioneer in the field and the market-leader, YouTube's dominance means that it stands in for the whole industry in the same way that Kleenex and Hoover became general terms for tissue or vacuum cleaner. At the time of writing (the summer of 2010), YouTube has passed a major milestone: it's now streaming a staggering two billion views per day, making it the third most visited website on the planet. Every minute another twenty-four hours' worth of video gets uploaded, and it would take the individual viewer 1,700 years to watch all of the hundreds of millions of videos on the site.

YouTube isn't just a website, though, or even a technology, but more a whole field of cultural practice. Media theorist Lucas Hilderbrand uses concepts like 'remediation' and 'postbroadcasting' to pinpoint what is innovative about YouTube. The 're' in remediation indicates that it is largely, if not completely, dependent on the output of the mainstream corporate entertainment industry: music promos made by and paid for by major labels, network TV programmes, Hollywood movies. Of course, there is a lot of other stuff 'up there' that is non-mainstream and DIY: esoteric and underground music/art/film/animation, amateur videos of babies and cats doing cute things, teenagers goofing around in their bedrooms or in the street, footage of bands playing live documented by fans using cellphones. But a high proportion of the content of YouTube is mainstream entertainment and news re-presented, in excerpted form, by its consumers: talk-show snippets, period-piece TV commercials, theme songs, long-lost vintage footage of bands performing on TV, favourite sequences from movies. As for 'post-broadcasting', the 'post' has two connotations: 'post' as in leaving behind the era of a cultural mainstream (the dominance of the big TV networks) and entering a consumer-empowered era of niche-audience narrowcasting; and 'post' as in postmodern (art that's based around pastiche and citation). YouTube teems with fan fiction-style treatments of mainstream entertainment: parodies, people doing karaoke versions of pop songs, mash-ups and other forms of 'culture jamming' based on the re-editing of footage. These mocking travesties recall the sample-based audio pranks of outfits like the KLF, Culturcide and Negativland.

59

Looking at YouTube from a purely musical perspective, two things are particularly striking about this new (post-)broadcast medium. The first is the way that YouTube has become the repository of ultra-rare TV appearances or bootleg live footage that once upon a time were treasured and traded by hardcore fans. Advertising in the back pages of *Goldmine* or *Record Collector*, communicating via fanzines and pen-pal networks, fans would swap or sell video cassettes, copied and recopied so many times that the image of Elvis or Bowie could only be dimly perceived through a blizzard of dubbed distortion. Nowadays this stuff lives on YouTube, freely available to anybody who cares enough to click. When I think of how useful this would have been to me when writing my post-punk history *Rip It Up* (which was finished about eighteen months before YouTube launched in the winter of 2005), I have mixed emotions: retrospective frustration offset by a strange feeling of relief. For as much as it would have been a great resource, I could easily have lost myself in the endless clips of live footage, ancient promo videos and TV appearances.

The other really interesting development affecting music has been the way that fans have transformed large swathes of this video archive into a purely audio resource, uploading songs accompanied by abstract, screen-saver-type moving patterns or a still image (in many cases, just a still of the record cover or label, or a grainy shot of the record playing on a turntable). Whole albums are being put up on YouTube by fans, with each track accompanied by the same generic and desultory image. YouTube's combination of promo videos and audio uploads means that it has become a public library of recorded sound (albeit a disorganised, messy one, with few omissions but plenty of repetition and 'damaged copies'). You can even 'borrow' without returning, using tools like Dirpy to convert YouTube videos into MP3s.

YouTube is much easier to consult than my huge and disorganised record collection. On some occasions I've actually downloaded albums off the Web that I already own, just to avoid the bother of rummaging through boxes for them. No matter that the CD or vinyl will sound so much better. MP3s are good enough if you're in a hurry (in my case, I'm usually looking to check something for reference purposes, so effectively treating the music as information rather than an immersive sonic experience). YouTube itself is an example of this kind of digital culture trade-off between quality and convenience. The medium has 'crummy image and sound quality', notes Hilderbrand, describing how the tolerable quality of the picture when in small-screen mode is exposed in all its true lo-res crapness when you click on 'full screen'. But just as listeners have accepted the 'lossy', thin-bodied sound of MP3s because of the advantages of compact storage and ease of exchange, nobody seems to mind the reduced fidelity of television viewing via computer screen (even though it is running in the opposite direction elsewhere with high-definition TV, 5.0 surround-sound home-movie theatres, 3D movies, and so forth).

In compensation, we have the vastly enhanced access and the quantity-over-quality volume and range of the online archive. We also have the consumer-empowering convenience of the time display at the bottom of the video, which allows the viewer to drag the scroll bar and jump within the video clip (or song) to get to 'the good bit' sooner. YouTube, based around excerpts, is already in the business of fragmenting larger narratives (the programme, the movie, the album), but this function actually encourages us, as viewers, to break cultural fragments into even smaller sub-units, insidiously eroding our ability to concentrate and our willingness to let something unfold. As with the Internet as a whole, our sense of temporality grows ever more brittle and inconstant: restlessly snacking on data bytes, we flit fitfully in search of the next instant sugar rush.

YouTube encourages this kind of drift through its sidebar of videos deemed, often by skewed logic, to be related to the one you're watching. It is hard not to fall into an inattentive, easily detached mode of viewing somewhere between browsing and channel-surfing (except that you're always flitting within one channel, YouTube, itself now a province of the Google empire, which bought the company in October 2006). This lateral drift is not just from artist to artist or genre to genre but a wandering across time, since video artifacts from different eras are jumbled promiscuously and linked by a latticework of criss-crossing associations.

This kind of drift stems partly from the disorderly nature of YouTube, which is more like a jumbled attic than an archive, only laxly framed and annotated. But elsewhere on the Web, all kinds of official organisations and amateur associations are assembling well-managed cultural databases whose contents are available to the general public. The British Library, for instance, recently made its huge collection of ethnographic music available online free of charge: approximately 28,000 recordings and 2,000 hours of traditional music, ranging from wax-cylinder documentation of aboriginal songs made by the anthropologist Alfred Cort Haddon in 1898 to the Decca West Africa label's mid-twentieth-century recordings of calypso and quickstep. The National Film Board of Canada operates a similar stream-for-free archive of its renowned documentaries, nature shows and animations by luminaries such as Norman McLaren. Then there's UbuWeb, a gold mine of avant-garde cinema, sound poetry, music and text administered by fans but presented with a scholarly meticulousness. UbuWeb is dedicated to making works that would otherwise languish in the storage chambers of art museums or the recesses of university collections, perhaps making very occasional public appearances at festivals and exhibitions, globally and permanently available.

Beyond organisations like UbuWeb, there's a teeming hinterland of blogs like The Sound of Eye, BibliOdyssey, 45cat and Found Objects, operated by individuals or small groups of like-minds, amateur curators who are frenetically hurling all manner of esoteric images and sounds up onto the Internet: curios and lost classics of twentieth-century book illustration, graphic design and typography; short avant-garde films and animations; scanned articles and, increasingly, entire issues of obscure periodicals, journals and fanzines; ancient public-information films and the intros to innumerable long-lost children's shows; and so forth. If I had a second life (one that was also blessed with a private income), I could happily while away my days feasting on all this culture carrion.

On the Internet, the past and the present commingle in a way that makes time itself mushy and spongiform. YouTube is quintessentially Web 2.0 in the way that it promises immortality to every video uploaded: theoretically the content could stay up there for ever. You can flit from the archaic to the up-to-the-minute in a click. The result, culturally, is a paradoxical combination of speed and standstill. You can see this manifested on every level of Web 2.0 reality: an incredibly rapid turnover of news (current-affairs and politics blogs updating every ten minutes, trending topics on Twitter, blog buzz) coexisting with the stubborn persistence of nostalgic crud. Into the chasm between these two poles drops both the recent past and what you might call 'the long present': trends with staying power, bands with careers longer than an album, subcultures and movements as opposed to fads and flavours. The recent past drops away into an amnesiac void, while the long present gets chiselled down to wafer-width, simply because of the incredible pace with which the pages of the current and the topical are refreshed.

OUTSELLING THE PRESENT

'Pop music is more fleeting nowadays,' says Ed Christman, the senior retail editor at *Billboard*. I contacted Christman because

I wanted to find out if consumers were buying more old music these days. He explained that the industry divided releases up into 'current' (which spanned from day one of release to fifteen months later) and 'catalogue' (from the sixteenth month onwards). But catalogue itself was divided up into two categories: what was relatively recent, and what was 'deep catalogue', to which music was assigned three years after release. Christman's sense was that the category of relatively recent catalogue (releases between fifteen months and three years old) was 'not as strong as it used to be'. And it's true that bands do seem to have shorter careers, with blockbuster debuts followed by flops; the greater proportion of bands with real staying power seem to be leftovers from the sixties, seventies and eighties.

When it came to my main area of intrigue – the relative ratio between old-music purchases versus new-music purchases – Christman dug up some statistics for me. In the year 2000, he said, catalogue sales (including both recent catalogue and deep) accounted for 34.4 per cent of total album sales in America, while current stood at 65.6 per cent; by the year 2008, catalogue had increased to 41.7 per cent, while current was 58.3. That didn't seem such a dramatic change, but according to Christman this steady, year-by-year shift all through the 2000s towards older music was very significant. It contrasted with an absolutely static ratio between current and catalogue that was maintained during the entire nineties (there are no figures for prior to that).

What made the increase in catalogue sales even more significant was that it was actually harder for consumers to get hold of non-current releases thanks to the appalling decline of record retail. 'All the traditional record stores that had deep catalogue and lots of it have been going out of business,' Christman said. He added that the ones that survived had been forced to carry non-musical products (such as games), which meant they drastically reduced the number of music titles they kept in stock. For instance, in 2000, Borders carried fifty thousand titles; by 2008, that figure had gone down to under ten thousand.

But if the traditional breadth of deep catalogue had been disappearing from record stores, which themselves had been drastically thinning in number, that begged the question: how had sales of old music managed to increase during the past decade? Part of the explanation was the rise of online retailers like Amazon, who could maintain vast back stock because of their economies of scale and warehouses in low-rent zones. You also had specific catalogue titles being reissued as 'new spiffy things', as Christman put it: anniversary editions and deluxe double CDs that were packaged and promoted as if they were new releases, and accordingly got prominent display in record stores. Finally, there was the rise of digital sales: the iPod explosion reawakened a lot of lapsed music fans' ardour for music (some of which would be old music, a catalogue boom similar to the CD-reissuing of classic albums from the mid-eighties onwards), who were also able for the first time to buy tracks rather than whole albums. Christman told me that 2009 was 'the first year that Soundscan separated out current and catalogue for its digital figures', and this had revealed that catalogue accounts for 'the majority of digital-track sales, 64.3 per cent compared to current's 35.7 per cent'. I suspect there must be a similar heavy slant towards old music in illegal downloads. It stands to reason: the past can't help but outweigh the present, not just in sheer quantity but also in quality too. For argument's sake, let's assume that approximately the same amount of great music is produced each year (averaging out the fluctuations within specific genres). That would mean each new year's harvest of brilliance must compete with the past's ever more mountainous heap of greatness. How many records released in 2011 will be as worthwhile an acquisition for a neophyte listener as *Rubber Soul*, *Astral Weeks*, *Closer*, *Hatful of Hollow*?

The concept of back catalogue is a key element of Chris

Anderson's much-discussed, and sometimes disputed, theory of the Long Tail. The slant of the argument is the familiar techno-utopian narrative we've seen so often in *Wired*, where Anderson's original article ran before it was expanded into the best-selling book *The Long Tail: Why the Future of Business Is Selling Less of More*. He claimed that the retail environment created by the Internet shifts the balance in favour of the little guy (the plucky individual entrepreneur, small independent publishers and record labels, minority-interest artists), as opposed to corporate-entertainment conglomerates with their orientation towards blockbuster hits and megastars, big first-week sales and expensive promotional campaigns.

The intriguing subtext to the Long Tail theory is that the new-media environment also shifts the balance in favour of the past and to the disadvantage of the culturally current. Right at the start of his original October 2004 *Wired* article, Anderson tells the story of a currently best-selling memoir about mountaineer-ing (*Into Thin Air*) whose success directed consumers towards a much older book on the same subject by a different author (Joe Simpson's *Touching the Void*), thanks to Amazon.com's 'If you like that, try this' algorithm and readers' recommendations. Simpson's book had only ever been moderately successful and was actually on the verge of going out of print, but thanks to *Into Thin Air* it resurged and became a best-seller. Anderson describes how Amazon 'created the *Touching the Void* phenom-enon by combining infinite shelf space with real-time informa-tion about buying trends and public opinion', and characterises the resulting 'rising demand for an obscure book' as a victory of the margins against the mainstream, of quality against force-fed, top-down pap. But when Anderson crows that 'now *Touching the Void* outsells *Into Thin Air* more than two to one', he is actually describing an instance of the past defeating the (then) present: 1988 eclipsing 1999.

The central thesis of the Long Tail is that 'the tyranny of physical space' has been overthrown by the Internet. Retailers in the pre-Net era were limited by the number of consumers that could physically reach the store. They were also limited by the amount of stock they could keep, because the closer you are to densely populated areas, the more expensive storage space becomes. But the Web allowed companies to locate in remote, low-rent areas where they could warehouse huge volumes of back stock, allowing for unprecedented range. They could also aggregate geographically dispersed niche audiences, overcoming the problem of 'an audience too thinly spread' being the 'the same as no audience at all'. But the Long Tail syndrome also represents a victory over the tyranny of time: the dominance in retailing of the current and the brand new. In traditional retail, storage space and display space are paid for by a certain rate of sale, which is what makes it worth keeping a CD on the racks in a record store or a DVD on the shelves in a video store; at a certain point, older stock must be marked down or got rid of. When storage space gets dramatically cheaper (operating out of low-rent, extra-urban areas) or infinitesimally small through digitisation (Netflix's online repertory of films and television series, digital-music companies like iTunes and eMusic), the result is that inventory can expand vastly. If the store display areas are online and virtual, there is also absolutely no pressure to get rid of older, slow-selling items to make space for newer releases.

'From DVDs at Netflix to music videos on Yahoo! . . . to songs in the iTunes Music Store and Rhapsody . . .' Anderson exults, 'people are going deep into the catalog, down the long, long list of available titles, far past what's available at Blockbuster Video, Tower Records, and Barnes & Noble.' Going 'far past' means going *far into the past*, as much as it can also mean extending way beyond the mainstream (to esoteric independent-label-culture releases and exotic imports). Because small sales over a long period count as profit when storage costs are infinitesimal, Anderson believes that the Long Tail approach should entail making available 'huge chunks of the archive' at a budget price. He specifically instructs the music industry to re-release 'all the back catalogs as quickly as it can – thoughtlessly, automatically, and at industrial scale'. Which is more or less what was happening all through the last decade and going back to the nineties, either actively instigated by the labels themselves or licensed out to specialist companies who trawl through older and bigger labels' back catalogues for Famous Band's Bassist's solo albums, offshoot projects, before-they-got-famous early stabs and after-the-fame-faded-away has-been releases.

The result has been a steady encroachment by past production on the window of attention that current production had hitherto dominated. In a sense, the past has always been in competition with the present, culturally speaking. But the terrain has gradually shifted to the past's drastic advantage, thanks to late-nineties and early-2000s developments such as satellite and internet radio (some of whose huge array of channels are formatted to vintage genres or generational cohorts) and the internet-connected 'infinite jukebox' that allows bar patrons to select from as many as two million tunes.

Underlying these recent innovations is the fundamental switch-over from analogue to digital: from recordings based around analogues of waveforms (vinyl, magnetic tape) to recordings that work through the encoding and decoding of information (compact discs, MP3s). This revolution was pushed to the hilt by the music industry in the eighties, apparently quite oblivious to its Achilles heel: it is so much easier to copy audio and video when it is encoded as data. A vinyl analogue recording can only be copied in real time; the magnetic information on an audio cassette or video tape can be copied at only slightly sped-up rates (otherwise there's a drastic loss of fidelity). Digital encoding enables much faster copying with minimal depreciation of quality. A copy of a copy of a copy is basically the same as the original, because it is information, the digital code of zeroes and ones, that is being replicated.

The implications of this fatal flaw became apparent not long after the launch of software for encoding MP3s in July 1994, followed a year later by the first MP3 player (WinPlay3). Developed by the German research institute Fraunhofer with the goal of being the worldwide standard medium for digital audio/video entertainment, the MP3 gradually spread during the late nineties. But it only really took off as bandwidth increased and a succession of peer-to-peer file-sharing networks and services (Napster, BitTorrent, Soulseek, etc.) took turns to flourish and wither. The essence of the MP3 is compression. Space (the sonic depth of a recording) is squeezed into a vastly smaller physical area than a vinyl record, an analogue tape cassette or even a laser-inscribed compact disc, while time is similarly compressed in the sense that the time it takes to copy or transmit through the Internet a piece of music is much briefer than the actual duration of the musical experience.

According to music-technology scholar Jonathan Sterne, Fraunhofer developed the MP3 by devising 'a mathematical model of human auditory perception' to work out what data they could get away with discarding because it would not be heard by the average listener in the average listening situation. The technicalities of this process are complex and somewhat mind-boggling (for instance, parts of the frequency spectrum are converted into mono, while other parts – the stretch of the audio spectrum that most listeners notice – stay in stereo). Suffice to say that the result of the process is the characteristic flatness of sound-picture and the thin-bodied textures we've all grown accustomed to through hearing music as MP3s. (Of course, any sense of diminishment of sonic richness only really applies to those of us old enough to have had a history of listening to music as vinyl or compact disc; for many younger listeners, MP3 and music heard through computer speakers and iPods is simply what recorded sound sounds like). The sheer convenience of MP3s, in terms of sharing, acquiring and portability (what the industry calls 'place-shifting', moving your music between playback devices and contexts of use), has encouraged us to adapt to the lower-quality sound. Besides, most music fans aren't audiophiles hung up on sound reproduction and intangible qualities like 'presence'. Audiophiles are usually analogue fanatics, into 180-gram vinyl and turntables that cost thousands of pounds. But the fact is that even within the realm of digital music there's a pronounced difference in quality between an MP3 and a pre-recorded CD. Every so often I'll get the proper CD version of an album I've fallen in love with as a download, and I'll get a rude shock when confronted by the sense of dimension and spatiality of the music's layers, the sculpted force of the drums, the sheer vividness of the sound. The difference between CD and MP3 is similar to that between 'not from concentrate' orange juice and juice that's been reconstituted from concentrate. (In this analogy, vinyl would be freshly squeezed, perhaps.) Converting music to MP3 is a bit like the concentration process, and it's done for much the same reason: it's much cheaper to transport concentrate because without the water it takes up a lot less volume and it weighs a lot less. Yet we can all taste the difference.

SURFING AND SKIMMING

What the inventors of the MP3 were banking on was that most of the time most of us are not listening that closely, and we aren't listening in ideal circumstances. According to Sterne, the MP3 was designed with the assumption that the listener is either engaged in other activities (work, socialising) or, if listening immersively, doing so in a noisy environment (public transport, a car, walk-ing on a busy street). 'The MP3 is a form designed for massive exchange, casual listening and massive accumulation,' he argues. Just as 'concentrate' is not a drink to savour, zipped-and-opened sound files are not music to roll around your ears. The audio equivalent of fast food, the MP3 is the ideal format for an era where current music, with its high-turnover micro-trends and endless give-away podcasts and DJ mixes, is increasingly some-thing you *keep up with*.

So many of the consumer-friendly advances of the digital era relate to time management: the freedom to be inattentive or interrupted during a television programme (pause, rewind), to reschedule the viewing of programmes to when it's more conve-nient and to stockpile televisual time for a rainy day (recordable DVDs, TiVo). The arrival of the CD player in the mid-eighties was an early glimpse of how music would be affected by digitalisation. Unlike record players and most tape decks, the CD player usu-ally came with a remote control. The record player is an unwieldy mechanical device for extracting sound waves etched into vinyl grooves; the CD player is a data-decoding machine, and therefore much easier to pause and restart, skip to a different track, and so forth. The CD player made it vastly more tempting to disrupt the flow of musical time: to answer the door or go to the toilet, to leap ahead to your favourite tracks or even your favourite *bit* of a track. The CD remote, essentially the same device as a TV remote, brought music under the sway of channel-surfing logic.

This was the dawn of a new digital-era way of experiencing time, something we've since become totally familiar with. And every gain in consumer-empowering convenience has come at the cost of disempowering the power of art to dominate our attention, to induce a state of aesthetic surrender. Which means that our gain is also our loss. It is also becoming very clear that the brittle temporality of networked life is not good for our

71

psychological well-being; it makes us restless, erodes our ability to focus and be in the moment. We are always interrupting ourselves, disrupting the flow of experience.

It's not just time that is affected, it's space too. The integrity of 'here' is being fractured just as much as the integrity of 'now'. Research by Ofcom, the organisation with authority over Britain's telecommunications, suggests that families congregate in the living room to watch TV but are only partially present, because they are busy texting or surfing the Web via laptops and handheld devices. They are plugged into social networks even while nestling in the bosom of the family, a syndrome that's been dubbed 'connected cocooning'. Just as the Internet makes the present porous with wormholes into the past, so the intimate space of the family is contaminated by the outside world via telemetric streams of information.

The final years of the 2000s saw a spate of hand-wringing articles about the pernicious effects of webbed life on one's ability to concentrate, along with testimonials from people who'd tried to break their addiction to the Internet by going offline permanently. In his famous 2008 *Atlantic* essay 'Is Google Making Us Stupid?', Nicholas Carr mourned his de-evolution from 'a scuba diver in the sea of words' to someone who 'zip[s] along the surface like a guy on a Jet Ski', and quoted the pathologist and medical blogger Bruce Friedman's plaintive admission that his thinking had taken on a 'staccato' quality: 'I can't read *War and Peace* anymore, I've lost the ability to do that. Even a blog post of more than three or four paragraphs is too much to absorb. I skim it.'

Carr's essay, which he developed into the 2010 book *The Shallows: What the Internet Is Doing to Our Brains*, generated a huge amount of commentary, some predictably characterising him as a Luddite and Gutenberg throwback, but more frequently chiming in with a sense of recognition about the ways in which webbed existence was interfering with capacity for focused work and fully immersed enjoyment. Writing in the webzine *Geometer*, Matthew Cole picked up on Carr's point about hyperlinks ('unlike footnotes . . . they don't merely point to related works; they propel you toward them') to characterise net life in terms of 'a perpetual state of almost-deciding': a vacillatory suspension of skipping and skimming that offered 'the *illusion* of action and decision' but was really an insidious form of paralysis.

In lots of ways, though, this flighty state of distraction is the appropriate response to the superabundance of choices. The horrifying (to a writer) meme 'tl dr' (too long, didn't read) has yet to be joined by 'tl dl' and 'tl dw' (too long, didn't listen; too long didn't watch), but it can only be a matter of time, because as many of us can attest, we're already at the point of, for instance, dragging the scroll bar ahead when checking out a video on YouTube. Attention-deficit disorder is the name of this condition, but like so many ailments and dysfunctions under late capitalism, the source of the disorder is not internal to the sufferer, not his or her fault; it's caused by the environment, in this case the datascape. Our attention is dispersed, tantalised, teased. So far there is no real equivalent in music to skim-reading; you can't speed up listening itself (although you can skip ahead or break off midway through and never pick up where you left off). But you can listen while doing other things: reading a book or magazine, or surfing the Web. Carr's 'shallows' refer to the experiential thin-ness of music or literature consumed in this multitasking fashion, the fainter imprint it leaves on our minds and hearts.

The rearrangement of time and space in the Internet age seems to be mirrored by distortions in one's sense of self, which feels splayed and stuffed. The playwright Richard Foreman used the image of 'pancake people' to describe what it feels like to be 'spread wide and thin as we connect with that vast network of information accessed by the mere touch of a button'. He contrasts this with the rich interior depths of the educated self shaped by a predominantly literary culture, where identity is complex and 'cathedral-like'. Certainly as I sit in front of this computer I feel stretched and stressed by the options available. My self and the screen are one; the various pages and windows simultaneously open add up to a picture of 'continuous partial attention' (the term coined by Microsoft executive Linda Stone to describe the fragmented consciousness caused by multitasking). It's the 'present' I inhabit that really feels stretched thin, a here-and-now pierced by portals to innumerable potential elsewheres and elsewhens.

A while ago I felt a strange pang of nostalgia for boredom, the kind of absolute emptiness so familiar when I was a teenager, or a college student, or a dole-claiming idler in my early twenties. Those great gaping gulfs of time with absolutely nothing to fill them would induce a sensation of tedium so intense it was almost spiritual. This was the pre-digital era (before CDs, before personal computers, long before the Internet) when in the UK there were only three or four TV channels, mostly with nothing you'd want to watch; only a couple of just-about-tolerable radio stations; no video stores or DVDs to buy; no email, no blogs, no webzines, no social media. To alleviate boredom, you relied on books, magazines, records, all of which were limited by what you could afford. You might have also resorted to mischief, or drugs, or creativity. It was a cultural economy of dearth and delay. As a music fan, you waited for things to come out or be aired: an album, the new issues of the weekly music papers, John Peel's radio show at ten o'clock, *Top of the Pops* on Thursday. There were long anticipation-stoking gaps, and then there were Events, and if you happened to miss the programme, the Peel show or the gig, it was *gone*.

Boredom is different nowadays. It's about super-saturation, distraction, restlessness. I am often bored but it's not for lack of options: a thousand TV channels, the bounty of Netflix, countless

74

net radio stations, innumerable unlistened-to albums, unwatched DVDs and unread books, the maze-like anarchive of YouTube. Today's boredom is not hungry, a response to deprivation; it is a loss of cultural appetite, in response to the surfeit of claims on your attention and time.

NO TIME LIKE THE PRESENT

In one of the most famous scenes in Nicolas Roeg's movie *The Man Who Fell to Earth*, David Bowie's alien Thomas Jerome Newton is seen watching a dozen televisions stacked on top of each other at once. That image – the super-advanced being capable of assimilating all these separate yet simultaneous data streams – seems a potent emblem for where our culture is heading. By the end of the movie, Newton is stranded on Earth, prevented by the human authorities from returning to his family on the distant home planet. He becomes an alcoholic, but also a cult musician, releasing eerie records under the name The Visitor. I'm not sure we actually get to hear what his music sounds like; I've always imagined it might be reminiscent of the second side of *Low*, melancholy vapours of Satie-esque sound, wintry and emaciated. But what would Newton's music have been like if it had in some way paralleled the saturated, overloaded gaze with which he watched those multiple TVs? It might have foreshadowed some of the music produced in the later years of the 2000s, which suffers from the syndrome I call 'glutted/clotted'.

Musicians glutted with influences and inputs almost inevitably make clotted music: rich and potent on some levels, but ultimately fatiguing and bewildering for most listeners. The problem is most acute on the hipster fringes of music-making: free of commercial considerations, which push musicians towards accessibility and simplicity, they can explore the info-cosmos of webbed music, venturing into remote reaches of history and distant corners of the globe alike. Two recent examples of this hyper-eclectic approach are Hudson Mohawke's *Butter* and Flying Lotus's *Cosmogramma*, from 2009 and 2010 respectively. *Butter* is prog rock updated for the Pro Tools era, a CGI-like frightmare of garish and overworked sound. *Cosmogramma* is hip-hop jazz for the ADD generation.

If it takes time to get to grips with this music, it's because, in some ways, too much time has been squeezed into it. Time in the sense of musical labour: musicians working in home-studio conditions, using digital-audio workstation programs, don't have financial restrictions on the amount of man-hours they can lavish on their work. But also time in a cultural sense: each of the musical styles these artists digitally splice together represents a tradition that evolved and mutated over decades, that in some sense contains embedded historical time. Naturally it requires many hours of fully attentive listening to unpack its complexities.

FLYING LOTUS AND THE WEB OF SOUND

Critics concur: there's something quintessentially webby about the music of Flying Lotus, aka Steve Ellison. *The Quietus*'s Colin McKean, for instance, described *Cosmogramma* as 'a sprawling, post-Web 2.0 cacophony . . . like hurtling through the digital darkness of Spotify with everything blaring at once'. FlyLo is at once locally rooted and a post-geographical entity. Ellison is the hub of a Los Angeles scene that includes the club Low End Theory, artists like Gaslamp Killer and Gonjasufi, and Ellison's own Brainfeeder label. But FlyLo are also considered part of an amorphous, transcontinental genre known as wonky (a controversial term accepted by few of the artists) that includes UK artists such as Hudson Mohawke and Rustie. Prominent in this music's super-hybrid DNA are strands of glitchy electronica, experimental hip hop and spacey seventies jazz fusion. Its off-kilter beat structures and mutant funk grooves are further spiced with day-glo synth tones and snazzy riffs that hark back to eighties electro-funk and video-game music. It's this omnivorousness that makes FlyLo and its genre so characteristically Web 2.0. As Ellison put it in one interview, 'Why not just have all these things from our past as well as all of the newest technology from today in one, and just really come up with the craziest shit we can?'

Time, of course, is the one thing that most listeners don't have at their disposal these days.

Artists and listeners are in the same boat, and that boat is sinking in 'the mire of options', to use the Zen Buddhist term. 'Restriction is the mother of invention,' said Holger Czukay of Can, pointedly defining the group's minimal approach against the maximalism of their prog-rock and jazz-fusion contemporaries. But you might also say that 'restriction is the mother of immersion'. In other words, truly experiencing music in any kind of intimate depth means reconciling oneself to the reality of finitude: you'll never be able to listen properly to more than a fraction of the torrent of music being made today, let alone across the span of human history.

This is one of the big questions of our era: can culture survive in conditions of limitlessness? Yet as much as the Internet's instant access overwhelms, it also presents opportunities. There

---

What makes the music timely, then, is not its components (which are from everywhere and everywhen) but the way it is put together ('We have the technology!' exults Ellison) and the sensibility it mirrors. FlyLo is made by and for nervous systems moulded by online culture; this music is drifting, distracted, assembling itself according to an additive logic of audio greed. When Nicholas Carr writes in *The Shallows* about how the 'calm, focused . . . linear mind is being pushed aside by a new kind of mind that wants and needs to take in and dole out information in short, disjointed, often overlapping bursts', this could be the opening paragraph of a *Cosmogramma* review. FlyLo music seems to contain its own hyperlinks (multiple stylistic jump-cuts can occur within a single track) and windows (up to eighty layers in a single *Cosmogramma* track). It's the skittering scatterbrain sound of networked consciousness, repeatedly interrupted by cutaways, freeze-frames and zooms in and out of focus.

Most listeners find *Cosmogramma* to be daunting and overwhelming initially. *Pitchfork*'s Joe Colly described the music as 'frustratingly unstable until you hear it a few times and the pieces begin to interlock and congeal'. I hated *Cosmogramma* at first. Eventually I found a way into it. But the 'good bits', for this listener, occur in the idyllic moments of clarity and resolution: particular

are artists who are navigating the Web's choppy info-ocean and, specifically, sifting through YouTube's immense flea market of memory, finding new possibilities for creativity.

Nico Muhly, a rising young composer who started as a protégé of Philip Glass, often draws on source material from the Web in his work. Some of his pieces were initially sparked by YouTube finds. He might, for instance, compose a violin concerto based around Renaissance ideas about astronomy, an interest first triggered by stumbling on eighties educational videos about the solar system uploaded by some nameless nutter onto YouTube, complete with voice-overs from now vaguely kitschy figures like Carl Sagan. Or he'll work on a piece designed to accompany bizarrely banal YouTube clips, videos of someone's backyard or a person doing housework.

When I went round to Muhly's apartment in Manhattan's Chinatown to interview him over lunch (an expertly prepared cauliflower cheese), he told me he was working on an 'internet opera' inspired by the true story of a 'younger boy who invents seven online identities to seduce an older boy, and then he gets stabbed in the chest'. On the subject of the influence of YouTube

---

portions of multisegmented songs, or occasionally whole tracks like 'Mmmhmm', sleepy hollows of melodic repose that offer a haven from the *Koyaanisqatsi*-like on-rush.

The paradox of *Cosmogramma* is that it is a classic 'grower', that old-fashioned term for an album that requires many plays before it unfolds its magic. *Cosmogramma* reflects the dispersed, fractured sensibility of digital modernity, but it really demands a mode of contemplative listening associated with the analogue era. FlyLo music clearly has spiritual intent, yet it mirrors and exacerbates the kind of jittery mind-state least conducive to meditative consciousness. *Cosmogramma*, Ellison explains, means 'the studies that map out the universe and the relations of heaven and hell'. Perhaps what he is trying to 'say' with his music is that what seems like hell (the stimuli overload of the Web, where everything becomes porn) could be heaven, if we could just find a way of grooving with and through the chaos.

and the Web in general on his music, Muhly talked about how he would disappear down 'Internet wormholes. The Web is really scary for that! If you start checking out people who dress up their miniature ponies like works of art, there's five hundred thousand things like that!'

The *New Yorker* profile that first brought his name to wide attention made much of the fact that Muhly was a Web 2.0 generation composer, writing his music onto a virtual score in his computer while replying to emails, chatting via instant messaging and participating in several simultaneous online Scrabble games. Clearly a high-functioning creature of the multitasking era, Muhly's approach to composition is characteristically webby in its associational drift. He calls it 'penetrative narrative', but it is really more like an anti-narrative. And Muhly's mode of research is the same as his mode of composition: non-linear. 'Plunging through things in another way, like putting a knife through a telephone book,' is how he describes it. 'A particular area, like, say astronomy, leads to something else, and that in turn will lead to something else altogether. This endless thing where there's no beginning and there's no end, and the narrative of it is just your *path through it.'*

Where Muhly moves through the world of Carnegie Hall and the English National Opera, Daniel Lopatin exists in a totally different milieu of modern music: the experimental electronic underground of Brooklyn squat gigs and vinyl/cassette-only micro-labels. Yet these two talents are responding to similar macro-cultural shifts: the emergence of the Internet as a landscape of the sublime, occupying a roughly equivalent place to Nature in the imagination of the eighteenth- and nineteenth-century composer, and to the city for the twentieth-century composer.

In his cramped Brooklyn bachelor pad, Lopatin's arsenal of vintage synths and rhythm boxes is just an arm's reach away from his giant-screen computer. He spends most of his time indoors, either doodling on the synths or surfing the Web. The recordings he's released under the name Oneohtrix Point Never – like 2009's *Rifts*, voted the no. 2 album of the year by *Wire* magazine – are for the most part amorphously abstract yet harmonically euphonious instrumentals created using arpeggiated synth melodies and pulsating sequencer patterns. But the 'echo jams' he did under aliases like KGB Man and Sunsetcorp are what made the widest impact: mash-ups of audio and video material he's scavenged on YouTube. In particular, 'Nobody Here' – built out of a tiny loop of vocal from Chris De Burgh's 'The Lady in Red' and a vintage eighties computer-animation graphic called 'Rainbow Road' – became a YouTube hit in its own right, chalking up over thirty thousand hits over the course of several months. Not massive compared to Lady Gaga, but in the context of the underground scene he comes from, 'Nobody Here' was a *Thriller*-level smash.

Part of its appeal is that listeners accustomed to thinking of Chris De Burgh's late-eighties chart-topper as putridly sentimental find themselves moved by the desolate yearning in the tiny excerpt that Lopatin zooms in on. Combined with 'Rainbow Road' (a color-spectrum ramp of fluorescent light that sways back and forth across the screen against a backdrop of skyscrapers), the effect is an eerie melancholy. A fan of vintage 'vector graphics and cad-cam eighties video art', Lopatin was drawn to this particular 'found visual' because the 'Gothic urban skyline' undercut the 'sappy, sentimental associations of rainbows'. It also crystallised his alienated feelings about his own life in the city. Hence the aching resonance of the Chris De Burgh loop: 'There's nobody here.'

Lopatin has been echo-jamming for years. It started as a way to bunk off from his dreary day job without actually leaving his office cubicle. 'I was a total 9-to-5er, so bored, and this was the kind of music I could make at work, just ripping stuff from YouTube. Back then I wasn't doing it to impress anyone, it was just a really cathartic thing to do while I was doing menial office labour.' An 'echo jam' is not just a straightforward montage of an audio loop and a video loop. After isolating the micro-excerpts he finds compelling – a splinter of longing from an old Kate Bush or Fleetwood Mac song, a heartbroken pang from Janet Jackson or Alexander O'Neal, the dreamy vocal-only breakdown of a Euro-trance anthem – Lopatin coats it with 'a ton of echo'. Because he's 'not a party animal', he'll also slow the music down, a technique derived from Houston's legendary DJ Screw, whose 'screwed' mix-tapes involved playing gangsta rap at narcotically torpid tempos. Lopatin also slows down the video loops, which are all sourced from YouTube and then converted and edited using Windows Movie Maker. Among his favourite sources are eighties TV com-mercials from the Far East or from the Communist bloc promot-ing new video and audio technology. In one echo jam, a young Soviet couple blissfully share a 'his and hers' portable cassette player with twin headphone sockets.

Lopatin likes to downplay the creativity involved in echo jams. 'It's really simple. I'm uncomfortable with the idea that I'm an author of this stuff. I'm just participating in stuff that's happen-ing all across YouTube, kids doing similar things all over.' That may be true, but the surplus value Lopatin brings is the concep-tual framework to his projects, which relates to cultural memory and the buried utopianism within capitalist commodities, espe-cially those related to consumer technology in the computing and audio/video entertainment area. Gathering together his best echo jams for the 2009 DVD *Memory Vague*, Lopatin argued in the liner note that 'no commercial work is outside of the reach of artistic reclamation'.

These preoccupations came to fruition with a long piece Lopatin created in 2010 for an exhibition of sound art: a decon-structive unravelling of a 1994 infomercial he found on YouTube. Sixteen minutes of corporate propaganda for the Performa ('the family Macintosh from Apple, with the future built right in') is converted into a thirty-minute echo-jam symphony. 'The Martinettis Bring Home a Computer', as both the original infomercial and Lopatin's treatment are titled, captures a moment in the early nineties when the information superhighway held out the same promise of emancipation and expanded horizons that the creation of the interstate freeway system once did.

What originally snagged Lopatin's Web-surfing eye was the high production values and 'Robert Altman-movie-level' acting of the infomercial, probably deposited on YouTube as an online resumé by its director (although these days it's perfectly possible that there are actually fans of infomercials, auteurist connoisseurs assiduously curating the genre on the Web). Lopatin's deconstructed version starts with snippets of the elegiac music on the original score, which he loops into an endless wistful-yet-gaseous refrain. Gradually, some alarming slithering and retching sounds insinuate themselves into the idyll, along with the restless tap tap tap of computer keys. The slimy sounds reveal themselves to be grotesquely slowed-down dialogue from the family scenes in the infomercial: 'We were having the time of our lives with the computer'; 'There's a whole other world out there'; 'The funny thing was, the computer fit right into our family just like it belonged.'

Lopatin describes this section of the piece as 'an exploding mess of cultural noise, all these voices and desires overlapping, as the family members express their desire to own this computer and why they want it. The infomercial's angle is that it's a kind of Renaissance machine and it'll make the whole family into this holistic entity. Every member will get what they need out of it. It'll bring them together but it'll also bring out the individuality.' But what the computer ultimately represents is a new stage in the disintegration of the family: the networked family is promiscuously intermeshed with external systems, plugged into remote streams of data. 'Nil Admirari', a cacophonous track on Oneohtrix Point

82

Never's 2010 album *Returnal*, explores the same idea: it's a sound-painting of a modern household, where the outside world's violence pours in through the cable lines, the domestic haven contaminated by toxic data. 'The mom's sucked into CNN, freaking out about Code Orange terrorist shit,' says Lopatin. 'Meanwhile, the kid is in the other room playing *Halo 3*, inside that weird Mars environment killing some James Cameron-type predator.'

If 'The Martinettis Bring Home a Computer' is about the sinister side of information technology, it's also about its seductiveness: the bright future that a new computer or digital gadget seems to herald. Yet the speed of technological advance means that each beloved machine is rendered obsolete with ruthless rapidity. With individuals and businesses throwing out info-tech every two or three years, obsolete computers are a huge environmental problem. 'I'm super into formats, into junk, into outmoded technology,' says Lopatin. 'I'm super into the idea that the rapid-fire pace of capitalism is destroying our relationships to objects. All this drives me back, but what drives me is a desire to connect, not to relive things. It's not nostalgia.' He argues that the idea of 'progress' itself is driven by the economic requirements of capitalism as much as by science or human creativity. In a 2009 manifesto-like article, he decried the fixation on linear progress, proposing instead the opening up of 'spaces for ecstatic regression . . . We homage the past to mourn, to celebrate, and to time travel.'

Disappearing down 'Internet wormholes' – Nico Muhly's quippy description of his meanders across the Web – also contains the idea of time travel. The subject of endless speculation by physicists and a popular device in science fiction, the 'traversable wormhole' cuts through a fold in the fabric of the space–time continuum and creates a short cut; theoretically, it could work as a time tunnel. Muhly's wormhole metaphor brings out a quasi-astrophysical dimension to the Web: this is cyber*space*, a cosmos of information and memory. Which is also how archives work

83

– through the spatialisation of time. They are systems for orderly storage that distribute objects in subdivided space. What computers and the Web have done is to speed up drastically the process of retrieval and to make the past more accessible to everyone, no matter where they are located or whether they have institutional privileges.

For young artists like Lopatin and Muhly, YouTube presents amazing opportunities for 'ecstastic regression' and for time-tourist trips to exotic pockets of cultural strangeness. Lopatin uses the analogy of archaeologists stumbling on a lost civilisation. 'We approach the ruins and we look for symbols on the wall. We try to piece together what their culture was, their purpose. Those hieroglyphs are our window into that culture. Little images of daily activities, or athletics, or whatever.' YouTube, he reckons, is the image bank of our civilisation, 'a reality vault'. He imagines people one or two thousand years from now treating it like ancient Egyptian hieroglyphs. 'It's basically the inventory of who we are. All our mundane and insane dreams, collected. Things we're interested in and things we found funny. Especially as a lot of YouTube seems to be diaries or weird confession-booth stuff. It's so sad to me, but beautiful too. At the end of the day this is what people seem to need. That's what they want to leave behind.'

YouTube is almost like a new continent that suddenly emerged only half a decade ago, rising out of the data sea. This New World keeps getting larger as more and more culture stuff gets stuffed into it: imagery and information, audio and video from every corner of the globe and every crevice of our past, and increasingly from the pasts of all those foreign cultures as well. This retro-exotica is already drastically expanding the horizons of influence for contemporary bands. For instance, on Ariel Pink's *Before Today*, 'Reminiscences' is an instrumental cover of an eighties Ethiopian pop song. Sung by Yeshimebet Dubale, the original can be found, alongside other low-budget videos made covertly during the Derg military dictatorship, on a YouTube channel with the inadvertently amusing title DireTube.

The crucial point about the journeys through time that YouTube and the Internet in general enable is that people are not really going *backwards* at all. They are going *sideways*, moving laterally within an archival plane of space–time. In a very real sense, a YouTube sequence from some 1971 Latvian light-entertainment show – girls in hot pants dancing to what sounds like an ersatz Soviet version of the Tom Jones sound – exists *in the same space* as a this-minute YouTube clip of black Chicagoan teenage dancers doing bizarre footwork to the high-speed electronic rhythms of 'juke'. The Internet places the remote past and the exotic present side by side. Equally accessible, they become the same thing: far, yet near . . . old yet *now*.

3

LOST IN THE SHUFFLE

Record Collecting and the Twilight of Music as an Object

I don't go for the most obvious forms of conspicuous consumption – no flashy cars or expensive designer clothes or high-end gadgets. Nonetheless, it has to be said, I've managed to acquire an awful lot of material goods over the years, mostly books and records. Perhaps that made them seem somehow nobler than mere possessions. Still, for a 'non-consumerist', I've done a lot of *shopping* – albeit of a particular record-geek and book-nerd kind. In fact, in this area I'm something of a virtuoso consumer, sifting through the dross to find the overlooked and abandoned.

The fact that most of what I buy is old stuff probably allows me to make a pseudo-distinction between my version of consumerism and the normal mall-zombie sort. Shopping for clothes, furniture or appliances bores me rigid. But the other kind of shopping is an adventure. I still get a little rush of excitement and anticipation when I walk into a second-hand store. Whether I find something I've been seeking for ages or come across something bizarre I'd never known even existed, these purchases seem less like commodities than capsules of possibility.

Still, until recently, I never really thought of myself as a collector. Collectors were people who cherished rare artifacts like coins, postage stamps, antiques; if they were record collectors, they were oddballs who fetishised format and packaging – coloured vinyl seven-inch singles, Japanese versions of albums. For me it was all about the music, and anyway, I wasn't collecting for its own sake. This was professional research material, part of my effort to expand my knowledge of musical history.

But one day it smacked me full in the face: I'd amassed an immense private archive of audio artifacts. I could blame this sorry plight on the endless stream of freebies arriving in the mail-box, but in truth I had been headed down this path well before I joined the rock-critic profession. As an ex-student living off the dole in mid-eighties Oxford, I'd tape LPs from public libraries 'just in case'; later, when the freelance money started coming in, I'd buy all kinds of records I was curious about, a few of which to this day shamefully remain in their shrink-wrap. (Mind you, according to Walter Benjamin, the twentieth century's great phi-losopher of collecting, browsing and what we'd now call vintage shopping, 'the non-reading of books' is a defining characteristic of serious bibliomaniacs; he cites Anatole France, who blithely admitted that he'd barely read one-tenth of the books in his library.) When vinyl fills shelves and closets in every room of your apartment, and there's more recordings still stashed away in lockers in your building's basement, and there's even a storage unit in London largely filled with CDs, tapes, LPs and singles left there when you moved to the US fifteen years earlier . . . it's time to face facts. You're a collector, a chronic one, well past the point where it's a manageable, wholesome pastime.

Such a gargantuan accumulation of recorded music starts to exert subliminal pressure. You inevitably begin to think about whether there's actually enough life ahead of you to listen to all the stuff you *like* one more time, let alone make new discover-ies. The music obsessive's version of a midlife crisis is when all those potential pleasures stacked on the shelves stop representing delight and start to feel like harbingers of death.

Which is a cruel irony, because the standard psychoanalytic interpretation of obsessive collecting is that it is a way of warding off death, or at least a displacement of abstract, inconsolable anxieties, often rooted in childhood feelings of helplessness. Having all this *stuff*, the unconscious logic goes, protects you against loss. But eventually having all this stuff keeps on reminding you of the inevitability of loss. 'I dread the day that I die,' Gareth Goddard, collector and the man behind the reissue label Cherrystones, has said. 'Because I think, "*What the hell's going to happen to my collection?*"'

I must admit, the fate of my records after I'm gone flickers across my mind every now and then. It's not like my wife won't have much more pressing things to deal with, but I've urged her repeatedly not to take them to the nearest Salvation Army centre. Partly because I know they are worth something but also because I'm troubled by the thought of these precious discs being roughly treated. On a deeper level, it seems that Gareth Goddard and I are really mourning ourselves in advance. Records *are us*: they represent a significant portion of what we've done with our time on this planet, untold hours of labour and love.

CONSTANT CRAVING

Some studies suggest that the impulse to collect is at its strongest between the ages of seven and twelve, the prepubescent phase when the child is seeking to individuate himself and establish control over his environment. A second phase of obsessive collecting occurs in men in their forties. In between is a long period in which a different kind of hunting and capturing dominates, one driven by sexuality. That would seem to confirm the traditional view of collectors as asexual nerds. Walter Benjamin, in fact, noted that there was a 'childlike element' to collecting. But he wasn't being disparaging: on the contrary, he admired the way children re-enchant the world through play, fantasy, daydreams, anthropomorphic projection, drawing and other ruses. For collectors, Benjamin wrote, 'the most profound enchantment . . . is the locking of individual items within a magic circle in which they are fixed as the final thrill, the thrill of acquisition, passes over them'.

I see this on a daily basis with my ten-year-old son, witnessing the anticipation and delight, total absorption and insatiable lust that infuses his collecting of Pokémon cards. Kieran is smack dab in the middle of that seven to twelve age group, in the same way that I am – as a forty-something man – in the prime demographic for collecting's second wind. He has no interest in my collecting, and doesn't involve his parents in Pokémon, apart from when trying to wheedle some money for a new deck or make the case for a trip to some out-of-the-way store that stocks the latest cards. Still, there was a time when I joined him in an obsession: his first one, at the age of five, for bus maps.

New York buses carry leaflet-sized maps for individual routes; there's usually a bunch of different ones in a pouch at the front as you board the bus. Kieran started picking them up every time we took a bus. Soon his obsession escalated to the point where he and I would hang around at bus stops: while the line of people boarded, I would reach inside and grab the ones he hadn't got. There were various types and colour schemes depending on which borough of greater New York they covered, and I must admit they did look attractive splayed out on the rug en masse. Kieran devised a number of supplementary activities, like drawing his own brightly coloured versions of the routes, but the primary goal was to get the complete set.

There was no rhyme or reason to which maps any given bus would be carrying (indeed, it rarely furnished the map for its own route). So one excursion might result in a good score (several maps that Kieran had never even seen before) or we might go away empty-handed. Soon we were going on expeditions to particularly busy intersections, parts of town that were the bus equivalents of railway junctions, and increasingly further afield, to Brooklyn or Queens. Kieran would get very excited and sometimes overwhelmed when too many buses came at once and we couldn't get to them all.

As any collector knows, the more you get of a particular set (or genre, in music), the harder it is to fill in the remaining gaps. I was getting a bit worn out by Kieran's hobby (winter was approaching, making it more arduous), but the main concern for me was that each new mission was producing the same old maps, leading to disappointment for my little boy. So one day near the end of a particularly fruitless session, I suggested that we find out where the central bus depot was and go scoop up all the remaining bus maps in one fell swoop. Kieran thought for a while, and then said, 'No. I don't want to do that. I want to collect them one by one.'

I stood there by the bus stop looking at him with some amazement. I thought to myself, 'You really are a chip off the old block.' Because if I was confronted with a sort of magic record store that contained my entire want list, I'd spurn it too. The true collector's desire is to remain within the state of constant craving. In her book *On Longing*, Susan Stewart argues that 'it is not acceptable to simply purchase a collection in toto; the collection must be acquired in a serial manner . . . "Earning" the collection simply involves *waiting*, creating the pauses that articulate the biography of the collector.' For Kieran, the pauses had gotten longer, the ratio of disappointment to euphoria had increased, but he was determined to persevere.

Then one day, he just lost interest. Eventually all those bus maps that represented hours and days of his and my time were chucked out in a household spring clean. Collecting seemed to fade, for a while, in Kieran's life. Then it returned with Pokémon. The cards depict an endlessly expanding menagerie of anime creatures with different powers and weaknesses that they deploy in the super-complex Pokémon game (although hardly anyone seems to play it). But the primary appeal is not aesthetic. Trading the cards enables socialisation (largely among prepubescent boys). Pokémon is also a system, with sets to complete, cards that are rare or have some kind of design quirk, and so forth. Analysing the psychology of the collector, Jean Baudrillard and Susan Stewart concur in finding that the hallmark of true collecting is what they respectively term 'systematicity' and 'seriality': a 'formal' interest eclipses the attraction to specific objects for their intrinsic and particular qualities.

Once Kieran's Pokémon obsession got beyond his captivation with individual cards, it did become abstract. He sorted and reorganised the collection according to different criteria, expanding it constantly through new purchases and advantageous trades. He got involved in the YouTube scene, where collectors video themselves opening a fresh pack of Pokémon cards and go through their new acquisitions one by one, narrating in real time their feelings of surprised delight or disappointment.

As a parent who has to deal with the stacks of cards scattered around the house, Pokémon seems like a demonic scheme for parting children and their parents from cash, particularly since there is no limit to the number of new characters and new sets that can be created. Baudrillard argues that 'the collection is never really initiated in order to be completed', and that 'the most important piece in the collection is the missing one'. Where Pokémon surpasses sports trading cards is in the fact that the series is infinitely extendable. Theoretically, if you have enough money and determination and moved fast enough, you can complete the series; but in practice they have always designed and manufactured more. This ensures that there is always a 'missing card'; the endpoint to one's desire always recedes out of reach. But the drive to collect is as much about anxiety as desire: it's driven by a will to mastery, to create order. If you completed the collection, this would interfere with the displacement of anxiety achieved through the neurotic activity of collecting itself. The spectre of death and the void would loom up again.

Perhaps it's not the fear of emptiness, though, but of overwhelming plenitude that collecting is a defence against. In 'Orchid Fever', her famous 1995 *New Yorker* profile of the law-breaking orchid hunter John Laroche, Susan Orlean muses that the problem with reality is that 'there are too many ideas and things and people, too many directions to go. I was starting to believe the reason it matters to care passionately about something is that it whittles the world down to a more manageable size.' In Orlean's portrait, Laroche is a serial obsessive in the same way that some people are serial monogamists or serial addicts who move from drug to drug. He started with turtles, moved to fossils, and then to tropical fish. One day, out of the blue, he decides he's 'done with fish . . . fuck fish', even vowing never to go in the ocean again, and launches full-tilt into a new obsession: the pursuit of rare, often government-protected orchids, including the famous Ghost Orchid.

You could talk of the collecting personality in the same way that people talk of the addictive personality. Collection would be a kind of elective version of addiction (except that in some cases junkies seem to *choose* to get hooked, while some collectors feel like it's all out of their control, involuntary, a passion visited on them). Where collection and addiction converge is in their relationship to time. Addiction is sometimes diagnosed as an unconsciously motivated attempt to simplify life and to structure time: drug use creates a rhythm to existence (the routine of cop, shoot, nod); it fills the void by killing time.

In his oft-quoted essay 'The System of Collecting', Baudrillard talks of collecting as a way of domesticating time, making it 'docile' (an echo of his analogy, earlier in the essay, between collected objects and pets, who are seen as extensions of their owners, mute mirrors of narcissism). Time crops up a lot in theoretical writing on collecting, ideas to do with permanence and finitude (the collection outliving the collector) but also time slowing down in the reverie of sensuously sorting (fondling, almost) the objects. Sometimes the specific nature of the things collected further intensifies this childish revolt against the 'irreversibility' of time's flow. Figures like Robert Opie and Alex Shear build private museums of bygone packaging and consumer goods from eras that seem halcyon from the present's vantage point. Shear describes his collection of fifties ephemera as an ark preserving 'the soul of America'. The apolitical, mundane material of everyday life – mustard jars, bathing caps, food blenders, children's toys – exudes an aura of integrity and 'innocence': precisely the trustworthy, dependable qualities that are hard to find in people but that can be projected onto and sought in inanimate objects.

It's easy to see the fit here with certain kinds of record collectors, renegades against the irreversibility of pop-time's flow, taking a stand against the way that styles go out of fashion or run out of steam, leaving in their wake a legion of cruelly forgotten performers. All things must pass; by definition, an era is finite.

Thoughts of Time bring me to my saddest moment as a record collector. Musing about a hard-to-find, expensive series of records I started to think about how great it would be if you could go back in time and buy them when they came out. They'd cost what a normal, brand-new release cost, and best of all, they'd be in mint condition. Soon I was daydreaming an elaborate science-fiction scenario, a story about time-travelling record collectors, hurtling across the aeons for rare records at bargain prices. Perhaps they'd be true music fiends. Or maybe they'd be dealers who would artificially engineer rarity for the future by buying up most of a pressing (which they could sell back in the present in controlled amounts, to avoid saturating the market). They could even be record-plant saboteurs, engineering the defects and quirks of packaging that future collectors would pay top dollar for. They'd have to be careful to dress inconspicuously, in period-appropriate clothes, and not do anything anachronistic in terms of the way they spoke or carried themselves.

How pathetic, though. So you have the power to travel through time, and you're not heading straight to the cradle of Adolf Hitler to smother him with a pillow? Or to Memphis in 1968 to warn Martin Luther King not to go out on the motel balcony? Surely you'd want to witness, oh, Lincoln's Gettysburg Address, or take a gander at ancient Rome in all its splendour, or dinosaurs stalking Earth? OK, you're obsessed with music, fine . . . at least go see The Beatles in Hamburg, or whizz far into the future and discover what's going to be hot in the hit parade in the year 3000.

THEORIES OF COLLECTING

In the surprisingly substantial literature on collecting, certain themes crop up again and again: order, neurosis, control, time, death. Certain figures crop up, too. Walter Benjamin is oft-quoted, largely because of a single essay, 'Unpacking My Library', a 1931 talk in which his meditation on the collector's drive to capture and care for possessions is triggered by his own experience of moving to a new apartment and opening the cases containing thousands of volumes he's amassed. Benjamin sees the collector as having 'taken up arms against dispersal' (the confusion and scattering of things in this world), yet his passion, being insatiable, itself inevitably 'borders on the chaotic'. As a result, the collection, and the collector's life, is characterised by a 'dialectical tension between the poles of disorder and order'. Benjamin's wry, self-mocking tone lends dignity and existential depth to what from outside can seem demented. At the time of writing 'Unpacking', he was several years into his great unfinished work, *The Arcades Project*, named after Paris's iron-and-glass-covered passages, whose boutiques and bric-a-brac made for a browser's paradise. What survives is a kind of collection itself, a vast, shapeless scrapbook of quotations, text fragments and

TOO MUCH IS NEVER ENOUGH

Up until the turn of the millennium, obsessive record collecting seemed like a minority pursuit. Most people's collections of
records and CDs numbered in the hundreds, not thousands. In
the nineties, when I'd discreetly appraise people's CD cabinets, it
was striking how haphazardly accreted they were (lots of semi-
trendy albums bought while at college, a few token classical and
jazz CDs) and how, more often than not, there'd be a cut-off point,
when the intake of new music tapered to a trickle. In the 2000s,
though, obsessive collecting of music seemed to spread from the
fringe to the mainstream, thanks to the new technologies of distribution and storage. It became a modern-day folk tale: gushing
testimonials from people whose dormant or lapsed passion for
music was reignited by the iPod. The device launched them into
a second adolescence as they avidly checked out new music and
ventured into unexplored corners of the past. iPod/iTunes and

---

jottings . . . a book in the process of forming itself out of other books, complete
with his margin-scribbled annotations.

Freud frequently makes an appearance in the theoretical writing about
collecting, not because he devised a psychological explanation for the
compulsion (he barely references it in his work) but because he was such a
rampant collector himself (accumulating by the time of his death in 1939 several
thousand antiquities, things like statuettes and scarabs) and because his own
collecting is easy to psychoanalyse (it started shortly after his father died). But
theorists of collecting often sound Freudian notes. In 'The System of Collecting',
Baudrillard talks of it in terms of narcissism ('it is invariably *oneself* that one
collects') and 'regression to the anal stage, manifested in such behavior patterns
as accumulation, ordering, aggressive retention' (which sounds both true and
trite). More intriguingly, he compares collectible things to pets, who exist at the
midpoint between person and object, companion and chattel.

Others see collecting as a futile displacement of the fear of mortality, a
screamed denial of the truth 'you can't take it with you'. Jacques Attali, for
instance, writes in his treatise *Noise: The Political Economy of Music* that 'the

countless other forms of accessing music (Spotify, Rhapsody, illegal file-sharing, etc.) allowed people to divorce the pleasures of collecting (not just listening but categorising, compiling playlists, and so forth) from the 'downsides', such as the physical effort of finding the stuff, the problems with storage space and organising the collection.

New technology has naturally affected the hardcore collector scene too. Selling over the Internet has been a huge boon for record dealers, while also robbing some of the romance and random epiphanies from record shopping in the real world of stores and record fairs. Online mechanisms for finding, auctioning and price-comparing like eBay, Gemm, Discogs and Popsike have radically transformed the collecting experience, while decreasing the likelihood of finding a bargain in a second-hand record store – since the market value of a record is only a few mouse clicks away for the owner.

Facilitated by eBay, collecting of every kind – not just music

---

stockpiling of use-time in [recordings] is fundamentally a herald of death'. In *To Have and To Hold*, his magisterial survey of five centuries of collecting, Philipp Blom argues that collectors often seem to be building 'fortresses of remembrance and permanence'. The inspiration for *Citizen Kane*, William Randolph Hearst had a massive fear of death; like so many plutocrats of his era he was an uncontrollable ransacker of Old World treasures, most of which remained in their crates in his giant folly of a mansion. Blom suggests that 'the greater the collection [and] the more precious its contents', the more the collector can seem like a pharaoh, entombed with his treasures.

But elsewhere Blom offers a more positive, even heroic vision of the collector. Tracing the connection between the alchemist's idea of *spiritus mundi* to Hegel's 'world spirit' (the spirit of history), he argues that 'we find echoes of . . . alchemy in every attempt to capture the wonder and magnitude of everything around in the realm of personal possession . . . This practical alchemy is at work whenever a collection reaches beyond appreciating objects and becomes a quest for meaning, for the heart of the matter . . .' Collecting, in other words, can be a way of telling a story.

– has become more and more widespread, and this increasing friction between the pack-rat impulse and the limitations of living space has helped the storage industry to become one of the fastest growing sectors of the US economy, expanding 700 per cent over the last decade. Like me with my storage unit in London, loads of people seem prepared to pay in order not to have to scale down their collecting habit or get rid of the stuff they've already acquired.

The annals of collector culture are crammed with tales of dysfunction, people who've gone way, *way* too far. Among those I've personally known whose passion bordered on the unhinged, one figure stands out: Steve Micalef, a friend from my days at Oxford University. Steve was a student at the Ruskin, the city's trade-union college, where as a working-class youth from Bermondsey in South-East London he'd won a scholarship. But instead of seizing the opportunity to make something of himself, the brilliant but incorrigibly anarchic Micalef (he'd been an original punk rocker and part of the team behind the legendary DIY fanzine *Sniffin' Glue*) continued to misspend his youth with endless feats of Dadaist mayhem. Typically he spent his entire student grant in the first week on albums. In collector terms, he was way ahead of his time, purchasing Arthur Lyman's faux-Polynesian easy-listening classic *Taboo!* a decade before 'exotica' became fashionable, and anticipating the current vogue for field recordings with records of Amazonian shamans tripping out on the hallucinogen DMT. But there was a random aspect to these discoveries. Like those huge 'bottom-trawling' nets used in modern-day deep-sea fishing, Micalef's indiscriminate shopping frenzies would dredge up all kinds of lesser musical matter, and the gems were embedded amid mounds of barely listenable tat and piffle: brass bands, Highland jigs 'n' reels, nursery rhymes, schmaltzy light entertainment of every kind.

As much as Micalef loved music and enjoyed owning so many

records, he had an utterly un-prissy and non-precious relationship with vinyl. The floor of his room – the attic of a shared house – was shin-deep in an undulant ocean of unsleeved records, the discs layered like shingles on a cottage roof. On the turntable, a grotesquely warped album, damaged when left against a piping hot radiator, would often be left to rotate silently, the freaky folds and kinks in its surface rippling to unsettling effect. Micalef made a point of playing every purchase at all three speeds – 33, 45 and 78 rpm – to extract maximum entertainment potential from the record. Eventually, when he had to move in a hurry, the collection was divided up and left in the care of various different friends and ultimately forgotten.

Micalef utterly lacked the other side of the rampant collector: the anal obsession with storing and classifying. In Ian McEwan's short story 'Solid Geometry', the intimacy-starved wife of an emotionally repressed antiquarian insults him with the put-down, 'You crawl over history like a fly on a turd.' Serious collector culture – the world of record fairs, pricing guides, discographies, auctions – is the kingdom of flies.

When I open a magazine like *Record Collector* or *Goldmine*, I feel queasy – this is passion misdirected, a monomania that began with pure devotion to music but which has somehow detached itself from the original object and become a treadmill of runaway desire. Here you find the completists who accumulate every single thing that a band has put out (remixes, B-sides, mono seven-inch mixes from the sixties), plus anything in bootleg form (out-takes, demos, unofficial live albums). At least this is based on the desire to hear every variation, every version. But beyond this lies the pitiful realm of those who've really missed the point, the collectors who chase down every last format and packaging incarnation: coloured vinyl, promos, foreign editions with different covers or track running orders, test pressings. Deeper still into the mire, there's the trade in ephemera: concert programmes, tour posters, badges, press kits, tickets, promotional items, spin-off merchandise.

Fred and Judy Vermorel, pioneering analysts of fandom, would diagnose obsessive collecting as one form of what they call consumer mysticism – the literal idolatry of pop stars. Collecting is a substitute for connecting, a fantasy of total possession through hyper-consumption. Mind you, collectors tend not to resemble Saint Teresa of Ávila that much. Keeping any mystic tendencies tightly leashed, they talk a drier, droning language. For instance, collectors are always complaining about a dearth of 'documentation'. I came across the *reductio ad absurdum* of this viewpoint in an issue of *Goldmine*: reviewer Jo-Anne Greene enthused about a live Vibrators recorded in 1976 on a portable cassette player, despite its atrociously shitty sound, arguing that 'so many of rock 'n' roll's crucial moments have been lost forever, that, even if this were absolutely unlistenable . . . its existence would still be a cause for celebration'.

'Lost moments, captured forever' is the big lure behind bootlegs, along with the notion that the definitive versions of songs occur in performance rather than in the lifeless studio environment. A few artists do endlessly and significantly rework their material onstage, like Bob Dylan and The Grateful Dead. But most rock bands aren't capable of, and aren't particularly interested in, improvisation. The spark of spontaneity is then located in the between-song banter. But as one veteran bootleg collector, Roger Sabin, notes, even here redundancy can kick in: 'On the Black Sabbath boots, Ozzy Osbourne would say to the audience . . . "Are you high?" The audience would scream, "Yeah!" and he'd respond, "SO – AM – I!" The first time you hear it you think it's really funny, but it's not so funny when you've heard ten bootlegs and he says it on each one.' So what does motivate the fans who scroll down the tiny print of whole-page ads in *Goldmine*, checking out, say, the 117 Springsteen bootlegs offered by a single dealer?

It reminds me of those Roman feasts where gluttons would withdraw to the vomitorium mid-banquet to regurgitate the first six
courses, in order to make room for more of the same.

Obsessive collecting also recalls the mild autistic condition known as Asperger's Syndrome, which combines difficulty
with relating to other people with an obsessive need for things
to stay the same and an immersion in arcane knowledge. When
you look at the more extreme manifestations of music fandom
online, there's something Asperger-y about the hoarding of data:
catalogue numbers, changing line-ups, details of recording sessions, the locations and dates of gigs (including in some cases
the minutely varying set lists playing on each date of a tour). In
Britain, they use the term 'trainspotter' to describe this breed
of fact-fiending fan, after the teenage boys who spend their
Saturdays on platforms at train stations collecting the serial numbers of locomotives. 'Trainspotter' means someone who's missed
the point, whose obsession has detached itself from the thing that
actually matters (in this case, the music itself) and fritters energy
in the stockpiling of pointless data.

There's an argument about trainspotterhood, what you might
call the Hornby Thesis: that it's basically a way for emotionally
repressed males to relate without really relating. Whether it's
sports or music, these external obsessions provide men with a
safe outlet for passion – something they can get worked up about
emotionally, even shed tears over, while avoiding the too-real
stuff: sexuality, love, relationships. In Nick Hornby's novels *Fever
Pitch*, *High Fidelity* and *Juliet, Naked* there's a critique – a partial
self-critique on the part of the author – of masculinity in retreat
from the mess and risks of adulthood into a more orderly world
of obsessive fandom. Philipp Blom notes that 'the characteris-
tics of emotional paucity and the language of collecting overlap
in many ways: holding on to one's feelings, bottling it up, being
retentive, not letting go'. He misses the big one: the old-fashioned

term 'collect yourself', meaning to pull yourself together after you've gone to pieces emotionally.

Most of the ardent collectors I know *are* married or involved in long-term relationships, hardly running scared of intimacy or commitment. If their collector selves represent a form of arrested adolescence, this is a protected zone of retardation (a sort of 'nerd-life sanctuary') that runs in parallel with their relatively emotionally mature lives. Professional provocateuse Elizabeth Wurtzel once argued that women would do better to develop more impersonal obsessions, as opposed to those related to appearance, health and relationships. In effect, she suggested, women would be happier if they were less like Bridget Jones and more like the trainspotters of Hornby World.

It's not that some women don't collect stuff. Some do – art, antiques, vintage clothes, dolls. Indeed, according to researcher Susan M. Pearce, a slight majority of women self-describe as collectors. But her research also showed that the obsessed, out-of-control, living-to-collect collectors were generally male rather than female. Record collecting certainly remains a male-dominated field, as one glance surveying the stalls and aisles of a record fair will tell you. Canadian academic Will Straw, the author of several incisive essays on record collecting, recalls being interviewed for the documentary *Vinyl* and learning from its director that despite his best efforts, only five of the hundred collectors interviewed were women.

Straw argues that record collecting offers a kind of alternative masculinity in which mastery is based around knowledge and discernment. This appeals to those who are either alienated from, or feel inadequate to, the more traditional masculine ideals (leadership or physical strength, for instance). Nerds don't wield authority; they *become* authorities through their taste and cultural expertise. They put in the work to find obscure records and accumulate esoteric knowledge. This can actually involve physical effort (graft, discomfort, flicking through mouldy boxes in dusty basements), but mostly it's about persistence, mental stamina. Obscurantism can take on a heroic aura: it means you are sticking up for the underdogs of underground, non-commercial music. Collecting may also seem like a quest, 'an expedition into the . . . wilderness of discarded styles', as Straw puts it. But why is this particular area of esoteric expertise so gendered? There's no evidence that men love music any more intensely than women. If there's a distinctively masculine sickness here, it's perhaps related to the impulse to master what actually masters you; containing music within a grid map of systematic knowledge is a form of protection against the loss of self that is music's greatest gift.

Music is conventionally regarded as the soundtrack to a life: the favourite song as commemoration, a Proustian trigger that sets you adrift on memory bliss. But for collectors, the obsession increasingly becomes independent of anything going on in their lives. Collector friends of mine often seem impelled to create a narrative about their collecting, talking about turning points, the record purchases that 'changed my life' – meaning both that their ideas about music were transformed and that new vistas of obsessive consumption were opened up. As with any obsession (sports, say), this operates almost as a second life running in parallel to the 'real' one of romance, family and friendships.

One collector acquaintance talks about 'the thrill of the hunt'. As Straw notes, 'hunting' masculinises what would otherwise be understood as a feminine activity: shopping. Other terms connect collecting to ideas of treasure and prospecting, like the title of collector magazine *Goldmine* or the acronym Gemm, which stands for Global Electronic Music Marketplace.

Record collecting lends itself to serendipity: its intensified version of everyday consumerism's 'purchase of the moment' is the epiphany rush of spotting something of value amidst a pile of dreck. When arcane records become easier to obtain after

102

being reissued on CD, they lose their allure. Collectors are deeply invested in the notion that buried treasure is (still) *out there*. Dealer and collector meet in a kind of mutual confidence trick. Having coughed up lots of dough for mediocre records, collectors have an incentive for gulling themselves into believing they're exceptional; convinced, they become capable of convincing others. And so begins the cycle of inflation (of reputation and price) whereby albums achieve a 'lost classic' status that's quite undeserved. Original copies of third-rate records go for astronomical prices.

SHARITY BEGINS AT HOME

The Internet and MP3 culture has both amplified and undermined the whole notion of secret knowledge. Now, with comparatively little expenditure of time, money and effort, anyone can

---

UNCOLLECTABLE RECORDS

Some years ago, as a byproduct of countless hours poring over dusty used vinyl, I became fascinated by the notion of the Least Collectable Records of All Time – those unlovable albums that have left the most grime on my fingertips over the years. In the early noughties, I posed the question on I Love Music, the hyper-intelligent discussion board, defining 'least collectable' as not simply bad music but specifically where there was an excess of supply over demand; typically, the sequel to a mega-platinum blockbuster, where millions were confidently pressed up only for the album to underperform drastically (Led Zeppelin's *Presence* is a classic example). Millions of copies, some still shrink-wrapped, the corner snipped off ('cut-outs' as they were called in America), circulating in perpetuity. 'Least collectable' could also encompass genuinely popular records that have dated terribly or suffered from a capricious reversal of mass taste.

The response revealed interesting transatlantic differences. America's unfaves included many that had scant impact in the UK: Seals and Crofts, The Alan Parsons Project, Styx, Chuck Mangione, Asia, Bob Seger. Britain, meanwhile, has its own unique anti-pantheon of novelty tack, expired teen crazes and light entertainment: Chas & Dave, Mud, Bros, Geoff Love, Leo

103

amass immense collections of music and have access to expertise. The disincentives that used to exist – limits of living space and disposable income – have disappeared, and this is allowing ever more people to become obsessive collectors.

I didn't dive into the whole music-for-nothing scene until the mid-2000s. I never got into the file-sharing communities like Napster and its more decentralised (and less prosecutable) successors like Morpheus, Kazaa, Grokster et al. Torrents, as pioneered by Pirate Bay, sounded a bit off-putting, evocative of 'going under', 'drowning in sound', the breaching of psychological dams, etc. What pulled me in finally was the rise of the 'whole album blog', where a post on a particular artist or obscure record would link to its upload at a file-hosting service like Megaupload, Mediafire, Rapidshare and countless others. It was easy to do, especially if you got a subscription to one of these services,

---

Sayer, Bert Kaempfert, Winifred Atwell, Mrs Mills. Overall, though, Herb Alpert's *Whipped Cream and Other Delights* clinched the title of least collectable record of all time. Its cheesy, nude-concealed-in-white-goo cover is horribly familiar to all vinyl rummagers.

The record industry's throw-shit-against-the-wall-and-see-if-it-sticks approach means that there's a lot of shit that sticks around. Recently the blogger Kek-W wrote of trends in 'unfame' that he noticed while trawling through the 'discardia' of charity shops, i.e. what records people were suddenly getting rid of for no apparent reason. Then there were the hardy perennials: 'Some artists – like Paul Young, Terence Trent D'Arby and Five Star – seem to never go out of Unfashion.' But the first critic I know to seriously ponder the fate of all the failed product is the Canadian academic Will Straw. (Mind you, it could be said we're all trudging in Walter Benjamin's footsteps here.) In his 2001 essay 'Exhausted Commodities: The Material Culture of Music', Straw writes about the stuff that people *dig through* when they're digging in the crates. He noted the emergence of a parallel economy – car-boot sales, thrift stores, flea markets, stoop sales and yard sales – in which items of culture-matter 'persist and circulate', their value depleting even as their physical forms refuse to biodegrade. In New York, the lowest rung of all is represented by those plucky entrepreneurs who set up shop on the street,

allowing you to avoid the delays and limitations (e.g. only one download at a time) that many file-hosting companies built in to encourage people to cough up for premium membership.

'Sharity', some people called this new blog network: a three-way pun on 'share' + 'charity' + 'rarity'. In sharity's grand give-away bonanza, barely a genre seemed unrepresented, from the most readily available mainstream fare (fancy the complete discography of Iron Maiden? Every last Pink Floyd bootleg demo?) to the most inaccessible arcana (West African guitar-pop cassettes, 100-edition eighties power-electronics tapes, complete catalogues of library music labels . . .).

The ethos of sharity is captured rather neatly in the phrase 'one of the best, most obscure' – as if the two things were identical – as uttered by the Japanese guy behind the folk-specialist blog Time Has Told Me to describe some choice item he'd uploaded. Over

---

splaying on the sidewalk a choice array of soiled LPs (baked and warping on the griddle-like pavement), scuffed paperbacks, used magazines, semi-functioning appliances and even garments.

In Straw's home town of Montreal, the usual suspects – seventies prog-lite and soft-rock singer-songwriters, hair metal, budget classical, mediocre musicals, club music, etc. – are augmented by local Quebecois delicacies: 'the fake Tijuana brass albums produced in Montreal, the French-language Hawaiian records, the disco symphonies celebrating the 1976 Olympics'. But wherever in the world you live, what you can glean from this sad parade is a shadow history of pop culture, the massive-selling tack that never makes it into the official account. Most of the records churned out in such insane volume during the twentieth century still exist in the world: they can't be pulped like books or recycled like glass; people seldom put them out for the garbage-disposal men – they persist in seeing some value in them even if only for some Other, and give them to charity shops or deserving causes like the school fair, where most of them become a burden, a drag, taking up space.

The unloved collectivity of all these records that don't belong to anybody's collection could be dubbed the Dejection. It's possible that in its orphaned immensity the Dejection outnumbers the grand total of all the records that do

the course of a year or so, the collector dynamic drove Time Has Told Me on a strange, cranny-of-History-rummaging journey through British folk (not the trendy psychedelic Incredible String Band end of things but true woolly-jumper, wood-whittling, pipe-smoking traditional music, minstrels like Cyril Tawney) and into French folk, Dutch folk, Quebecois folk, Christian folk and even Christian psychedelic folk.

The impetus behind record collecting used to be: 'I want to have something that no one else has.' But with the advent of sharity that's shifted to: 'I've just got hold of something no one else has got, so I'm immediately going to make it available to EVERYBODY.' There's a weird mix of competitive generosity and showing off how cool and esoteric your taste is. What made the sharity blog circuit different from the peer-to-peer file-sharing communities that preceded it is the exhibitionism. Knowledge became cultural capital and bloggers became cult figures, 'faces'

---

have owners and homes. Yet, inevitably, the record-collector impulse, with its penchant for esoteric knowledge, has motivated some to make incursions into the taste wasteland. The Dejection is gradually shrinking, nibbled away at here and there as genres get re-evaluated: second-division glam rock and glitter, eighties Goth, half-forgotten dance styles like New Beat, Hi-NRG, Freestyle and Electronic Body Music. But the Dejection is also shrivelling because some people go looking specifically for bad music: collectors and bloggers who specialise in 'Crap Records', especially when they have atrocious or bloody peculiar cover art. These anti-connoisseurs install themselves in the most uncool corners of music history, like the whimsical, softly bearded student I met some years ago who professed to *genuinely* love Andy Williams and Perry Como.

Ultimately, the digitisation of culture will change all this totally. You can't sell on or donate a sound file or e-book. You can only delete. There can't be a second-hand economy for digitised culture. This means there will no longer be an unofficial public record of unsuccessful records. We won't be able to visit 'museums of failure' (Straw's term for used-record stores) in which the 'monumentality' of the music that never made it or whose moment passed is available to our pitying yet fascinated gaze.

on the scene, even though their real-world identity was shrouded.

Take the blog Mutant Sounds, justly celebrated for its prolific output of esoterica, most of which is out-of-print and extremely hard to find. Founded in January 2007 by a guy called Jim, the blog soon expanded into a collective, enabling Mutant to sustain its ferocious rate of posts and expand its weirdo-music range. Like the best sharity blogs, Mutant Sounds puts a lot of effort into not just finding obscure stuff but presenting it well (high-quality sonics, scans of the artwork, which is often lavish and intricate). Mutant Sounds operative Eric Lumbleau (unusually for a sharity case, happy to use his full real name) sees the motivation for all this work as 'self-aggrandising altruism . . . blog authors anointing themselves as gurus and presiding over their own little kingdoms of cool'. Which sounds rather vain and pompous, except there's also been the handy side effect of 'throwing open the floodgates to decades worth of occult knowledge for casual perusal.' Lumbleau predicts that this explosive 'unleashing' of arcane knowledge is going to seed a new generation of 'adventurous music-making'.

Jim, Mutant Sounds' founder, distinguishes between the record collector and the music enthusiast. This is actually a very common distinction made by record collectors, both on- and offline: they like to distinguish between those who are into rarity for its own sake (especially if format- or packaging-related) and people like themselves who just love music and want to turn other people on. Sometimes these self-proclaimed enthusiasts, who spend a good chunk of their lives at record fairs or perusing set-sale lists, even refer disparagingly to 'collector scum'.

Sharity proponents often talk of how blog coverage has led to certain long-overlooked artists being rediscovered, even leading to official reissues in a few cases. But will people really go to the bother and expense of buying the reissue if they've already downloaded the music free of charge, I wonder? I can only think of a few cases where I've paid money for something I've already downloaded. In fact, sharity in particular, and the interweb in general, has screwed up my enjoyment of record collecting: often I'll be in a used-record store, see something cool or intriguing, then think, 'I could probably find this on the Web . . . Do I really want to pay twenty bucks for a record I'll only play twice, just to have it cluttering up my house?'

With the Web, there's no cost and the file is infinitesimally compact and inconspicuous. It's no secret that downloaders get into chronic binge mode; it's hard to see a reason not to indulge one's mildest twinge of curiosity – at least until you need to get a second external hard drive. What's more intriguing, though, is that the sharity bloggers themselves seem to suffer from a reverse binge syndrome. Some blogs disgorge music at such velocity it's impossible for regular visitors to keep up with them. 'Extreme music' blog Sickness-Abounds is one of the most torrential sharity spots I've come across. The person behind it, \m/etal\m/inx, admits, 'I've received comments like "Slow down!!!" or "You're going too fast!"' Some sharity bloggers seem to have a thoroughness fixation, a compulsion to fillet a particular artist's discography down to its every last B-side compilation and stray split seven-inch.

When I first came across the sharing scene, I was fascinated by the oddball shut-in characters and cul-de-sac-like communities. In their own minds, their generosity makes them almost saintly, and they are truly shaken when trolls leave abusive messages in the comments box or when record labels and recording artists threaten legal action. One particular figure, almost a cult hero on the scene in its early days, was actually hounded into retirement. He would close down one blog, after an eruption of hatred in his comments box from anti-file-sharing vigilantes, and then open another one, only for the same thing to happen. Seemingly a fifty-something hippy, he was genuinely bewildered by the hostility:

he only wanted to 'share' the music he loved – mostly sixties psychedelia.

In the topsy-turvy world of sharity, making stuff available to total strangers is a noble act, and many bloggers pride themselves on the care they put into copying the artwork, liner notes and box-set CD booklets. The word 'share' puts a high-minded, altruistic spin on the legal reality of what they're doing – infringing on someone's copyright. Consumerism and communism unite. The mindset is redolent of that early nineties cyberculture/*Mondo 2000* maxim 'information wants to be free'. In sharity, the abstract idea of dissemination itself takes on a utopian tinge; the kick is the rush of connectivity itself.

In his Benjamin-homaging essay 'Unpacking My Record Collection', Julian Dibbell wrote about the early 'warez' traffickers at the turn of the millennium who were 'dedicated to moving pirated digital goods – software, games, movies, music – as fast as high-bandwidth Net lines allowed'. One young man, talking fast, his knee bouncing with nervous energy, called it 'the zero-day scene . . . It's a competition. A race to see who can get the latest stuff up first.' Dibbell sensed that the boy wasn't interested in the music itself or even the size of his collection: 'what he collected was the speed with which they'd traveled from their corporate origins to his computer . . . The whole obsessive idea, in fact, was to compress a record's history to nothingness, to a vanishing sliver of time: zero days.' In the years that followed, that quest went below zero: blogs competed to get hold of albums before their release, through pirate promo copies and leaks from within the record company. When Dibbell talks of the 'almost sexual frisson at their sudden connectedness and vulnerability to the wired population of the world', I'm reminded of a Napster-era confessional from a downloading convert, who wrote in peculiarly eroticised terms about his addiction to 'nude music' (sound liberated from any kind of material form). His piece climaxes with the declaration: 'I'm open 24-7. Suck me dry.' File sharing can some-times seem like an orgy or a bathhouse, where the spectacle of erotic bounty, the idea of instant, total access and no limitations to desire, is as exciting as any specific sexual transaction that takes place.

What's the harm in it? Well, obviously artists are suffering, and so is the music industry, as well as ancillary industries dependent on them, like music magazines and record stores. But perhaps the biggest danger represented by sharity/the Internet is actually to music fans. Writing in *Old Rare New*, an anthology of elegiac paeans to the record store, Johan Kugelberg described how the net-stalking music fan succumbs to 'Falstaffian gluttony', 'eating at the biggest buffet, heaping and piling exotic foodstuffs not only from all around the globe but spanning history, on your plate' and coating the intestines of one's hard drive with 'noxious build-up'.

I'd always had this ravenous appetite for new stuff, combined with a neurotic anxiety about missing out on anything. Absolute access corrupts absolutely, and I went about it like a pig at a trough. I think my record was to have thirty simultaneous down-loads streaming into my computer at once: over a day's worth of listening, acquired in a little over an hour. It was a dark time, actually. Like the proverbial kid in the candy shop, or Augustus Gloop, that fat German boy in *Willy Wonka* who drowns in the chocolate river, I got lost.

Downloading can all too easily open up a kind of abyss, the dimensions of which are in proportion to the emptiness of your life. It quickly becomes a compulsion that distils consumerism down to its addictive essence. You're stockpiling so many albums, live bootlegs and DJ sets that you never have time to unzip the files and play them. Like crack follows cocaine, the stage after downloading vast amounts of music you will never listen to is when you start skipping the tiny but irritating interval of wait-ing while the files enter your computer and start saving the links for later, building up these massive documents stuffed with the intent to download. Only now am I getting around to deleting some of the stuff I downloaded.

Most collectors know deep down that quantity is the enemy of quality, in the sense that the more you amass, the less intensive a relationship you can have with specific pieces of music. As my friend, blogger-turned-musician and *serious* collector Matthew Ingram, puts it, 'I can't help thinking that if one really *listened* to one's records, one would have a lot *less* of them.' It's easy to imagine that as the collection's size approaches infinity, the appetite to listen to music shrinks to infinitesimal.

And sometimes the sharers get fed up with it too. Here's a post from early in 2010 that struck me as symptomatic:

> Real post: I don't even read blogs anymore. This thing is played out. I deleted 400 [gigabytes]-worth of my music a week ago and I don't miss it. Obsessively downloading/collecting every obscure noise-release you can get your hands on is pointless. Stop it: let it go. Think to yourself and ask 'how many times will I listen to the album I'm about to download?' Just skip it. Buy a tape instead; a fetish object is infinitely more interesting than a pile of mp3s on a hard disk inside your computer. Buy a tape. Buy a record. Fuck it; buy a cd too. Have fun. This isn't 'goodbye;' this is just realchat. Realtalk. Y'know?

The guy was back at it a few months later, though, uploading music as frenziedly as ever on behalf of people unknown to him.

FRANTICITY

There's a mind-state that chronic downloaders get caught up in, a tense vacancy familiar from the slot-machine junkies in Las Vegas and Atlantic City combined with repetitious actions (clicking, dragging, typing titles and info) that resemble the behaviour of laboratory rats nudging the switch for their next cocaine dose over and over. 'Franticity' is what I call this brittle mood of impatient fixation. Franticity is the neurological pulse of the wired life. I can't really see a way to escape it, other than to withdraw to some kind of monastic existence or bucolic haven. Because that's what disconnecting from the Internet would be: a pastoral retreat from the city of information.

I stumbled on the word 'franticity' after seeing a TV commercial for iTunes, appropriately enough. I was fascinated by the imagery – a self-assembling cityscape of skyscrapers and apartment blocks built out of CD covers – and soon found out (via the Web, how else?) that the advertising agency's title for the spot was 'Frantic City'. Lose one of the 'c's and there you have it. In the commercial, the buildings made of music collapse like houses of cards and deliquesce into a dazzling stream of audio-visual data that's then decanted at a furious bit rate into an iPod. The commercial's soundtrack is Rinocerose's 'Cubicle', digitalised garage punk with a chorus that sneers, 'You spend all your time/ in a little cubicle/ *a cubicle.*' The implication is that iTunes will free you up into a world of hearing *outside the box*, a brave new multiverse of listening without prejudice.

'The city of sound' is the governing metaphor of Paul Morley's *Words and Music: A History of Pop in the Shape of a City*, his 2003 book about pop music in the modern era. The spine of *Words and Music* is an imaginary journey taken by Morley and Kylie Minogue on a highway to what the author variously describes as 'the capital city of Pleasure' and 'the concrete city of information'. As evoked by Morley, this glittering metropolis almost immediately struck me as no place I'd want to visit: an unimaginably vast, shiny-sterile music megastore, or the interior of an iPod. I don't think the word 'iPod' actually appears in *Words and Music*, but at one point Morley describes the place that he and Minogue are driving towards as 'a city of lists', which suggests he already had the machine in mind when writing the book in 2002, even though it was still a pretty obscure piece of consumer electronics (the iPod's sales graph only really started to soar in 2005). Either way, *Words and Music* could be a *Das Kapital* for music and the record industry in the age of MP3s and the iPod, a diagram of a new-millennium reality of total abundance and instant access. The city is somewhere 'all that's solid melts into air', to use the famous phrase from *The Communist Manifesto*. Music has become *insubstantial* – not just in the sense of becoming dematerialised code but because all the various forms of 'substance' with which rock critics and rock fans have dignified and validated pop music (in the process tethering it to the Real of social and biographical context) have now vaporised.

Here and there Morley seems ambivalent about this utopia/dystopia of free-floating data, writing at one point about 'a rootless post-reality heaven and hell, where desires can be satisfied instantly, where pleasure can be constant . . . where our lives are run by remote companies in remote control of our needs and wants'. But elsewhere the tone of *Words and Music* is surprisingly close to the technotopian rhetoric you'd have found in an early-nineties edition of *Mondo 2000* or *Wired*, at the height of the information-technology boom; writing that often verged on a kind of capitalist mysticism. A good example is *Wired* senior writer Steven Levy's paeans to Apple boss Steve Jobs (who 'builds his brand the way Michelangelo painted chapels') and to the iPod Nano ('so beautiful that it seemed to have dropped down from some vastly advanced alien civilization'). What Morley envisions – the city where 'everything that has ever happened is available, all at once, all around us' – is identical to the notion of a Universal Library (also known as the Celestial Jukebox) heralded by *Wired*'s co-founder and former executive editor Kevin Kelly in a 2004 *New York Times* article: a vast cultural database containing every book and magazine article ever written, in all languages, and eventually every movie/TV programme/cultural artifact EVER. Kelly went further still and imagined the Universal Library being miniaturised and compressed into an iPod-size device that anyone can carry around with them wherever they go. Of course, seven years after Kelly wrote his article Wi-Fi and ubiquitous cellphone access have rendered obsolete this idea of the portable omni-encyclopedia; smartphones and iPads and other handheld devices mean that it's possible to be connected to the Internet virtually every waking minute of the day. The stated goal of Google's creators is to put everything ever written into the Datacloud, to map not just physical reality (Google Earth) but every square inch of cultural reality too, and place it at our fingertips.

MEMORY ALMOST FULL

In 1989, summing up the decade that was coming to an end, *Musician* writer Bill Flanagan concluded that the lesson of the eighties 'may be musical trends are now shaped more by delivery systems than by any act. The next . . . Beatles may be a technology.' He was talking about the compact disc, but his prediction came true with the iPod, which really did revolutionise the music industry like the Fab Four (just via a different Apple).

Unlike The Beatles, the iPod didn't change music itself. So far the machine – or more precisely, the download-and-share MP3 culture of digitised music – has spawned just one genre of music unique to itself, the mash-up (more about this fad later in the book). Still, the iPod was definitely the biggest thing to happen to music in the first decade of the twenty-first century – both in terms of its own impact and how it crystallised the whole culture of dematerialised music. My wife was an enthusiastic, relatively early adopter, but I was very resistant, partly because I was never that keen on the Walkman (I don't like to be insulated from the sounds of the city as I pass through it; equally, I dislike the way the outside noise interferes with the music). Indeed, some of the very same complaints about the iPod's privatising of social space were mounted against the Walkman; one critic tagged users 'the Walkman dead . . . The eyes flicker with consciousness but they don't *see*.'

But mainly I avoided the iPod because I had this immediate visceral sense that the little white box was an emblem of the poverty of abundance. The idea of carrying your collection with you wherever you went didn't seem at all appealing. It felt freakish. Cramming all that energy, passion, creativity, exuberance and pleasure into a tiny space touched the same superstitious part of my psyche that I evidently have in common with primitive peoples who feared the camera as something that robbed your soul.

In its brief existence, the slim (and getting slimmer every year) music player has generated a mini-genre of iPod lit, from popular-science-style non-fiction books, like Steven Levy's *The Perfect Thing*, to personal testimonials from user-believers, like Dylan Jones's 2005 confessional *iPod, Therefore I Am: Thinking Inside the White Box*. The latter is a fascinating account of one man's unhealthy obsession with a gadget. Hardly the first example of the consumer-confessional genre, *iPod, Therefore I Am* is nonetheless a document that ethnologist-historians in the far future will find invaluable in terms of understanding our times. This lucid anatomy of consumerist desire sometimes reads like a spiritual memoir, a *Pilgrim's Progress* for the twenty-first-century music fanatic.

A journalist and editor who rose from the edgy British street-fashion mag *iD* to running mainstream men's magazines like *GQ*, Dylan Jones retraces in *iPod, Therefore I Am* the trajectory by which seventies punk evolved into eighties style culture, which in turn led to the current state of play, where nothing is subcultural any more and ideas of 'underground' and 'subversive' seem untenable, at least within popular music. 'Why be willfully different when you can consume with impunity?' Jones writes,

seemingly without irony. But more than a celebration of affluent complacency and freedom defined as the right to buy, *iPod,
Therefore I Am* is a candid confession of perverse attachment to
a commodity. Jones *knows* there's something unwholesome and
auto-erotic about his identification with the little white box:
'It sits in my office, daring me to play with it, like some sort of
sex toy,' he says, only four pages into the book, and later admits,
'The feelings I have toward my iPod . . . toward the iPod's iconic
white headphones, toward everything associated with it, are
almost unnatural.' All the ancillary gadgets – the Macally mouse,
PowerBook G4, Altec Lansing travel speakers – are evoked with a
loving, tactile sensuality. Steven Levy likewise recalls his first time
with an iPod: 'It felt very good to hold. Spinning my thumb on
the scroll wheel was satisfying. The smooth silvery back felt so
sensual that it was almost a crime against nature.' But Jones goes
further still, describing the tedious process of ripping CDs into
iTunes as 'sexy'.

Even as it abolishes record collecting in the traditional sense,
the iPod represents the ultimate extension of its mindset: the
compulsion to hunt, stockpile and endlessly reorganise. For Jones,
this technologically enhanced collecting takes on an ontological
dimension (hence the jokey-but-not-really-Cartesian title, *iPod,
Therefore I Am*). 'My whole life is here, 40 GB of memory, thirty
years of memories,' he notes. This suggests that for Jones the iPod
arrived in timely fashion to serve as a way of managing midlife
crisis, that point when memories of youth enter your consciousness involuntarily and the lostness of *temps perdu* starts to weigh
heavily.

'Could I get an entire lifetime's experience into this little white
rectangle?' Jones ponders. Perhaps because of his job at the helm
of magazines the metaphor of 'editing' particularly appeals to
him: 'what I was really enjoying was editing my life'. After ripping
the CDs, he starts the laborious process of converting his vinyl

116

collection, all the import rarities, ancient seven-inch singles and flexi discs: 'If I was seriously going to pour my whole life in to my box, I had to squash it all in, and not just the bits that had been deemed acceptable for the CD generation.'

Soon, Jones's 'box of memories is full, fit to bursting'. When he gets requests from lazy friends to fill up their iPods for them, the metaphor that springs to mind is memory transfer, a creepy notion redolent of the memory implants given to the androids in *Blade Runner*: various top UK media folk, he notes with delight, 'are now walking around with my memories bouncing around inside their heads'. It's not true, of course: the music is perfectly blank to these friends, devoid of the associations it has for Jones. But the fixation on music as an aid to remembering, or as a form of memory preservative, is revealing. Collection and recollection are entwined.

The iPod may be a memory box, but it is not a memory *maker*: it is hard to imagine the device playing the same kind of role as the radio did in the past, in terms of entwining music with everyday life, especially as often it involves the use of music to screen out the outside world and avoid unwelcome social interactions. In *iPod, Therefore I Am*, Jones's reminiscences of the role music played in his life at various points are vivid and stirring, ranging from the rowdy communion of a punk-era squat to the bustle and racket of Jones's art-school residence halls with all sorts of music blaring out into the corridors (Genesis and Talking Heads, Barry White and Lynyrd Skynyrd, roots reggae and The Ramones). 'In the playlists on the left-hand side of my iTunes display panel, all human life is there for my listening pleasure. It's like the halls of residence all over again . . .' he writes. Except that the social aspect is completely absent. Instead of the chance encounters and risky collisions, the friction and epiphany, the iPod offers by way of compensation the solitary thrill of total mastery.

'Right now, I am exerting complete control, keeping a tight

hand on the tiller,' exults Jones. He revels in all the empowering conveniences that the iPod offers, like being able to 'correct' albums by removing their weak tracks (even on Beatles LPs, where he removes all the Ringo songs), boiling them down to their essence or rearranging the track sequence. He gurgles with delight over the time read-out that tells you that 2.15 minutes have elapsed and there's 1.12 left to go. This function not only abolishes the 'lost in music', timeless quality of immersive listening but has an insidious tendency to encourage the listener to skip to the next track rather than wait for the song to unfold in its own due time. It's the porno-logic of franticity striking again, always 'the next, the next, the next'. In both cases ('correcting' the album and the skip-ahead impulse), you witness consumer empowerment disempowering both artist and Art. Instead of being an experience to which you submit yourself, music becomes something *useful*.

The most chilling element of *iPod, Therefore I Am* is the subliminal sense that what Jones wants most of all is to be *done with desire*. He skips between dizzy delight at the future vistas of insatiability and a dream of somehow reaching the *end* of music (the little white box full to the brim, the best bits of every genre neatly arrayed). The fantasy is to be want-less and loss-less (Apple Lossless is the name of a superior digital encoding that he adopts belatedly, forcing – or is it really enabling? – him to rip and upload all his music again, to go through the whole months-long anal-erotic procedure once more). This idea of the iPod as a magic charm to ward off death becomes very clear by the end of the book, when Jones talks about absent friends and how 'while some people might not be with me now, the records we listened to together are all here in my little white memory box, all lovingly compiled and curated, just waiting for that time when I might need them again'.

iPod fans always go on about how the machine is like having your own personal radio station. Exactly: the iPod is Radio Me, where there's no nasty surprises and the programmer magically knows what you want to hear. Which means it's the *opposite* of the radio, which is a medium for surprise, for connection with people you might have nothing else in common with, for creating strange social alliances.

What in the end is more antisocial: blasting your in-car sound system or boom-box, or walking through a city wearing iPod headphones? The former is a contribution to civic vitality, even if it feels like noise pollution; the other is withdrawal from street life. Music was meant to spill out into public space. You think of hip hop (with its block parties and park jams, literally music of the streets) and rave (appropriating buildings or public land), but also the poignant stories of people huddling in silent awe around the radio or someone's record player the week that *Sgt Pepper's* was released. The iPod is fundamentally asocial. OK, you get people who plug their iPods in at parties, but at best this is an update of the host's mix-tape, at worst the vastly expanded update of the boor who takes over the music centre and imposes his taste on everybody else. Matthew Ingram notes how common it is for people at dance parties nowadays to accost the DJ and insist on plugging their iPod into the mixer because they *have* to hear a certain tune; this is consumer empowerment turned toxic, the impatience to hear 'my music NOW' overriding the collective experience of the dance floor as lovingly guided by the expert DJ. It's a poignant clash between two different forms of collection and their attendant mediums, vinyl and digital.

I was fairly committed to skipping the iPod era altogether. But then . . . I got one, as a gift. And sure enough I went through all the processes that everybody else goes through: enchanted, in a peculiarly kinky sort of way, by it as a silky-sensual object; geekily absorbed by the process of loading it and organising it. But I quickly found that having all that choice didn't sit well with me, like being in one of those restaurants with excessively long menus, page after plastic-coated page, or cable TV with its hundreds of channels almost *forcing* you to keep skipping through them.

Shuffle offered a reprieve from the problem of choice. Like everybody, at first I was captivated by it and, like everybody, had all those experiences with mysterious recurrences of artists and uncanny sequencings. The downside of shuffle soon revealed itself, though. I became fascinated with the mechanism itself, and soon was always wanting to know what was coming up next. It was irresistible to click onto the next random selection. Even if it was something great, there was the possibility something greater still would flash up next. Soon I was listening to just the first fifteen seconds of every track; then, not listening at all. Franticity strikes again. This was a kind of ecstasy of optionality, consumerism with the boring bit (the consumption, the product itself) vaporised right out of the picture. Really, the logical culmination would have been for me to remove the headphones and just look at the track display.

Although magazines such as *Wired* like to present technology as the unstoppable force of necessity, technologies never catch on unless and until the climate is right: there has to be popular desire and consumer need that the machine answers and fulfils. The cultural invention of the use always precedes the machine, if not as an invention then as a successful phenomenon. The iPod took off because it slotted right into the new-millennium Me generation, where the insistence on having it your way right now reflects the huge existential-political weight that has been invested in consumerism (just about the only real zone of control in people's lives). The 'i' at the start was put there for a reason: because this is *my* music, not *our* music.

The shuffle function seems particularly telling: eliminating the need for choice, yet guaranteeing familiarity, it relieves you of the burden of desire itself. And that's what all these digital-era music technologies propose: pop without fandom. This is exactly the kind of consumer – omnivorous, non-partisan, promiscuously eclectic, drifting indolently across the sea of commodified sound – that the music industry prefers. Obsession doesn't fit this scenario because it asserts the irreplaceableness of the object of desire and rejects the idea of 'plenty more fish in the sea'. Devout fans of a particular band or bygone subculture (Teddy Boys, Deadheads) have opted out of the market: at a certain point, there are simply no more things to buy.

The promise of the iPod and of the download culture in general is that people will become open-minded, into music as a whole as opposed to a specific nook or niche of it. Yet the abundance, diversity and ease of access that we now enjoy seems to have actually had the opposite effect. As the end of the 2000s approached, more and more blog posts, magazine columns and message-board discussions testified to appetite loss induced by excessive downloading. In a June 2008 article for *Phoenix New Times* headlined 'When Every Song Ever Recorded Fits on Your MP3 Player, Will You Listen to Any of Them?' Karla Starr confessed: 'I find myself getting bored even in the middle of songs simply because I *can*.' Barry Schwartz's book *The Paradox of Choice: Why More Is Less* was frequently cited, while the anecdotal accounts of jaded palates and MP3-choked hard drives were given scientific support in the form of a research study conducted by music psychologists at the University of Leicester which suggested that downloading led to apathy and indifference. 'The accessibility of music has meant that it is taken for granted and does not require a deep emotional commitment once associated with music appreciation,' argued the project's leader, Adrian North. 'In the 19th century, music was seen as a highly valued treasure with fundamental and near-mystical powers of human communication,' he elaborated, before glumly concluding that nowadays, even though people listened to much more music *in toto* than in the past, and to a much wider range, their listening was 'not necessarily characterised by deep emotional investment'.

This depreciation of the value of music observed by Dr North and his team can ultimately be traced back to the shift from analogue to digital. First music was reified, turned into a thing (vinyl records, analogue tapes) you could buy, store, keep under your own personal control. Then music was 'liquefied', turned into data that could be streamed, carried anywhere, transferred between different devices. With the MP3, music became a devalued currency in two senses: there was just too much of it (as with hyperinflation, banks printing too much money), but also because of the way it flowed into people's lives like a current or fluid. This made music start to resemble a utility (like water or electricity) as opposed to an artistic experience whose temporality you subjected yourself to. Music has become a continuous supply that is fatally susceptible to discontinuity (pause, rewind/fast-forward, save for later, and so forth).

In a sense, digital music has simply taken the inherent tendency of recorded music to its logical limit. All recorded music, analogue as well as digital, has the effect of desanctifying and desocialising the experience of music, because what was once an event becomes repeatable and what was once collective becomes privatised. As the theorist Jacques Attali argued, the ritual role and the function of social catharsis that music once had is eroded by the ability of individuals to stockpile recordings and play them whenever they wish. We are living through the era in which music sheds its last vestigial traces of '*kairos*' (the ancient Greek word for peak time, the time of the event or the epiphany) and its final subordination to '*chronos*' (the quantitative time of work and leisure).

DAMMING THE STREAM

This subordination of music to the values of utility was the spur for Bill Drummond to launch his No Music Day campaign.

Inspired by his own jaded audio palate, he invited music fans to join him on an annual sonic fast on 21 November (the day before St Cecilia's day, she being the patron saint of music). Like everything the man behind The KLF has done, the idea was simultaneously mischievous and deadly earnest. Drummond talked about how we'd arrived at a point 'where we can (in theory and almost in practice) listen to any recorded music, from the entire history of recorded music, wherever, whenever while doing whatever we want'. While acknowledging the upsides to this, he argued that this represented an utter voiding of music's meaning and purpose. 'As we edge our way deeper into the twenty-first century we will begin to want music that cannot be listened to wherever, whenever while doing whatever. We will begin to seek out music that is both occasion and place specific, music that can never be merely a soundtrack.' Drummond argued that the MP3/iPod era was actually the death throes of 'recorded music', which he predicted would be 'perceived as an art form very much of the twentieth century'. Music would become something you either made just for yourself and perhaps a few friends, or it would be experienced in the unmediated presence of the musicians. Either way, it would be returned to the present tense, to real time.

When Drummond wrote these words in 2006 as a prequel to the first No Music Day, it was already noticeable that a resurgence of live music had been quietly building. Attendance at gigs was booming, despite the rising ticket prices; festivals were more important, more plentiful, more well-attended than ever (and by people of all ages, from teenagers to middle-aged parents dragging their infants and toddlers with them). Live performance had also become the principal way that bands could make a living, a reversal of the way it used to be when tours lost money but were undertaken in order to break bands and promote new albums. The live-music resurgence must be due to a semi-conscious craving for the unrepeatable event, something you have to be there to experience. While recorded music became free and thus valueless, live music rose in value because it wasn't something you could copy or share. It was exclusive. The audience might even get a sense of itself (potentially at least) as a community. Part of the appeal of live music is that it enforces a fully immersed state of concentrated listening through the loudness and enveloping nature of the sound, but also because if you've paid through the nose for an experience you're probably going to make an effort to stay in the moment rather than distract yourself. You can't press pause, rewind or save it for later. Live music not only insists on, it *imposes* undivided attention and uninterrupted listening. To today's option-overloaded music fan, that kind of subjugation feels like liberation.

During the course of the 2000s, the music business turned inside out. Bands and DJs got more gigs if they put out records, so recordings became a kind of calling card or non-specific flyer, a loss-leader way of promoting the live performances or club sets where the money was actually made. A journalist friend, Andy Battaglia, told me he'd noticed that the audio quality of recordings was getting worse because bands and electronic-music producers alike weren't spending so much time making them; to make a living, they had to be on the road most of the time.

Another music-journalist buddy, Michaelangelo Matos, worried more about the quality of his own listening experience and launched a one-man Slow Listening Movement. Like No Music Day, this was humorous yet utterly serious. But Matos wasn't making a polemical gesture like Drummond so much as trying to devise a practical programme for a better way of life. So what he proposed was not a fast, like No Music Day, but a diet. Matos vowed that from January to November of 2009, he would only allow himself to 'download one MP3 at a time; the next MP3 can only be downloaded once I listen to the first one'. There were various other limitations, but the general principle of intake restriction struck me as not just a cool idea but quite possibly a vital sanity-preserving measure: the creation of a filter, or perhaps a dam, to protect against the rising sea levels of the ocean of sound.

LOST IN MUSIC

There are various other ways of resisting the info tsunami. One is to go back to vinyl, which quite a lot of people have been doing, resulting in a resurgence of the format. Personally, I generally pay for music these days only when it is vintage vinyl from a second-hand store. But even buying a CD gives me a strange frisson; it feels like an enjoyably perverse act of swimming against the tide of history. Coughing up hard-earned cash also ensures you'll listen to the bloody thing, and listen intently. Vinyl seems more dissident, though, and more of a defiant throwback: it means that you're literally re-entering analogue time. With CDs you can skip tracks, you can pause and restart at will. That's far less easy to do with vinyl records (or cassettes, also resurgent). The absence of digitally enabled consumer convenience means that analogue formats enforce a more sustained mode of listening, more contemplative and reverent.

Still, as time goes by and the folk memory of music as a material object fades, record collecting is bound to become an increasingly aberrant lifestyle choice, an arcane exertion of money and effort. The idea that people kept their music splayed across shelves and crammed into cupboards, and that they lugged it from dwelling place to dwelling place, will seem quite preposterous. Sooner than we imagine, even the idea of actually keeping the stuff in your computer will be considered quaint.

With the extinction of the idea hovering on the horizon, it's worth considering what was at stake in the notion that you could 'own' music. As with other consumer purchases of non-essential things that give life meaning and colour and excitement (clothes being the parallel that springs to mind), the commodification of music meant that investing one's cash and investing one's emotion became totally wedded. When music came clad in a cherishable husk of packaging and the recording medium itself had a material heft, it asserted itself as a tangible presence in your life. It was easier to form an attachment to music when it was a thing.

The fact that most people had limited spending resources made the decisions freighted with meaning and fraught with anxiety. I can remember a time when the decision of what album to buy that month (as a teenager) or that week (as a student) was weighty; you made the wrong choice, you were lumbered with it. Or rather, even if a record was disappointing on first listen, you would persevere with it in the hope that it would open up and reveal its qualities to you. Under capitalism, money is the product of labour time sold (for most of us, at a poor price). When you spent hard-earned money on cultural goods, logic dictated that you would spend further time extracting value from them.

Most people lived in an 'either/or' reality. You bought one record, which meant that you couldn't afford this other one you craved, and lots of others would have to go unheard. This fitted rather well with a music culture organised around partisan identification, where if you loved one kind of music, you abhorred (or at least ignored) another. A time of movements and warring style tribes.

Nowadays 'either/or' thinking, or even 'either/or' *feeling*, is considered passé. 'Plus/and', a philosophical term of uncertain origin (I'm told Deleuze and Guattari used it), is the buzz concept. 'Plus/and' means you don't have to choose, because you can choose both; you don't have to take sides, because everything has its point and its positives.

'Either/or' is the logic of difficult choices in an economy of scarcity. The extreme example is the folk myth of the person who skips a meal in order to buy the record they really, really *have* to have. 'Plus/and' is the logic of downloading. File-sharing culture – and the things that have enabled it, like increased bandwidth, ever-expanding computer memory, etc. – have removed music from the scarcity economy. If there's no cost, and no issues to do with storage, there is no earthly reason to desist from the 'and this . . . and this too' imperative. 'Plus/and' is the logic of the all-you-can-eat salad bar. It's also the logic of liking a really diverse range of music, but not having that exclusive monomaniacal (or do I mean monogamous?) relationship with a specific genre. It's breadth, rather than depth.

Unfortunately (or is it in fact fortunately?) life remains subject to the rule of 'either/or'. Life itself is a scarcity economy: you only have so much time and energy. What's missing from all the techno-utopian scenarios of access and choice is the reality of limits – on resources, on an individual's time, on our brain's ability to process information beyond a certain speed. To the extent that 'plus/and' is becoming the dominant principle of culture (so many options, so much information, so much entertainment), it could be that it is actually killing music, because its ultimate tendency is towards a kind of indifference. Again, 'glutted/clotted' springs to mind as the common predicament of the age. 'Glutted' captures that over-sated sensation, the aural equivalent to chronic-fatigue syndrome, where the auditory pleasure centre of the brain is fried after years of trying to process, absorb, *feel* too much music in too little time.

In the era of scarcity – which is all of human history, pretty much – utopia was usually identified with plenty: El Dorado, the Land of Cockaigne, the Big Rock Candy Mountain, the Happy Hunting Grounds, and so forth. But as Christian Thorne notes in his essay 'The Revolutionary Energy of the Outmoded', under late capitalism these visions of bounty start to seem like 'little more than hideous afterimages of the marketplace itself, spilling over with redundant and misdistributed goods'. That sounds like a good description of the charnel houses of the Internet, strewn with multiple pirated copies of the same albums, at various degraded levels of bit rate. The core abomination of the MP3 and the conversion of music into code is that there is no limit to copying. A single Rapidshare upload can be downloaded millions of times, and can be 'stolen' and uploaded by others: a virally spiralling miasma of dissemination. Thorne suggests that the society of hyper-consumption must paradoxically 'find utopia in its antithesis . . . dearth'. Less is more. And as Fredric Jameson points out, there is actually another literary tradition of utopias that are about seclusion and serenity: withdrawal from the promiscuous bustle and hyper-stimulation of the city in favour of pastoral stasis. A utopia that is not about wanting *for* nothing, but about wanting *nothing*.

4
GOOD CITATIONS
The Rise of the Rock Curator

I first noticed the buzz-phrase 'curated by' at some point in the early 2000s, when it started to infiltrate the left-field fringes of music. You'd come across it in press releases, flyers and concert programmes, or in profiles of musicians. Activities that once would have been humbly described as selecting a compilation or booking bands for a festival now came coated in the high-falutin' gloss of curation.

I'm really not sure how the trend began. It probably drifted across from the art world, thanks to the increasing number of intersections between experimental music and the museum and gallery circuit: artists doing work inspired by rock or incorporating elements of pop culture; musicians becoming involved in projects and exhibitions or doing performances in art spaces. The curatorial role had also gradually risen in prominence in the art world to the point where you could talk about star curators.

The aspirational use of the word 'curating' by musicians suggested that the same skill set required to run an art gallery or organise a museum exhibition was being applied to the formation of a band's sonic identity. It also elevated ancillary activities like making compilations, booking DJ nights or festivals, collating archival reissues, and so forth, by turning them into facets of the group's or musician's creative expression. Like the music, all these fronts of activity came out of one's taste and sensibility. The spread of 'curator' has gone hand in hand with the vogue for using 'creative' as a vague all-purpose noun (somewhere between occupation and existential identity) to describe people whose artistic expression is spread across a wide range of forms and outlets.

Brian Eno, something of a patron saint of creatives, has been moving back and forth between the music and art worlds for decades, splitting his time between making video art and giving lectures on one side, and making records and producing bands on the other. It's fitting then that Eno noticed the rise of the curator and grasped its implications way ahead of the pack. In 1991, reviewing a book on hypertext for *Artforum*, he proclaimed: 'Curatorship is arguably the big new job of our times: it is the task of re-evaluating, filtering, digesting, and connecting together. In an age saturated with new artifacts and information, it is perhaps the curator, the connection maker, who is the new storyteller, the meta-author.'

But Eno wasn't just elevating the stature of the curator, he was slightly demoting – or at least, *recasting* – the role of the artist. In a 1995 interview with *Wired*, he characterised the contemporary artist as not a creator so much as a 'connector of things . . . This is why the curator, the editor, the compiler, and the anthologist have become such big figures.' This idea had actually been germinating in his mind for some time: back in 1986, Eno argued that innovation was 'a much smaller proportion' of artistic activity 'than we usually think', and proposed the concept of 'remixing' as more suited to the postmodern age. The contemporary artist, he suggested, '*perpetuates* a great body of received cultural and stylistic assumptions, he *re-evaluates* and *re-introduces* certain ideas no longer current, and then he also innovates'.

The term 'curator' derives from the Latin word for guardian, and originally had an ecclesiastical meaning, referring to a low-level priest 'responsible for the care of souls'. From the late seventeenth century, it started to refer to the custodian of a library, museum or archive – any kind of collection maintained by a cultural-heritage institution. As the private amassing of cultural artifacts has become more and more widespread, it could be said that rather a lot of us have become curators of a sort, albeit with no professional training or sense of obligation to the public and a completely idiosyncratic policy in terms of 'acquisitions'. Still, quite a few famous museums began as the private collections of aristocrats and antiquarians, while many private collectors approach their area of obsession with a systematic thoroughness. Some of these private collectors are musicians.

In the early eighties, the *New Musical Express* featured a weekly column called 'Portrait of the Artist as a Consumer', in which a musician listed favourite records, books, films and TV programmes. Nowadays, magazines are littered with celeb-related space-filler of every kind, but back then this was an original move that revealed the star as a fan. At its most interesting, 'Portrait of the Artist as a Consumer' offered a map to a singer's or band's aesthetic. So when The Birthday Party's Nick Cave and Rowland S. Howard did one, their checklist – which included movies like *Wiseblood* and *Night of the Hunter*, singers like Johnny Cash and Lee Hazlewood, Morticia from the cult TV show *The Addams Family*, and so forth – made for a perfect cross-section of Southern Gothic and trash Americana. A display case of super-cool early-eighties taste, the chart helped explain The Birthday Party's transition from their early style circa *Prayers on Fire* (informed by *poètes maudits* like Rimbaud and Baudelaire and the primal-yet-quirky sounds of Pere Ubu and Captain Beefheart) to the pulpy guignol of *Junkyard* and the *Bad Seed* EP.

It's true that there were earlier rock artists whose music came attached with a kind of invisible reading and movie-watching list. In some ways, the cover of *Sgt Pepper's*, with its gallery of

131

people The Beatles thought were cool – Lenny Bruce, Edgar Allan Poe, Oscar Wilde, Albert Einstein – was a precocious example of this syndrome, but with a few exceptions (Stockhausen, Lewis Carroll, Dylan) few could be said to have been an influence on The Beatles' words and music. Still, the cover of *Sgt Pepper's* does loosely fit the concept of the 'portal' that critics like Mark Fisher and Owen Hatherley have recently used to describe the way a certain type of band directed their fans to rich sources of brain food, a whole universe of inspiration and ideas beyond music. Postpunk was a great era for portal bands. Song lyrics and interview comments by Magazine's Howard Devoto or The Fall's Mark E. Smith might turn their fans on to Dostoevsky or Wyndham Lewis. Being a Throbbing Gristle or Coil fan was like enrolling in a university course of cultural extremism, the music virtually coming with footnotes and a 'Further Reading' section attached. The Smiths edified their devotees through myriad allusions in the

---

COVER VERSIONS

A few years after doing the *NME*'s 'Portrait of the Artist as a Consumer' with his Birthday Party bandmate Rowland S. Howard, Nick Cave began to signpost the Deep Southern Americana influences across his early solo work, starting with the single release of a cover of Presley's 'In the Ghetto'. *The Firstborn Is Dead*, his second album, contained a mythopoeic song about Elvis named after his birthplace, Tupelo, while the album title alluded obliquely to Jesse Garon Presley, the King's stillborn twin. The album came wrapped in faux ethnographic sleeve notes that wittily pastiched the edifying tone of the Folkways record label. Then Cave literalised the artist-as-consumer/creator-as-curator notion with the 1986 covers album *Kicking Against the Pricks*, which laid out a smorgasbord of all the things from which he and his group The Bad Seeds drew artistic nourishment: blues, country and the epic balladry of Gene Pitney and Glen Campbell.

But *Kicking Against the Pricks* wasn't the first covers album, not by a long shot. In 1976, Todd Rundgren's album *Faithful* devoted an entire side to near-immaculate forgeries of sixties classics, with Rundgren applying his studio-wizard knowledge of production techniques to replicate the textures and ambience of songs like 'Strawberry Fields Forever' and 'Good Vibrations'. And

lyrics (many sampled verbatim from films, plays, novels) and the systematic iconography of the record-sleeve images.

Mark Fisher argues that the pop-group-as-portal works most potently when the connections being made cut across 'different cultural domains': from music to fiction or cinema or visual art. As the eighties proceeded, though, bands increasingly made reference to esoteric forms of music or to pop history; the portals rarely seemed to transport you outside the realm of music. By the early nineties I was calling this phenomenon 'record-collection rock', having noticed how a large proportion of interviews with bands seemed to be taken up with talking about influences and reference points. Most really interesting bands have a map of their taste buried within their music for obsessive fans to dig out. But what was different was that the taste map was getting ever more explicit and exposed, to the point where the aesthetic co-ordinates were right there on the surface of the sound. The Jesus

---

three years earlier, David Bowie and Bryan Ferry each released one at almost exactly the same time, *Pin Ups* and *These Foolish Things*. These late-1973 albums were extensions of the way that both glam icons had served as portals for their fans, with their music, lyrics and visual presentation indexed to a dizzying array of cultural reference points: Bowie wrote a song about Andy Warhol, while Ferry paid tribute to Humphrey Bogart in Roxy Music's '2HB', romped archly through a checklist of high-cultural name checks on 'Do the Strand', and elsewhere invoked Pop Art, Aubrey Beardsley, Nietzsche and F. Scott Fitzgerald.

Pin Ups was a straightforward 'these are my roots' exercise, similar to The Band's blues, soul and rock'n'roll covers album *Moondog Matinee* (also released in autumn 1973). Bowie pressed the pause button on his artistic evolution for a nostalgic flashback to his mid-sixties London mod days, serving up mannered renditions of songs by The Pretty Things, The Easybeats and The Yardbirds. The front cover featured Twiggy, the face and body of Carnaby Street circa 1965. Ferry's *These Foolish Things* drew on a wider pool of fifties and sixties rock and soul: classics by Presley, Smokey Robinson, The Beach Boys and Lesley Gore. The selection made a kind of argument: it rejected the prevailing rock belief that authentic artists were those who sang their own songs. Ferry treated songs by

and Mary Chain, Spacemen 3 and Primal Scream were pioneers of the new sensibility. These groups installed themselves as custodians of a canon of mavericks (and usually pop-marketplace failures) that included The Velvet Underground, The Stooges, Love, MC5 and Suicide. There was something inherently 'meta' about the Mary Chain. Their blissfully cacophonous shroud of feedback concealed the traditionalism of their songwriting (equal parts Ramones and Ronettes). Even the crowd disorder at Mary Chain gigs seemed like meta-riots: enactments of a desire to have a reason to riot, and historically informed by the folkloric memory of punk as passed on by the music press.

Spacemen 3 went one step further than the Mary Chain's heard-it-somewhere-before melodies by featuring actual citations in their songs: reworked riffs and tunes that, OK, didn't *depend* on the listener recognising them, but certainly became an integral part of the aesthetic response and pleasure for those listeners

---

rock-era icons like Dylan, The Beatles and the Stones as if they were Broadway standards, easily separable from the persona of their writer-performers. Rock was folded back into showbiz. This polemical gesture was intensified the following year on the sleeve of a *second* covers album, *Another Time, Another Place*: here Ferry wore a white tuxedo and black bow tie, a look suggestive of timeless elegance.

In the sixties, cover versions had generally been of contemporary songs, a way for a performer or group to fill up an album. In other words, the cover version was not particularly freighted with significance. That began to change in the post-punk era, when covers were often chosen to express a group's sensibility or make an argument about pop history. The Human League's covers of The Righteous Brothers' 'You've Lost That Lovin' Feeling' and Gary Glitter's 'Rock and Roll' were pointed gestures indicating their pro-pop allegiances and their ambition to be chart stars. The 2-Tone groups' covers were tributes to their sixties ska ancestors. Elvis Costello recorded a whole album of country-and-western covers, *Almost Blue*, showcasing a less-known aspect of his musical make-up while making the case for country as a form of white soul music unjustly scorned by hip taste. Hüsker Dü would signal the shift of post-post-punk music towards

who did know their underground rock history. Released in 1986 (a year after the Mary Chain's *Psychocandy*), Spacemen 3's debut, *Sound of Confusion*, featured a song called 'Losing Touch with My Mind' based on a riff borrowed from The Rolling Stones' 'Citadel', and a second side that began with a cover of The Stooges' 'Little Doll' and rewrote their 'TV Eye' as 'O.D. Catastrophe'.

Once, rock'n'roll was a commentary on adolescent experience; over time, rock itself became that experience, overlapping with it and at times substituting for it entirely. Formed by one-time Mary Chain drummer Bobby Gillespie, Primal Scream typified the new breed of eighties bands who spent their youth cooped up in dark bedrooms drowning in vinyl and steeped in the music press, in the process amassing enormous knowledge about rock and fierce convictions about 'what went wrong'. Primal Scream's music evolved (and improved) as Gillespie's record collection expanded, from their early overly canonical incarnation as fetishists of

---

sixties influences with covers of 'Eight Miles High' and 'Ticket to Ride'. Soon, in addition to covers, you started to get tribute songs: Psychic TV's Brian Jones paean 'Godstar', The Replacements' 'Alex Chilton' and The House of Love's 'The Beatles and the Stones'.

By the late eighties, covers and covers albums were all the rage. Often they seemed to serve as a way for bands who'd lost their way and run out of steam to recharge their batteries, as with Siouxsie and the Banshees' *Through the Looking Glass* or Guns N' Roses' album of punk covers *The Spaghetti Incident?*. In the case of This Mortal Coil – a project helmed by the boss of 4AD Records, Ivo Watts-Russell, and involving multiple singers – the release of three albums of esoteric cover versions, punctuated by wispy ambient instrumentals, was a form of canon-making. In the mid-eighties, Watts-Russell's choices were polemical: maverick minstrels from the pre-punk era such as Tim Buckley, Tom Rapp, Roy Harper, Gene Clark and others.

Covers albums could be mischievous exercises ambiguously poised between iconoclasm and homage, as with The Residents' 'The American Composers Series', a giant project intended to take them to the end of the twentieth century and to cover the works of at least twenty American musical greats. In the end,

VelvetsByrdsLove to their 1991 peak *Screamadelica*, whose songs like 'Higher Than the Sun' layered a more esoteric, wide-ranging taste span (Tim Buckley, Augustus Pablo, Parliament-Funkadelic, Smile-era Brian Wilson, John Coltrane) over contemporary techno and house rhythms.

At the time I enjoyed all these bands, and to this day still adore certain of their works (*Psychocandy*, *Playing with Fire*, 'Higher Than the Sun'). I also believed, back then, that their out-of-time sound was a righteously renegade response to the eighties pop mainstream. Jason Pierce of Spacemen 3 later characterised their stance as a kind of passive-aggressive defiance of the present: 'We sat the '80s out, really. We weren't in tune with what was going on musically or politically at all . . . We mined a world of music that wasn't mainstream – taking from '50s and '60s music – then just sat on it and made it our own.'

Nonetheless, it was clear even at the time that none of these

---

they only managed to honour four giants – George Gershwin, James Brown, Hank Williams and John Philip Sousa – across two albums, *George & James* and *Stars & Hank Forever*. Earlier in their career, The Residents had perpetrated a kind of cover *per*version of the Stones's 'Satisfaction' and created 'Beyond the Valley of a Day in the Life', a montage of Beatles 'samples' and soundbites from Fab Four interviews. This spawned an entire eighties mini-genre of parodic plagiarism, from Culturcide's *Tacky Souvenirs of Pre-Revolutionary America* (Top Forty hits defaced and at times almost completely drowned out by noise) to Negativland's mockery of U2 and Laibach's transformation of songs like Queen's 'One Vision' and The Rolling Stones's 'Sympathy for the Devil' into bombastic epics of totalitarian kitsch.

The next step in tribute-through-desecration was to cover an entire album. Laibach did *Let It Be*, and in recent years we've seen efforts like Japancakes's chamber-pop instrumental version of My Bloody Valentine's *Loveless*, Petra Haden's simulacrum of *The Who Sell Out* (which she spun entirely out of her vocals) and Jeffrey Lewis's acoustic folk translations of anarcho-punk on *12 Crass Songs*. Probably the most interesting whole-album-cover in recent years was The Dirty Projectors' *Rise Above*, described by the band's leader Dave

groups pointed a way to the future. In a non-specific sense (as opposed to how the word is generally used) they were tribute bands. Where they really failed was on the expressive level; you rarely got the sense there was anything much in the way of felt emotion behind the songs; they seemed born of fandom, a love for the stylisation of emotion in music. This peculiar detachment was most evident in the lyrics, with their fruit machine-like rotation of time-honoured words and phrases: 'honey', 'heaven', 'candy', 'soul', 'Jesus', 'how does it feel', 'Lord', 'sweet', 'dark', 'high', 'come down slowly', 'shine', 'angel', 'tears'. The intent was to achieve an edgy (yet also spiritually profound) conflation of the languages of love, religion and drugs; a big idea around at the time was that clichés imparted more truth than clever-clever wordsmithery. But the ultimate effect, more often than not, was just a highbrow hipster's counterpart to the way songs got written by hair-metal Guns N' Roses-style bands on the Sunset Strip.

Longstreth as an attempt to 'rewrite *Damaged*, an album by Black Flag, from memory'. He deliberately avoided listening to Black Flag's album or reading the lyrics during the making of *Rise Above* because he 'wanted to see if I could make this album myself – not as an album of covers or an homage per se, but as an original creative act'.

The rise of the cover version and the covers album is an index of the increasingly inter-referential nature of pop. Look at the trend for bands naming themselves after an album, song or lyric – Starsailor, Ladytron, Death Cab for Cutie and *pièce de resistance* Scott 4, after the fourth Scott Walker solo record. This phenomenon was virtually unknown until the nineties but is now out of control. A variant of it is the album title that melds the names of legendary groups and classic albums: Japan's neo-psych-prog ensemble Acid Mothers Temple are repeat offenders here with titles like *Starless and Bible Black Sabbath* and *Absolutely Freak Out (Zap Your Mind!!)*. In a sort of cannibalistic assimilation of one's influences and icons, groups will even incorporate an earlier performer's name into their own: Brian Jonestown Massacre, The Mooney Suzuki (the latter combining the names of Can's first two vocalists). On the name front as with everything else, pop is greedily eating itself up.

The only difference was that in this particular School of Rock, the textbooks were the Velvet's third album and The Stooges rather than Aerosmith's *Toys in the Attic* and Hanoi Rocks' *Two Steps from the Move*.

BRIC-A-BRAC COLLAGE

If music is a self-portrait of the artist as consumer, the places that groups go to get the raw materials out of which they fashion their sonic identity are record shops, flea markets, thrift stores, record fairs and, nowadays, eBay, online record markets like Discogs and Gemm, sharity blogs, and so forth. Saint Etienne are a good example of a band constituted out of the practice of elevated consumerism. Jon Savage nailed the sensibility in his sleeve note to their 1990 debut *Foxbase Alpha*, which describes a trek to Camden Market trawling for Northern Soul compilations, roots reggae tracks and 'overpriced UK psych singles'. The pop aesthete weaving through this overcrowded bazaar of cultural jetsam becomes a figure for navigating through the chaos of urban postmodernity itself. What Savage was describing was a form of sonic antiquing. Saint Etienne's collecting feeds both into their music and into a range of parallel activities; one of the trio, Bob Stanley, writes music journalism and liner notes, compiles anthologies of obscure vintage music, and so forth. They are classic curator-as-creator types, in other words.

The music that comes out of this bricolage is, at its best, like the creation of an alternative pop universe: hallucinations of the hybrid styles that could have happened if pop had gone down a different fork in time. In this game, the more you know about pop history, the more possibilities you have for coming up with new reconfigurations of the known into the unforeheard. 'It's a lot more limiting when you get someone forming a band who's only heard music from the last two years,' Stanley told me. 'If someone's got a large record collection, there are so many loose ends in pop history that nobody's ever followed up that there's limitless work to be done reinterpreting the past. It's never gonna be a dead end.'

But one downside of sonic antiquing is a certain detachment. Saint Etienne's songs aren't torn from the soul so much as lovingly pieced together from sounds either inspired by or sampled from their favourite records. It's pop as objective artifact ('What a fab single!') as opposed to pop as subjective expression ('That really moves me'). Stephin Merritt of American outfit The Magnetic Fields could have been speaking for Stanley and partner Pete Wiggs when he talked about his song writing in terms of making 'pretty objects I can treasure forever'.

This is a 'gay' (quote marks because as far as I know Saint Etienne are actually straight, although Merritt isn't) pop aesthetic of 'passionate irony' that sets itself against the straight rock ethos of blustery authenticity. And in fact there is a historical connection between antiquing and gay masculinity, one that inspired the academic treatise *A Passion to Preserve: Gay Men as Keepers of Culture*. Author Will Fellows originally thought the notion was a stereotype but decided it was actually an *archetype*: there really was an unusually strong gay attraction to antiquarianism and collecting, along with related fields like house restoration and interior decoration. The appeal was partly the obvious lure of a life dedicated to aestheticism. But it also held out the prospect of a life apart from the more traditionally macho work cultures in industry or finance, promising a daily existence in which a lot of the people you dealt with would be women.

That said, in music there's no shortage of heterosexual collector-curator types, and even a few heterosexist ones (parody hard rockers and meta-metal bands like Zodiac Mindwarp, Monster Magnet, Urge Overkill, The Melvins, Boris). It is also true that irony and heterosexualised camp had filtered into the mainstream by the late nineties. That's what enabled The Darkness to hit really big. Deliberately histrionic and over-the-top, their metal was inoculated with a kind of internal *Spinal Tap* – singer Justin Hawkins squealing 'geeetar' just before the lead solo kicks in, and so forth. Celebrations of The Darkness invariably highlighted the group's 'healthy sense of metal's ridiculousness'. But that always struck me as rather malignant: a tumour of not-really-meaning-it that eroded any actual power that metal still possessed. The Darkness's real counterparts in the noughties music landscape weren't other hard 'n' heavy groups like Queens of the Stone Age or Mastodon (grimly earnest, in the main) but pop stars like Robbie Williams (prone to archly rolling his eyes during a performance, as if distancing himself from the song's passion) and The Scissor Sisters.

'Irony and reference points are the dark destroyers of music,' railed Bill Drummond in the early nineties. Clearly, Drummond was conflicted about his own knowingness, which permeated projects like The KLF and The Justified Ancients of Mu Mu. Perhaps histrionically – and certainly with a similar feeling of self-disgust – I've also written about 'the cancer of irony' that has metastasised its way through pop culture. Metastasis, the word for the spread of disease through the body, inadvertently pinpoints the malaise of postmodern pop: there is a profound connection between meta-ness (referentiality, copies of copies) and stasis (the sensation that pop history has come to a halt).

At a certain point, music seemed to become disconnected from History and to reflect inwards on itself, on its own accumulated history. When I 'joined' rock (it really was almost like signing up) in the post-punk late seventies, bands didn't really talk about the music much in interviews; they spoke about politics or the human condition, or about 'the state of pop' in a very general way. If they discussed inspirations, they referred to literature, cinema and art. Critics likewise tended not to break down a group's sound into its constituent parts and identify precursors, but to operate on the assumption that the group was 'about' something. But as the eighties rolled into the nineties, increasingly music began to be talked about only in terms of other music; creativity became reduced to taste games. Drifting off into its own self-referential universe, record-collection rock made music into something separated off from real life. Neither drawing from deep within their personal life nor engaged with the world outside music, so many hip groups assembled their identity within a kind of economy of influences. Where financiers invested in futures, bands of this kind speculated in pasts. You can really see it as a kind of stock market in which hot influences, high-risk options and reliable perennials jostle: at the time of writing you'd want to sell your British folk shares and invest in German early-eighties art-punk, maybe. But by the time this book comes out, your influence broker will probably recommend something else altogether.

'Subcultural capital' is what they call this kind of thing in the academy, a concept derived from Pierre Bourdieu's theories about taste and class, which explore how aesthetic preferences help us distinguish ourselves from others. The simplest, shallowest version of this is where taste becomes a form of social display. So bands, just like individuals, select their influences to create a flattering impression, or situate themselves within the ever-shifting landscape of hip. But the Bourdieu view is more than a little reductionist and cynical. For many artists, the process of self-creation involves the creation of a pantheon of heroes. Littering your music with citations from these godstar predecessors, then, is not really a form of showing off or connoisseurial conceit; it's more about paying tribute, about ancestor worship. Reference is deference, mixed with a bit of reflected glory.

Neo-psychedelic rocker Julian Cope is a paragon here. He talks candidly about his artistic self as a composite of heroes. During his Teardrop Explodes years and early solo career, Cope was on what he dubbed the 'white male fuck-up' trip, modelling himself on figures like Syd Barrett, Roky Erickson and Jim Morrison: holy fools who risked absurdity in their pursuit of total experience. 'The idea was that the accumulation of all my heroes would be one hell of a god to be!' Cope told me. Following his shift into a mature phase of sobriety, non-recklessness and political (especially ecological) passion with 1991's *Peggy Suicide*, Cope began to frame what he did explicitly in terms of curation and antiquarianism, under the humorous but actually spot-on concept of 'Head Heritage': the preservation of the monumental achievements of the psychedelic and freak-rock tradition.

Cope has always been as good (arguably better) a critic of music as he's been an exponent, starting with a celebrated 1983 *NME* article on garage punk and psychedelia and blossoming with 1995's *Krautrocksampler*, his rabidly enthusiastic and vividly written paean to German *kosmische* rock. This self-published book purported to be the first in a line of 'Head Heritage Cosmic Field Guides'. Styled as a pocket-portable volume similar to the *Observer's Book of Birds*, it was jam-packed with colour plates of tripped-out album sleeves. Later there was the Head Heritage website, written by Cope and like-minded scholars of freak music, and an online successor to psych-specialist print zines *Bam Balam*, *Strange Things*, *Bucketful of Brains* and *Ptolemaic Terrascope*.

But Cope wasn't just a sixties rock antiquarian. He was a proper antiquarian in the more accepted sense of the word: a fanatical researcher into the history of Britain and Europe's stone circles and prehistoric monuments. He published not one but two lengthy (approaching five hundred pages) full-colour tomes on the subject: *The Modern Antiquarian* (which spawned a BBC2 documentary and a website) and *The Megalithic European*. Then he returned to music, penning another music book, *Japrocksampler*, that looked at the seventies freak-rock scene in

Japan. Much longer than the slim, breezy *Krautrocksampler*, *Japrocksampler* had the densely researched weightiness of the stone-circle books. Its scholarly, at times rather windy tone was more evocative of donnish tweed and leather-patched elbows than loon pants and long hair.

The concept of Head Heritage started out as a bit of fun, a jest on the idea of the National Trust's monuments and listed buildings, protected areas of outstanding natural beauty and blue plaques marking the homes of the famous dead. But this became a genuine mission not just to preserve and commemorate the forgotten pioneers of underground rock history but to carry on their good work. Cope organised (I should say 'curated', shouldn't I?) a two-day mini-festival at London's South Bank Centre in 2000. Named after the mythological 'horn of plenty', Cornucopea juxtaposed venerable seventies legends like Ash Ra Tempel and The Groundhogs with new bands. Unlike other retro-psychedelic bands who sever the music of the counterculture from its utopian politics, Cope has also tried to reactivate the political militancy of the late sixties and early seventies. His current outfit Black Sheep is a sort of primal protest band modelled on The MC5. Figures like The MC5's manager and leader of the White Panther movement John Sinclair have become as much a part of his pantheon as Syd and Roky.

REFERENTIAL TREATMENT

The first time I consciously noticed the term 'curated' used in a music context was in a press release announcing the launch of Protest Records, a label founded in 2003 in response to the invasion of Iraq and intended as an outlet 'for musicians, poets, and artists to express love and liberty in the face of greed, sexism, racism, hate crime, and war'. Offering all-free, not-for-sale tracks from Cat Power, The Fugs, Eugene Chadbourne and others,

Protest was co-curated by New York designer Chris Habib and Thurston Moore of Sonic Youth.

Moore and his band are this past decade's most relentless curators. Their first big splash in this area was curating the first All Tomorrow's Parties festival to take place in America, a four-day event in 2002 at UCLA in Los Angeles. This relationship with ATP continued with several more events over the next four years, while Moore also oversaw the *NOISE/ART* exhibition in New York, 'a visual survey' of the artwork of noise-cassette releases. Then Sonic Youth itself became an exhibition in 2008. Curated by somebody else (one Roland Groenenboom), *Sensational Fix* was a detailed map of the 'multidisciplinary activities' engaged in by the band since its 1981 formation. Seven separate areas explored the group's collaborations with visual artists, film-makers and designers, as well as other musicians; exhibits included album covers, flyers, fanzines, posters, T-shirts, photographs, underground poetry, broadsheets, videos and films. The exhibition's emphasis was less on their own work than the constellation of their influences and the extended network of people they'd either influenced or worked with (Spike Jonze, Sofia Coppola, Stan Brakhage, Jonas Mekas, Jack Goldstein, Gus Van Sant, Gerhard Richter, Mike Kelley, Todd Haynes, Raymond Pettibon, William S. Burroughs, Vito Acconci, Glenn Branca, Dan Graham, Richard Prince, Tony Oursler, Patti Smith, Rita Ackerman, and on and on. Pretty fucking impressive, I must say!) The result was a cross between an artist's career retrospective and an address book.

Sensational Fix revealed Sonic Youth to be the ultimate portal band. And it made a wonderfully neat loop back to the group's dawn, when Thurston Moore organised (nobody would have used the word 'curated' back then) a June 1981 showcase of post-No Wave bands at the downtown New York art space White Columns: a week of performances under the banner Noise Fest that included Sonic Youth's first live show.

'Multidisciplinary activities' is a peculiarly anaemic phrase to describe a band that's sung about murder, psychosis, hallucinatory chaos and other extremes. But as the White Columns association shows, Sonic Youth belonged to a downtown New York milieu where the punk underground mingled with the art world; the group's singer/bassist Kim Gordon worked at art galleries and wrote critical essays for *Artforum* and similar journals. *Sensational Fix* was not a case of a renegade band having their music gentrified but the logical culmination of the group's approach from the beginning.

This was underlined by the album that Sonic Youth released around the same time as the career-retrospective exhibition. Their first in half a decade, *The Eternal* was intriguing precisely because, more blatantly than any previous release, it constituted an act of sonic curation. Virtually every song nodded towards an artist that Sonic Youth admired. 'Sacred Trickster', for example, doubled as a salute to artist Yves Klein and the musician Noise Nomads, while 'Leaky Lifeboat (for Gregory Corso)' was based on the Beat poet's metaphor for life on Earth. 'Thunderclap for Bobby Pyn' took its title from an alter ego used by Darby Crash of LA punk legends The Germs. Even the artwork, a painting by the late John Fahey, was a homage to him, a hero of theirs.

'What scares me is people who don't have a sense of history,' Kim Gordon once said. Sonic Youth could certainly never be accused of that. Their 1985 album *Bad Moon Rising* took its title from a Creedence Clearwater Revival single, while a guitar riff from another 1969 song – 'Not Right' by The Stooges – appears as a distorted citation, as if it's being played on a malfunctioning tape machine, in between two other songs. Sonic Youth's rock-scholarly obsession with the year the sixties turned dark (Altamont, Manson, etc.) carried through to the accompanying EP, *Death Valley 69*, inspired by the Manson Family murders. Elsewhere in the group's late-eighties/early-nineties discography there's allusions to The Beach Boys ('We're going to kill the California girls . . .' in *Sister*'s 'Expressway to Yr Skull', that title itself an obscure reference to an album by Hendrix sideman Buddy Miles) and a song inspired by Karen Carpenter called 'Tunic (Song for Karen)'. The video for 1988's 'Teenage Riot' montaged fragments of an aborted earlier video, handheld footage of Sonic Youth goofing around on tour and ultra-brief clips from their video collection to create a kaleidoscope that merged the band with their pantheon: Patti Smith, Mark E. Smith, Henry Rollins of Black Flag, Sun Ra, Iggy Pop, Blixa Bargeld, Tom Waits and, bizarrely, Susanna Hoffs of The Bangles.

But it was the side project Ciccone Youth that really displayed the band's curatorial bent. The name was originally coined for the 1986 release of 'Into the Groove(y)', a noise-drenched cover of the Madonna song featuring brief snippets of the original 'Into the Groove'. Initially, the plan was for Ciccone Youth to do a cover of the entirety of *The Beatles*, aka *The White Album*. Their New York noise pals Pussy Galore had already done a cassette-only cover of *Exile on Main Street*, the Stones' own double LP. But Ciccone Youth's *The Whitey Album* ended up being something different altogether. There was a cover of John Cage retitled '(silence)' (a sped-up version of his '4' 33"', i.e. a couple of minutes of silence) and a song called 'Two Cool Rock Chicks Listening to Neu!' (Gordon and a female friend chatting about Dinosaur Jr while Neu!'s 'Negativland' drones in the background). Attempting to trump the mischief of their Madonna cover, the album included a version of Robert Palmer's sexist MTV hit 'Addicted to Love', with Kim Gordon entering a make-your-own-record booth and singing karaoke-style over a pre-recorded session-band version of the song.

These sorts of ideas – the ironic cover version, the irreverence of plagiarism, sampling-as-theft-as-subversion – were very much in the air during the late eighties, a knock-on effect of the rise of hip hop and the new availability of affordable samplers. But the conceptual japes on *The Whitey Album* also owed a lot to the New York art world, ideas and techniques that dated back to the late seventies: the appropriation art of the Pictures Generation movement. Named after the 1977 *Pictures* exhibition at New York's Artists Space, this milieu's prime movers were Sherrie Levine and Richard Prince, whose work involved copying famous paintings or rephotographing photographs (sometimes famous shots, sometimes iconic adverts), then cropping, enlarging, blurring or otherwise reframing the images. In particular, Ciccone Youth's karaoke remake of 'Addicted to Love' recalls Levine's famous 'After' pictures, where Levine rephotographed photographs by Walker Evans that had been reproduced in an exhibition catalogue, then presented these at-third-remove images as her own work. With both Levine and Gordon, there's a feminist subtext: Gordon is goosing the drooling machismo of Robert Palmer; Levine is expropriating the Masterworks of the Dead White Males that have marginalised female art in museums, galleries and auction houses alike.

The word 'After', as in 'After Walker Evans' or 'After Egon Schiele', traditionally means 'in the style of'. But it also evokes a sense of artistic belatedness, a postmodern pathos. Early in her career Levine wrote a short manifesto entitled 'Statement' that conveyed the mixed emotions of the 'late' artist entering a field already crowded with masterpieces. The contemporary artist is unavoidably made anxious by the overwhelming torrent of influences that flood the self, but – in Levine's case – can fight back with a defiant celebration of non-originality and non-priority. 'The world is filled to suffocating . . . We know that a picture is but a space in which a variety of images, none of them original, blend and clash. A picture is a tissue of quotations . . . Succeeding the painter, the plagiarist no longer bears with him passions, humours, feelings, impressions, but rather this immense encyclopaedia from which he draws.'

It seems no coincidence that the Pictures Generation artists rose to prominence at a point near the end of the seventies when the Fairlight sampler went on the market as a high-end digital sound-copying machine. Levine had drawn a lot of her inspiration from her days working in commercial art, where sampling of a sort was widespread. 'I was really interested in how they dealt with the idea of originality,' she recalled in a 1985 interview. 'If they wanted an image, they'd just take it. It was never an issue of morality; it was always an issue of utility. There was no sense that images belonged to anybody; all images were in the public domain and as an artist I found that very liberating.' Richard Prince – after Sherrie Levine and Cindy Sherman, the most famous of the appropriation artists – used commercial art as his raw material, rephotographing the Marlboro cigarette ads for his famous *Cowboys* series. Prince characterised his pictures as 'ghosts of ghosts . . . three or four times removed [from the original]' – a description that anticipated the way that samples of samples would drift across hip-hop and dance culture, becoming more distorted and mutated through copying.

Influenced equally by appropriation art, postmodernism and the wave of French critical theory that was starting to come into translation, New York downtown writers like Kathy Acker explored similar approaches all through the eighties. In her infamous 1984 novel *Blood and Guts in High School*, Acker 'sampled' texts by Nathaniel Hawthorne, Jean Genet, and Gilles Deleuze and Felix Guattari. In 1986, she published *Don Quixote*, her rewriting of the Cervantes classic; something was clearly in the cultural air, as this was the same year that Pussy Galore covered *Exile on Main Street*, while Sonic Youth started to think about the *Whitey Album* project. In a 1989 interview, Acker pinpointed Sherrie Levine as her major inspiration, saying that with *Don Quixote* especially '. . . what I really wanted to do was a Sherrie Levine painting . . . it was the simple fact of copying that

148

fascinated me. I wanted to see whether I could do something similar with prose.'

Sonic Youth's music has often been a 'switching center', in Baudrillard's words, the place where all their influences criss-cross. Inveterate contributors to tribute albums for artists like Neil Young and Captain Beefheart, they've occasionally made their own tribute albums, like 1999's *Goodbye 20th Century*, with its interpretations of avant-garde classical works by John Cage, Steve Reich, Christian Wolff et al. *The Eternal*, likewise, resembles a display case for Sonic Youth's touchstones and talismans. What I find disconcerting about the album is how close it approaches a kind of bohemian consumerism – the collecting of ideas, gestures, insurrections, deviances. Disconcerting, perhaps, because it's so close to what I do, as a fan and as a writer. But it's an odd place from which to write songs, if you look at songs as the expression of personal experience. That was the approach of just about all the artistic, literary and musical icons Sonic Youth honoured on *The Eternal*. You can't really imagine Gregory Corso or Darby Crash operating with that kind of curatorial detachment.

The closest British counterpart to Sonic Youth is probably Stereolab, another long-running ensemble centred around a married couple which has walked the line between the avant-garde and rock'n'roll first traced by The Velvet Underground. Douglas Wolk hailed them as 'pop's leading historian-utopians, a band for whom record collecting and trying to change the world are roughly the same thing'. That's a great formulation, but it leaves you with the nagging worry that record-collection rock might be the exact inverse of the kind of rock that once sought to change the world. Unlike beat-poet-besotted Sonic Youth, Stereolab aren't really bohemians (bohemia was once memorably defined as the attempt to change one's world through art rather than politics) but socialists. Laetitia Sadier sings of how capitalism is 'not imperishable, oh yes it will fall'. Where Sonic Youth followed the Velvet

Underground/Stooges/punk/No Wave lineage with excursions into the parallel stream of the avant-garde and free jazz, Stereolab jumbled things up with a 'musaic' that tiles together various strands of retro-cool: Krautrock, Moog music and EZ listening, Françoise Hardy-style French pop of the sixties, lite jazz, the scores to Czech animation, and more. The resulting unlikely fusions are signposted by titles like 'John Cage Bubblegum' and 'Avant Garde M.O.R.'.

Stereolab are the ultimate record-collection rockers. Most of their song and album titles have arcane references secreted within them: 'Jenny Ondioline' is an allusion to an obscure proto-synthesizer of the early twentieth century, while the group's own name nods to a series of records (including stereo demonstration LPs) released on Vanguard. That's the label that put out the cult-classic Jean-Jacques Perrey and Gershon Kingsley albums *The In Sound from Way Out! Electronic Pop Music of the Future*. Stereolab let their record-collecting discoveries drive the evolution of the group's sound. Their interviews are invariably couched in terms of what the group's been getting into lately. When I spoke to Sadier and partner Tim Gane in 1996, the co-ordinates for the new album *Emperor Tomato Ketchup* were Yoko Ono and Don Cherry. But in an earlier interview in 1994, around *Mars Audiac Quintet*, Gane was still in full 'space-age bachelor-pad music' mode, delightedly showing me the kitschy album artwork. Often the back covers featured photographs of early synthesizers, huge unwieldy things with banks of dials, switches and meters. Gane said he was drawn to the music and its iconography precisely because 'it was about the future. Being done in the fifties and sixties, that idea of the future was quite crass – but also full of optimism and infinite possibilities. Which is different from now, where the future isn't about infinite possibilities at all.' Again, we see Stereolab's historian-utopian streak, the wistful attraction to sixties utopianism – just a different aspect to that decade than the one that enthrals Sonic Youth or Julian Cope.

INVENTED GENRES AND RETRO-EXOTICA

Andrea Juno, co-author of the *Incredibly Strange Music* series, which played a big role in making space-age bachelor-pad music trendy, described the record collectors interviewed in the book as heroic explorers venturing into the terra incognita of music history and bringing back weird treasures. Juno also argued for the collector as a kind of critic or renegade historian: 'Popular culture has generated so much stuff this century, and there's a real need for people with discrimination and categorization skills to sort through it all. There's also a transgressive aspect to tweaking the aesthetics of "good taste".' Record-collector culture needs to open new frontiers, and it does this by reinventing the past: redrawing the map of pop history and valorising the disregarded and discarded.

It's no surprise then to find curator-creator types in bands branching out as reissuers and compilers, and even retroactively creating genres that never actually existed as recognised entities during the period in question. Saint Etienne's Bob Stanley is a good example: he's either coined or pushed figments such as 'junkshop glam' (second-division, failed-to-make-the-charts glitter bands as compiled on *Velvet Tinmine* and *Litter from the Glitter Bin*, the latter featuring extensive sleeve notes from Stanley), 'wyrd folk' (LSD-tinged British pastoralists of the late sixties and early seventies) and most recently 'English Baroque'. As corralled on the compilation *Tea and Symphony: The English Baroque Sound 1967–1974*, this is Stanley's term for a style of johnny-come-lately psychedelia, groups like The Left Banke of 'Walk Away Renee' fame, who took their lead from The Zombies and from the Paul McCartney side of the latter-day Beatles, and who made big use of string quartets, harpsichords, woodwind and other orchestral embellishments, defying the general drift in the underground rock scene after 1968 towards heavy and bluesy sounds.

151

The 'genre-as-retroactive-fiction' arguably goes back as far as Northern Soul and garage punk, both terms coined at the start of the seventies but not actually used at the time. Later came semi-figments like freakbeat (mod meets LSD) and 'sunshine pop' (groups who imitated The Beach Boys, The Mamas & the Papas and The Fifth Dimension). All these resemble the names invented by real-estate dealers who hope to hasten the gentrification of an area, as with the substitution of the term 'East Village' for the northern end of what was once called the Lower East Side of New York.

Dealers and collector-explorers share an interest in pushing invented genres in order to make the price of the original records rise. Recent growth areas include Italo-disco and minimal synth. The latter describes a seemingly inexhaustible seam of do-it-yourself electronic music from the early eighties that was low-budget and usually self-released, often in cassette-only form. Minimal synth consists of groups who would have been Depeche Mode or Soft Cell if they could have come up with a tune, plus Suicide/DAF/Fad Gadget clones. Mutant Sounds' Eric Lumbleau says that he recalls first seeing the term used on eBay circa 2003 and believes it was 'developed by canny record dealers in order to recontextualise yesterday's bargain-bin private-press synth pop/new wave albums as tomorrow's mega-rare treasures'.

If you can get fans to buy into the idea that these semi-invented sounds really existed as a distinct category in rock history, you've created a market. So as well as serving the profit margins of collector-dealers, genre creation has an obvious attraction to compilation curators and specialist reissue labels. That's the cynical view. Obviously, enthusiasm for the music plays a large part, as does the deep-seated compulsion to keep on discovering new things. Besides, there's not a huge heap of money to be made in this game; it's a niche economy.

Many people wear multiple hats in a scene: collecting and

dealing records, DJing, doing compilations, putting out reissues via their own independent 'salvage label' (a term coined by the writer Kevin Pearce). Gareth Goddard of the Cherrystones label is just such a retro-polymath. Along with like-minded compiler/collector/DJ/club host/producer types like Andy Votel (of the Finders Keepers label and B-Music DJ collective), Goddard has identified a fuzzy zone of late-sixties and seventies music that overlaps psychedelia, prog rock, funk, jazz fusion, Latin music and the more rhythmically dynamic end of soundtrack music. The lust of these British beat-headz for ever rarer grooves and exotic orchestrations has led them to Eastern Europe, Turkey, South America, the Indian subcontinent . . . and also to Wales (for Votel's *Welsh Rare Beat* compilation). When I asked Goddard if he thought there was still scope left for remapping music history, he guardedly offered some examples of retroactive genres under development: drunk rock ('like junkshop glam but without the niceness') and ted beat ('anything with a hard-drum rock'n'roll shuffle').

Reissuing, in the 2000s, is increasingly bound up with the creation of markets for invented genres and exotic sounds. It is about stirring up desire: there was no pre-existing consumer demand for 'Welsh Rare Beat', for West African psych and Ethiopian James Brown imitators until labels, DJs and journalists made them seem cool. This is a big shift from its early days, when reissuing emerged to cater to those fans of a particular style who were left behind when pop music moved on.

Most people say that reissuing began in the sixties with doo-wop collectors, and specifically the Times Square label, founded in 1961 off the back of a record store of the same name that specialised in obscurities. But record collector/DJ Peter Gunn alerted me to a much earlier example: the UHCA label, started in the early thirties by Milt Gabler, owner of the Commodore Music Shop (also near Times Square in New York, and said to be the first specialist jazz retailer). Gabler began reissuing early New Orleans jazz (UHCA is short for United Hot Clubs of America, as in 'hot jazz'). He moved from re-pressing out-of-print classics to excavating unreleased music by the pioneers of jazz.

After the sixties doo-wop cult, the next major phase of reissuing, according to Gunn, was in the early seventies, with figures like Shelby Singleton, 'who reissued all the classic Sun country and rockabilly on a revived version of the Sun label', which in turn prompted RCA to reissue Elvis's *Sun Sessions*. By the late seventies, the first really serious operations dedicated to repackaging and anthologising the recent musical past emerged: labels like Ace, Charley and Edsel. The latter, an offshoot of Demon Records, was named after an unsuccessful line of automobiles introduced by Ford in the late fifties – a resonant symbol for the salvage ethos of rescuing music that had failed in the pop marketplace of the day but was at the very least deserving and occasionally even superior to the stuff that had succeeded.

Ace, Charley and Edsel established an approach that would become the industry standard: meticulously detailed sleeve notes, period-style design, good-quality sound. Their model was followed by a swarm of reissue labels during the late eighties and nineties, from Sundazed and Yazoo to See for Miles, Little Wing and Blood and Fire. Almost every area and era of music soon had its specialist salvage operations. But black music of the fifties, sixties and seventies has always been the strongest zone, partly because of the fanatical, mostly white collector scenes that developed in the UK and other European countries, but also because of the sheer amount of fine music that was made, sometimes for major labels (who tended to delete black records quicker than white ones, making their neglected back catalogues ripe for the picking) and sometimes for black independent labels (more often than not run by hustler types who didn't take good care of their archives).

154

Blood and Fire are your archetypal Brit custodians moving in to protect and cherish the heritage of a black style fallen into neglect. Founded in 1993 by a clutch of British reggae fans (including roots expert/DJ Steve Barrow and Simply Red singer Mick Hucknall), the label made available renowned yet frustratingly out-of-print classics like The Congos' *Heart of the Congos* and anthologised super-obscure singles by producers like King Tubby. Before this, reggae reissues had generally been shoddy affairs, with ugly packaging, no information and dismal sound (often mastered from a vinyl copy of the record, the master tapes having long gone astray). Blood and Fire set itself apart by its careful sound restoration and attractive vintage-aura artwork. The packaging was crucial to the label's success as a brand. The colour palette and 'weathered' look suggested Jamaica in the seventies: painted wooden signs bleached in the tropical sun, fences with faded and torn posters for sound-system events, and so forth. The shtick was similar to the way Jack Daniel's advertises itself in the UK: old-timey fonts and sepia-toned photographs of men in overalls working at the Daniel's distillery in Tennessee, taking their time and letting the whisky mature in oak barrels the old-fashioned way. And it was hugely effective.

So totally did Blood and Fire own that particular reggae-salvage look that rival label Soul Jazz had to take a completely different tack with their own line of seventies roots'n'dub reissues, such as the hugely popular Dynamite series: bright, full-gloss colours and solarised photographs, a gaudy style in some ways truer to the dancehall aesthetic. Emerging from the same London black-music connoisseur milieu as the DJ Gilles Peterson, Soul Jazz took the heritage concept to the next level with releases so thoroughly annotated and edifying they were almost daunting: projects like the double-CD-plus-100-page-booklet package *Can You Dig It: The Music and Politics of Black Action Films 1968–75* (which sounds more like a paper at an academic seminar or a season at the National Film Theatre). Soon enough they were publishing actual books like *Freedom, Rhythm & Sound: Revolutionary Jazz Original Cover Art*, a deluxe feast of retro-radical chic compiled by Soul Jazz boss Stuart Baker and Gilles Peterson.

SALVAGE AND HERITAGE

In terms of reverse-missionary zeal – bringing culture and the true musical faith to ignorant white folks – the undisputed world champion is Chicago's Numero Group. They place the same emphasis on a consistent design aesthetic and top-quality sound restoration as Soul Jazz, but surpass their rivals through sheer obscurity. Numero Group specialise in music that barely even came out in its own day, recordings that are often hardly more than rumours in hardcore collector circles. Co-founder Ken Shipley told me that the label's brand aura – the identical-looking CD spines – helps them sell music that's devoid of even a smidgeon of name recognition or reputation.

Numero Group is less your standard niche-market-milking (and bilking) salvage operation, and more a grand sonic-reclamation project that blends aspects of archaeology and anthropology. Like Folkways, their releases document what Shipley calls 'vernacular music culture'. Threading through the label's catalogue are series that focus on a particular genre or city-based scenes. Shipley describes *Eccentric Soul: Smart's Palace*, which focuses on a particular nightclub, as 'taking a picture of what it was like to make music in Wichita, Kansas, in the sixties and seventies. It's stuff for the library of the future.'

Along with 'Eccentric Soul', there are several other Numero Group 'series'. 'Cult Cargo' looks at the impact of American music on foreign (usually Caribbean) music cultures; 'Wayfaring Strangers' trawls through the singer-songwriter boom of the seventies, folky Americana often released as privately pressed albums in small editions. But it's the 'Local Customs' series that seems most to express the idealistic core of Numero Group. 'In the old days a custom studio would be the one recording studio in a town, and people came in and made a record, and then a few weeks later they went to pick up anywhere from fifty to two hundred albums,' Shipley explains. 'So all kinds of music were getting recorded, and the guys who owned the studio and produced and engineered the recordings, they would effectively become these Alan Lomax figures, without necessarily intending to be.' The word 'customs', then, doubles to mean both the site of music-making and the ethnographical notion of music as part of the fabric of a community's life. The series' debut release, *Downriver Revival*, sifted through the late-sixties/early-seventies catalogue of Ecorse, Michigan's Double U Sound studio, which was owned by Felton Williams and largely self-built in his family basement. Double U's backlog of released and unreleased recordings (300 reels of tape) offers a cross-section of virtually the entire musical activity within one black American community over the course of a decade. Confronted with such an ethnomusicological bonanza, Numero Group went overboard: accompanying the CD there's a DVD containing a thirty-minute documentary, plus 'a digital tape vault' of some two hundred bonus audio recordings, from sermons and rehearsals to church recordings and a steel-guitar tutorial.

Talking with Shipley, I got a sense that what's driving Numero Group isn't just the reclamation of lost music but a kind of redemption, an impulse to make right. Numero operate a sort of reparations programme, compensation for the little guy who most likely once dreamed of being a big guy, the next Motown or Stax. The consolation prize is recognition, their story being preserved for Posterity. The music industry is a harsh, cruel business at the best of times, but it seems particularly so in black music, if only because there is such an overflowing wellspring of talent that who gets to succeed can seem arbitrary. So many of the groups unearthed by Numero are only a notch away from being Booker T. and the MGs, or The Temptations, or Martha and the Vandellas.

'Masses of music was put out then and not everything could get to be number 1, or number 10, or even number 100,' says Shipley. It's exactly this musical overproduction that has made the boom of reissue labels possible. According to Shipley, 'We've a long way to go before it's all tapped out. Just recently, we opened up something that nobody ever knew about. *New shit has come to light.* At Numero we're trying to pursue as many projects as possible, just to stockpile stuff. People are dying, and it's like we've got ten or fifteen years before the last of a generation is gone. You're in trouble if the guy who owned the label or the studio dies, because they have the information in their heads, they've got photos they can tell you about, and you can piece together the story. You can talk to the children or other secondary sources, but it's much harder to piece together the story. And our releases exist at that nexus between the song and the story. Sometimes the music is great but there's no story.'

Reissue mania is constantly pushing back barriers, both geographically and in terms of that other 'foreign country' – the past. Curator-compiler types, as they run out of ways to remap the relatively recent pop musical past through invented genres, are going further back in time and further out geographically from the anglophone music world. In Britain, collector-compiler types like Bob Stanley have lately taken an interest in English music hall. In America, labels like Yazoo, Revenant and Dust to Digital have for some time now been excavating American music from the pre-World War II period: blues, country, gospel, ragtime, 'sacred song and oratory' (spirituals and sermons, in other words), plus assorted bizarre oddities like kazoo choirs. Typically these are all field recordings rather than studio documents. In some cases, as with Dust to Digital's *Victrola Favorites: Artifacts from Bygone Days* and Revenant's *American Primitive, Vol. 1 and 2*, they've been sourced directly from 78 rpm platters rather than long-lost master tapes: the crackles and pops of worn shellac add to their bygone aura.

More recently, though, these 'American Rural'-oriented labels have started to feel the pull not just of the past *as* foreign country but the past *of* foreign countries. Yazoo was ahead of the pack: in the late nineties, the label launched the series 'The Secret Museum of Mankind', dedicated to ethnic music from the early decades of the twentieth century and offering 'pictures of a gone world' (as compiler Ivan Conte put it). More recently, Dust to Digital released *Black Mirror: Reflections in Global Musics*, a motley assortment of tracks dating as far back as 1918 and scattered as far afield as Java and Jugoslavia. West London label Honest Jon's entered the game when it achieved access to EMI's massive archive in Hayes, where a monstrous quantity of pan-global recordings dating as far back as 1901 had been languishing in dusty disorder: everything from the street songs of Bengali beggars to a World War I recording of public-warning bells to be rung after a poison-gas attack. Donning a kind of invisible pith helmet, Honest Jon's Mark Ainley found himself retracing the blistered footsteps of recording engineers like Fred Gaisberg (who went on field trips to Russia, India, China and Japan in the first few years of the twentieth century) or the EMI teams who journeyed to British-controlled Iraq in the twenties to record local musicians and then sell the music back to the indigenous populace.

Archival labels like Numero Group and Honest Jon's raise difficult questions to do with cultural heritage: the extent to which it is possible or desirable to preserve and remember everything. Maybe we need to forget. Maybe forgetting is as essential for a culture as it is existentially and emotionally necessary for individuals.

The opposite of 'letting go' is the box set: music as memorial, as monument. There's some confusion over who invented the box set: the German label Bear Family, founded in 1978, was an early pioneer, initially with extravagant packages of country and rock'n'roll and later moving on to colossal projects like its ten-CD collections of protest songs, calypso, thirties Yiddish entertainers, etc. But in the US the outfit that became synonymous with the deluxe, often quirkily packaged box set was Rhino Records. Originally the offshoot of a hip Los Angeles record store, the label started out putting out novelty records and releases by contemporary South Californian bands, but according to co-founder Harold Bronson, Rhino discovered that the only projects that didn't lose money were reissues and single-artist anthologies. They also realised that major labels were not really motivated to exploit their own back catalogues. 'In the late seventies and early eighties, the majors were making so much money from block-buster albums they weren't interested in making ten thousand sales of a Spencer Davis Group "best of"', says Bronson.

Fans as much as businessmen, Bronson and partner Richard Foos took care over the repackaging of the music with which they'd grown up, emphasising high-quality remastering, informative liner notes, rare photos and new interviews with the bands. The box set was the next step, augmenting the tracks fans already knew with demos, live tracks and unreleased songs, and expanding the liner note into a full-colour, in-depth history book. British labels like Ace were moving in this direction too, but where the Brits and other European reissuers tended to focus on the esoteric, Rhino's focus was the major-label main-stream: acts that had been famous in their day but had never been given the back-catalogue refurbishment they deserved, figures like The Monkees and Ritchie Valens. They also specialised in genre-spanning sets that scooped up tracks by groups that had one or two killer hits but would individually not really warrant a 'best of', genres ranging from disco to Goth to 'cheese'.

For various reasons – journalistic assignments over the years, compensation for a sleeve-note debacle – I've ended up with a large number of Rhino boxes in my possession, along with sets put out by major labels. I can't be the only person who ferociously covets these box sets yet finds them strangely repellent once they've got them. With its packaging resemblance to a coffin or tombstone, the box set is where an old enthusiasm goes to die: a band or genre you loved frozen into an indigestible chunk. The audio glut forming a kind of clot in your living environment, a box set is invariably bloated with out-takes, which is to say songs that simply weren't good enough to make the original cut of albums. With a few exceptions, they are impossible to listen to all the way through, and in a lot of ways don't seem to be actually made for listening purposes but for ownership and display, as testaments to elevated taste and knowledge. If music is a library, as Bobby Gillespie once suggested, these are the leather-bound volumes that nobody ever cracks open; music that's been curated to death.

5

TURNING JAPANESE

The Empire of Retro and the Hipster International

There was a time, in the early nineties, after CD-reissue pro-grammes had gotten under way but before reissuing went into absolute overdrive, when a lot of records by major artists and cult icons remained out of print. Things that nowadays you take for granted as easily accessible – Miles Davis's jazz-rock-era LPs of the early seventies, for instance – were unavailable everywhere in the world. Except for Japan. The only way to get those particular CDs was to buy horribly expensive imports from the land of the rising sun.

In Japan, seemingly everything ever recorded was still in print. No other country on Earth, not even anal-retentive England, has dedicated itself so intensively to archiving the annals of Western popular, semi-popular and downright unpopular music. And no other music-producing nation has blurred the border more thoroughly between creation and curation. Roland Barthes called Japan the 'empire of signs'; you could just as aptly dub it the 'empire of retro'.

Earlier, in the chapter on museums and memorabilia, the con-cept of 'historicity' – the intangible aura of era that infuses a vin-tage artifact – made an appearance. The first time I came across this concept was in the writing of science-fiction legend Philip K.

Dick, specifically his 1962 novel *The Man in the High Castle*, which is set in an alternative-history world in which the Axis powers won World War II. Most of the story takes place in San Francisco, capital city of the Japanese-controlled West Coast of the former USA. One character is a dealer in antique Americana, everything from Civil War-era weapons and utensils to the popular-culture ephemera of the twenties and thirties. The bulk of his clientele are Japanese visitors from the Home Islands (Japan itself), who avidly collect pre-war jazz and ragtime shellac 78s, vintage base-ball cards or signed movie-star photographs. Demand is so strong for these relics of a lost world that a sub-industry of forgeries and fakes has developed to exploit the collector market. It's this that occasions the meditations by Dick, voiced through the novel's characters, about 'historicity', the elusive quality that differenti-ates an original from a facsimile but which has to be largely taken on trust by the purchaser.

Writing in the early sixties, Dick seems to have tapped into something characteristic about the Japanese sensibility and to have inadvertently prophesied the way that the Japanese would curate, assimilate and reprocess Western popular culture. The notion of a Japanese genius for esoteric record collecting is famil-iar to most people who've spent time in the world of left-field music culture, thanks to bands like The Boredoms, Acid Mothers Temple and Boris. Monsters of meta-rock, even their most out-there or heavy music feels like it's wrapped in invisible quota-tion marks. But the stereotype (or is it in fact an archetype?) even crept into the television mainstream recently with *Tremé*, the drama series conceived by *The Wire*'s producer David Simon and set in post-Katrina New Orleans. One of its minor characters is a wealthy Japanese jazz fanatic who arrives in the Crescent City offering alms to struggling musicians, only to try their patience with his constant know-it-all stream of information about obscure band line-ups and discographical quirks.

From Dixieland jazz combos to Elizabethan madrigals, Japan has an extensive history of ersatz domestic versions of Western music. In his study *Japrocksampler*, Julian Cope notes this Japanese facility for mimesis, which in rock terms began with the 'Eleki' craze for Shadows-style twangy instrumental rock, developed through the 'Group Sounds' movement (suit-wearing bands modelled on the British Beat boom) and blossomed with the main subject of his book, the seventies freaks (aka Futen), bands like Flower Travellin' Band, Taj Mahal Travellers and Speed, Glue & Shinki. These bands often had a single specific Western precursor/model: Blue Cheer, for Les Rallizes Denudes, or The Moody Blues, for the Far East Family Band. Cope argues that the West-to-East translation process creates 'a peculiar copy of the original', a wrongness that in some instances allows the Japanese version to surpass its inspiration. What's more striking to me, though, is not the wrongness but the *rightness* of Japanese takes on Western pop forms: the unstinting attention to stylistic detail.

W. David Marx, a journalist and the man behind the website Néojaponisme, told me that almost every rock band in Japan starts as a cover band before they begin to work original songs into their set. He explained that 'artistic tradition in Japan has always been about following Old Masters' until the point of 'creative confidence is reached. There is no penalty for being seen as "copycat" or "derivative". In fact, that's exactly what brings legitimacy.' Appropriation artist Sherrie Levine made a similar point, noting that originality was a relatively recent invention, even in the West, with copying only starting to be seen as uncreative around the time of the Renaissance: 'It was a different relationship to history at that time. It was more like an oriental belief in tradition. You strove to be fully mature in your tradition. Originality was not an issue.' Anthropologist and indie-rock scholar Wendy Fonarow likewise observes that 'for the Navajo Native Americans, there is only one correct way to sing a song and new songs are not desirable'.

According to Marx, in Japan style is not personal, a matter of cultivated quirks and differences, but impersonal, an external standard to which you have to measure up. Musical authenticity, he says, comes from an obsessive commitment to getting the details right, and that in turn is indexed to 'the degree of consumerist effort' expended by a fan-turned-musician. Which is one reason why Japan has some of the best-stocked esoteric niche record shops in the world. Remote culturally and geographically from the source subculture, a Japanese punk, for instance, could 'never actually *be* punk rock in some kind of existential sense', Marx explains. 'The closest you can get is to collect as much punk-rock stuff as possible and prove fandom by expertise.' He roots both the mimetic tendency and the über-expertise impulse in Japanese religion's belief in 'correct practice'. 'The Japanese believe that "God is in the details" – it's about how you act and what you practise, not what you believe. You can't "be hip hop" just by having a "hip-hop spirit" – you have to look perfectly hip-hop and own all the records.'

DAVID PEACE ON JAPANESE RETRO-PUNK

Author David Peace recently returned to his native Yorkshire after fifteen years in Japan. He didn't move there in 1994 out of any great fascination for the culture: it was to pay off his student loans by teaching English as a foreign language. But in Tokyo he fell in love: with a woman, and also with its underground music culture. 'She's a big fan of seventies punk, and our first date, in fact, was going to see The Sex Pistols when they did the Filthy Lucre reunion tour. The Pistols were great, but even more amazing were the support bands, these Japanese punk groups.' Through his wife-to-be, Peace learned about the extensive history of punk in that country. 'The first band I really thought was fantastic was The Stalin. The singer was a fascinating character: he'd been involved in the anti-Vietnam War movement and so was quite old, but he heard the Pistols and then formed The Stalin. The thing with the great Japanese bands, often they'll take their cue from a Western group, but then they take it to the next level. I mean, the Japanese didn't invent the car, did they? But they perfected it!'

165

The lack of emphasis on originality and the obsession with details merged with the rampant consumerism of the great Japanese economic boom to produce a nineties musical movement unique to Japan: artists like Kahimi Karie, Cornelius, Fantastic Plastic Machine, Buffalo Daughter and many others, who were collectively known as Shibuya-kei by the Japanese media. The term came from the Shibuya area of Tokyo, in which were clustered record stores like Tower and HMV that stocked a lot of imports, along with ultra-hip record boutiques. The upper-middle-class, privately educated kids who frequented these stores bought loads of import records from the UK and esoteric reissues of all kinds, then created music that was a portrait of themselves as exquisitely discerning consumers.

Although they actually existed before the term was coined, Flipper's Guitar – the brainchild of Keigo Oyamada and Kenji Ozawa – were the foundational Shibuya-kei group. They influenced all the groups in the movement, and Oyamada's post-Flipper's incarnation Cornelius was one of the biggest Shibuya-kei successes. Before Flipper's Guitar, Oyamada had been in a Cramps

---

Every Western micro-genre has its Japanese adherents. 'Do you remember psychobilly?' Peace asks, referring to the eighties British scene of Cramps imitators. 'In Japan, you get groups copying The Guana Batz. They'll play their own tunes interspersed with covers of Meteors songs.' An even more bizarre example is the Japanese cult for right-wing, racist Oi! bands. 'You might wonder how a band like Skrewdriver could possibly have a fan base here, but they do. They even have copy bands. I once saw a CD by a Japanese skinhead group that consisted entirely of songs about West Ham Utd. On the cover they were wearing trilbys and West Ham scarves!' According to Peace, Japanese rock fans always 'take it to the nth degree'. When metal legend Celtic Frost re-formed, they played Tokyo, and Peace, a fan, attended. 'One of the most amazing gigs I've ever been to. The group were great but really it was the audience – the detail in their appearance, the jackets and T-shirts, and the corpse paint. It really was like stepping back fifteen years.'

This hyper-meticulous attention to detail can be found in every area of

and Jesus and Mary Chain covers band, a Richard Prince-like copy-of-a-copy in so far as so many Cramps songs were covers or originals heavily based on obscure rockabilly songs. As for the Jesus and Mary Chain, Scottish indie pop was a formative obsession of Oyamada and Ozawa. The name Flipper's Guitar was an oblique nod to Orange Juice, via the dolphins on the front cover of the Scottish group's 1982 debut album *You Can't Hide Your Love Forever*. Inside the record there were further Scottophile allusions with songs like 'Goodbye, Our Pastels Badges' and references to Aztec Camera, The Boy Hairdressers and Friends Again.

Later, Flipper's Guitar would follow the post-'Madchester'/ Stone Roses evolution of British indie pop into 'indie-dance'. They began to work sampling into their music, but even when not digitally quoting they were often copying melodies: 'The Quizmaster', for instance, was a rewrite of Primal Scream's 'Loaded'. As Marx points out, 'It does not just have the same instrumentation and tempo as "Loaded" – it has the same melody!' Emerging at the absolute peak of Japanese consumer affluence, Shibuya-kei bands 'were less concerned about *sui generis* creation and more about

---

Japanese fandom, not just music. 'There's an area in Tokyo called Golden Gai which has about a hundred little bars. Each bar is dedicated to a theme, like crime novels, or absinthe, or French art-house cinema. The bars are homages to certain people or to movements in art or music. People who are starting to get interested in one of these topics, they'll go to the bar to learn. Being a fan in Japan is about teaching each other and sharing information.' This explains why so many cults endure in Japan. 'It's not just a retro thing, because you have people who got involved when these styles originally kicked off. You go to a psychobilly concert, they'll be people who were fans back in 1982. Japanese audiences are incredibly loyal, whether it's music, sport, film. So you have the original fans and then people who got into it later on.' In Japanese culture the teacher/pupil relationship is very important, he explains, so older fans are revered by neophytes as founts of knowledge that is passed down to the next generation.

Because Japan's population is almost 130 million it can support a huge array

having their song catalogues represent their own personal tastes', says Marx. 'Theirs was a music that was literally built out of this collection process. The "creative content" is almost all curation, since they basically *reproduced* their favourite songs, changing the melody a bit but keeping all parts of production intact.'

The Shibuya-kei taste map shows a pronounced bias towards the dainty, the sprightly, the blithe, the borderline anodyne: French sixties pop, Italian soundtracks, bossa nova and especially 'sunshine pop' (Roger Nichols & the Small Circle of Friends, a sub-Fifth Dimension outfit, were a particular touchstone). The Postcard label and the tradition of Scottish indie pop it spawned was hugely admired, and there was a penchant for what the Japanese dubbed 'funk-a-latina': Haircut 100 (Flipper's Guitar actually wrote a song *called* 'Haircut 100'), Blue Rondo à la Turk, Matt Bianco. The composite of all these innocuous and already distinctly ersatz sources was a cosmopolitan hybrid that didn't draw on any indigenous Japanese influences.

Marx argues that this 'all-inclusive bricolage . . . thrown together under a rubric of sixties retro-future Internationalism' was something like the nineties pop equivalent of the International style

---

of subcultures, retro and contemporary, that exist completely outside the pop mainstream (which is dominated by home-grown boy bands and girl groups). Cult Western bands can play a couple of 5,000-capacity concerts and feel like they're 'big in Japan' without even denting mass consciousness. In recent years, an intriguing development has been the emergence of Japanese retro action that isn't so singlemindedly fixated on Western prototypes but instead merges Western rock styles from, say, the eighties with elements from early-twentieth-century Japan, in the process creating a trans-historical and post-geographical hybrid. 'The Japanese historical calendar is divided into eras, and one of them, the Taisho era, coincides with Weimar Germany,' explains Peace. 'And this subculture of Japanese bands emerged playing Gothic punk music but wearing clothes from the Taisho era. The music sounds a bit like Siouxsie and the Banshees, but the costumes and the graphic design are from 1920s Japan. It's all very theatrical and stunning looking.'

in architecture and design. *Fantasma*, Cornelius's 1997 album, was Shibuya-kei's crowning achievement and roughly equivalent to Beck's *Odelay*. Like the Pizzicato Five's albums, it was picked up for release in America by ultra-hip indie label Matador and released to critical plaudits and cult-figure-level sales. Still, Shibuya-kei never managed to match its massive success at home in Japan with equivalent mainstream breakthroughs elsewhere in the world; while its sources were totally international, the composite of them remained peculiarly parochial, attuned to Japanese tastes.

What was really international was the *underlying* sensibility. Japanese upper-middle-class hipster youth were very early and extremely adept practitioners of the curatorial skill set, as deployed in the West by groups like Saint Etienne, Stereolab and Urge Overkill. The Shibuya-kei approach to making culture was common to an emerging class of rootless cosmopolitans with outposts in most major cities of the world: young creatives who work in IT, media, fashion, design, art, music and other industries of aesthetics. You can find this curator/creative class – the quasi-bohemia known pejoratively as hipsters – in any city in the developed world that is large and affluent enough to support a decent-sized upper middle class.

For instance, when I went to São Paulo a few years ago, I was struck by how knowledgeable the twenty-something music obsessives I encountered were, how totally on top of their shit regarding not just the most obscure current music from overseas but also the most arcane recesses of rock history. Even with the majority of the city's inhabitants living in poverty, São Paulo's massive population – just under 20 million – creates a substantial upper middle class whose youth can afford expensive import records and which supports the existence of specialist stores catering to really narrow Europhile or anglophile music tastes. Really, location doesn't matter any more: members of the Hipster

International have more in common with each other than with their physical-world neighbours.

Shibuya-kei itself didn't spread across the globe, but music made on the same principles – pastiche, plagiarism, utter liberation from the anchors of geography and history – is the leisure soundtrack for a new worldwide class whose fundamental mode of operation is the reprocessing of culture. This is a neo-colonial class that refines the raw materials generated by rooted cultures. These can be found in the Second or Third Worlds, or in the urban ghettos that still lurk within the developed West. But increasingly the really rooted, really 'real' music can be found mainly in the archives. Like true imperialists, the postmodern hipsterati don't have any culturally generative power. That's because they don't live in cultures but in 'civilisation', to use the dichotomy that underpins Oswald Spengler's *Decline of the West*. Cultures are insular and bound by norms; music serves a social purpose, offering communal catharsis. Closer to the brute facts of life, cultures create new musical forms, from blues to country to reggae to rap; folk forms all, essentially. Civilisation refines and recombines those forms. It is attracted to their energy and expressive power, but too often undermines these qualities with detachment and irony. This is why, in Spengler's formulation, civilisation precedes decadence.

One of the problems with the Shibuya-kei model of elevated consumerism and curation-as-creation is its conversion of music into style signifiers and cultural capital. Once music is a reflection of esoteric knowledge rather than expressive urgency, its value is easily voided. When the Shibuya-kei groups became popular, their music – and music that copied their approach to copying – filled every boutique and cafe in Japan. The arcane reference points became common knowledge because, explains Marx, entrepreneurs 'sold manual-type reference guides and speciality books to help younger fans decode all the influences, inside jokes, and connections, what records were sampled and so forth'. People like Oyamada/Cornelius were forced to move on to something else, which in his case meant exploring more abstract, non-referential, electronic sound that no longer used samples.

THE RETRO VIRUS

Once upon a time, the idea behind that *NME* column 'Portrait of the Artist as a Consumer' was startling and even slightly transgressive. Rather than the Romantic idea of creativity as coming deep from within, the emphasis was on the way the performer assembled an identity through taste, through the conscious selection of influences. There was an implicit emphasis on the word 'as' in 'Portrait of the Artist as a Consumer': let's look at this in a *different* way. But the 'as' started gradually to lose its stress, until it seemed totally natural to think of artists in this way. What else *could* they be but consumers, shopping for an identity in the marketplace of ideas?

In a sense, the arty, hipster end of music culture in the West was gradually 'turning Japanese'. In Britain, the pastiche/recombinant ethos already had roots, thanks to the glam and art-school tradition. What was once a fairly restricted sensibility, pioneered by Saint Etienne, Stereolab and The High Llamas, has spread through almost the entire musical culture, such that you can detect a 'Japanese' tinge to everything from The Horrors to The Go! Team to The Klaxons. Britain even has a fake-Japanese outfit, Brighton band Fujiya & Miyagi, whose retro-chic music (Neu! and Can meets Happy Mondays and Stereolab) exhibits a fetishistic attention to detail.

In America, where the emphasis on authenticity and meaning remains strong in the heartland, you tend to find the Japanoid sensibility more in coastal cities like New York, home to The Strokes, The Dirty Projectors and Vampire Weekend. Probably the most interesting of these cool curator-type groups is the one most conflicted about its Japanese-like tendencies, LCD Soundsystem, the flagship act of the ultra-hip DFA label in New York. The brainchild of recording engineer James Murphy, LCD Soundsystem came to fame with 'Losing My Edge', the plaint of a cool hunter type – a musician or DJ or record-store clerk, or possibly all three – agonisingly aware that he's slipping, as younger kids outdo his recondite knowledge with even more obscure reference points.

'I'm losing my edge to the Internet seekers who can tell me every member of every good group from 1962 to 1978,' the character whines. 'To the art-school Brooklynites in little jackets and borrowed nostalgia for the unremembered eighties.' The ageing hipster's claims of priority and having been first on the block get more and more absurd, as he reels off a list of legendary musical events he claims to have witnessed, from the early Suicide practice sessions in 1974, through Larry Levan DJing at the Paradise Garage and Jamaican reggae sound clashes, to the earliest days of UK rave culture in Ibiza. A hilarious auto-critique of hipsterism, 'Losing My Edge' also obliquely captures the pathos of the modern era. All the advantages we have today in terms of technology and how to get good sounds have resulted in a crisis of 'well-made' music, where producers are scholars of production and know how to get a great period feel, yet it seems harder and harder to make music that actually *matters* in the way that the music that inspired them did in its own day.

Shibuya-kei-like techniques cropped up throughout LCD Soundsystem's debut album: 'Disco Infiltrator' doesn't sample but recreates the eerie synth riff from Kraftwerk's 'Home Computer' from 1980, while 'Great Release' is a pastiche of Brian Eno circa *Here Come the Warm Jets*. 'I just like the type of energy that some Eno/Bowie stuff got, and some of the space of Lou Reed stuff, like "Satellite of Love",' James Murphy told me. Then he got tetchy: 'Is there seriously some problem with there being too many songs that use sonic spaces similar to early Eno solo work? I mean, is this really something we need to talk about before it gets out of control?!? I *wish* I had that problem. Or is the problem just me – that I'm not being original enough? Because if it is, then let's just dump rock in the fucking ocean and call it a day, because I'm doing the best I can for the moment!'

What makes LCD Soundsystem interesting and moving, but also a timely and telling response to the present, is that my potential responses, as an old modernist-minded post-punk, already nag away inside Murphy's guts. Although quite a bit younger, he's someone who grew up on punk and art-rock values, who's torn between his attachment to rock's heritage and his equally powerful urge to create something completely new. The result is a volatile cocktail of rage and self-loathing, igniting songs like 'Movement', in which Murphy surveys the contemporary music scene: 'It's like a culture, without the effort, of all the culture/ it's like a movement, without the bother, of all of the meaning.'

The most acerbic meta-pop commentary of the decade didn't come from LCD Soundsystem, though, but from the cult British

ELECTROCLASH AND THE NOUGHTIES' ENDLESS EIGHTIES REVIVAL

Although it emerged from the boho zones of Western cities like London, New York and Berlin, the electroclash scene had something of a Japanese flavour in its emphasis on style over substance. Unlike earlier revivals, this eighties resurrection stubbornly resisted attempts to read anything into it in terms of resonance or broader cultural significance. The 2-Tone ska revival of 1979–81, for instance, offered a multiracial sound/ethos that aligned with the Rock Against Racism struggles of the era. But electroclash's return to the eighties – synthesizers, New Romanticism's obsession with style, artifice and posing – seemed neither to be in synch with or opposed to post-millennium culture. Rather, it felt like there was simply a kind of structural inevitability to an eighties resurgence arriving punctually twenty years to the day. Electroclash really was 'a movement, without the bother of all the meaning', to quote LCD Soundsystem.

comedy series *The Mighty Boosh*. A loving satire of hipsterism conducted from deep inside its mindset, *Boosh* is set in the trendy East London area of Dalston and is centred around two musicians, Vince Noir (a glammed-up fashion casualty played by Noel Fielding) and Howard Moon (Julian Barratt's earnest jazzbo). By the third series, this odd couple are working in a vintage bric-a-brac boutique by day, while also collaborating together in various musical ventures. The entire show has a retro-fantastical atmosphere. A prominent flavour is the Eighties Revival that stretched the length and breadth of the 2000s: Vince idolises Gary Numan (who makes several cameo appearances), and along the way we encounter an electroclash-like group called Kraftwork Orange. But there are also mod wolves doing Motown routines in sharp suits; a 'dead media' creature called the Betamax Monster; an episode set in the Desert of Inspiration where pop relics like Dexys Midnight Runners singer Kevin Rowland and Chris de Burgh search in vain for new ideas and where a Carlos Santana-like figure materialises. In *The Mighty Boosh*, pop history becomes

---

Eighties flavours actually began circulating on the underground dance scene a few years prior to 2000, in the form of a network of artists influenced by synth pop such as Dopplereffekt, I-f and Adult.. The latter's label Ersatz Audio caught the back-to-the-future spirit with compilation titles like *The Forgotten Sounds of Tomorrow* and *Oral-Alio: A History of Tomorrow*. The music was deliberately cold and repressed, the imagery evocative of technocratic sterility, 'desire and efficiency'. Daft Punk picked up on the fetish for the robotic and inorganic but gave it an unexpected warmth with 2001's *Discovery*, which melded early-eighties sounds with seventies pomp rock (Supertramp, ELO, 10cc, etc.) to create a sound of transcendent artificiality. The eighties connection here was the decade's association with 'plastic pop', the notion that synthesised sounds were analogous to man-made fabrics. In the actual eighties, indie rockers like The Smiths resisted this 'dehumanisation' (Morrissey, in 1983: 'Suffice to say if a synthesizer appeared on one of our records, I wouldn't') and instead embraced guitars and folky influences. But in 2001, Daft Punk and the emerging electroclash movement staged a transvaluation of plastic, shedding its negative

phantasmagoric, a hallucinatory bestiary of absurd and sometimes grotesque memory hybrids.

At various points in the series, retro rises to the surface as an
explicit theme. The 'Eels Song' hybridises music hall and techno,
with a boogeyman character singing the chorus 'Elements of the
past and the future/ combining to make something not quite as
good as either' and the couplet 'I had one foot in the grave/ but
now I'm nu-rave'. In another episode, Vince Noir and Howard
Moon are plagued by a plagiarist duo who copy their every
style move, catchphrase and even their names: they call themselves Lance Dior and Harold Boom. 'Harold Boom' is a wicked
wisecrack: a reference to literary critic Harold Bloom and his
famous theory of 'the Anxiety of Influence' (which the copycat
duo clearly don't suffer from). But then über-hipster Vince in his
own way is just as unoriginal, which makes his outrage at being
ripped off (he even reports the miscreants to the Fashion Police)
all the more funny. The rival duo give Vince and Howard some
deliberately unhelpful advice: 'The future's dead. Retro's the new

---

associations (disposable, inauthentic) and recovering its utopian promise as
the material of the future. Daft Punk's use of vocoder treatments was crucial
here, coating their voices in an angelic, otherworldly sheen, just like Kraftwerk
had done.

Spawned in the hipster precincts of Williamsburg, Shoreditch and Mitte,
electroclash was a full-blown early-eighties flashback of svelte young poseurs
sporting asymmetrical haircuts, skinny ties worn over T-shirts, and studded
bracelets. The first wave of electroclash groups (Fischerspooner, Miss Kittin,
etc.) didn't live up to the media's Next Big Thing hype. But the sound stuck
around as a trendy nightclub staple for the entire decade. People began to call
it 'electro'. This was confusing for those of us who had lived through the actual
eighties, when electro meant bass-bumping hip hop from New York designed for
break-dancing and body-popping. But in the noughties, electro came to mean
any kind of danceable electronic pop that was deliberately dated, avoiding the
sound-morphing capacities of digital technology (the programs and platforms
that underpinned most contemporary dance music) and opting for a restricted

thing . . . Everyone's looking back, not forward.' Rattled, Vince and Howard promptly drop their latest concept (a futuristic synthesizer sea-shanty sound) and decide to 'look further back into the past than anybody's looked before'. Overnight they develop a medieval-minstrels look of jerkins, codpieces and lutes, and write a song that climaxes with the boast: 'We are running backwards/ Running through time into the past/ Taking retro to its logical conclusion.'

When I look back at the development of pop and rock during my lifetime as an alert, conscious fan (i.e. from 1977 onwards), what perplexes me is the slow but steady fading of the artistic imperative to be original. At the start of that period, and right in the heart of the mainstream with artists such as Kate Bush, The Police, Bowie and Peter Gabriel, musicians were spurred by the desire to create something never heard before. But from the mid-eighties onwards, gradually but with increasing momentum, that changed into an impulse to create something very much heard before, and moreover to do it immaculately, accurate in every last detail: a lineage running from The Jesus and Mary Chain,

---

period sound of thin synth tones and stiff drum-machine beats. Electro now meant yesterday's futurism today.

Then, unexpectedly, electro broke into the charts at decade's end with Lady Gaga, Little Boots and La Roux (whose tunes could be played next to Yazoo and Eurythmics records without sounding the least bit temporally out of joint). The ultimate recombinant pop star, Gaga's persona and appearance mixed seventies glam decadence (Bowie), eighties costume excess (Grace Jones, Madonna, Vogueing, Leigh Bowery), nineties neo-Goth (Marilyn Manson) and early-noughties electroclash (Fischerspooner's pro-pretentiousness rhetoric, Miss Kittin's velvet-rope glitz fantasies). Gaga's music merged eighties retro-robotics with fully contemporary qualities of efficiency, ruthless hookiness and cosmetic perfection (vocals glazed and sugared with Auto-Tune). Collapsing past into future, and edgy hipsterism into mainstream showbiz, Gaga voided the meaning of either. Fittingly, she became the iconic pop performer of our time.

Spacemen 3 and Primal Scream, through Lenny Kravitz, The Black Crowes and Oasis, to The White Stripes, Interpol and Goldfrapp. David W. Marx says of Shibuya-kei that its strong point was 'the curation of imitative styles'. That's meant to be praise, but it's easily redirected to form a caustic assessment of most Anglo-American rock over these past twenty years. *Especially* the hipster/alternative/underground sector.

According to Harold Bloom's theory of creativity, outlined in books like *The Anxiety of Influence* and *A Map of Misreading*, a 'strong' poet is one who's heavily influenced by a predecessor but who resists that influence, fights it with every ounce of his strength. In Bloom's Freudian-mystical account, the resulting Oedipal struggle entails the younger poet (who will have been initiated, turned on to the glory of poetry by a primal encounter with the elder's work) swerving from the ancestor's style, wilfully misreading it or doing violence to it in some other way. The strong artist is impelled by a despairing sense of belatedness, the feeling that nothing new can be said because the precursor said it all. A titanic psychological struggle to self-birth oneself as an artist is required before the descendant ceases to ventriloquise the dead elder and finds his own voice. But a 'weak' poet (or painter or musician) is simply inundated, flooded by the ancestor's vision.

There are plenty of examples in rock history of performers who had a primal encounter with a particular predecessor's work and then had to push through an imitative phase before finding their own style. The ideal of originality and the injunction to evolve continually as an artist was fuelled further by the influence of art schools on sixties rock, along with the general ideology of progression and innovation that reigned across the culture at that time. So what changed? It's not that there weren't unoriginal performers and groups during the sixties and seventies – quite the contrary. They could often be hugely successful (e.g. Electric Light Orchestra, with their obvious debts to The

Beatles). But those sorts of acts tended not to get critical respect – that was reserved for genuine innovators. What changed from the mid-eighties onwards was the level of acclaim that blatantly derivative groups started to receive. Retro-styled groups had generally been a niche market, for people unhealthily obsessed with a bygone era. But now these kinds of heavily indebted bands – The Jesus and Mary Chain, The Stone Roses, Elastica, Oasis, The White Stripes – could become 'central': epoch-defining figures even when the substance of their sound referred back to a much earlier epoch.

It was almost like some kind of generational deficiency of 'the anxiety of influence' kicked in. 'Strong' groups began to be outnumbered by 'weak' ones: fans who internalised their influences to the point where they didn't so much replicate as uncannily write 'new' songs in an old, other's style. Another factor was the steady accumulation of history behind the music with each passing year. Accompanying this was a build-up of knowledge, through in-depth articles in fanzines and magazines, through biographies and music histories, such that fledgling groups could find out exactly how certain classic recordings had been made. Lee Mavers, the infamously perfectionist frontman and leader of The La's, took the obsession with period sound further than most, rejecting one vintage mixing desk on the grounds that 'it hasn't got original sixties dust on it'.

Not only has the anxiety of influence faded away, so has a sense of shame about being derivative. Even relatively innovative artists feel comfortable about taking detours into pastiche or homage. The brilliant UK electronic producer Darren Cunningham, who records as Actress, describes certain of his tracks as 'studies': 'Hubble', for instance, is a 'study' of Prince's 'Erotic City', while 'Always Human' is almost completely made out of sounds from The Human League's 'Human'. On the self-titled debut album by The xx, who deservedly won the 2010 Mercury Prize with their fresh mesh of skeletal post-punk and sombre dubstep, the track 'Infinity' is blatantly related to Chris Isaak's 1989 song 'Wicked Game': it really is a study, an exercise in technique, in the sense that the band have written a new song entirely within the very specific and immediately recognisable texture palette and emotional atmosphere of Isaak's original. Ironically, 'Wicked Game' itself is a highly stylised retro-chic affair, like a fifties ballad sluiced through the deluxe atmospherics of Roxy Music circa *Avalon*.

This gradual process of 'turning Japanese' was not limited to Western pop, of course, but was culture-wide. In a 2003 *Artforum* special issue looking back at the eighties, installation artist Mark Dion recalled that decade as the moment when a 'profound sense that the avant-garde was finally dead' kicked in. For the previous, seventies generation, 'ideas like "who did what first" were still important. Who could give a damn today? Nothing feels more irrelevant.' In some ways, pop music could be said to have held out against the onset of postmodernism the longest, from vanguards like hip hop and rave to isolated modernist hero figures within rock or pop itself (a Radiohead, a Björk, a Timbaland, an Animal Collective). Still, the first decade of the twenty-first century is truly when the tide decisively turned Japanese. The cycles of recycling have a senseless quality, uncoupled from History or a social reality beyond music. The mad merry-go-round of contemporary music culture can be played for laughs, as *The Mighty Boosh* and LCD Soundsystem have done. But it's the kind of slightly hysterical mirth that could easily turn to tears. Surveying the soundscape of rock and pop in the last ten years, amusement turns to bemusement. How on Earth did we get here?

2: 'THEN'

6

STRANGE CHANGES

Fashion, Retro and Vintage

Vacationing in London in the summer of 2006, I checked out a big exhibition of sixties fashion at the Victoria and Albert Museum. A fan of sixties pop who knew little about fashion per se, I found the exhibition enthralling in a way that went far beyond the 'Swinging London' grooviness of the era. A vivid sense of the sheer rush of the sixties – the bombardment of newness on all cultural fronts – cut through the quaint period charm. I was especially taken by the designs of André Courrèges, Pierre Cardin and Paco Rabanne. Who knew that Pierre Cardin had ever been cutting edge? And Paco Rabanne I had only ever associated with aftershave!

The mini-skirts (an invention credited both to Courrèges and Mary Quant) and the mod-girl look of white lipstick and op-art clothes were totally familiar from countless movies and documentaries, of course. But Courrèges's 1964 Moon Girl Collection blew me away. Inspired by the Age of Sputnik and the first manned missions into outer space, it featured white and silver man-made fabrics cut in geometric shapes, along with PVC boots, cosmonaut-style helmets, and goggles. The missing link between mod and modernism, Moon Girl resulted in Courrèges being hailed as fashion's Le Corbusier. Just as the Brutalist school of architecture turned Le Corbusier's machine-for-living vision into the look of municipal buildings and urban apartment blocks across Europe, Courrèges became 'the most copied and plagiarised dress-designer of his era', according to the Victoria and Albert exhibition catalogue. 'The market was flooded with plastic skirts and jackets, angular seaming, crash helmets, white boots, and goggles, for a boxy silhouette.'

Rabanne and Cardin were no slouches, either. Rabanne used Perspex discs and metal links to create dresses that looked like a cross between medieval chain mail and fishnet stockings – at once sexy (glimpses of flesh through mesh) and forbidding (unyielding and abrasive in an embrace). Cardin explored vinyl and silver fabrics, and made hats with plastic visors attached, an idea inspired by astronaut's suits. 'The clothes that I prefer are those I invent for a life that doesn't exist yet – the world of tomorrow,' he wrote in 1990, surveying the sweep of his career.

Some would concur with Karl Lagerfeld's retrospective verdict on mid-sixties future-shock fashion: 'In 1965, people were still far away from the end of the century, and they had a completely childish, naive vision of what the end of the century would bring.' And even at the time, plenty of people recoiled from the new youth style. In *The Neophiliacs*, a critique of the sixties mania for innovation, Christopher Booker lambasted the 'exhibitionistic violence' of mid-sixties style, which 'grabbed at the attention – the contrasts, the jangling colours, the hard glossiness of PVC, the show of thigh . . . [the] awkward, even ugly contortions of the models', who stared with blank affectlessness in photographs splayed across brutal urban settings.

Forty years after the fact, that ultra-modernist look blew my eyes. Wending through the exhibition, however, I noticed a shift circa 1966–7. Almost overnight, everything stopped looking futuristic. The change was subtle at first, things like Mary Quant basing a design on a garment worn by governesses between the two world wars. But as psychedelia kicked in, youth style started to revel in anything and everything that was neither modern nor from the industrialised West. The vocabulary of late-sixties fashion was based either in *exoticism through time* (Victoriana, Edwardiana, twenties and thirties influences) or *exoticism through space* (ideas from the Middle East, India, Africa).

This paradigm shift caught my attention because I'd been puzzling over something I called 'the Rift of Retro': the precise point at which looking backwards had become a dominant force in rock music. That question emerged from my book *Rip It Up and Start Again*, which had argued that, circa 1983, post-punk's futuristic spirit crumbled and the independent-music scene spurned the pop present (synthesizers, drum machines, the cutting edge of modern black music) in favour of the sixties. This was a little bit too neat and tidy, though. There had been retro-tinged operators during the post-punk era, groups like Orange Juice and The Specials who mixed and matched ideas from the pop archives. And then if you looked at postmodernist popsters of the early eighties like ABC, The Human League and Adam Ant, it became clear that their approach owed a lot to glam rockers like Bowie and Roxy Music. Every time I thought about the Rift of Retro, the date seemed to slip a bit further back in pop time. Now, at the Victoria and Albert, I wondered if I'd actually located the true historical pivot. Was 1965 the absolute pinnacle of Newness and Nowness? That certainly seemed to be the case with fashion. After that high point, postmodernist-like techniques of pastiche and recycling began to take effect in fashion many years before they would appear in pop music.

When I investigated the history of fashion, I was surprised and pleased to find that some theorists do actually point to 1965 as a pivotal year. In his book on London style culture, Alistair O'Neill says that there's broad agreement that 1965 was when 'the demand for ever-evolving newness forced a distraction from innovation and invention towards a plundering and interpretation of historical styles'. John Stephens, the king of Carnaby Street, needed to stoke the consumerist mania of the mods, a subculture where the signifiers of 'with it' changed on a weekly basis. 'Italy was exchanged for India, Op and Pop exchanged for the nostalgic and foppish.' In *The Neophiliacs*, the young fogey Christopher Booker lists with disdain the fads of the mid- to late sixties: art nouveau ties, grandfather clocks painted white, 'colourful playthings and visual "images" pillaged indiscriminately from a century of industrialised culture . . . the disintegration of the youthful collective fantasy into a more fragmented and inconsequential phase, in which no one look or fashion would prevail, but in which titillatory images would be seized on almost at random'. You can even see this creeping into psychedelic music, with archaic or exotic instruments (lutes, harpsichords, sitars) mingling with state-of-art technology and effects (the Moog synthesizer, phasing).

The mid-sixties moment when ultra-modernism flips into proto-retro is caught in *Blowup*, Michelangelo Antonioni's 1966 movie about a fashion photographer's fast-lane life driving flash cars and bedding twig-limbed models. The David Bailey-esque character has his finger on the pulse, which explains why he's toying with buying a bric-a-brac shop full of curiosities like vintage-aeroplane propellers. By the time the movie came out, there were London clothes boutiques that merged fashion and antiquarianism, the psychedelic and the passé. Opening on the King's Road in February 1966, Granny Takes a Trip was the pioneer. Catering to the new pop aristocracy – stars like Pink Floyd, The Small Faces, Jimi Hendrix, The Rolling Stones – the boutique sold antique garments along with new clothes inspired by late-nineteenth-century designs. One of the trio behind Granny Takes a Trip, Sheila Cohen, was a collector of Victorian clothes who scoured flea markets for army redcoats, velvet jackets, ostrich-feathered hats and pony-skin shirts. Like similar stores such as I Was Lord Kitchener's Valet, Cobwebs, Antiquarius and Past Caring, Granny Takes a Trip grew out of the emerging bohemian micro-economy based around Portobello Road and similar flea markets, which had benefited from the early-sixties popular boom in antique collecting. Sifting through the clutter of shabby tat for cool collectables – Blitz-era gas masks, hand-cranked gramophones, shop signs with chipped paint, brass bedsteads – required time, energy and a sharp eye. This made it (what we now call 'vintage') seem more elevated and alternative than mere consumerism.

In sixties fashion itself, there's one name that symbolises the big switch from looking forward to looking back: Biba. Before visiting the V&A exhibition, I had only a vague idea about what Biba represented: it bridged the hippy era and glam rock with a sensibility that mingled nostalgia, Art Deco and that fashionable early-seventies notion of 'decadence'. Profiled by the *Daily Telegraph* as a fashion face to watch in 1966, Biba owner Barbara Hulanicki declared: 'I love old things. Modern things are so cold. I need things that have lived.' The interviewer noted how odd this statement sounded from such a '"with it" designer', but concluded that 'with everything around her so fast, so uncertain, she needs to go home to . . . the comfort of dark red wallpaper and Edwardiana. It makes her feel safe.' The paradox of Biba is captured in the contrast between the *Chicago Times*' 1968 comment 'the whole Biba scene makes you feel like you're into tomorrow' and the 1983 elegy in *The Face* that hailed it as 'the first fashion house to define the present as a modern-baroque restatement of the past . . . As a trading company, Biba spanned the years 1964 to 1975. As a design factory it began around 1890 and ran a clear line through most of the Twentieth Century.'

The original Biba shop opened in 1964 in a dilapidated former chemist's in Kensington, West London. Hulanicki reversed the glaring white brightness of the mod mid-sixties, opting for dimly

lit interiors and vintage decor featuring aspidistras and brass hat
stands. 'Funereal', is how she later described the colour scheme of
Biba's clothing: sombre blues, stodgy browns, blackberry purples
and rust, the 'dull, sad Auntie colours I had despised in my young
days'. This palette was later extended in the form of Biba make-
up, all 'chocolate lipstick and fawn and mulberry eyeshadow',
according to one journalist. The store's huge success led to it
expanding repeatedly to bigger premises, climaxing with its take-
over of an old Art Deco department store on Kensington High
Street. Complete with a food hall and a concert space (where
The New York Dolls, Manhattan Transfer and Liberace all performed), Big Biba was London's first new department store of
the post-war period. At the 1973 opening, customers were handed
a Biba newspaper which included a mission statement defining
the emporium as 'a small museum devoted to Grave Lapses from
Good Taste. Everything in Biba's Kitsch department is guaran-
teed to be as camp as Aldershot. Nothing here will ever make the
Design Centre, but shrewd investors could buy now with an eye
on Sotheby's in 1993.'

But it was actually an earlier Biba store on Kensington Church
Street that was bombed by the Angry Brigade on May Day 1971
(after closing time, when nobody was on the premises). This
underground unit of 'libertarian communist' guerrillas usually
went for government ministries, the homes of MPs or police com-
missioners, the Imperial War Museum and such like. Biba was one
of their few 'non-political' targets. What was it about Hulanicki's
sensibility that made Biba explosion-worthy? Communique 8, the
Angry Brigade's 'press release' issued immediately after the attack,
explains:

'If you're not busy being born you're busy buying'.

All the sales girls in the flash boutiques are made to dress the
same and have the same make-up, representing the 1940's. In

fashion as in everything else, capitalism can only go backwards – they've nowhere to go – they're dead.

The future is ours.

Yet it wasn't. By the end of the seventies, the post-1968 para-military underground had either faded away or been smashed by state power. Biba had gone out of business (Hulanicki had been pushed out by the financial backers she'd partnered with), but it had nonetheless set the tone for fashion's future. Which has over-whelmingly been fashion's past, endlessly renovated and recom-bined. Revivals in clothing style were not a new thing, but they had generally looked to antiquity or the relatively distant past: fads for Greek or Roman styles (in the 1790s), or for a Renaissance look (in the 1820s). What Biba had pioneered (in mainstream, high-street terms), and what would flourish from the seventies onwards, was fashion retro: the cyclical recycling of styles from the immediate past, looks that had been à la mode within living memory. Nearly all of the most famous designers of the post-1965 era have gone in for retro to some degree. Yves Saint Laurent pio-neered the sensibility with his 1971 collection 'Forties' (actually a flop because too close to the French bone in its evocations of the Occupation era), and he would go on to design collections inspired by pre-Communist Revolution clothing, from Russian peasant attire to Chinese court dress.

Fashion theorists make a subtle distinction between retro and historicism. Whereas retro involves remaking and remodel-ling styles that were fashionable within living memory, histori-cism looks for inspiration further back in time: examples include Laura Ashley's Victorian English pastoralism, Ralph Lauren's use of nineteenth-century Americana, Jean-Paul Gaultier's Montmartre/Moulin Rouge-influenced 'French Can Can' collec-tion. Historicism, in turn, is carefully distinguished from 'cos-tume' or fancy dress. In musical terms, that distinction seems

189

similar to the difference between being deeply derivative of a specific band and being a tribute band that covers the band's songs as faithfully as possible. From a distance, though, retro and historicism blend into each other and look rather like inspiration-starved designers rifling through the past's wardrobe. It has become systematic, a structural element of the way fashion operates. According to Colin McDowell, Karl Lagerfeld – the guy who derided Courrèges and Cardin for their childish futurism – owns 'a library reputedly containing a copy of every book on costume and fashion ever written'. Other designers pore through vintage copies of fashion magazines for inspiration. When researching my post-punk history, the quest for eighties music magazines led me to a New York store called Gallagher's. Stepping into the basement-level premises, I found some horrendously overpriced *NME*s and *Melody Maker*s, but I was struck more by the shoulder-high stacks of decades-old *Vogue*s and *Elle*s, each issue sealed in protective plastic and extortionately priced. Clearly, Gallagher's did most of its business catering to the insatiable hunger of fashion designers.

Vivienne Westwood – one of the major 'historicist' designers of our era, creator of collections inspired by pirates, hobos, the styles of the eighteenth and sixteenth centuries, and so forth – told the *New York Times* in 1994 that she believed that 'going forward, things don't just get better – they can get worse. Modern is a question we have to abandon . . . Fashion might be an important indicator in the sense that there's something intuitive that people are after. Intuitively, they're going back to things in the past.' This rationale dignifies what has become a mad scramble to pillage the past as soon as a decent-enough interval has passed. Fashion journalist Lynn Yaeger observed that Anna Sui 'based an entire career on resuscitating, revamping, and rethinking the vintage fashions of the 1960s and '70s, the decades when she was young'. Valerie Steele, theorist and director of the Museum at

New York's Fashion Institute of Technology, told me that designers started referencing the eighties *as early as 1990*. 'No sooner is a period over than it starts to get referenced. Through the nineties, every three years or so a different aspect of eighties retro came into vogue.' There was even a wave of eighties-inspired fashion modelled on Vivienne Westwood's 'historicist' collections, like Nostalgia of Mud. Another twist on the manic recycling is 'nostalgia layering', fashion journalist Bethan Cole's term for 'a pile-up of eras: for instance, viewing the 1930s through the lens of the 1970s'. As an example, she cited the way British pop star Alison Goldfrapp filtered thirties Marlene Dietrich glamour through seventies glam rock and Biba. This parallels the way Goldfrapp's music itself is assembled, with a different sonic 'look' for every album, a new layering of old ideas plucked from pop's past.

Where Vivienne Westwood generally had lofty reasons for her various investigations of the historical past, retro-fashion's turnover of revamped ideas seems for the most part purely random. The vogues for period looks are not so much 'signs of the time' as floating signifiers that circulate endlessly within a relatively autonomous realm of taste and cool. 'These things exist within the world of fashion images, disassociated from any larger social context,' argues Valerie Steele. 'The impetus comes from individual designers, like Marc Jacobs, who have their own creative reasons for referencing that period, and from trends within what you could call "the world of craft" – fashion-makers and trend-setters.'

But isn't this true of all fashion? Fashion has its own cyclical history that is only rarely indexed to social change or currents within the broader culture. As Roland Barthes established in his seminal if turgid study *The Fashion System*, the oscillating lengths of skirts, the alternations of colours and fabrics, are almost completely arbitrary. 'Fashion is based on change,' argues fashion journalist Jamie Wolf, but 'which change, exactly, is quite unimportant'. I would extend Wolf's point further to claim that

fashion is about changes but not Change in the sense of progress. A restless yet fundamentally static system, fashion is not just
the opposite of, but in some profound sense *opposed to* change
in the artistic or political sense. We talk of artistic movements or
political movements because they are building towards something, and in the process they definitively jettison earlier stages
of development or outmoded ideas. But in fashion, everything
démodé becomes à la mode again, sooner or later. Equally, all chic
things must be stripped of that status, as the industry's seasons
turn in a grotesque, ecologically unsound (all that waste!) parody
of Nature's cycles.

Take this example I stumbled upon in a 2009 newspaper, an
article about what sunglasses to wear that summer. 'According to
the diktats of fashion, it's time for something new,' the journalist observes, advising the reader to chuck out last year's Ray-Ban
Wayfarers and replace them with something 'classic and retro':
the Ray-Ban Clubmaster, which came out originally in the eighties but 'were inspired by the 50s retro rockabilly style'. Here we
see fashion's 'all change' = no change exposed: we are encouraged
to dispose of a commodity that still has use-value, since it's only
one year old, for another one (made by the same corporation!).
And we see also how retro-fashion's auto-cannibalism opens up
an infinite recession of meaning: purchasing the Clubmaster is a
flashback to the eighties, except that this turns out to be a flashback to the fifties. In fashion, everything is transient except the
sweet music of the cash register.

VINTAGE CHIC

Alongside retro, the other big development in fashion within
the last couple of decades was vintage. The two are related but
not identical. Vintage is about the original period garments,
as opposed to brand-new clothes that rework old designs.

192

Sometimes this impulse can actually have an anti-fashion motive, captured neatly by the slogan of a London vintage store called Pop Boutique: 'Don't follow fashion. Buy something that's already out of date.' Kaja Silverman has argued that the vintage look was an empowering style for feminists, allowing them to oppose fashion in the haute-couture, fashion-industry-imposed sense, without denying themselves the pleasures of self-expression through style. Like retro, vintage can be traced back to the sixties, when bohemians and hippies broke with the taboo on wearing second-hand clothing, hitherto only worn by poor people who couldn't afford new clothes.

The word 'vintage' itself was something of a rebranding coup, replacing the notion of second-hand or 'used' (that even more off-putting American expression for previously owned goods). The word comes originally from the wine trade, where superiority is generally measured by how old a particular vintage is. It drifted across to refer to other things where age could be a seal of quality: musical instruments, early motor cars from between the world wars. By the fifties and sixties, old clothes were starting to lose their stigma, at least within bohemia. According to fashion historian Angela McRobbie, the Beats rummaged for thirties-style clothing, while the dormant flea markets of major European cities were made happening places again by hippies seeking fur coats, lace petticoats and velvet skirts. As with collectable knick-knacks, a micro-economy of traders and aspiring designers sprang up who foraged for salvageable garments in the markets, mending and sometimes tweaking the clothes they found.

Vintage wear keeps getting bigger, reflecting the fact that the past steadily accumulates behind us. In London a few years ago I passed a boutique called NOWretro whose window proclaimed that they sold forties, fifties, sixties, seventies and eighties clothes. By now they've probably added nineties to the list. According to Elaine Showalter, 'The new term for an overflowing wardrobe is "archive"; rummaging through your cast-offs has become a form of research, and, if you have shopped wisely, your archive may deserve an exhibition of its own.' The individual becomes a curator of their own life-in-style; nothing should be thrown out, because it may come back into fashion.

In an essay on seventies-style revivalism, Nicky Gregson, Kate Brooks and Louise Crewe distinguish between the connoisseur's approach and the 'so bad it's good' celebration of the garish, tacky seventies. The first involves witty, knowing reappropriation of salvageable elements from 'the decade that style forgot' and triggers a smile of appreciation from fellow cognoscenti. The second approach, closer to fancy dress or the theme party, detonates a shared howl of laughter. Gregson, Brooks and Crewe argue that the connoisseur approach is a form of resistance to the mass-produced, mass-promoted trends of the High Street, a form of 'beating fashion at its own game'. What's really interesting, though, is how the canny shopper's sifting transforms yesteryear's mass-produced, mass-promoted trends into self-expression. An

---

VINTAGE AND CLASS

Like antique collecting, vintage fashion is a largely middle-class game, a taste that has to be cultivated. The further down the class ladder you go, the more value is set on things being brand new. Look at the glimpses into rappers' homes on *MTV Cribs*, where spotless furnishings like white leather sofas and chrome lamps (decor that looks like it's been transplanted straight out of *Scarface*) jostle with the latest hi-tech home-entertainment systems. Some rappers boast that they only wear sneakers and dazzling white T-shirts once. You can see a similar preference for the crisp and box-fresh, the same slant towards man-made fabrics and glossy, garish colours, in the clothing styles and interior decor favoured by ethnic minorities on both sides of the Atlantic, as well as the UK's white working class, who would not be seen dead in anything that even looked old, let alone actually was second-hand.

Interestingly, and logically, this preference for the new over the old extends to music. In some ways chavs are Britain's last bastion of futurist taste, favouring

aura of uniqueness slips back into the vintage garment, thanks to the aesthete spotting something special about it as it languishes amid mounds of devalued and discarded clothing.

Retro and vintage are obviously related: they're two sides of the same coin, which is fashion's relentless drive for constant change. This fast turnover generates a mountainous heap of passé product, clothing that no longer gets thrown away or destroyed but lingers in the world. Based around the engineering of 'psychological obsolescence' through advertising and other forms of pressure, fashion insists that garments be discarded prematurely, long before their wearability is exhausted. The symbolic value of a garment expires long before its use-value is gone. When these clothes are resold or donated to charity, they enter a subsidiary economy, where they circulate indefinitely. Some of these clothes get a second life when they reacquire symbolic value.

There is a similar pressure within music for new stars, new product, new trends and scenes; it comes from the industry, from the media, and to an extent, from the fans and music fiends

---

R&B or lumpen post-techno styles like donk. US hip-hop radio is notable for its dearth of golden oldies. Young MC recently complained that his 1989 crossover rap hit 'Bust a Move' would get 'plays on pop stations. But there are no oldies rap stations.' The fixation on 'fresh' is a perennial force within black American music: writing in 1984 about changes in American radio, Ken Barnes celebrated the way that black stations '[run] records up and down the charts faster than any other format and generally [scorn] to play oldies. As a result, black music changes constantly, avoiding stagnation and generating a fresh crop of innovations that later become catalysts for pop changes.' Conversely, the same American middle-class and mostly white audience who love Americana and alternative-country or indie-rock styles based around sixties and seventies rock are likely to wear vintage clothing and to decorate their living spaces with vintage Americana: chipped painted signs from roadside diners, old-fashioned ceramic kitchenware, beverage bottles (i.e. things that were once commercial and mass-produced but now have the old-timey aura of the mid-twentieth-century antique). Brand-new is totally associated with nouveau riche; it's brash, vulgar, too brightly coloured.

themselves. But music's value doesn't get voided in quite the same way as fashionable garments. Jean Cocteau famously declared: 'Art produces ugly things which frequently become more beautiful with time. Fashion, on the other hand, produces beautiful things which always become ugly with time.' Pop music exists somewhere between fashion and art, but leans far more to the art side. Consumers can get temporarily tired of a song through overexposure, but music rarely becomes unlistenable over time in the same way that a garment becomes unwearable (too embarrassing, too dated to be seen in). People are moved by music in a way that is different to the feelings they might have for a pair of shoes or a jacket. They become attached to music in a more enduring and deeply felt way. Not that music is immune to the logic of fashion. For instance, from 1968 onwards the sonic mannerisms of psychedelia became passé; new groups still using them were deemed ludicrous, behind the times. But this didn't mean the musical high points of 1966–7 psychedelia were stripped of their stature. That particular form of beauty did not suddenly become ugly.

It is this very aspect of enduring aesthetic and emotional value that creates the problem of retro in music. If music had the 'purity' of fashion and was governed by arbitrary oscillations of style, pop would simply be discarded as used-up product. It would really be disposable in the way that its critics (cultural conservatives on both the political Left and Right) always believed it to be, mere product churned out by Theodor Adorno's despised 'culture industry'. The potency of 'cheap music' isn't just its emotional power but its hold on memory, its durability. Old songs don't lose value with the passing of time. The store of imperishably great music keeps accumulating. Indeed, informed pop fans are meant to acquaint themselves with as much of the past's greatness as possible, while also keeping up with the diverse onslaught of new music. In pop music, the frenetic turnover of fashion and commerce collides with the 'heritage' mindset of the higher arts. Pop is caught between two fundamentally opposed value systems: fashion and art. This in turn is rooted in the fundamental contradictions of popular culture: it is mediated through capitalism while often speaking to values that transcend capitalism.

Retro is a byproduct of what happens when popular creativity is enmeshed with the market. The result is a cultural economy organised around bipolar rhythms of surge and slowdown, mania and nostalgia. As we saw with fashion and the pivotal years of 1965/6, the hunger for the new creates an insatiable appetite for change that can't be sustained indefinitely, for aesthetic innovation can never be a steady flow and is subject to stalling, deadlock or exhaustion of ideas. At a certain point, it becomes tempting for artists to look back to the immediate past and reinvestigate ideas abandoned prematurely during the creative phase. Retro thus becomes a structural feature of pop culture: it's the inevitable down phase to the preceding manic phase, but it is also a response to the build-up of ideas and styles whose potentials have not been fully extracted.

In music, the first of these slowdowns occurred in the early seventies. Immediately following the massive neophiliac frenzy of the sixties, the period was widely felt as a dipping in energy and momentum on just about every level. Of course, in hindsight and from the perspective of our current inertia, the first half of the seventies looks remarkably vital. Partly this is because of the continued pursuit of sixties principles within genres like progressive rock, Krautrock and jazz rock. But it was also because the first backwards-looking movement within rock, glam, actually *felt new at the time*. Postmodernist moves had never been made before in rock. So not only did they seem fresh and bold, but to an extent they *were* more cutting edge and intellectually acute than the lingering sixties visions of the progressives. Still, at the time, the general sentiment overall was that the seventies was a period of stagnation compared with the preceding decade.

Punk and its aftermath (New Wave and post-punk) represented the next major surge. The entropy phase then started to take effect around 1983. Again, this sense of dwindling momentum and creativity was partly accentuated through contrast with the preceding seven years. In the indie-label underground, the leading edge of hip by 1983 no longer involved innovation and technophilia but their reverse: it was a *retreating* edge, looking to the sixties and rejecting synthesizers and sequencers for the traditional line-up of guitar–bass–drums. In the mainstream, the shift was not as marked; state-of-the-art technology prevailed. But there was a massive rediscovery of sixties and early-seventies soul, which became the template for white pop. This era was inaugurated by Phil Collins's redundantly immaculate cover of The Supremes' 1966 hit 'You Can't Hurry Love', which reached no. 1 in the UK in January 1983. It continued with Culture Club, Wham!, Wet Wet Wet, Peter Gabriel's 'Sledgehammer', The Style Council, Hall & Oates et al. Nineteen eighty-six to '88 was the absolute peak of sixties-into-eighties rock'n'soul, from the vintage R&B singles propelled into the higher reaches of the charts by the Levi's 501 commercials, to the cross-generational duet of George Michael and Aretha Franklin and their transatlantic no. 1 'I Knew You Were Waiting (For Me)', to U2's *Rattle and Hum*. The latter featured collaborations with Bob Dylan and B. B. King, and covers of The Beatles' 'Helter Skelter' and Dylan/Hendrix's 'All Along the Watchtower', while the video for the single 'Angel of Harlem' was filmed at the Sun Studio in Memphis in black and white, with photo portraits of Elvis looking down on the band.

Compared with the slowdown of 1970–5, this second entropic phase in the eighties was shaped by the filtering into pop culture of postmodernist techniques of pastiche. Collins's 'You Can't Hurry Love' is a perfect example: the artwork and typography for the single was styled to look like a Motown picture sleeve, and the promo showed the balding Genesis singer jiving in a sharp sixties suit and thin tie. To the right of the frontman are his two backing vocalists (Phil Collins again, through the wonders of special effects), one of whom wears sunglasses just like Dan Aykroyd and John Belushi in *The Blues Brothers*. That movie came out two years earlier in 1980, was crowded with R&B legends like Aretha Franklin, Ray Charles and James Brown, and may well have contributed to reactivating interest in black sixties pop.

As well as postmodernism, another factor affecting the eighties shift to retrospection was simply that there was now a lot more pop past to work with: that hardy perennial the fifties was joined by the rich and at that point relatively underexploited terrain of the sixties, and soon groups started venturing into the seventies. Only a few years earlier that decade was considered off-limits; it was what New Wave defined itself against. But now the repertoire of rehash started to incorporate hairy-and-heavy rock, thanks to nouveau hard rockers like The Cult and Zodiac Mindwarp. The mid- to late eighties succumbed to a sort of omnidirectional outbreak of retro faddishness: folk-punk outfits (most famously The Pogues), country-influenced 'cowpunk' acts (Lone Justice, Jason & the Scorchers, etc.), multiple different restagings of psychedelia, and many more. In part this was a response to the post-post-punk directionlessness, nobody really knowing where to go next or how to recharge the ebbing momentum of punk. But it was also a response to the fact that it was *possible* to go back in all these different directions, the fact that so much music had accumulated in the archives.

The third and most recent upsurge of innovation kicked off at the end of the eighties and carried through for nearly all of the nineties. Prosperity and technological innovation (the digital revolution) synergised to propel rave and club culture for a good decade, during which time electronic dance music became the dominant force in European pop culture for several years.

199

But it was strongly challenged, in the UK, by the retro-oriented counterforce of Britpop. America only briefly felt the impact of the techno rave-olution, partly because hip hop already supplied the role of radical dance music, and partly because of alternative rock, aka grunge. Like indie in Britain, alternative rock expressed its alternative-ness from contemporary pop by being deliberately not-contemporary. Grunge was based on early-seventies heavy rock and late-seventies punk rock, but it *felt* new because that sound had never had any presence in the mainstream. Nirvana's breakthrough into MTV and modern rock radio felt like the long-overdue eruption of eighties indie aesthetics (scruffy image, gnarly sound) into pop. But seen objectively, grunge was, like Britpop, another example of the accumulation of rock history stacking the odds against innovative sounds ever again being the dominant youth-favoured music of the day.

Rock history is now a gigantic archive, virtually every recess of the past accessible to us all. Reversing Elaine Showalter's observation (the idea that an individual's wardrobe can be re-envisaged as a curated clothes collection), you might say that this archive serves as a wardrobe into which new bands dip at will. Bands can do 'nostalgia layering' of sonic garments from different eras. They can try on personae like costumes. Rock's closet is very stuffed indeed and it is so very tempting for new artists to mix and match their clothes, or make small alterations, rather than try to create completely original designs.

Over the course of the last decade or so, rock music has gradually come to operate in a manner much closer to fashion. It hasn't quite reached the point of utterly arbitrary oscillations of period style, but it's getting there. All these dressing-up games can be played without the degree of emotional investment and identification that characterised the era when rock was seen fundamentally as art or rebellion. Musical style was not a consumer choice but a matter of expressive urgency, generational allegiance or identity politics.

Yet this is not the only way that the past can be used by contemporary musicians. Remember the Pop Boutique store in central London with its slogan 'Don't follow fashion. Buy something that's already out of date'? Just as vintage can have an undercurrent of recalcitrance towards fashion, similarly it is possible for rock nostalgia to contain dissident potential. If Time has become annexed by capitalism's cynical cycles of product shifting, one way to resist that is to reject temporality altogether. The revivalist does this by fixating on one era and saying: 'Here I make my stand.' By fixing identity to the absolute and abiding supremacy of one sound and one style, the revivalist says, '*This* is me.'

7

TURN BACK TIME

Revival Cults and Time-Warp Tribes

Arriving at university in the autumn of 1981, I was surprised to find a gang of hippies at my college. The boys sported beards and long hair; the girls had a raggle-taggle flower child look going on. They were into groups I'd never heard of before, records like Gong's *Camembert Electrique* and The Incredible String Band's *The Hangman's Beautiful Daughter*. Oxford student taste lagged behind the cutting edge at the best of times, but this was different from not keeping up with the latest music trends. This was a group of young people, aged between eighteen and twenty-one, making a statement. In a defiant gesture of untimeliness, they spurned the most recent youth revolution – punk rock – and embraced its predecessor, precisely the thing punk had scornfully defined itself against.

These out-of-time hippies were the most intriguing group of people at Brasenose College, so naturally I started hanging out with them. I didn't look the part and my musical leanings (post-punk and new pop, Public Image Ltd and Bow Wow Wow) were incompatible with theirs. In those days I just couldn't see the appeal of Gong and The Incredible String Band, finding them twee and goofy. But the hippies accepted me with open arms, thinking I was a potential convert, someone to 'turn on'. And I actually was fascinated by the sixties and had read Richard Neville's *Playpower* and a bunch of other books about the counterculture. I was also infatuated with Situationism and went to meetings of the university's anarchist group. As did a few of the hippies. Most of them, though, had no interest in the confrontational aspect of the sixties. They were into lifestyle nonconformism: music, clothes, mysticism, drugs.

Thanks to the hippies I got my first taste of cannabis (via a blow-back, where someone puts the joint between his teeth with the lit end inside his mouth and, locking lips, blasts smoky air into your lungs). But generally I was bemused by the giggly, meandering conversations that accompanied the spliff's transit round the room; there was something ritualised, or even placebo-like, about it. These hippies also experimented with LSD, which seemed outlandishly anachronistic. I vividly recall the day one of the hippies, Brian the blow-back specialist, burst into my room without knocking and, wild-eyed with panic, demanded my copy of *Playpower*. He needed the recipe for an LSD bring-down potion (FYI, a quart of orange juice + one cup of sugar) because one of the hippies was bad-tripping, curled in a foetal ball, convinced that Brian was his dad and wanted to kill him.

Strangely, the hippies weren't the only people at my college trying to relive the sixties. After becoming estranged from the long-hair set, I befriended Zaki, a thin, clean-shaven boy obsessed with a different corner of that decade: 1964–6, the apex of mod music and style just before the acid kicked in and the kaftans came on. Carnaby Street boutiques and Soho cappuccino cafes, sharp-suited young men popping pills and cutting shapes in dimly lit discotheques . . . all the clichés of Swinging England as seen in countless sixties movies and documentaries.

Zaki dressed the part, from his chisel-toe shoes (winkle-pickers, but less pointy) to his Nehru jacket with high-standing band collar. The collar doubly suited him because he was north Indian or Pakistani (I never asked – our relationship was entirely based around music). Looking so date-stamped and period-perfect, Zaki stuck out like a sore thumb at Oxford. Unlike the hippies, he didn't have a crew to roll with, so probably welcomed the company of someone like myself whose appearance most likely affronted his sense of aesthetics but who was keen to be hipped to the glories of sixties UK pop. Zaki had boxes of neatly arranged seven-inch singles, many in original sixties picture sleeves, others in yellowing paper sleeves and with jukebox-style cut-out label centres. His view of what was proper and acceptable out of the sixties was tightly policed: the white American sixties didn't really get a look in, but soul of the Motown and Wilson Pickett type was cool. And he had striking opinions: for instance, he didn't rate The Beatles, in large part because of Ringo, who spoiled the group's image by looking goofy and who was – he claimed, absurdly – a lousy drummer.

What Zaki loved above all were the groups who didn't make it. Like The Creation, an amped-up rhythm-and-blues outfit whose thrilling explosive tunes like 'Making Time' and 'How Does It Feel to Feel' ought to have made them as big as The Who, but who only grazed the Top Forty. Then there was John's Children, whose fey frenzy of acid-tinged mod completely tanked at the time, and who were so inept that manager Simon Napier-Bell salvaged their debut album by turning it into a fake live record (*Orgasm*) and splicing in audience screams from *A Hard Day's Night*. But the biggest historical injustice, according to Zaki, was the non-success of The Action, a more soul-oriented mod band produced by George Martin. Singles like 'I'll Keep on Holdin' on' and 'Shadows and Reflections' were so quintessentially sixties that they were almost characterless, a pure emanation of the zeitgeist.

Zaki and I drifted off on separate paths. The last time I saw him was a few years after I'd moved to London, as we were leaving the same Leicester Square cinema: appropriately enough, the film showing was *Scandal*, about the Profumo scandal of 1963, which even has a tiny glimpse of mod culture in the scene where Christine Keeler dances to ska in a shady club. Zaki still looked sharp as a pin, but in a different, non-sixties way: he was working, if I remember rightly, as a trainee at a law firm.

TRAD MAD

The Brasenose hippies and Zaki the Mod were the first time I encountered the phenomenon of the time-warp cult: young people taking a King Canute-like stand against the forward march of pop history. Zaki's special interest in The Creation and The Action typifies the time-warp cultist's drive to correct History. But it is also related to their need to somehow *expand* the lost golden age, make it last longer. This trick is pulled off by fetishising the second- and third-division groups of the era; in a sense, taking advantage of the overproduction of the music industry by retroactively overrating its unsuccessful products.

Zaki the retro-modernist and the nouveau hippies were time-warp cultists in the full sense, adopting the period costume and even the mannerisms, rituals and slang of the lost golden age. Others don't go quite so far, obsessing over the music but not expressing sartorial allegiance. But time-warp cultists of either persuasion have often gone that extra step and formed bands that recreate the vintage style, typically taking pains to use the correct kinds of guitar, organ and other instruments.

Revivalism of this kind is sometimes based purely on an intense attachment to a specific sound that's no longer made; nothing else compares. But usually there's another dimension to the fanaticism: an antagonism to the present day, the belief that something's been lost. Modern music lacks some vital intangible: purity, innocence, a primal rawness and rowdiness. It's lost its connection to the people through gentrification and the contamination of artistic seriousness, or it's simply been 'castrated', its rebellion converted to mere showbiz. It's the strength of this conviction that History went awry at some point that enables the time-warp cultist to contradict pop's imperative to 'live in the now' and to assert that *then* was better.

Ethnomusicologist Tamara E. Livingston argues that music revivals are generally middle-class phenomena that construct a collective identity for individuals 'disaffected with aspects of contemporary life'. Revivalists often disdain the commercial mainstream. The folk revival, for instance, originally regarded rock'n'roll as just part of the meaningless and corny pop mainstream. That's why they embraced traditional music: folk wasn't just the authentic music of the people, it was also a better vehicle for message lyrics, unlike rock'n'roll with its indecipherably slurred vocals and inane words. Other renegades from the modern world turned to early jazz, ragtime and blues. Like his friend and documentary subject Robert Crumb, film director Terry Zwigoff believes that music went into a sharp decline after 1933 owing to the influence of radio and phonograph recordings. 'By the early thirties most of the stuff was getting pretty slick and homogenised,' Zwigoff told me. 'Before that there were these little pockets of uniqueness and eccentricity and local difference, unaffected by the mass media.' In his movie adaptation of *Ghost World*, Daniel Clowes's comic book about the friendship of two alienated teenage girls, Zwigoff inserted a Crumb-like character called Seymour and a bunch of all-new scenes set in the fusty milieu of middle-aged cranks who collect 78 rpm shellac recordings. For the director and Seymour alike, pre-1933 music is a haven from corporatised America's soulless strip-mall sameness.

Time-warp cultists like Zwigoff and Crumb seem unable to recognise that the same energies they prize about the music of the remote past can be found in the present, and indeed often come from *exactly the same place*, socially and geographically. Fans of hot jazz and rural blues have no time for 'Dirty South' hip-hop styles like crunk and New Orleans bounce, which are associated with lowlife and strip bars. But jazz was originally brothel music, and was regarded by respectable black Americans of the upward-aspiring, by-your-own-bootstraps, Booker T. Washington type as a disgrace to the race. As nostalgia theorist Fred Davis observes, it is only the passage of time that transformed 'the tinny, Victrola-squelched jazz band sounds of the 20s' from signifying 'the tawdry and dissolute' to evoking a bygone spirit of sprightly merriment, as in Woody Allen's movies.

Like Crumb and Zwigoff, Allen plays in his own traditional jazz-preservation band. But when the music of twenties New Orleans was first revived back in the forties, it was a return to a sound that had existed in living memory. Revival jazz, or as it later became known, trad jazz, is the first example within popular culture of a time-warp tribe: young people rejecting what the commercial pop industry of the day (late forties and fifties) was offering, in the belief that music had strayed from the righteous path.

'Trad' versus 'modernist' was the big split among jazz buffs in the forties and fifties: modernists favoured bebop and cool modal jazz and sneered at the trad-jazzers as 'moldy figs'. But most of the trad-jazz fans weren't old: they were young people in their twenties and thirties who just preferred the New Orleans style's wild energy. In the period between 1945 and 1956 – after the war but before rock'n'roll arrived – revival jazz was the best thing on offer for young British people who wanted to get lively and party hard. The scene's combination of dance-crazy energy and bohemian informality (scruffy clothes, improvised dance styles, relative sexual freedom, lots of drink, even a little drug-taking) offered an escape from a stiff-necked, tight-lipped, post-war Britain where austerity and rationing reigned and the pre-war class system had been largely reimposed. Trad broke with conventional British

207

stuffiness in ways that looked ahead to the sixties pop explosion.

Trad wasn't traditional just for the sake of it. Looking back to New Orleans and the first few decades of the twentieth century was a *positive negation* of the present, both in terms of the broader pop mainstream (starched, sentimental) and the two directions that jazz had pursued in the thirties and forties: the genteel blandness of big-band swing and the cerebral subtlety of bebop. Interviewed by *Picture Post* in November 1949, Humphrey Lyttelton, one of the revival's top band-leaders, talked about an impulse to 'unearth the principles which distinguished the early jazz forms, which had become almost obscured beneath an accumulation of decadent influences, and to re-establish these as a basis for future development'. He scorned bebop's self-conscious attempts at innovation, arguing that true progress could 'only be achieved by constant reference to first principles'. For Lyttelton and his fellow traditionalists, the essence of jazz pertained to its function as dance music. 'We don't believe that it should be dressed up in a starch shirt and hustled on to a concert platform. Jazz never was and never will be a highly intellectual music. But it can be a dance music which is worthier of the dancers' intelligence . . . than the dreary products of Tin Pan Alley.'

In his classic book about the prehistory of the British counterculture *Bomb Culture*, Jeff Nuttall describes the trad scene as a minority sect who believed New Orleans jazz's rambunctious vitality was 'unclouded by the corrupting touch of civilization'. Nuttall describes how the early trad clubs 'were totally outside of commerce, running at the start . . . on a non-profit-making basis, employing amateur bands . . .' This do-it-yourself aspect of trad jazz blossomed with the spin-off cult for skiffle, a crudely rhythmic hybrid of folk, blues and jazz that had originally been all the rage in twenties America, with bands using washboards, one-string bass fiddles made out of broom handles, and kazoos. Popularised by the chart-topping banjo player and singer Lonnie

Donegan, skiffle became a huge craze, with thousands of skiffle clubs and bands springing up across the land. One of them, The Quarrymen, evolved into The Beatles.

Donegan had originally played in the same band as Ken Colyer and Chris Barber, the two central figures on the UK revival scene. A schism developed between the two and Barber left to form his own group (taking Donegan and his mid-show 'skiffle segment' with him). These two bands came to represent the divergent paths that divided trad into rival camps. Colyer, a cornet player, was a fundamentalist who believed true jazz was the sound made by the New Orleans musicians before they left the Crescent City to pursue careers elsewhere in America. Trombonist Barber stood for a less purist approach that would ultimately encompass ragtime, blues and swing, as well as hot twenties jazz.

'The great incorruptible' (as critic and musician George Melly described him), Colyer was obsessed with the trumpeter Bunk Johnson, whose style he admitted to 'slavishly' copying. A big part of Colyer's own mystique to his acolytes was that he'd actually *been* to New Orleans. A former seaman, in 1951 he re-enrolled in the merchant navy purely in the hope that his boat would make a stop at the birthplace of jazz (he had no choice about the ship's route). Over a year later, the boat docked at Mobile, Alabama, near enough for him to journey to New Orleans. As jazz scholar Hilary Moore relates, Colyer felt that his arrival in the Crescent City was a spiritual homecoming: one of the few original songs he ever wrote, 'Goin' Home', declared: 'If home is where the heart is/ Then my home's New Orleans/ Take me to the land of dreams.' Befriending the local legends, he overstayed his visa and ended up in prison for a month. During his entire pilgrimage, Colyer sent back epistles that were published in *Melody Maker* and *Jazz Journal*.

Like Moses and the tablets, Colyer returned to England with an armful of Bunk Johnson records and told his fellow jazzmen

209

that this was what they should be playing. He would spend hours on end playing particular Johnson tunes over and over. 'I was trying to get beyond the notes and inside the music and find what is to us the elusive ingredients, the alchemy,' he recalled of one session, listening to 'Lowdown Blues', that lasted until dawn. But Colyer was also painfully aware that 'when you hear a New Orleans musician, there's a whole lifetime of experience, wisdom, and sometimes depression, coming through that horn'. There was a creeping undertone of futility to these attempts to unlock the music's secrets, a pathos captured in Colyer's plaintive admission: 'I was born fifty years too late, in the wrong country, and the wrong colour. An outcast.' In a way, this actually *was* the authentic 'blues' of the white man, or white fan: the anguish of being never able to be completely inside the music that exerted such a powerful pull on you.

Trad jazz is part of a grand tradition of British musical subcultures based on an intense projection towards black America, a continuum that includes the blues clubs that spawned groups like John Mayall's Bluesbreakers, The Yardbirds and The Rolling Stones, through the soulboys and jazz funkateers of the seventies and eighties, to the deep-house headz, Detroit techno buffs and underground hip-hop cognoscenti of the nineties onwards. The British fan of these black American styles strives to overcome the distance between himself and the music through a Herculean drive to know everything that is rivalled only by the Japanese and that involves collecting the records, compiling discographies, re-releasing obscure recordings with detailed annotations, evangelising for the music as a radio or club DJ or as a specialist critic and, in some cases, making new music fastidiously faithful to the original sound. The dream is that knowledge and devotion can compensate for being white. And indeed from blues and jazz to reggae and soul, the custodians of black musical heritage have to a great extent been white middle-class men, and often British.

210

There's an inherent contradiction to musical cults of authenticity: fixating on a style that is remote either in time or space (and sometimes both, with the UK trad-jazz revival) inevitably condemns the devotee to inauthenticity. Either he strives to be a faithful copyist, reproducing the music's surface features as closely as possible, risking hollowness and redundancy; or he can attempt to bring something expressive and personal to it, or to work in contemporary influences and local musical flavours, which then risks bastardising the style. Tamara E. Livingston astutely observes that all revival movements reach a kind of structural impasse, a crisis point where this fundamental contradiction reveals itself. At this point, the scene bifurcates. Confronted by the fork in the road, Ken Colyer followed the right(eous) path of exactitude; Chris Barber swung left, opening up the sound to other inputs. As a result, Barber's band would popularise the revival sound, leading to the trad-jazz boom that took off in the late fifties and early sixties, when it became, for a few years just prior to Beatlemania, chart pop. But even as it crossed over commercially, trad jazz retained its link to bohemian left-wing politics: it was the soundtrack for the 1958–63 marches organised by the Campaign for Nuclear Disarmament between Trafalgar Square and Aldermaston, Berkshire, the location of the Atomic Weapons Research Establishment.

Trad's pop boom kicked off in 1959 with Chris Barber's Jazz Band scoring a no. 3 hit with 'Petite Fleur'. Then, in 1960–1, Mr. Acker Bilk and His Paramount Jazz Band, The Temperance Seven and Kenny Ball and His Jazzmen romped into the charts with tunes that increasingly trampled on the ideals of New Orleans purism. Clarinet-wielding Acker Bilk scored with covers of showbiz tunes like 'Stranger on the Shore', 'Buona Sera' and even 'White Cliffs of Dover'. Bilk's image was pop too, or at least gimmicky: bowler hats and striped Edwardian waistcoats, meant to evoke his background as a cider-swigging blacksmith from the west of England county of Somerset.

Trad started to get a reputation as music for drunken students into stomping their feet and daft antics. At the 1960 Beaulieu Jazz Festival, inebriate rowdies jeered a modernist jazz band off-stage in their impatience to hear Bilk and his boys. The disorder swelled into a full-blown riot, with bottles thrown, TV cameras toppled, even some minor arson. A boy grabbed a BBC microphone and addressed the nation with the demand: 'More beer for the workers.' In an essay on Beaulieu, George McKay describes a fifteen-strong trad gang called the Barbarians, who wore fur loincloths and brandished caveman clubs, and a girl whose long white shirt was daubed with the slogan 'IDIOTS OF THE WORLD UNITE!' These young roustabouts bingeing on Bilk and beer were members of a fully fledged subculture known as 'ravers'. The word had been in common parlance on the scene back in the early fifties, with promoters throwing All Night Raves in cramped Soho cellars. By 1962, trad had got so popular that there was an All Night Rave at the voluminous Alexandra Palace. There was even 'rave gear', a trad look of 'stylised shabbiness', according to George Melly. Reporting for *New Statesman*, Melly zoomed in on one couple at the Alexandra rave: the boy sporting 'a top hat with "Acker" painted on it, a shift made out of a sugar sack with a C.N.D. symbol painted on the back, jeans, and no shoes', and the girl wearing 'a bowler hat with a C.N.D. symbol on it' and a man's shirt over black tights. Meanwhile, the dancing had degenerated into a manic stomping on the spot 'like a performing bear, preferably out of time to the beat'.

Trad peaked in 1961–2, with a BBC TV series, a spate of books such as *Trad Mad* and even an exploitation movie, *It's Trad, Dad!* Directed by Richard Lester, who would soon make The Beatles' first movie *A Hard Day's Night*, the film had to be hastily adapted as the trad fad started to wane during its making: twist king Chubby Checker was worked into the plot. When Beatlemania took off in the autumn of 1962, trad faded fast, a passing fancy that had brightened a few young lives before England started swinging for real, as opposed to swinging 1923 N'awlins style.

In *Revolt Into Style*, George Melly defines pop culture as 'the country of "Now"', a teenage nation that 'denies having any history' and regards the words '"Do you remember"' as 'the filthiest in its language'. For that reason, he disqualified trad jazz from consideration as a true pop phenomenon, despite its exuberance and irreverence. Writing in the late sixties, Melly declared that pop was founded in a 'fanatic rejection of the past and equally obsessive worship of the present'. Yet curiously it is one of the defining features of pop music – its orientation towards records more than live performance – that allows it to revive earlier styles. Fans can spurn the record-industry product of the present if it doesn't appeal and listen to records from the past. They can form bands and learn to play in the out-of-time style.

In a throwaway phrase in *Picture Post*'s 1949 profile of Humphrey Lyttelton, the journalist Max Jones refers to jazz-revival bands who play songs 'old enough to be new'. The early trad-jazz bands didn't get these songs from sheet music but from their record collections. Another critical factor in the scene's genesis was something of an historical quirk: the fact that during the revival's early years, a Musicians' Union ban prevented groups from overseas playing in the UK. Because they'd usually never heard the original New Orleans bands in live performance, trad jazzers had a distorted notion of what the music sounded like when played in a nightclub. As a result, Hilary Moore notes, they would faithfully mimic the 'distorted instrumental balance and faulty intonation' of the music as reproduced via 78 rpm discs.

There is a poetic aptness to a music revival (an attempt to bring back to life a dead sound) being so dependent on phonograph records, which were originally conceived by Edison as a means of preserving the voices of the dearly departed. Despite this, the orientation of British trad jazz itself was initially primarily about

213

audiences dancing to live bands; only towards the end of its life-time did the hit albums and chart singles come. The next major time-warp tribe would take phonographic fetishism much further. Its gurus were disc jockeys rather than musicians. Northern Soul was organised almost entirely around records. Its equivalents to Ken Colyer and Acker Bilk – purist preservationists versus bastardising popularisers – weren't performers, they were DJs. But their stature and mystique weren't founded on DJing skills as we nowadays understand them, but on their skill at finding records nobody else knew about, digging up rare nuggets from the lost golden age.

KEEPING THE FAITH

I've never totally understood the appeal of Northern Soul, that strange English cult for uptempo sixties soul in the classic Tamla Motown style. Motown itself – yeah, fabulous . . . But fetishising the sub-Motown wannabes? Northern Soul came about at the end of the sixties, when British taste in black American dance music split regionally. The south of England followed black American music's evolution to slower, funkier grooves: Sly Stone, James Brown, and so forth. But the north and the Midlands, for reasons that are slightly mysterious, preferred the high-energy Motown sound, with its brisk, clip-clopping beat and stirring orchestration. Sticking with a style that had gone *out* of style in its homeland, the Northern fans pledged allegiance to music that had been left behind by History. Hence Northern Soul's big slogan, 'Keep the Faith'. Gradually they built an entire subculture, with its own clothing style, slang and rituals, around this bygone music.

The first time I encountered the Northern Soul mentality – not that I recognised it as such then – was at university in the early eighties. Through Zaki, I got to know some other sixties cultists at a different college. They didn't dress mod like Zaki, but in some ways were actually closer to the original mod sensibility: they were into the original rhythm-and-blues records from America, rather than the bands like The Creation and The Action who came up with a British take on R&B. I swapped tapes with these Northern-minded students, but the C-90 containing what I considered to be vintage soul (early-seventies Stax stuff by Shirley Brown and The Dramatics, tunes by Bobby Womack and James Brown) did not meet with their approval. It was past their cut-off point: too funky, too earthy and too midtempo, lacking the pounding beat they loved in The Four Tops and Wilson Pickett.

These perfectly pleasant puritans had an equivalent to The Action: a touchstone singer called Major Lance, who'd recorded for the Okeh label and had a couple of US hits produced by Curtis Mayfield, along with a bountiful string of flops. His songs struck me as surpassingly mediocre, but as far as they were concerned he was *the* great lost singer of the era. Years later I discovered that Major Lance was one of Northern Soul's pantheon of godstars. So revered and popular, in fact, that he actually moved to the UK for a couple of years in the early seventies.

My one experience of Northern Soul as a dance-floor scene was accidental. In spring 1988, my friends and I journeyed to Shoom, the pioneering acid-house club in South London. The media was buzzing about the acid phenomenon, and I was already a fan of the music, having written a piece largely based on the records at the start of 1988. Shoom had an infamously strict door policy, though, and we were turned away. Heading back across Southwark Bridge to the north side of the Thames, feeling disconsolate and vaguely humiliated, we wondered what to do with the suddenly empty night ahead. Someone suggested a club night they'd heard was going on in Kentish Town. But when we got there, it turned out to be a sixties soul night. Standing morosely on the edge of a dance floor full of period-styled boys and girls stepping to that Motown-soundalike beat, I reflected that the music originated from the exact same regions of America that produced Detroit techno and Chicago house, but was a good twenty-five years behind the times. I had wanted to embrace the phuture but ended up in the retro-zone. What I wonder about now, though, is all the young people at the Town and Country who'd come there on purpose. What makes actual young people stop chasing tomorrow's music today (like the acid ravers at Shoom were doing) and pursue yesterday's music today?

The paradox of Northern Soul is that it began as an offshoot of the mods, which was originally short for 'modernists'. In the north of England, mods broke with the mod credo (keep on keeping up with the cutting edge of black music) and instead kept faith with the sounds danced to by mods during the movement's early- to mid-sixties heyday. For the Northern fans, this was the unsurpassable peak of black dance music. But DJs and dancers didn't just stick with the classics, the well-known golden oldies. On the contrary, the Northern scene retained and intensified mod's characteristic restlessness, its chase for the latest records. It just did this by redirecting the impulse into the past. The quest was for *new old songs*, what DJs and fans called 'unknowns': discoveries from the vast deposits of Motown-like music laid down during a short stretch of time in the mid-sixties. Low production costs and the immense reservoir of black talent in urban America encouraged a host of small R&B labels such as Ric-Tic and Wheelsville to churn out singles in the hope of scoring a hit. A few became regional successes; most flopped. But as a result there was a staggering amount of decent-quality uptempo soul music still lingering in the world as vinyl singles. This historical bulge of musical overproduction enabled Northern Soul fans to perpetuate that mid-sixties moment indefinitely.

Everything about the scene in its early days was a pure extension of mod: scooter-riding, pill-popping, obsessing about clothes. The basic look for boys was three-button suits fastened at the top button and with a single vent at the back, Ben Sherman shirts and tight-pegged pants. Neatly combed hair with a parting was de rigueur and the men all wore aftershave: the atmosphere in clubs was thick with the pungent whiff of Brut. One unique style quirk that distinguished the scene from its mod precursor was the wearing of a motorist-style black glove on your right hand, a fad adopted by dancers at the Twisted Wheel in Manchester. This was because dancing was becoming increasingly acrobatic, with back-flips and twirls, and the concrete floors of the Wheel got slippery and sticky with sweat.

Like mod, Northern Soul was a white British fantasy of American blackness. 'We wanted to pretend we were black, we danced like we were black,' recalled one 'face', Tony Bremner. Visiting the Twisted Wheel in 1971, Dave Godin – the *Blues & Soul* journalist and London record-shop owner who actually coined the term Northern Soul – marvelled at the fluent grace of the dancing and noticed that everyone on the floor 'was an expert in Soul clapping! In the right places, and with a clipped sharp qual-ity that only adds an extra something to appreciation of Soul music.' Yet like trad jazz, the Northern fantasy of blackness was already out of date: in America, the new street style at the start of the seventies was Afros and bell-bottoms and garish colours, while the soundtrack was psychedelic soul and funk.

Two songs distil the essence of the Northern Soul dream, and both were sung by Dobie Gray. Nineteen sixty-six's 'Out on the Floor' celebrates the transcendence over the workaday grind that could be found at the dance club, while 1965's 'The "In" Crowd' glories in belonging to an aristocracy of sharp-dressed stylists. The song celebrates being ahead of the pack ('other guys imitate us') through the cultivation of special knowledge: what to wear, where to go, the new dance steps. Northern Soul was all about making that extra effort to set oneself apart from the herd. Club promoter David Thorley described it as a 'secret society', and thus a means by which 'a working class person' could be 'an elitist, which they could hardly achieve any other way'. Normal kids went to dance at the local High Street nightclub; Northern fans made long-distance pilgrimages to special clubs in other cities, like the Torch in Tunstall, Stoke-on-Trent, or the Mecca in Blackpool, travelling by car or chartering a coach. Ordinary kids jigged about to Top Forty hits spiced with the occasional golden oldie. Northern Soulsters were obsessed with 'secret sounds', knowledge that was exclusive and excluding. Ironically, Tamla Motown's own music was regarded by Northern fiends as too 'commercial', which is to say, 'common knowledge' and not something you could be elitist about.

In the earliest days people didn't talk about 'Northern' but about 'rare soul'. Hundreds of R&B singles came out each week during the sixties, and independent labels would often press up a small batch of records to see if club or radio DJs would bite. Those that never made it to a bigger second pressing had a scarcity value to collectors. Rare-soul fiends chased down this commercial-sounding but commercially unsuccessful music, scouring second-hand record stalls and junk shops for used jukebox seven-inches or trekking to the handful of specialist shops across the UK that maintained a large back stock of soul 45s. The very first 'rare soul' retailer was a man called Gary Wilde, who ran a cigarette kiosk in Blackpool. At the back he kept a box of rare soul singles, which he sold for £5 each. That's fifteen times the standard price of a single then (which retailed at 35 pence). This was at a time, circa 1967–8, when your average working-class youth earned about £5 a week. For that special soul rarity, fanatics were willing to cough up a week's wages.

The record industry is predicated on overproduction and wastefulness. The bulk of its products don't get bought and most of its signings fail to deliver a return on the investment. But the strategy of 'throw shit against the wall and hope some of it sticks' worked – at least in the industry's prime – because of the high profit margins when a record became a blockbuster. Northern Soul found a strange liberating gap within this system; it transformed redundant waste into the knowledge base and means-to-bliss of a working-class elite. A frenzied market for rare soul singles threatened to eclipse the scene's focus on dancing: dealers brought boxes of records to the clubs and mini-marts of swapping and selling sprang up on the edge of the dance floor or on the balcony area. Where only a handful of copies of certain singles were known to exist, they were traded for increasingly large sums. By the early seventies, the rarest singles would be going for up to £50.

Northern Soul became a scarcity economy. The rarity of the records governed the status of DJs, the competition between clubs and what ruled the dance floor. If a DJ had a record no other jock had and that fans couldn't find, the only way to hear it was to go to that club. This gave DJs a vested interest in turning obscurities into anthems. It also meant it was vital to protect one's secret knowledge. Hence the phenomenon of the cover-up. This idea

---

IAN LEVINE – NORTHERN SOUL LEGEND AND ÜBER-COLLECTOR

DJs in Northern Soul weren't celebrated for their mixing skills (the technology for that didn't exist then) but for their knack of reading the crowd and picking the right tune at the right moment, and above all, for their ability to unearth nuggets of rare soul. Ian Levine was unsurpassed as a 'digger'. He started out as a teenager, initially providing tunes for DJs at the Blackpool Mecca, before graduating to the decks himself and becoming a star on the scene.

Levine and his Mecca colleagues revelled in the obscurer-than-thou, high-turnover ethos of the Northern scene. 'Our rule was that as soon as a record was bootlegged' – and thus rendered too widely available to punters and rival DJs – 'we dropped it like a hot potato.' Levine would score the biggest haul of 'unknowns' ever when he scooped up four thousand singles from a gigantic thrift store in Florida while on a vacation with his wealthy parents. He spent the entire fortnight schlepping back and forth to the warehouse, sifting through the vinyl in

was developed independently by many dance scenes, often involving the use of Tipp-ex to white out the label. But the Northern scene came up with a supremely cunning ruse, which was to cut out the label centre of an inferior, more easily obtained record and stick that over the rarity, in the process sending rival DJs off on a fruitless quest for the wrong record. But if a DJ, or a spy working for him, somehow managed to work out the true identity of an anthem and get hold of a copy, things got even more dastardly. That DJ could then sell the record to a bootlegger, who would press up several hundred knock-offs that sold for £1.50. Flooding the market with bootlegs of a hitherto exclusive song had the vicious double-whammy effect of disarming a key weapon in the original DJ's arsenal and also massively deflating its resale value.

Northern Soul's cult of the non-hit would eventually become a cult of the substandard. It's a route followed by all collector cults, but Northern Soul took it further than most. By the mid-seventies, clear-eyed members of the scene were complaining about the elevation of third-rate records purely for their obscurity

---

sweltering heat all day long. In the process he found 'records like Don Gardner's "Cheating Kind" that are worth £3,000 today' but for which Levine paid the bulk-buy rate of 15 cents.

Sensing that the scene couldn't keep on mining the mid-sixties, Levine spearheaded an initiative to let in more contemporary releases by outfits like The Carstairs, whose sound was more shuffly and less driving than the classic Motown-style rhythms that hitherto defined Northern. The music-policy shift was controversial and spawned the 'Levine Must Go' campaign: a contingent of disgruntled Mecca regulars who wore anti-Levine T-shirts and badges, and even, in one case, held up a twelve-foot banner in protest on the dance floor.

In the early eighties, Levine pioneered the gay club sound of Hi-NRG through his sets at London nightspot Heaven and productions like Miquel Brown's 'So Many Men So Little Time'. Although made using synths and drum machines, it bore the imprint of Northern Soul in its uptempo euphoria, soul-diva vocals and funkless four-to-the-floor beat. In 1989, Levine organised the reunion of sixty Motown stars in Detroit. It was the first in a steady stream of nostalgia-oriented

value. Some DJs, like the Blackpool Mecca's Ian Levine (see side-bar), started to work into their sets contemporary soul music that was compatible with the Northern ethos of 'no funk please' but had a less pounding rhythm than the archetypal Northern sound. This did not meet with universal acceptance, and the diehard purists in the scene converged around the Wigan Casino, an all-nighter where the classic Northern 'stompers' still reigned.

The crowd at Wigan developed a distinctive look that left behind mod sharpness for singlet vests, tank-top sweaters and pants that were baggy around the legs but tight-waisted and butt-hugging. It was clothing suited to the ever-more athletic back- and front-flips, high kicks and leg splits that had become de rigueur. Wiganites arrived at the club around midnight clutching hold-all bags adorned with commemorative patches (slogans like 'Keep the Faith' or 'Night Owls') and containing essentials for an all-night dance: a change of clothing, talcum powder to stop your feet slipping on the sweat-shiny floor, and chewing gum to allevi-ate the teeth-grinding caused by amphetamines.

---

initiatives that includes the Motorcity label, a six-hour DVD documentary on Northern Soul, various disco and Hi-NRG compilations and, in 2002, with the Rocket, the first major Northern all-nighter since Wigan Casino.

Levine's flair for collecting and nostalgia isn't limited to music, though. In 1996, he organised the largest family reunion of all time after tracking down over six hundred members of his mother's side of the family, the Cooklins. Four years later he staged a bizarre re-enactment of his childhood, reuniting all thirty of his classmates from Blackpool's Arnold School, along with the original teachers, garbing them in authentic sixties uniforms and recreating a typical school day complete with morning assembly, gym lessons and a game of rugby. A compulsive collector of comics, Levine eventually managed to acquire a copy of every book that DC Comics issued from the thirties onwards. And his love of *Dr. Who* led him to offer a reward (a life-size Dalek) to anyone who could supply a copy of any of the 108 early episodes that the BBC notoriously deleted. All these fandoms manifest the same obsession with turning back the clock and salvaging 'lost time' that animates Northern Soul.

Problems with the drug squad had led to the closing of the early Northern clubs the Twisted Wheel and the Torch. By the time of Wigan's ascendancy, stimulants, or 'gear', were more central than ever. As leading Northern Soul DJ Neil Rushton recollected in a myth-burnishing 1982 piece for *The Face*, punters would fervently discuss 'the respective merits of blues, green and clears, black and whites, sulphate and bombers'. Barbiturates were popular too. Soft Cell's David Ball recalled that 'every so often the Drug Squad would raid a club and as they came in you'd hear the crunch of tablets under-foot . . . The dance floor would be covered in little white powder dots and afterwards people would pick them up and use them! It was no joke really though . . . kids were always over-dosing.'

Northern Soul's reverberations spread wide, from Soft Cell's no. 1 cover of the scene anthem 'Tainted Love', through the gay Hi-NRG sound, to the early support in the north of England for house music (another uptempo sound from mid-America that went well with stimulants). But the movement itself shrank to a diehardcore during the eighties, the torch kept aflame by clubs like Stafford's Top of the World. Ironically, another stronghold for Northern was in the heart of the south: London's 100 Club, which hosted the long-running 6Ts night. Here the DJs prided themselves on playing tunes that nobody knew, nicknamed 'Sixties Newies', which meant records that had come out in the sixties but had not been played during the Northern scene's seventies prime, despite the frenzied fossicking for lost soul gold that had gone on then.

The scene waxed and waned through the nineties and into the 2000s. New recruits who'd read about the myths of the Wheel, the Torch and the Casino rubbed shoulders with forty- and fifty-something veterans returning for nostalgic reasons. Northern Soul's keep-the-faith spirit has doubled on itself: today's scene pays tribute to both the original sixties soul and the 1968–75 hey-day of the scene built around that music.

Running all the way through Northern Soul is a logic of redemption. The original black music was all about the weekend of dance/dressing up/romance that would redeem the working week. The mods built an amplified version of that black fantasy, accelerating the style turnover and creating a scene in which working-class drones could become Faces. Northern Soul found a new facet to the secret knowledge that separated them from the dull-witted nobodies who were otherwise members of the same working class: rare soul. In the process, the DJs became stars. But so too, in a marvellous twist, did the original black performers, who, years after giving up on their dreams of fame, found themselves the focus for a strange cult in a distant land. Soon they were flown over to sing to packed clubs and treated like stars. Performers like Rose Battiste, who'd quit singing to work in the advertising department of General Motors and then as a typist at Motown, but whose flop single 'Hit and Run' on the Revilot label became an anthem at the Twisted Wheel. There was a wonderful mirroring effect, a mutually glorifying symbiosis between the desire for transcendence on the part of the Northern fans and the disappointed dreams of stardom and escape from poverty that had inspired the original performers, writers and producers of the music.

Perhaps alongside the defiance of Time that is integral to Northern Soul – one fan at a nineties reunion event declared, 'It won't change, it won't stop, it's *incessant*' – there is also a defiance of Fate. Northern Soul is pop history rewritten by the losers.

ALL MOD CONS

Just as the original wave of Northern Soul flagged in the final years of the seventies, the UK saw a full-blown Mod Revival. This effectively meant that you had a tradition that developed out of mod (Northern Soul) co-existing with a retro reconstruction

223

of it. The Mod Revival was almost entirely a south of England phenomenon, however, and its focus was radically different from Northern Soul. It didn't recreate sixties mod's orientation towards black American music. The Mod Revival was about bands wielding electric guitars and bashing drums: mod according to The Who, in other words. Indeed, some Mod Revival bands specifically drew inspiration from The Who's 1973 concept album *Quadrophenia*, which depicted the modyssey of an alienated young man in the early sixties.

Just as important as The Who, though, were The Jam. Their stylised sharpness stood out against the anti-fashion ugliness of punk. The Jam appealed to British kids who liked punk's high-energy sound but didn't care for either the yobbish element or the art-school theory-and-politics contingent. The inner sleeve of The Jam's 1978 album *All Mod Cons* featured a montage of mod fetishes: singles like 'Biff Bang Pow' by The Creation and 'Road Runner' by Motown's Jr. Walker & the All-Stars, a *Sounds Like Ska* compilation, plus Union Jacks and a cappuccino (a nod to Soho cafe culture). All this provided vital clues for those fans who were in the process of forming their own Jam-style combos.

The Jam had actually started as a school band way back in 1972, doing American rock'n'roll covers, songs by the likes of Chuck Berry and Little Richard. But when singer, guitarist and leader Paul Weller discovered The Who, he decided that mod could be 'a base and an angle' from which to write songs but also something that would set the group apart from everybody else. Punk was coalescing and its initial orientation was very American: The Stooges, New York Dolls, sixties garage punk. Mod was totally English. It was also, Weller decided, the antithesis of rock'n'roll, even though groups like The Who used guitars, bass and drums. This notion actually had roots in the dichotomy that the original mods had felt existed between 'their bands' (The Who, Small Faces et al.) and The Rolling Stones, whom they considered 'dirty, undesirable, long-haired art school beatniks', to quote *NME* writer and genuine sixties mod Penny Reel. Weller himself would later rail against 'elegantly wasted wankers like Keith Richards', and assert that 'I've never really seen us as part of the rock thing. I see us outside of that . . . I believe in . . . *clean culture, real culture.*'

The Jam, revealingly, would never break America, never winning over more than a niche anglophile following. Weller talked of being indifferent to America and its music (apart from soul, of course). And there was something inherently English and neurotic about mod, from its neat-freak ethos to its fractured, combustible guitar pop. Built around Pete Townshend's slashed power chords and Keith Moon's flailed cymbal crashes and tom rolls, The Who weren't a groove band. Taking their cue from The Who's wiry, tension-wracked sound, The Jam and the Mod Revival bands that followed them further stripped the sexuality from R&B.

The secret of The Jam's influence, and their creative remodelling of mod for a post-punk world, was the disillusionment in their music, a bleak vision rooted in Weller's sour personality. The Jam's defining songs weren't the motivational anthems like 'Start!', 'Absolute Beginners' or 'Beat Surrender' – all of which harked back to the sixties idea of youth as a new classless class – but desolate ditties like 'That's Entertainment', 'Eton Rifles', 'Funeral Pyre' and 'Down in the Tube Station at Midnight'. Even 'When You're Young' – the 1979 hit that pushed them towards being a phenomenon, the kind of band whose every single enters the chart at no. 1 – is not about possibility but constrictions: 'The world is your oyster/ but your future's a clam,' Wellers sings, aware that the kid's open-hearted passion ('used to fall in love with everyone') will eventually contract into wary, weary cynicism. For Weller, youth was a glorious but tragically short-lived sensation of total possibility, curtailed almost immediately by adult responsibility: settling down, settling for less.

The Jam's following was large enough to constitute a significant movement in its own right, but they also influenced younger, punk-inspired groups like The Chords and The Purple Hearts to 'go mod'. Fuelled by the fanzine *Maximum Speed*, the revival took off in the late summer of 1979, helped by the release of the movie version of *Quadrophenia* (in which some Mod Revival groups and fans had roles as extras). There were hits for The Merton Parkas and The Lambrettas (both considered bandwagon-jumpers), and for Secret Affair, who rapidly became the scene's leaders. Like Dexys Midnight Runners and their 'young soul rebels', Secret Affair had originally intended to start a movement of their own, the Glory Boys, and pulled together a look inspired by the movie *Performance* (which starred Mick Jagger) and suggestive of Kray twins-style East End gangsters (Chas, the smooth-criminal protagonist of *Performance*, was a bit of a mod, with his short hair, thin ties and sharply creased suits). When small-faced, skinny boys wearing parkas with Union Jacks and target signs on the back began turning up to the early Secret Affair gigs, the group realised that the movement they were looking for already existed.

Although most of Secret Affair's anthems were written by guitarist Dave Cairns, singer Ian Page became the spokesman for the band and for the scene. In a *Sounds* feature, he defined mod as social revenge exacted through a sort of superiority complex: dressing 'rich' was a way of resisting the wealthy's 'right to feel superior, or treat [ordinary working-class people] like a soiled pound note. Powerful people – businessmen in suits, take their clothes, retain your identity.' The point was not egalitarianism, though, but the creation of an alternative hierarchy based on style and suss: 'I do not believe everyone is equal. I believe everyone should have equal opportunity to be top dog.' Looking back on the revival decades later, Page said the idea of calling the band Secret Affair was to suggest a secret society: 'special, separate and elite'.

The Mod Revival is not a British pop moment that's garnered much respect or attention from historians. Even at the time, the new mods were regarded sceptically by most music journalists, being seen as retrogressive and tribalistic. *Sounds* championed the sound initially but moved swiftly to other kids-on-the-streets movements like 2-Tone and Oi! that had more social resonance. So what was it all about, then, the Mod Revival? Just a strange blip in the after-punk confusion?

According to Kevin Pearce, a music writer who was involved in the revival as a teenager, even though the original mod scene occurred a bare fifteen years earlier, 'It seemed like a lost era. There was nothing to draw on for information except for a couple of books and the records, if you could find them.' The original mods, by then in their mid-thirties, had been subsumed into the suburban normality they'd dreaded. 'It was too big a gap for your older brother to have been one, and not enough of a gap for parents to have been involved in,' says Pearce. Yet part of the appeal was precisely that it required considerable effort and dedication. 'You couldn't just walk down the road and get all the records; there weren't thirty Northern Soul compilations like there are now. Same with the clothes. Later on, when it all took off, there were loads of bandwagon exploiters selling mod wear. But at the start, you had to search through charity shops and jumble sales. Even the books you were getting information from, you had to find second-hand. That was the fascination: you were putting together the jigsaw pieces from very few source materials.'

Pearce describes the new mod as 'a revival of *interest* rather than a recreation', and therefore more comparable to 'the folk revival of the early sixties' than to a retro fad. It was also very much shaped by the post-punk context. This is what made it different from Northern Soul, which carried on the sixties mod approach of transcending workaday dreariness through music and style. The Mod Revival bands focused more on the bleakness that necessitated the escapism than on the escape itself. They had assimilated the dashed hopes of the seventies that gave birth to punk.

The Purple Hearts, formerly a punk band called The Sockets, found their name – slang for a brand of amphetamine tablet – on the back of a Small Faces album. They came from Romford, Essex, the same kind of London-periphery zone of commuter towns that produced The Jam (whose home town was Woking in Surrey). One of The Purple Hearts' best tunes, the brittle 'Frustration', features singer Robert Manton stuttering like Roger Daltrey in 'My Generation' about how he's suffocated by all-engulfing mediocrity: 'I get frustration/ I wear it like a suit/ But the jacket fits too tightly/ And there's lead inside my boots.' Even more jittery with angst in tight-pegged pants, 'I Can't Stay Here' chafes at the claustrophobic rut of small-town life and the routine of commuting to the office job in the city: 'Waking up is a big comedown/ I'm going to work with a crowd of people/ Who make me feel as if I'm nothing.'

Of all the Mod Revival's would-be anthems, The Chords' 'The British Way of Life' comes closest to Jam-level greatness. Surveying a panorama of predictability, the verses weirdly combine exuberance and grimness. Weekday work at the office (where 'they don't even know my name/ I feel so cold/ They watch me grow old') alternates with visits to the pub ('I swallow my dreams like my beer'), and every weekend brings the local football match and Sunday roast with the wife. But at the chorus – 'This is my life!' sung choirboy-pure and rising-high like The Small Faces on 'Itchycoo Park' – it's as though the narrator's having an out-of-body experience, soaring above the plain of the mundane, looking down on his petit-bourgeois life with an exultant disdain for just how petty it is.

But if the message in 'The British Way of Life' about UK society at the end of the seventies was that 'nothing new happens here . . .

nothing will ever change', that begged the question: why did the nouveau mods contribute to the stagnation by filling the airwaves with such musty familiarity? Why not drop those guitars and pick up forward-looking synths? Or at least try to play modern black music and contribute to the south of England's thriving jazz-funk scene? This was the contradiction of the Mod Revival: its betrayal of the original principles of modernism, which involved being into the latest, coolest thing.

Why did the new mods dress up in the glad rags of a second-hand subculture and listen to faint copies of yesterday's sounds? You might say that they took punk's 'no future' literally, and acting like pop's clock had stopped, rewound to relive its brightest day. Or perhaps the real explanation is simply that enough time had elapsed for the past to seem exotic. 'For The Purple Hearts, hearing The Creation for the first time, it was a totally brand new thing for them,' says Kevin Pearce. Like Max Jones's casual insight about the New Orleans jazz songs being 'old enough to be new' by 1949, this was the crucial shift within pop music that solidified during the seventies. With age came history, a heap of memories. In 1979 – long before the boom for rock documentaries and photo books – the memory bank consisted of records. This steadily accumulating phonographic archive could serve as a resource, a catalyst to the imagination. But equally it might lead to lameness and laziness. You could explore it like an undiscovered land and bring back exotica to enrich the present. But you could also use it as a hiding place.

THE LIVING DEAD

On the face of it, it's difficult to think of anything more distant from mod and Northern Soul than the Deadheads, that tie-dye tribe who followed The Grateful Dead on their arena tours all through the seventies, eighties and early nineties. The turn to psychedelia in the mid-sixties was precisely what turned off many mods and led to Northern Soul. It's easy to imagine a Northern Soul or Secret Affair fan's disgust at the Deadhead's sense of 'style': the long straggly hair and face fuzz, the cut-off shorts and loose-flowing garments with their unappetising mix of garish colours and Whole Earth-y shades of brown. The Dead's music – all meandering guitar solos, rootsy grooves, weak white-bread harmonies – could hardly have been more offensive to the mod sensibility.

Still, there are a surprising number of parallels between Northern Soul and the Deadhead scene. Both are style tribes whose members travelled on pilgrimages to particular clubs or one-off events, 'temples of sound' where they congregated to create an ecstatic ritual space. At the Dead's long arena shows and the Northern Soul all-nighters loud music and drugs meshed to overwhelm listeners and transport them to a collective high. Dead shows were famous for the ripples that traversed the crowd-body in response to certain shifts in the music. As journalist Burton H. Wolfe observed, the Dead's music was 'action sound for dancing' just as much as it was head music designed to 'blow the mind'. A different kind of dancing, for sure, to the fastidious steps and acrobatic twirls on display at Northern nights. Free-form and fluid, Deadhead dancing was the continuation of the 'freaking-out' style that emerged in sixties San Francisco at former ballrooms like the Fillmore and the Avalon, as well as at the Be-Ins and similar trip-tastic happenings. Orgiastic yet asexual, this sacred frenzy of undulant gestures matched The Grateful Dead's 'search for the form that follows chaos', as guitarist Jerry Garcia characterised it. But like Northern Soul, the Dead's concert audience was mostly on its feet, moving and grooving.

The main thing that the Deadheads and Northern Soul have in common is their fixation on a particular moment in the sixties, keeping it alive in defiance of the passage of historical pop time. Neither scene was really retro but rather an example of sub-cultural persistence. 'Keeping the faith' is the central principle in both fan cultures. So too is an emphasis on community – a sense of togetherness defined against the mainstream, that unlucky majority who aren't in the know. As the Dead's Tom Constanten put it, 'Back in the sixties, there was a great sense of community, and I think a lot of the energy and the steam, the wind in the sails of the Grateful Dead phenomenon is from that commu-nity.' There are even parallels between Northern Soul and the Deadheads in terms of the way a rhetoric of anti-commercialism was combined with a bustling entrepreneurial activity, as with the markets for handcrafted goods (hemp bracelets, jewellery, tie-dyed clothes) and Dead memorabilia that sprang up in the park-ing lots outside the arenas where the Dead played, which aren't that far removed from the record dealers selling and swapping rare soul singles at the Northern Soul all-nighters. In both scenes there was also a bustling illegal trade going on rather less openly: amphetamines and barbiturates with Northern, and at Deadhead shows, marijuana, 'doses' (LSD) and other psychedelics, like pey-ote, mushrooms and MDMA.

All this parking-lot activity was as much a part of the total experience of a Dead show as the band's performance. These out-door bazaars, teeming with backpack-lugging peddlers and gaud-ily daubed, Merry Prankster-style micro-buses and vans, offered a kind of nomadic surrogate for Haight-Ashbury circa 1967–9. And they had the same upsides and downsides: familiar faces that you'd see at every show, people passing around the pipe and shar-ing stuff with strangers, an atmosphere of trust and tranquillity . . . but also rip-off deals, scam artists, hardcore drug casualties, kids flipping out on bad trips.

Deborah J. Baiano-Berman, who's both an academic and a Deadhead, characterises the band's following as a 'moral com-munity' and argues that the Dead's concerts allowed their fans 'to live out their interpretation of a hippie-like communal value system, based primarily on freedom, experimentation, solidarity, peace, and spontaneity'. Inside the auditorium, the crowd created the atmosphere as much as the band or the lighting crew. The emphasis on tie-dye and clashing colours, the painted faces and beads turned the whole shimmying, swaying audience into a paisley ocean, a spin-art kaleidoscope. Baiano-Berman points out that almost nobody sat in their assigned seats in the concert hall: they moved out into the aisles and danced, drifted around the auditorium, settling in different places, creating an effect of 'incessant movement and circulation'. To an audience sensitised on drugs like LSD, which intensifies peripheral vision, to be in the midst of this flickering multitude was entrancing and magical.

Another aspect of Deadhead culture that's about communality and circulation is tape trading. From very early on Deadheads started recording shows, a practice that was first tolerated by the band and then encouraged, with The Grateful Dead making provisions for a special area for tapers at each of their shows. There was a huge demand for cassette recordings of the band's performances, in part because The Grateful Dead's official studio albums were airless affairs that failed to capture the electricity of the band in full improvisational flow. Deadhead culture's communal ethos meant that if anyone requested a tape, the taper had to make them a copy. Tapers also got into trading recordings with other tapers in different parts of the country. All the resulting excessive documentation and redundancy anticipated aspects of today's retro culture, like the multiple clips of the same gig videoed on cellphones and uploaded to YouTube.

The taping phenomenon has a paradoxical aspect. The angle on the Dead has always been that you really had to see them live to 'get it': you needed to experience the flow of the moment, the pure quicksilver magic of Garcia's soloing as it rippled out into the cosmos. Taping the shows attempts to capture that evanescent

232

beauty but in the process goes against the 'be here now' spirit of psychedelia. Indeed, the tapers became obsessed with recording quality. Instead of dancing and getting lost in music, they would spend the show crouched beside their tape-recording equipment, constantly adjusting the recording levels (sometimes listening to the show through headphones plugged into the machine) or repositioning the microphones. They'd admonish dancing Deadheads for bumping into the equipment or chatting too loudly on the periphery of the tapers sections. Like the dad with a video camera welded into his eye socket at his kid's birthday party, the tapers were not fully present; they missed, partially at any rate, the very event they were attempting to save for eternity.

The fact that obsessively stockpiling audio documentation of the live Dead is so central to the Deadhead subculture seems to resonate with its deepest impulse: to freeze-frame History and artificially keep alive an entire era – the late sixties. The Deadhead scene is a preservation society. Or perhaps it was actually a *reservation*, a zone of cultural territory set aside for an outcast tribe. The gentle frenzy of the Deadheads is a ghost dance: an endangered, out-of-time people willing a lost world back into existence.

BACK TO THE OLD SKOOL

American rock culture has always placed more emphasis on live performance than records; in Britain, it's the opposite. The UK's phonographic orientation explains the key role played by recorded music in trad jazz and Northern Soul. It may even account for why there have been so many revivalist scenes in the UK compared with the US. But the slant towards records also contributes to something that is the absolute opposite of nostalgia: the forward-looking, fast-turnover world of UK club and rave culture, where disc jockeys (non-musicians who entertain audiences using recordings) enjoy greater status than the musicians who actually make the records they spin. In its early days, UK club culture was oriented around that week's batch of import tracks from America. Later, as domestic production outstripped the original home towns for house and techno – Chicago and Detroit – the dance scene was fuelled by the very latest white-label pre-releases and promos. By the early nineties, UK dance culture was so obsessed with innovation and freshness, ravers were dancing to music that was literally from the future, thanks to the dubplate phenomenon: DJs would press up metal acetate versions of tracks, either ones they'd made themselves or had been given by producers, and play them in their sets. These dubplate anthems would not get released to the general public as proper vinyl singles for another six months or even a year.

In its early years, 1988 to 1993, rave was like a flash flood-engorged river bursting its banks and scattering off foaming side-streams in a dozen directions. The era's sense of runaway momentum was stoked by the energy flash of Ecstasy and amphetamine. By the mid-nineties, though, rave's engine of drug/music synergy was sputtering; the participants had hurtled down the road of excess at top speed only to crash into various aesthetic and spiritual dead ends. Once so future-focused, ravers began to look back wistfully.

Like everyone else who got swept up in the collective rush, I never dreamed that the culture would ever slow down, let alone succumb to retrospection. 'Rave nostalgia': the idea would have seemed unthinkable, abominable, a contradiction of everything techno was about. So many of the hardcore rave anthems had titles like 'Living for the Future' or samples that proclaimed 'We Bring You the Future'. But inevitably, all genres reach a midlife crisis, when the early days start looking better than the present. Sure enough, around 1996, you started to hear talk about 'old skool hardcore': veterans waxing wistfully for a golden age of rave *only four years earlier*.

'Old skool' comes from hip hop, but it's spread through pop culture as a shorthand for notions of origins and roots. It's a term used by epigones, scene patriots who believe that the present is less distinguished than the illustrious past. A classic example of old skoolism is the rap group Jurassic 5, whose 2002 hit 'What's Golden' celebrated their allegiance to hip hop's 1987–91 belle époque, which doubled as a rejection of contemporary gangsta rap: 'We're not ballin' or shot callin'/ We take it back to the days of yes y'all-in'/ We holding onto what's golden.' People who venerate 'old skool' often seem to believe that things could be righted if only the ignorant and insufficiently reverent new generation that's emerged would let itself be schooled by wiser elders.

The old-skool mindset – curatorial, pedantic, pedagogic – is about as far as you could get from the heedless spirit of rave, which was all about being oblivious to History. Having been swept up in the early-nineties hardcore madness, I responded to the emergence of 'old-skool hardcore', initially as a collector's market for the old music and later actually as nostalgia raves, with queasy ambivalence. In principle I despised the development. But I also felt the 'let's go back' impulse tugging at me too. I'd started to collect old hardcore records myself as early as 1994. It became a rampant obsession that was clearly about more than the desire to get hold of music I'd missed at the time. It was as if grabbing hold of the tangible vinyl incarnation of the music could somehow stop time slipping through my fingers, arrest the fading of those magic memories.

In their original heyday of 1990–3, hardcore rave records were at their lowest value ever. A few months after coming out, nobody wanted them: certainly not the outside world, which despised rave as barbaric drug-noise, but not the hardcore kids either, because this was a fast-moving scene and they were only interested in the very latest tunes. 'Oh, that track's *old*,' the sales assistants at specialist stores would say when I'd ask for a record more than a

235

couple of months old. This wasn't because they accepted the outside world's view of the music as disposable trash. It was because hardcore was hurtling forward so fast it discarded its recent past like a rocket jettisoning fuel stages as it leaves the Earth's atmosphere. The idea of 'old skool' was inconceivable in those days; the best was still to come.

When I started scooping up all these old tunes, things heard on pirate radio that I'd never been able even to identify at the time, they were still pretty cheap. A few years later, around 1996, the prices had gone up dramatically thanks to the emergence of a fully fledged collector's market, with mail-order dealers sending out catalogues and cassettes with bursts of tracks to help nostalgic ravers identify their favourite 'mystery tunes'. Certain anthems or hard-to-find gems were fetching what then seemed substantial amounts, up to £15. Today, that's chicken feed: twelve-inch singles that were worthless in 1992 can sell from anywhere between £30 and £200. Specialist traders also sold or swapped vintage DJ mixtapes, video packs of shoddily filmed footage of raves that the promoters originally sold as mementoes, and rave flyers.

Old-skool hardcore was not just a collector phenomenon, though. By the late nineties, it became a genuine time-warp cult, as a circuit of 'Back to 91' and 'Back to 92' raves emerged. Leading promoters from the original rave era such as Fantazia transformed themselves into nostalgia operations, throwing massive events with line-ups of veteran DJs and groups like Ratpack who perform as golden-oldies acts. Fantazia boast that they 'own the largest collection of rave footage in the world', but at the same time advertise themselves with the slogan: 'Do come and join the future. The Future is Fantazia.' There were even pirate-radio stations that transported listeners back to '92 jostling on the FM airwaves with stations playing current post-rave styles like UK garage, drum 'n' bass and dubstep.

The old-skool rave scene eventually ran into the problem that afflicts all retro-based scenes: the finite-ness of the past. Hardcore rave had been a DIY explosion generating thousands and thousands of tunes released in small pressings, along with white-label promos that were in stores for just a few weeks and never saw a proper release. But as with sixties psychedelia and Northern Soul, the true nuggets were excavated quite quickly. 'People who've been collecting for a while are moaning at old-skool events that no one is playing any "undiscovered" anthems,' DJ Twist, a prime mover on the retro-rave scene, told me. 'This partly kicked off the thinking that for the scene to survive we need new music pumped into it. So people are writing new "old" stuff.'

The idea of 'new old' seems absurd, on the face of it. To get the right sound and vibe, you'd have to shun deliberately the superior music-making technology available to modern dance-music producers, just like Lenny Kravitz, with his reproduction antique rock in the style of John Lennon and Hendrix, deliberately used valve amplifiers and other late-sixties recording gear. But there was a logic to the 'new old' development: the next stage in the struggle against Time, a desperate strategy to stretch out the past and make it last a little longer.

While I continued to hunt down the old records, I could never quite take the next step and join the time-warp cult itself. Living in New York helped me here, because retro-rave was a predominantly UK phenomenon. Then temptation came in the autumn of 2002, when DB – a British expatriate DJ who'd played a big role in starting the East Coast rave scene – started an old-skool event called Sorted. This event was essentially a reunion for people who'd attended NASA – not the space-flight agency but DB's pioneering New York hardcore club of the early nineties. I was pushing forty then, but most of the Sorted attendees were still young, in their late twenties and early thirties, succumbing to nostalgia for their teenage adventures.

Two years later, DB threw NASA Rewind at the original venue

in Tribeca that hosted the club in 1992–3. Punningly linking retro with the jungle tradition of rewinds (DJs spinning tunes back to the start in response to audience clamour), the name NASA Rewind asserted that the early nineties were back *by popular demand*. And indeed the party was jammed. Surprise guest Moby – originally a rave-scene hero for his 'Go' anthem but now a multimillion-selling purveyor of sample-based mood music – played a glorious set that made up for the non-appearance of scheduled artists Kicks Like a Mule, famous for their cheeky comedy rave smash of 1992, 'The Bouncer'. But then again what could be more realistically retro-rave than a no-show, the failure of the flyer to live up to its extravagant promises? Another authentic period touch was the massive queue outside the venue, owing to a messed-up guest-list system.

Once you finally got inside the venue, NASA Rewind was a fantastic party, full of hands-in-the-air fervour. But like the earlier Sorted events, it showed how old skool falsified the past. The quality of the music was *way better* than at any rave I'd been to back in the day. This salutary illusion was created by the cherry-picking approach of old-skool DJs. During rave's early-nineties heyday, DJs played the very latest tunes. Eighty per cent of their sets consisted of white-label tracks in the shops that week; inevitably, a high proportion of that crop would be filler, not killer. Old-skool DJs weeded out all that run-of-the-mix stuff and played the crème de la crème from across the three-year, 1991–3 span of hardcore. The resulting wall-to-wall exhilaration makes an old-skool rave unfaithful to the very thing with which it's keeping faith.

The historical focus of old skool has gradually inched its way up through the nineties and into the early 2000s, with Back to '94 (jungle), Back to '97 (UK garage) and Back to '99 (2step) events, and even the odd event dedicated to the early days of dubstep. You can see similar revivals of earlier sounds throughout dance culture (like acid house, which has returned umpteen times). All this reverent retrospection from a culture once so uncontrollably innovative used to puzzle me. Then I realised: it's *just like me*. I've often decried nostalgia but I'm also highly susceptible to that emotion. I can remember being five and looking back wistfully to how great things were when I was four. Perhaps rave's succumbing so quickly to retro is actually somehow integral to its future-mania, with both being different facets of an acute sense of temporality, two sides of the same coin.

Nostalgia gets a bad rap, but it can be creative, even subversive. The fact is, certain periods in the life of an individual or a culture are more intense, exciting . . . simply *better* than others; the impulse to go back there may be ultimately counterproductive, but it's perfectly understandable. Nostalgia-driven movements can function as ways of getting through doldrum eras, keeping faith until the next 'up' phase. And as we'll see in the next chapter, the past can be used to critique what's absent in the present.

8

NO FUTURE

Punk's Reactionary Roots and Retro Aftermath

There is a paradox right at the heart of punk: this most revolutionary movement in rock history was actually born from reactionary impulses. Punk opposed itself to progress. Musically, it rejected the sixties idea of progression and maturity that had led to prog rock and to other sophisticated seventies sounds. A concerted effort to turn back the clock to rock's teenage past, to fifties rock'n'roll and sixties garage, punk rock also rejected the notion of progress in a broader philosophical sense. Driven by an apocalyptic appetite for destruction and collapse, its vision was literally hope-less. Hence the vindictive glee with which Johnny Rotten promised 'no future' in 'God Save the Queen'.

Punk is usually seen as a bolt from the blue, an eruption of rage that was also a rupture abruptly dividing past from present. But when you delve into punk's prehistory, it becomes clear that punk was a long time a-comin'. Finally achieving lift-off after a drawn-out process of damp squibs and false starts that dragged on for *a good seven years*, punk really ought not to have been a big shock.

How something so incremental and rehearsed became a Year Zero Event is hard to reconstruct in hindsight. That punk then snowballed into a genuinely transformative, world-historical force is even more puzzling. Because when you look at the cast of prime movers who laid down the intellectual and infrastructural groundwork for punk – embittered rock critics and nostalgic fanzine editors, obsessive garage-punk compilers and professional reissuers, dusty-fingered record collectors and discographers, second-hand vinyl dealers and vintage-clothing retailers – well, it doesn't look particularly promising. This bunch seem less likely to start a revolution than to launch a magazine called *Mojo*.

One of the most important of these collector-historian types, Greg Shaw, actually *did* co-found a magazine called *Mojo*. Launched in late 1966, the San Francisco-based *Mojo Navigator Rock and Roll News* – to give it its full title – focused largely on the acid rock of the day and featured early interviews with bands like The Doors and The Grateful Dead. But by 1970, Shaw switched to publishing an overtly backward-looking periodical, *Who Put the Bomp!*, that he filled with wistful paeans to the mid-sixties British Invasion groups and American garage bands like The Standells. Alongside *CREEM* magazine, *Bomp!* would be the major spawning ground for punk ideology: Shaw gave swathes of space for Lester Bangs to write seminal, super-influential pieces like the 1971 diatribe/manifesto 'James Taylor Marked for Death'. At a time when *Rolling Stone* was championing singer-songwriters and Laurel Canyon-style country rock, and various forms of heavy rock, progressive music and jazz-rock fusion were getting critical acclaim elsewhere, *Bomp!*'s gospel of raw primitivism and perpetual teenagerdom was more or less heresy.

The word 'rock'n'roll' itself became a rallying cry for all those discontented with the direction music was heading in at the start of the seventies. Historically, rock'n'roll preceded 'rock'. To affirm the earlier term and all its juvenile associations was a renegade stance, because it meant you were rejecting the self-important artiness and self-conscious adultness of post-*Sgt Pepper's* music. *CREEM*, founded in 1969, dubbed itself 'America's Only Rock'n'Roll Magazine' (a jibe at *Rolling Stone*). *Who Put the Bomp!*'s slogan was 'rock & roll, all rock & roll, and nothing but rock & roll'. But where *CREEM*, as a nationally distributed publication competing with *Rolling Stone*, covered contemporary, commercially successful manifestations of the 'true' rock'n'roll spirit of vulgarity and aggression (Alice Cooper, Black Sabbath, heavy metal and glitter bands), *Bomp!*'s outlook was almost entirely retrospective. As Mick Farren put it in an essay for the anthology *Bomp! Saving the World One Record at a Time*, Shaw and his acolytes were 'plainly flying the flag for what seemed to be an age that had passed'.

'Revisionist rock history' was *Bomp!*'s primary activity during its first five years. Shaw's hope in those days, he later recalled, was to reach 'rock fans who shared my own taste for oldies, distaste for the contemporary scene, and hopes for something better someday'. This was a Dark Ages scenario: Shaw and acolytes as equivalents to the monks of Lindisfarne. Shaw also got directly involved in custodianship of the past, compiling deluxe anthologies of rock'n'roll, surf music and mid-sixties British beat for United Artists and Sire. Gradually, he grew more optimistic about the prospect of actually 'getting back to where we started', envisioning the creation by fans of an alternative economy to the mainstream music industry: indie labels and fanzines.

Keeping Shaw's spirits elevated all through this pre-punk lull was *Bomp!*'s mascot band, The Flamin' Groovies. Active in the present but defiantly non-contemporary, they were the embodiment of the alternate rock history that *Bomp!* wishfully proposed: a world where *Sgt Pepper's* never happened. The Groovies started out in the mid-sixties as The Chosen Few, an honest-to-goodness high-school garage band. But where most garage groups followed the trajectory of the times and went first psychedelic, then heavy, The Flamin' Groovies were a cause célèbre for *Bomp!* because they'd stayed in 1965, sidestepping all the late-sixties folderol of sitars, concept albums and blues jams. Like Shaw's magazine,

The Flamin' Groovies were from San Francisco, but were one of the few Fillmore Ballroom bands not scooped up in the major-label frenzy for Bay Area acid rock. Instead they started their own label, and in 1968 released *Sneakers*, a ten-inch mini-LP recorded in lagging-behind-the-times mono. Albums like *Flamingo* and *Teenage Head* followed on proper labels, but their mix of early-Stones and fifties rockabilly pastiches earned them only a cult following of rock critics and Frenchmen (one of whom, Marc Zermati – later to organise the First French Punk Festival – put out their 1973 EP *Grease* on his Skydog label). The Groovies moved to the UK for a period, gigging furiously and hooking up with Welsh rockabilly purist Dave Edmunds, at whose Rockfield Studios they recorded songs like 'You Tore Me Down'. This would be the debut single release for Greg Shaw's Bomp! label.

VIVE LE ROCK!

The idea of bringing back good old rock'n'roll was in the UK air during 1972–3, with a spate of rockabilly revivalist groups and a full-blown Teddy Boy revival. I recall seeing as a nine-year-old these outlandish figures mooching down the High Street of my home town: young men with Brylcreemed hair, drape jackets and brothel creepers, and now and then an original Teddy Boy who'd been stuck in a style time warp since the fifties. Right at the heart of this most reactionary of subcultures was a figure who'd play a crucial role in the punk revolution: Malcolm McLaren. The first clothing boutique he and partner Vivienne Westwood opened, Let It Rock, had a clientele consisting largely of Teddy Boys. McLaren had originally spotted the 430 King's Road premises when it was the Americana-oriented shop Paradise Garage. He persuaded owner Trevor Myles to let him use the back of the store to sell vintage radios and other period-piece ephemera of the sort he and Westwood had been flogging from a Portobello

Market stall. They gradually took over the entire premises. A fan of fifties rock'n'roll, McLaren filled the jukebox with old seven-inch singles by Eddie Cochran and Billy Fury, and decked out the store with vintage accoutrements, such as a pink and black fridge and James Dean posters.

Initially, McLaren and Westwood stocked the store with vintage clothes, which they mended and altered, using dye to brighten the faded colours or adding new velveteen or leopard-skin collars. Soon they were making all-new garments in the Teddy Boy style. Flyers and brochures for the shop bore slogans like 'Teddy Boys for Ever!', 'The Rock-Era Is Our Business' and 'Vive Le Rock'. The store's 'Vive Le Rock' T-shirt was later made famous by Sid Vicious, and the slogan resurfaced as the title of a rockabilly-style single by Adam Ant, a fervent McLaren admirer.

In his memoir *Apathy for the Devil*, legendary *NME* writer Nick Kent recalls McLaren as a 'real fifties purist', 'hopelessly trapped' in that era, and says that McLaren regarded Gene Vincent as the 'ultimate musical reference point, the figure that best summed up his vision of rock as something truly untamed and seditious'. Kent hung out with McLaren quite a bit during the early to mid-seventies (and later briefly belonged to a prototypical version of The Sex Pistols). When he discovered that McLaren had, upon The Beatles' arrival, simply 'turned his back on rock . . . and buried his head in the ground like an ostrich', Kent took it upon himself to hip McLaren to things like Hendrix and The Doors, describing it as 'just like teaching a bloke who'd been living in a cave for ten years about what had transpired during his absence'.

McLaren loathed hippies and saw the flamboyant but tough working-class delinquency of the Teddy Boy revivalists as vastly preferable to the mellow mindset of the longhairs, still a dominant force in London. Championing a subculture associated with violence and vandalism was his attempt to get back at the peace and love generation. Soon, though, he started to get fed up with Teds, whom he found frustratingly thick, narrow-minded, and in some cases, racist. Feeling 'lost in dead tissue', like he was uncomfortably close to the decrepit rag-and-bone men of TV's tragicomic *Steptoe and Son*, McLaren 'wanted something *new*'. Yet his discontent with seventies stasis could at this point still only express itself through the youth rebellions of the pre-Beatles era. He changed Let It Rock's name to Too Fast to Live, Too Young to Die and shifted its orientation to the Rockers, that British sub-culture of leather-clad, motorbike-riding hooligans inspired by the Marlon Brando movie *The Wild Ones*. Only with SEX, the subsequent incarnation of 430 King's Road, did he and Westwood start to come up with fashion ideas never seen before (at least outside the seedy world of specialist-taste porn). And this was also when the boutique started attracting some modern-day renegades rather than fifties retreads, among them future members of The Sex Pistols.

Around the time of the Too Fast to Live/SEX shift, McLaren got a taste for managing an anarchic rock band when he became involved with The New York Dolls. They had been one of a string of glam-era luminaries to visit Let It Rock. The vintage look appealed to a band whose whole shtick was a historically savvy collision of the Stones and The Shangri-Las. Recalling how the Dolls came up with their vampy, gender-bending image, frontman David Johansen declared: 'We were just very ecological about clothes. It was just about taking old clothes and wearing them again.' The music was equally recycled, a mish-mash of Chuck Berry and Bo Diddley, the British Invasion bands and the Spector-style girl groups. One of the Dolls' big anthems, 'Looking for a Kiss', starts with 'You'd best believe I'm in love L-U-V', a direct quote from The Shangri-Las' 'Give Him a Great Big Kiss'. For their second album, *The New York Dolls In: Too Much Too Soon*, they even hired Shadow Morton, The Shangri-Las' producer.

Strip away the flashy image, and the substance of the Dolls' raunchy hard rock was not far from The Faces'. But what gave the Dolls edge and made them prime punk precursors alongside The Stooges was their elevation of pose above proficiency. Drummer Jerry Nolan, who was a fan before he joined the band, told his sceptical buddies: 'You're missing the fucking point. They're bringing back the magic of the fifties!' The songs were short, solo-free, stripped raw and swaggering.

The New York Dolls made their debut British TV appearance playing live in the studio on *The Old Grey Whistle Test*, a BBC programme oriented towards all things progressive and muso. As the camp yet intimidatingly thuggish 'Jet Boy' careened to a halt, presenter Bob Harris dismissed them as 'mock rock', a quip that earned him eternal infamy among the punk generation-to-come, everyone from transfixed teenager Steven Morrissey (soon president of the UK chapter of the Dolls fan club) to future Pistol Steve Jones (who largely based his guitar style on Johnny Thunders's translation of Chuck Berry). At the height of punk rock, Sid Vicious would actually assault the bearded hippy Harris in a pub.

Take away Harris's simpering condescension, though, and his comment was spot on: The New York Dolls *were* rock'n'roll in quotation marks. They'd emerged out of an earlier outfit called Actress, a name that captures their transgender shock value and their theatricality. Like transexual rocker Wayne County (whose bad-taste-drenched shows were the missing link between Alice Cooper and John Waters), the Dolls were a transitional group, bridging the post-Warhol, glitter-and-decadence scene and the punk-rock movement emerging at clubs like CBGB.

Hearing past the crudity and clumsiness of the sound perversely required a refined sensibility, which is why the Dolls became a cause célèbre for New York's rock critics. They were 'one of the first bands . . . the critics felt they owned', recalled Todd Rundgren, producer of the Dolls' debut album. The punters didn't buy the hype, though, and within a few years the Dolls crashed

246

back to Earth in druggy disarray. Malcolm McLaren caught the band on their downward arc but was impressed by their trashy disregard for musicianship, later describing the debut album as 'the worst record I'd ever heard'. He recalled being 'shocked by how bad they were . . . By the fourth or fifth track, I thought they were so, so bad, they were brilliant.' McLaren applied all his energy and imagination towards launching them as an Alice Cooper-style shock-rock sensation, coming up with a subversive image makeover: the Dolls as un-American commies dressing in red patent leather and playing in front of a giant hammer-and-sickle flag. But to no avail.

Leaving the disintegrating Dolls, McLaren returned to England and to SEX, where he started to take an interest in some uncouth youths who hung out at the store and wanted to form a band. By this time – 1975 – a full-blown rebellion against hippiedom and progressive music was already stirring in London in the form of pub rock: a loose coalition of bands, including Brinsley Schwarz, Ducks Deluxe, Chilli Willi and Roogalator, who shared a passion for rhythm-and-blues and rootsy American sounds. As with The Flamin' Groovies, the rockabilly revivalists, and the Dolls, pub rock was very much couched as a return to basics, to how things should be done. The primary motivation was egalitarian, 'a backlash against the big megatours and flashy guitarists of the time', as Brinsley's Bob Andrews put it. In the shabby swelter of crowded taverns like the Tally Ho and the Hope and Anchor, a band was on the same level as the audience, sometimes literally, and at most performing on a small stage a foot or two above the floor. If you stood in the front row you'd get spattered with sweat-drops flicked from the band members and smell the beer on the singer's breath. It was this intimacy, rather than any substantive musical differences, that differentiated the pub-rock groups from sixties rhythm-and-blues-based survivors like The Faces.

Pub rock wasn't really a genre but a hotchpotch of mid-sixties

R&B, fifties rock'n'roll and country rock. But it was a movement, a sort of rival underground to the Underground. That was the name people in those days used to describe the longhair college-gig circuit, where folky blues minstrels like John Martyn and jazzy proggers like Hatfield and the North played to wispy-bearded students, a realm presided over by BBC hippies like John Peel and Bob Harris and covered in magazines like *ZigZag* and *Melody Maker*. Rather than offering something new to define themselves against all those late-sixties ideas turned mouldy, pub rock went back to the early- to mid-sixties sound of white rhythm-and-blues. Pensive drift and cosmic flatus were chucked aside in favour of aggression and brevity; dope and acid were supplanted by alcohol and amphetamines. Distinctly deficient in innovation, the pub-rock bands often played sets largely composed of cover versions. This was 'a reversal of the "progressive" idea', according to Dai Davies, manager of Ducks Deluxe. 'The school of thought [was] that if your own material wasn't brilliant you could do somebody else's song that was.' But even the original material tended to be derivative.

The most impressive pub-rock outfit, and the most influential in terms of preparing the ground for punk, was Dr Feelgood. Hailing from Canvey Island in the Thames estuary, they drew on mid-sixties rhythm-and-blues from America and the toughest of the British beat groups. But the amphetamine-wired energy of the group in performance gave Dr Feelgood a fixated intensity that would inspire everyone from The Jam to Gang of Four. Shuttling back and forth across the stage as if on invisible tracks, guitarist Wilko Johnson's jagged and clangorous rhythm-as-lead style was widely imitated. The group's sharp image, like mods grown slightly old and scary – short hair, tight pants, winkle-pickers, jackets and, for clothes-obsessed singer/harmonica player Lee Brilleaux, a tie – contrasted with both hippiedom and glam.

Relative latecomers to the London pub scene, the Feelgoods

rocketed ahead of their peers. In 1974, they signed to United
Artists and put out their debut, *Down By the Jetty*. The 'dirty
water'-style title evoked Canvey's history as an oil and gas termi-
nal, its landscape of refineries, giant storage tanks and infamous
mile-long but never-actually-used jetty. The album was recorded
in mono, which UA used as a marketing ploy, making out that
the group were striking a stance against the post-*Dark Side of the
Moon* state-of-the-art of forty-eight-track overdubs and stereo-
phonic intricacy. Actually, the group tried to record in stereo, but
it sounded bad so it was redone in mono. More revealing of the
Feelgood essence was their third album, *Stupidity*, which was the
group's commercial breakthrough, hitting no. 1 in October 1976,
just as punk was making music-paper headlines. *Stupidity* was a
live album, and seven of its thirteen tracks were cover versions,
tunes like Bo Diddley's 'I'm a Man' and Rufus Thomas's 'Walking
the Dog'.

Dr Feelgood had to fend off accusations of being throwbacks.
Speaking to *Trouser Press* in 1976, Wilko Johnson complained,
'we get pissed off at people talking about . . . how we're reviving
the '60s. We're not reviving anything. It's now. It was great then,
and it's great now.' Brilleaux chipped in with a testy remark to
the effect that nobody would ever ask a classical orchestra, '"Are
ya still playing that fucking old Beethoven stuff?" Why should
they say the same to us?' Supportive critics danced around the
issue. The *NME*'s Mick Farren described them as 'far from a rock-
revival band', even as he noted that 'their choice of songs comes
mainly from the period 1960–65'.

But pub rock did pave the way for one of punk's genuinely
revolutionary aspects: the reinvention of the independent label.
Stiff Records was co-founded by Jake Riviera, who had organised
the pub-rock package tour Naughty Rhythms in 1975, and the
label's roster largely consisted of graduates of the pub-rock scene
like Ian Dury, Nick Lowe and Elvis Costello. One of the label's

many cheeky slogans was 'Mono Enhanced Stereo'. Chiswick, the other key pub-rock label, was founded by Ted Carroll and Roger Armstrong in 1975 as an offshoot of the record store Rock On and its satellite record stalls in London street markets, all of which specialised in back catalogue and reissues of rockabilly, sixties garage and sixties soul.

Chiswick's third release was 'Keys to Your Heart' by The 101-ers, whose singer, Joe Strummer, would go on to front The Clash. The 101-ers came out of the West London squat underground, but instead of your typical Hawkwind-style space rock they played scrappy, high-energy Americana that mixed originals like 'Letsagetabitarockin'' with Slim Harpo and Chuck Berry covers. Strummer's Damascus moment came when The Sex Pistols supported The 101-ers. Recalling the gig years later, Strummer described the Pistols as 'light years different from us . . . on another planet, in another century'. He characterised 1976 as a historical pivot, a choose-sides moment: 'You were suddenly faced with the present. And the future, and you had to make a decision.' Yet the Pistols' set was as laden with cover versions as The 101-ers', mostly mod-era tunes like The Who's 'Substitute' (which, as it happened, The 101-ers also covered). But something about Rotten's delivery, his presence, heralded the new.

BACKWARDS INTO THE FUTURE

Back in America, the post-Dolls milieu in New York was inching its way towards punk rock. Along with The Ramones, Patti Smith was the key catalyst of the New Thing coalescing at CBGB and Max's Kansas City. One of her most famous sayings is the boast: 'I don't fuck much with the past but I fuck plenty with the future' (a lyric from 'Babelogue'). But the truth is completely the opposite: few rock'n'rollers have been as preoccupied with rock history as Smith. Her debut album, *Horses*, released in November 1975, was the spark that lit punk's blue touch paper. But the paradox of *Horses* is that it gallops into the future backwards, eyes firmly fastened on the past.

Before forming the band, Patti Smith was a poet and rock journalist, while guitarist Lenny Kaye was a rock critic and music archivist. Kaye had pulled together *Nuggets*, the hugely influential 1972 double-LP compilation of American garageland's one-hit wonders (groups like Count Five, The Seeds and Chocolate Watchband). The idea for *Nuggets*, and the comp's name, actually started with Elektra boss Jac Holzman, who'd got hold of an early cassette machine, had been making mix-tapes, and liked the notion of an album that scooped up choice cuts from LPs that only contained one or two morsels of solid gold. Kaye steered the *Nuggets* concept towards one-hit-wonder sixties garage bands, the sound that people like Lester Bangs and Dave Marsh had started calling 'punk rock'. In the sleeve notes, he referred to *Nuggets* as 'a continuing archeological dig into the bizarre splendor of the mid-Sixties'. The compilation's subtitle is '*Original Artyfacts from the First Psychedelic Era 1965–1968*', which means that since *Nuggets* came out in 1972, Kaye's archaeological dig into rock antiquity involves music as recent as *four years* previously.

Nonetheless, at a time when everything in rock was about subtlety, *Nuggets* was a dissident gesture, paralleling the revisionism of *Bomp!* and *CREEM* and the way they deposed the post-*Sgt Pepper's*/Cream virtuosos ('"tasty licks", and all that Traffic twaddle', snarled Bangs) in favour of forgotten garage bands who could barely play. *Nuggets* was a favourite record for many of the bands who would spearhead punk, like Television and Pere Ubu, and many would slip covers of *Nuggets* songs into their live sets.

Fast-forward a couple of years and Kaye is *in* one of these proto-punk bands: The Patti Smith Group. Because we know what happens next in the sequence of rock history, we cannot but hear *Horses* as a herald of the coming convulsion. But if you try to listen to this late-1975 album without thinking about what happened a year later, *Horses* more closely resembles the preceding decade. Kaye himself later admitted, 'Sometimes I think of us as the last of the sixties bands. We liked those long rambling songs, we liked twenty minutes of improvisation. We weren't the Ramones.' He compared The Patti Smith Group to The MC5. 'We had a lot of that revolutionary kick out the jams, motherfucker, fervour.' And Smith would actually end up marrying The MC5's guitarist, Fred 'Sonic' Smith.

The Patti Smith Group's orientation towards the sixties was obvious from the git-go. The group's 1974 debut single, 'Hey Joe', was a garage-band standard, but the cover mainly signified as a tribute to Jimi Hendrix; the track was even recorded at Electric Lady, the New York studio Hendrix had built, although he died before he could use it. *Horses* kicked off with 'Gloria', originally recorded by Van Morrison's first group, Them, but probably the song most widely covered by American garage bands. When 'Gloria' was released as the group's second single, the B-side was The Who's 'My Generation'. That tune was the group's barnstorming set-closer at their shows, climaxing with Smith's battle cry: 'We created it, let's take it over.'

When I interviewed Smith in 2006, she talked about the sense of dispossession she felt in the early seventies, the feeling that rock'n'roll had been taken over by corporations and had degenerated into showbiz. 'It felt like our greatest voices were snuffed out. Dylan had a motorcycle accident and retreated. Joan Baez disappeared. Jimi Hendrix and Jim Morrison were both dead. The new artists coming through were very materialistic and Hollywood, not so engaged in communication. As a citizen, I was very concerned about what was happening to my genre.'

Teeming with invocations and channellings, *Horses* is one long exercise in rock mythography. The gloriously surly swagger of white R&B that was 'Gloria' distilled the entire 'argument' of

Nuggets into a few minutes of rough-hewn excitement. On the second side, three iconographic songs amounted to an attempt to 'work through' the legacy of the sixties. Smith's original ambition as an artist, she told me, was to 'merge poetry with sonicscapes. The two people who contributed so much to that were Jimi Hendrix and Jim Morrison. With *Horses* I really wanted to thank them.' 'Break It Up' is a swashbuckling epic based on Smith's dream about Morrison being literally petrified – turned to stone – through his having become an icon, a monument in the rock pantheon. 'I get out of a car and there's a big clearing, and on this slab in the middle, there's Jim, half-human and half-stone, in chains. And I stand over him and realise: "Oh God, he's half human, he's still alive." And that's when I keep saying, "Break it up, break it up."' Finally, the Lizard King smashes 'through the marble and flies away', his unshackled spirit presumably irrigating and renewing rock like the Fisher King of T. S. Eliot's *The Waste Land*. 'Elegie', the album's closer, is a 'requiem for Jimi Hendrix' recorded on 18 September 1975, the anniversary of his death. And both dead Jims haunt the celebrated song suite 'Land', whose first section, 'Horses', nods to 'Horse Latitudes' (The Doors' pioneering slice of rock-poetry-meets-studio weirdness) and whose closing 'La Mer (de)' pays oblique tribute to Hendrix's oceanic '1983, A Merman I Should Turn to Be'.

Strangely, virtually nobody at the time noticed that *Horses* was in large part all about Smith's Freudian 'family romance' with her sixties fathers. 'I'm shrouded in the lives of my heroes' is how she once put it. *Horses* made her an icon, but she started out as an iconographer, patterning her persona and practising the art of 'presence' through close study of her heroes. 'Patti lived her whole life pretending to be John Lennon . . . or Brian Jones or some other rock star,' claimed her New York contemporary Penny Arcade. '[She] wanted to look like Keith Richards, smoke like Jeanne Moreau, walk like Bob Dylan.'

Smith was a recombinant star of the kind that only became possible when rock became self-reflexive. As such her real peers were figures like David Bowie or Bruce Springsteen. Like Smith, Springsteen was from New Jersey and obsessed with the sixties. His sound was a consolidation of sixties styles that aimed to restore the lost community and confidence of that golden moment. Like Smith, in 1975 he was hyped as the second coming; unlike her, he'd break through big-time with 'Born to Run'. Smith's own mainstream triumph would come in 1978 with a song she and 'the Boss' wrote together, 'Because the Night'.

It's hard to believe now, but at the start of his career Springsteen was often described as a 'punk'. Indeed, in Jon Landau's famous May 1974 live review for Boston's *The Real Paper*, the one that declares 'I saw rock & roll future and its name is Bruce Springsteen,' the writer describes him as 'a rock & roll punk'. In a sympathetic passage from *CREEM*'s 1976 book *Rock Revolution: From Elvis to Elton – The Story of Rock and Roll*, Lester Bangs likewise characterises Broooce as 'the American streetpunk hero in the classical mold we've been waiting for for so long he seems almost corny by now'.

Everybody remembers the 'I saw rock & roll future' line but nobody ever quotes the previous sentence in Landau's review: 'at the Harvard Square Theatre, I saw my rock & roll past flash before my eyes'. Rock's future turns out be a *restoration* – of the music's lost powers (and the reviewer's lost youth). 'I do feel old but the record and my memory of the concert has made me feel a little younger,' wrote Landau. In his *CREEM* appreciation, Bangs concedes that Springsteen 'seems somewhat anachronistic to many – black leather jacket, street-poet, kids-on-the-run, guitar as switchblade – but perhaps the definitive characteristic of all the most vital new rock is that it is not innovative in any avant-garde sense; rather, it's a brilliant rearrangement and reassessment of where we've already been. Which is more than mere nostalgia.

If we're gonna move out of this bog of despair we've known, we're gonna have to know our history well.' Not everyone was convinced by this argument. Reviewing *Born to Run*, Langdon Winner observed that Springsteen 'has gone to the finest pop schools. He respects his elders. He bears the finest credentials and upholds the highest standards. Like all dutiful epigones, he threatens to become the consummate bore . . . [*Born to Run* is] the complete monument to rock and roll orthodoxy.'

Born to Run and *Horses* came out within a few months of each other, towards the end of a year (1975) when rock's narrative seemed to have ground to a halt. We all know now that this was just a pause. But it's interesting to go back and see how Lester Bangs compared Patti Smith not just with Springsteen but with southern rock bands like Lynyrd Skynyrd and Wet Willie: 'What all these artists share is a love and respect for their own rock'n'roll history, a conviction that the power and vitality that made the fifties and sixties such thrilling decades to live through have (musically, at least) not petered out . . .' Bangs's essay was titled 'Rages to Come: Creem's Predictions of Rock's Future', but it was hardly an eve-of-revolution rallying call: 'It's no lament to say that the future lies behind us – the question, crucially, is what we will do with it, where we will take it.'

Other sharp-eyed commentators were equally tentative in their assessment of the energies stirring in downtown New York. James Wolcott's August 1975 *Village Voice* report on the scene at CBGB bore the decidedly non-incendiary headline 'A Conservative Impulse in the New Rock Underground'. Wolcott did describe the venue's three-week festival of unsigned bands as 'perhaps the most important event in New York rock since the Velvet Underground played the Balloon Farm'. But he astutely drew attention to the New York bands' reliance on rock's past. Quoting Pete Towshend's recently made remark that rock'n'roll 'is not really contemporary to these times. It's really the music of yesteryear,' Wolcott came up

255

with only a qualified rebuttal: 'What's changed is the nature of the impulse to create rock. No longer is the impulse revolutionary – i.e. the transformation of oneself and society – but conservative: to carry on the rock tradition . . . The landscape is no longer virginal – markers and tracks have been left by, among others, Elvis, Buddy Holly, Chuck Berry, and the Beatles – and it exists not to be transformed but cultivated.' His final flourish – 'these bands don't have to be a vanguard in order to satisfy' – sounds rather close to settling for less.

This idea of New York punk as a patchwork of what came before was shared by John Holstrom, co-founder and editor of *Punk* magazine, whose debut issue came out on 1 January 1976. 'One of the Punk things was going to the past to pick the right influences out . . . we weren't starting anything new,' he told Jon Savage. *Punk*'s initial spur was a New York group called The Dictators, whose 1975 debut album *Go Girl Crazy* caught the imagination of Holstrom and his partner Legs McNeil because it was the first rock record that seemed to be 'describing our lives', as McNeil put it – lives that apparently consisted of 'McDonald's, beer, and TV reruns . . . comics, grade-B movies'. The Dictators were even more of a critics' group than The New York Dolls had been. In fact, bassist/songwriter Andy Shernoff *was* a critic, writing for *CREEM* and doing his own fanzine, *Teenage Wasteland News*. That was rather close to what Holstrom originally wanted to call the magazine he and McNeil started: *Teenage News*, a title borrowed from an unreleased New York Dolls song.

Before they could get much further than being a critics' pet, The Dictators' thunder was stolen by another teenage-obsessed New York group: The Ramones. Where the Dictators sound was blustery and anthemic in the Who style, The Ramones had a far more tautly focused and original sound: a relentless, pummelling monotony.

The group's very name was evidence of an almost scholarly

passion for sixties music. 'Ramone', adopted by every member of the group as their stage surname, came from the alias 'Paul Ramon' that Paul McCartney used in the earliest days of the Beatles and later when moonlighting on records by The Scaffold. Producer Craig Leon modelled the sound of The Ramones' self-titled 1976 debut on *A Hard Day's Night*, to the point of trying a mono mix. Along with their minimalism, what made them both distinctively seventies and hugely influential was The Ramones' attitude and sensibility: the irony and black humour that led the group, despite being Jewish, to play with Nazi imagery in songs like 'Blitzkrieg Bop' and 'Today Your Love, Tomorrow the World' (whose original title was 'I'm a Nazi, Baby'). Ramones scholar Nick Rombes pinpoints the source in television (particularly cable), 'with all the repetition ("repeats"), irony, and camp that the medium engendered'. WWII films, reruns of sixties series, late-night B-movies all seeped into the group's lyrics. The Ramones' latent retro tendency finally burst free on their fifth album, *End of the Century*: here they teamed up with Phil Spector, covering The Ronettes and writing new songs that were overtly nostalgic, like 'Do You Remember Rock'n'Roll Radio?'.

For all their indebtedness and orientation towards the fifties and sixties, the debut albums by The Ramones and Patti Smith, which were released within a few months of each other on the cusp between 1975 and 1976, created a giant fissure in rock history: punk. Smith herself says she always saw *Horses* as being 'more concerned about the future than the past'. But she adds that 'our mission was to make space for the new guard. And the new guard came rather quickly, and when they came, me and my people were almost instantly obsolete. Because I'm fairly rooted in history. We sort of went this way, and the new bands went that way.'

Punk started out as the ultimate time-warp cult, but what was intended as a restoration escalated, almost inadvertently, into a revolution. How did such a diverse range of 'futures' emerge out a movement born out of largely reactionary impulses? Somewhere in the transition from New York to Britain (as well as to other cities in the US, like San Francisco and Los Angeles) other factors came into play. Unexpected disaffections and ambitions attached themselves to the word 'punk', creating a runaway momentum that propelled the movement far beyond what people like Greg Shaw and Lester Bangs, the Dolls and The Ramones ever envisioned. Musical influences from outside rock'n'roll, as well as non-musical catalysts from the worlds of politics, art theory and avant-garde fashion, entered the picture. Everything came together in a surge of energy, and then, Big Bang-like, exploded outwards into new galaxies of sound and subculture.

Arguably, the non-sonic aspects of punk were more crucial in terms of generating all these 'futures' than the music itself, which was just a stripped-down, intensely focused form of the hard rock that runs through the first half of the seventies. Patti Smith's image – androgynous, aloof, super-cool – was probably more influential than her music or her Beat poet-like lyrics, inspiring an influx of feminist ideas and feminist musicians (of both genders). Likewise, Johnny Rotten's attitude, persona and taste (he didn't like rock'n'roll or sixties music in general, but loved reggae and Krautrock) opened up more possibilities than the Sex Pistols sound, as powerful as it was. The Clash introduced into rock a new kind of political content and social realism. McLaren threw in Situationist ideas, while his disdain for musicality spawned the idea of incompetence as a virtue and thereby contributed to the explosion of do-it-yourself culture. Elsewhere, the very shortfall between the rhetoric surrounding punk and the vigorous but ultimately conventional substance of the sound inspired the hunger for genuine musical extremism, which spiralled off into directions like No Wave and Industrial.

'Punk' started out as a brief moment of unity and then became a contested term, something people have been fighting over ever since. One of the crucial splits was between post-punk's experimentalism and 'real punk' (also known as Oi!), which stuck with the first-Clash-album idea of punk as the sound of working-class anger. But there was another major division: between those who saw punk as a fresh start for rock and those who saw it as a return to the past.

GARAGELAND

Prominent among those turned off by the politicised and arty–experimental directions that had come out of punk was *Bomp!*'s Greg Shaw. In the November 1977 issue he'd patted himself on the back for his role in paving the way for the revolution: 'None of this just *happened* . . .' But the pride soon faded as punk turned out not to be the kind of uncomplicated teenage fun whose resurrection he had evangelised for all those years (eight, by his counting). So in early 1978, he switched to Plan B, the idea of a 'pop revival'.

Shaw had been kicking the idea around for several years, and it was very much part of *Bomp!*'s rewriting of rock history. He argued that 1967 and *Sgt Pepper's* had created a fatal split between rock and pop, leading to a schism between FM radio-oriented underground rock, 'built on eclecticism, extended pieces, long jams – in short, abandonment of form and structure', and AM radio pop, which had lost all its rock energy and become saccharine. When Shaw first started talking about a pop-that-rocks renaissance, there wasn't much in America to base it on, apart from Cleveland, Ohio's hooky-but-punchy The Raspberries. The tumult of 1977, though, had spawned a legion of New Wave groups with short songs and short hair, but who also liked melody and weren't really into the confrontational, extremist aspects of punk: UK bands like The Boys and Generation X, plus American

259

outfits such as 20/20, The Pop, The Nerves and The Sneakers. Shaw christened the movement 'power pop', a phrase he found in a 1967 Pete Townshend interview that seemed to express his ideal of 'explosive energy within a pure pop structure'.

The idea was picked up in the UK, where the Sex Pistols split had left something of a vacuum and some people were already wondering whether punk was dead and what was going to come next. *Sounds* journalist Chas de Walley was power pop's big champion, corralling under its banner not just the groups Shaw had extolled but a motley array of New Wave bands (XTC, Squeeze, The Rezillos, Blondie), ex-pub-rock artists (Nick Lowe, Wreckless Eric) and a clutch of English combos who were overtly revivalist: the so-called Thamesbeat scene of The Pleasers, The Stukas, The Boyfriend and The Look. A pun on Merseybeat, the tag was inspired by the way these groups wore matching suits and sang sub-Lennon/McCartney choruses that recalled the likes of Freddie & the Dreamers.

The hype fizzled out fast in Britain (most critics despised it as toothless, backwards-looking, apolitical). In America, though, power pop briefly was the Next Big Thing. Suit-and-skinny-tie creeps The Knack reached no. 1 with 1979's 'My Sharona', a hideously catchy song about lusting after teenage jailbait propelled by pelvic-jutting riffs. Greg Shaw's concept reverberated for years to come, with *Billboard* success for catchy, sixties-redolent New Wavers like The Romantics, The Go-Gos and The Bangles. But although *Bomp!* tried to get in on this chart action by putting out The Plimsouls' single 'A Million Miles Away' on their eponymous record label, Shaw's disenchantment was deepening. And it was *Bomp!*'s old mascot band The Flamin' Groovies that showed him the way forward, which turned out to be the way backward.

In the early seventies, the Groovies hadn't been retro so much as they'd just trailed behind the times. But in 1976, returning to the scene after a hiatus with a brand-new LP, *Shake Some Action*,

The Flamin' Groovies had remodelled themselves as a revival act. They not only sounded like a time warp, they now looked like one too, wearing Cuban heels and velvet-collared three-piece suits made by a tailor in London. 'You can't find tailors who can capture that style and spirit in America,' guitarist Cyril Jordan told *ZigZag*. 'We just wanted to get back to the flash of that era, which were the best years, as far as I'm concerned.' The front cover of *Shake Some Action* deliberately imitated the underexposed, murky menace of the photographs on the early Stones albums. Today it's a perfectly commonplace thing to mimic the graphic design of earlier eras, but in 1976 this was a striking move. For the first and only time, The Flamin' Groovies were ahead of their time – by being so overtly, meticulously behind it.

Shake Some Action was a massive record in the *Bomp!* milieu. No matter that the group's next album, 1978's ironically titled *Now*, sounded sapped of inspiration (original songs were outnumbered by eight covers); the Groovies had shown that turning your back on the present could be a heroic repudiation of contemporary music. Sharing the sentiments of the Groovies ditty 'Take Me Back' ('Take me back to times when I was young/ So much fun that we had'), Greg Shaw soon decided that words weren't enough any more; it was time for action. He folded the magazine *Bomp!* and injected all his energy into Voxx, a Bomp! subsidiary label dedicated to the new breed of post-Groovies garage bands.

Shaw's first signing was The Crawdaddys, a San Diego group so obsessed with sixties Brit combos like The Pretty Things and The Downliners Sect that their mono-recorded debut was 'virtually indistinguishable from the real thing'. That's the verdict of Mike Stax, who joined the band after hearing the record and would later launch the long-running retro-zine *Ugly Things*. Stax freely conceded that The Crawdaddys weren't 'original in any shape or form', but their music's 'total purity was thrilling in its audacity'.

Total purity became the watchword of this scene. Groups like The Chesterfield Kings went to incredible pains to get period-precise hairstyles, clothes, shoes, instruments, fuzzboxes and amplifiers. Fans dressed the part too. They clustered inside Los Angeles's Cavern Club, a time-warp enclave established by Shaw on Hollywood Boulevard in 1985. Thanks to Shaw's efforts, Los Angeles for a while had the biggest garage-punk revival scene in the world. But retro-punk was also popping up on the East Coast, where The Fleshtones were almost as crucial as The Flamin' Groovies in spreading the garage gospel. In 1983, seven years after the band formed, singer and tambourine basher Peter Zaremba could plausibly assert that The Fleshtones were 'one of the most influential bands of our time', even though the group was a complete throwback and non-original in every respect.

In the after-punk vacuum at the end of the seventies and early years of the eighties, revivals of every kind sprang up: ska, rockabilly, sixties soul, psychedelia, the country/punk hybrid known as 'cowpunk', and more. This retreat to established forms was in part an expression of innovation fatigue, a flight from the more forbiddingly experimental directions explored by post-punk groups. But there was also a kind of utopian impulse motivating the retro-ists. The future or unknown that the post-punk vanguard reached for was necessarily abstract, as well as harsh on the ear. Looking back to a bygone golden age was a more achievable form of utopianism because there were concrete things to fixate on: a quiff, the shape of a car's tailfin, the cut of a suit. This paradise of style and perfection had once existed, and it left behind sacred relics in the form of actual artifacts or iconic images stored in the archive of popular culture.

The avant-garde and the 'retro-garde' (Elizabeth Guffey's term) actually shared a similar temperament: absolutist, fanatical, questing. Motivated by a disatisfaction with the present, they both pursued the impossible, mirages destined always to recede from their grasp: further into the future, deeper into the past. Just as the avant-gardist has to push towards new extremes, the retro-gardist must always hunt holy grails secreted in ever more remote recesses of antiquity. This shared quest for an elsewhere/elsewhen explains why some people could jump so easily between avant and retro modes, or even operate in both zones simultaneously. Arto Lindsay, for instance, led the supremely fractured and atonal No Wave trio DNA but also played in the retro-styled 'fake jazz' outfit The Lounge Lizards, while Lydia Lunch oscillated between abrasive primitivism (Teenage Jesus and the Jerks, Beirut Slump) and more accessible period-styled phases (cabaret on the solo record *Queen of Siam*, swamp rock in the band 8-Eyed Spy).

I can testify to the competing appeal of the avant- and retro-garde options, having gone through a period of being obsessed with sixties garage punk. In the early eighties, when the energy of post-punk had faded, there was a lull during which contemporary pickings were slim and some of the only exciting stuff around was a flood of compilations documenting sixties garage. The entry point for me, as for so many, was the first few volumes of *Pebbles*, the leading compilation series, which originally launched in 1978 and was, I discovered only recently, the anonymous handiwork of Greg Shaw. As the title – a play on *Nuggets* – suggests, the focus of *Pebbles* was the garage groups too obscure for Lenny Kaye: the no-hit wonders of mid-sixties America, bands who'd put out one or two singles on regional labels and then disappeared. By the early eighties, there was a flood of *Pebbles* imitators, compilation series with names like *Boulders* (get it?) and *Mindrocker*.

Vinyl was the sole source for the music on these anthologies, either because the group had lost the original master tapes or, more likely, the compilation was put together without notifying the band (who were in many cases impossible to find anyway). As a result, what you heard usually reproduced the surface noise of well-worn, often poorly treated vinyl: pops, crackles, and now and then a scratch (like the skidding jolt that breaches The Litter's 'Action Woman' as it appeared on *Pebbles* #1). These sixties obscurities weren't exactly hi-fi recordings in the first place, having often been captured in one or two live takes in a cheap local studio. But the energy that burned through was electrifying, from the paranoid delirium tremens of 'Talk Talk' by The Music Machine to the sensual inferno of fuzztone that is 'You Burn Me Up and Down' by We the People.

I never graduated to the next three levels of garage-punk fanaticism: hunting down the original ultra-rare singles; following the revival bands that sprang up in the wake of The Flamin' Groovies and *Pebbles*; forming my own retro-garage band. Ultimately, as immortal as the greatest garage-punk music was, it couldn't distract me from the present for too long. But a lot of people did dedicate their whole lives to living in this particular past. In 2009, I took the train to Brooklyn to meet one of them, Tim Warren, the owner of Crypt Records, a specialist garage record store and reissue label, and the man behind the legendary compilation series *Back from the Grave*.

Warren and I chat in the stock room of his record store, located in a grim stretch of Manhattan Avenue in Brooklyn that's directly opposite an intimidating-looking housing project. The stock room doubles as his living quarters and the workplace for one of his main money-spinning activities: 'de-noising' compilations and albums for other reissue labels. Or at least it would be a money-spinner if he wasn't such a perfectionist, working a ninety-hour week. There's a bunch of computers that he uses for digitally removing the crackles and pops, and a Linn turntable with a $2,000 stylus for mastering his own compilations, an audiophile obsession that strikes me as incongruous given how raw and cheaply recorded the garage-punk singles were. Warren tells me that he's going to be winding up the Brooklyn store very soon and moving his business (the label, the de-noising, the record retail) lock, stock and barrel to Germany, where the garage-punk scene is stronger than in America. He already operates one satellite store in Hamburg and is in the process of purchasing a new one in Berlin to serve as Crypt's operational base

Although the Brooklyn store has no kitchen (Warren cooks on a hotplate) or bath (he showers by pouring water over himself while standing in a large plastic trough), the bedroom/office is homey and characterful, with vintage lamps and framed B-movie and pulp-novel posters covering every inch of the wall. A gigantic poster for the rat poison Warfarin makes me jittery, but it's just another period piece in a frame. Wearing sunglasses despite the indoors murk and chain-smoking Camels, Warren reminisces about the early golden days of the garage-punk retro scene.

'It all started with *Pebbles*,' he says. 'Greg Shaw changed my life. The guy changed a *lot* of people's lives.' Warren had previously been into Ramones-style punk, but once he heard the sixties garage bands he completely lost interest in the present-day music scene. He started collecting the original records, having been hipped to the existence of an oddball called Fieldler – a New Jersey dentist by day who mailed out sale lists of obscure garage 45s going for about $5–10 (a lot of money in 1980) and who would hold auctions for the rarest, most sought-after ones. 'A huge record in those days was $45. There's records I bought then for twenty bucks which I sold many years later for four grand.' The market for rare originals just keeps escalating: recently an Australian collector paid $7,500 for one single, while Warren himself sold a hundred of his best punk singles to raise a few hundred thousand dollars to buy a house. The remainder of his collection he describes as 'my retirement plan, basically'.

The eighties garage-collector scene was an incestuous milieu, and Warren soon got to know just about everybody involved. Some became lifelong friends and allies; others became bitter rivals and thorns-in-the-side. Like all obsessive collector subcultures, it had its fair share of weirdos, rip-off merchants and congenital liars. Some of these legendary collectors, like Monoman of Boston's The Lyres, started garage revival bands. Others, like Warren, were content to launch compilation series. This not only spread the garage gospel but served to ratchet up the market value of the original singles they owned.

The first volume of *Back from the Grave* came out in August 1983. Warren decided to specialise in really hopelessly obscure bands, explaining that he loved not just the 'frustration, the energy level, the naivety' but also the pathos. One of his touchstone garage singles is Ty Wagner & the Scotchmen's 'I'm a No-Count', 'no-count' meaning 'of no account': someone who'll never amount to anything, a worthless, low-class nonentity, a 'punk' in its original meaning. If garage punk is in essence 'loser music', the *Back from the Grave* bands were the super-losers. 'Most of these groups only put out maybe one record. Like this band The Chancellors, who did a song called "On Tour" but probably never went further than fifteen miles out of upstate New York. It's like these dreams that never came to any fruition . . . It's beautiful. Those big fucking doofuses at the local sports bar having successful lives and driving successful cars, they listen to Phil Collins . . . But me, I'll listen to a group like The Kegs and it makes me feel like a winner.'

Unlike some other garage series, *Back from the Grave* drew a firm line at psychedelia. 'It goes horribly wrong with *Sgt Pepper*,' Warren chuckles. 'You know, flugelhorns *are not rock'n'roll*. I got stricter and stricter. The record had to be stripped down, just this *wail*. Musically, I became a fascist.'

After doing the first few *Back from the Grave*s with completely made-up liner notes about the original bands, Warren decided to actually find out the truth. Every three months or so he'd go on the road, driving all across America to the towns where these bands were from, knocking on doors. A music-industry lawyer tipped him off about the Library of Congress, and several times a year he'd go down there with a big stack of garage-punk singles and rifle through the file cards from 1958–72 for any unusual performer or writer name that appeared on a record label or sleeve. Then he'd go across the street and look through vintage editions of the *Yellow Pages*. 'I'd be racking up a tab of $400 a month on the phone bill doing things like call up every Ed Stritt in the state of Indiana.' Often the former garage punkster assumed the call was a prank and hung up on Warren. 'So I'd retrace through Directory Assistance, get the guy's address and mail out a royalty cheque, a contract and an interview questionnaire. The money was a way to get their attention. A week later I'd try phoning again.'

STUCK IN THE PAST

Like most fiends for a period of music, Tim Warren is an enthusiast rather than a theorist: the superiority of garage over all other forms of music is self-evident, something hardly worth arguing about. But revivalism does have a great ideologist in the form of Billy Childish, Britain's leading exponent of retro-punk and probably the biggest single influence on the second wave of garage revivalism that crossed over into the mainstream in the early 2000s with bands like The White Stripes and The Hives.

Across a vast discography that ranges from solo records and collaborations to the series of groups that serve as his main outlet (Thee Milkshakes, Thee Mighty Caesars, Thee Headcoats, The Buff Medways et al.), for three decades now Childish has mined a restricted seam of sound in the space between Link Wray, the Cavern/Hamburg-era Beatles and British beat bands like The Downliners Sect. Unlike many of the neo-garage bands who were his peers in the early days and whose releases were compromised by eighties studio sound, Childish quickly realised that to get the feel of the music right you had to work with the same limited

267

technology that the groups who inspired him used. But what really distinguished him from his peers then and now was that he developed a rationale for retrogression. Moreover, Childish's theories cut across and justify all his artistic activity – in addition to playing live and making records he is a prolific painter, poet and film-maker – to the point where it amounts to a full-blown philosophy of how life should be lived. When I came across Childish statements like 'originality is over-rated in our society. Originality usually means gimmick', I knew I'd have to speak to him.

Predictably, Childish recoils from the word 'retro' and denies that nostalgia is one of his motivations. Still, right from the start, in his first band The Pop Rivets, there were songs like 'Beatle Boots', a frantic toe-tapper about how he was a man-out-of-time in Merseybeat-era clothes: 'I know you'll say/ That I'm living in the past/ But those Beatles boots/ They were made to last.' The song ends with a medley of quoted riffs from early Fab Four tunes. Recorded in 1977, the tune was both autobiographical and (in hindsight) a mission statement. 'I stopped listening to music when it stopped being a vital force,' Childish told me. 'I followed The Beatles when I was about three. Didn't really like music in the seventies, so I listened to rock'n'roll, Buddy Holly and things like that. Then in 1976 punk came around and I thought, "This is exactly like the music I like." But then in 1977 I stopped liking punk, and I've not been into music much since then. I preferred punk when it was a minority thing, bands playing in small rooms on the same level as you. But it got to be about large concerts again.'

Along with these egalitarian principles, the main thing that Childish took from punk rock was do-it-yourself. Fixated on the process not the product, Childish makes the kind of music he does in part because it's the music he's *capable* of doing. For him, the point is to free up the creative process, to do it quick, whether it's recording an album in a few days or painting a picture 'in fifteen minutes, maybe twenty, sometimes three-quarters of an hour'. This anti-perfectionism enabled a three-decades-long torrent of expression bearing the signature 'Billy Childish': forty poetry collections, over one hundred albums, nearly three thousand paintings, plus numerous Super-8 films and a stream of novels, manifestos and other writings. All this restless productivity has a variety of motives and purposes, but at least partially fuelling it is a cathartic and therapeutic impulse related to the childhood and adolescent traumas Childish sometimes addressed in his songs.

For Childish, the essence of rock'n'roll is live performance, so the job of recording is to capture that as much as possible. 'If you listen to the guitar solo in The Kinks' "You Really Got Me", it sounds like it's going to fall apart. It might go wrong. It's alive and vital and uncontrolled and unbridled. It's got a huge amount of humanity and spirit in it. As did a lot of early rock'n'roll, a lot of early blues, a lot of early punk rock.' For Billy, The Beatles' *Live! at the Star-Club in Hamburg, Germany; 1962* is a touchstone. 'John Lennon said the best music The Beatles ever did was before they recorded. Which shows that John Lennon, no matter how stupid he was, understood something: the elemental energy. It was all downhill once they turned into a recording group.' The whole history of rock that involves the art of phonography – overdubs, multitracking, effects, all pioneered by The Beatles themselves from *Rubber Soul* onwards – means *nothing* to Childish.

By the time Billy's second group, Thee Milkshakes, started getting attention with records like *14 Rhythm and Beat Greats* and *Thee Knights of Trashe*, he was formulating an aesthetic similar to pub rock but more fanatically focused on using antiquated recording methods and avoidance of virtuosity. In a 1983 *Sounds* piece about the London neo-garage scene, which included bands like The Prisoners, The Cannibals and The Stingrays and was centred around a Brixton club called The Garage, Childish talked of recording a Milkshakes album in sixteen hours and deliberately simplifying their music. 'The Kinks have three chords, we try to keep ours down to two . . . I think our chords are A and D . . . Is that what they are? I don't know what they're called.' He also admitted that 'we listen to records purposefully adapting songs which already exist', and said Thee Milkshakes were investigating 'early recording techniques with the valve sound'. This approach to recording – using antiquated equipment that has analogue 'warmth' not digital clarity, opting for mono over stereo, recording live in the studio with minimal overdubs or postproduction – has subsequently become hugely influential and widely adopted. As Childish notes wryly, 'Huge amounts of money are being spent trying to get modern equivalents of all the old gear, like valve mixing desks and valve microphones and valve limiters, that studios had gotten rid of. People pay a fortune to get hold of the few originals that are left, or they buy the retro replacements, which have become an entire industry.'

When I suggested that there was some fetishising at work in this approach, Childish demurred. 'New' does not necessarily equal 'better', he insisted. 'I like trams because they're electric and it's a public-transport system. It shows that Victorians were slightly more advanced than us. It's not "retro". It was very easy for recordings to sound good in the fifties and sixties, and that's because it didn't require discipline: the discipline was given to you by the limitations of the material or the technology. But what happened next is that people decided those limitations were a problem rather than the *life*. Nowadays, to have any sensible life, you have to artificially impose limitations. Otherwise you have limitlessness, and limitlessness is the opposite of freedom. So the best thing to do is have your own absolute discipline.' Childish applies this Zen-like spiritual regime of reduction to everything he does, from cooking eggs in an iron frying pan to the materials he uses in his art.

'They call what we do lo-fi. I'm supposed to have bought into all of that because I've released albums that were recorded onto cassette. But that's just ignorance, like saying I'm a caveman because I do drawings using charcoal. What I do is embrace the limitation, because the limitation is my freedom, and I know that charcoal is the best thing for drawing, because the charcoal *loves to draw*.' Childish argues that 'it's always essential to stay with the primal, the thing closest to the ground. I would say I am totally original, because all I'm interested in is the Origin.'

The *New York Times* dubbed Childish 'the undisputed king of garage rock', which amused him because he doesn't actually like the American sixties punk sound, let alone the latter-day garage revivalists. Still, it's true that he's a real hero to the swarm of retro-styled rock'n'rollers who bubbled underground all through the late eighties and into the nineties on labels like Estrus and Sympathy for the Record Industry, then unexpectedly burst into the mainstream at the turn of the new millennium. All seemed to have short, sharp-sounding names starting with 'The' and often

---

THE EIGHTIES' ENDLESS SIXTIES REVIVAL

The *Pebbles*-meets-Kinks scene that Billy Childish and Thee Milkshakes helped create wasn't the only sixties action going on in Britain at the time. The eighties had started with the buzz about Liverpool's neo-psychedelic groups The Teardrop Explodes and Echo & the Bunnymen. By 1982, there was another buzz about a completely separate scene based in London and calling itself the New Psychedelia. Where the Liverpudlians had worshipped mostly American groups (The Doors, The Seeds, Love, etc.), the London revival was besotted with the 'splash of colour' optimism of Carnaby Street circa 1967. Foppishly dressed groups like Mood Six, Shelle Dolance & the Amazing Sherbert Exposure and Marble Staircase gathered at Soho club The Clinic. Here the DJ called himself The Doctor and also fronted his own band, Doctor and the Medics, later to score a huge UK hit with a campy cover of Norman Greenbaum's 'Spirit in the Sky'.

Not aligned with any particular scene, The Television Personalities were just as infatuated with the English sixties, putting out singles like 'Smashing Time' (named after the classic Swinging Sixties movie) and 'I Know Where Syd Barrett Lives' and sticking a photograph of The Avengers on the cover of their

connoting some kind of pain, irritation or abrasion: The Strokes, The Hives, The Hotwires, The White Stripes, The Vines, The Beatings. 'We used to collectively call them The Strives,' laughs Childish. 'Because it sounds like all their names combined into one. Also because they're all wannabes, striving to be authentic.'

The most Billy-besotted of the wannabes was Jack White of The White Stripes. He asked Childish to appear with the band on *Top of the Pops* and paint a picture in the background; when Childish politely declined, White appeared on TV with 'Billy Childish' written in big letters on his arm. White was so infatuated with Childish that he did some recording at the same vintage-equipped Toerag studio where Childish made his records, and which quite a few people assumed Billy owned. 'The White Stripes wanted to record where we recorded, except they'd want to spend a few months, whereas we'd use a *day*,' Childish says,

---

debut album, *And Don't the Kids Just Love It*. Their offshoot group The Times maintained the sixties cult-TV fetish with 'I Helped Patrick McGoohan Escape'. Robyn Hitchcock's original band The Soft Boys had pipped everybody to the post by going psychedelic back in 1977 (the ads for that year's debut Softs single had proclaimed 'First psychedelic record release in 10 Years'), and by the early eighties the solo Hitchcock was emitting sub-Syd whimsies such as 'Brenda's Iron Sledge'. He became a cult figure in America, worshipped by the sort of anglophiles who adored XTC. The latter perpetrated their own pointless psychedelic pastiche under the names The Dukes of Stratosphear.

By 1984, another, different wave of sixties revivalism was taking off in the UK, centred around Creation Records, whose name came from mod gods The Creation. Early releases included 'Flowers in the Sky' by The Revolving Paint Dream and '50 Years of Fun' by Biff Bang Pow! (founder Alan McGee's own group, named after a single by The Creation). The label's most famous groups were The Jesus and Mary Chain and Primal Scream, who together catalysed into being the scene known variously as C86 and cutie: British bands who fused The Velvet Underground's wall of noise with the wimpiness of The Byrds. Meanwhile, American college radio was being overrun by home-grown flocks of Byrds clones, who'd hatched in the wake of R.E.M. In Los Angeles, there was

waspishly. 'I always say the difference between us and The White Stripes is we were trying to close the fifteen yards between us and the audience, and they were trying to get fifteen yards *between* them and the audience. They're going for the stadium. I think Jack knows that the first recordings they did on their own were their best.'

Fifty years old in 2009, Childish still bashes out the big-beat sound with his latest ensemble, Wild Billy Childish & the Musicians of the British Empire, complete with a Lord Kitchener-style handlebar moustache and World War I clothing. What's fascinating is that while he was crusading for fundamentalist rock'n'roll, Childish also co-founded a kind of retro art movement: Stuckism. The name came from Stuckism's other founder, Charles Thomson, who had been really struck by a passage in Childish's 1994 'Poem for a Pissed Off Wife (Big Hart and Balls)',

---

The Paisley Underground, a scene of neo-psych outfits led by rock scholars that included The Dream Syndicate, who took their name from the La Monte Young ensemble John Cale played in before joining the Velvets, and The Rain Parade, whose big song was rather revealingly titled 'This Can't Be Today'.

Alternative rock in the eighties defined itself through its refusal of the pop present: drum machines, synthesizers, discofunk influences. The sixties appealed not just for musical reasons but because they were the antithesis of the values of Thatcher–Reagan (who reviled the sixties and tried to roll back that decade's gains). The game of hip in the eighties would consist of shifting position within the sprawl of sixties music, setting up shop in a particular pocket of sound: garage punk or mod, psychedelia or folk rock. Later in the decade, as certain options got rendered 'obvious' through overuse, the more daring groups, such as Sonic Youth and Butthole Surfers, started making tentative steps into formerly *verboten* zones like acid rock and heavy rock (the very music that *Nuggets* acolytes frowned upon). By 1987, guitarists like Dinosaur Jr's J. Mascis or Butthole's Paul Leary were unfurling long, ecstatic, Hendrix-y solos. Long hair was back in, and it even became permissible to admit to enjoying The Grateful Dead. Inevitably, as the end of the eighties approached, you started hearing sounds emerging from the alternative scene that hinted at the seventies.

which documented a bitter argument about art Childish had with his former girlfriend, Tracey Emin, culminating in her outburst:

> Your paintings are stuck,
> you are stuck!
> Stuck! Stuck! Stuck!'

'She wanted me to go to an exhibition where a friend was taking cocaine live on stage,' Childish explained in a 2005 interview. 'And I said to Trace, "Look, I'm not interested in this piss-poor version of Dadaism which has got no balls to it." Tracey had a hissy fit . . . Charles [Thomson] loved it because it reminded him of the Fauves and the Impressionists, whose names also originated as insults, I believe. And art movements are always based on these insults.'

Stuckism was a revolt against the trendy conceptualism and provocations of Brit Art: cows in formaldehyde, tents decorated with the names of former lovers, child mannequins with penises protruding out of eye sockets, etc. Childish and Thomson railed against the *Sensation* exhibition generation, especially Damien Hirst, fingering them as mercenary careerists who exploited gimmicks and reduced art to wisecracks and visual puns (what some people in the art world mock as 'one-liner art'). 'To me the Brit Art movement was "retro" in the proper and bad sense of the word,' Childish explains. 'When Tracey and I had that argument, I said that Dada had knocked a man off a horse in 1916, and all that Tracey and her lot were doing was kicking that man in the head.'

Defiantly defending the continued validity of figurative painting, Stuckism rejected any art that didn't involve pigment on canvas. Out went installations, videos, readymades, performance art, body art et al. Childish and Thomson threw themselves into generating manifestos and mission statements, with Billy revealing a major talent for snappy slogans such as 'Artists who don't paint aren't artists' and 'Art that has to be in a gallery to be art isn't art' (both from *The Stuckist Manifesto*, 1999). Stuckism opposed everything that ultimately descended from Marcel Duchamp. In short, they were 'anti Anti-Art'.

What were they 'pro', then? The whole apparatus of authenticity, expression, vision, self-discovery, catharsis, angst and spirituality. Childish and Thomson celebrated figurative painting as a primal form of expression that went all the way back to the caves of Lascaux. Their heroes included Turner (they bitterly complained at the travesty of his name wrought by the Turner Prize), Van Gogh, Munch and the German expressionists. Just like his ideas about what's righteous in music, Childish's philosophy of art was basically a defence (through attack!) of the kind of painting and drawing he liked to do, and had indeed been doing for decades (he'd briefly attended St Martin's College of Art, only to be expelled for his obstreperousness). Childish actually wanted to take things much further than Thomson and get into direct action, do things like smash up Hirst's dead shark.

Stuckism is almost too perfect as an overall rubric for anti-modernist tendencies in art and pop culture, all those movements of resistance against the present-day, the fashionably futuristic. 'Stuck', because they try to rewind the tape of pop history and hold down the pause button on a moment, hoping to make it last for ever. But 'stuck' also in the sense of 'stuck on you': in love for eternity, undyingly faithful to a golden memory, unable to move on.

9

ROCK ON (AND ON) (AND ON)

The Never-Ending Fifties Revival

In hindsight, another strange thing about punk is that all the while this protracted underground struggle to launch a renaissance of rock'n'roll was taking place, a massive fifties revival was happening on the pop overground. Let's look at just one year, 1973, a crucial moment in terms of punk achieving critical mass: The New York Dolls released their debut album; pub rock was starting to make waves; Iggy Pop and The Stooges reunited and released *Raw Power*; the future Pistols Steve Jones and Paul Cook were hanging out at Malcolm McLaren's Too Fast to Live boutique, and that summer thieved a bunch of top-grade PA equipment after a Bowie concert, a major step towards forming a band; Patti Smith and Lenny Kaye played their first performances together; and, at the end of the year, CBGB opened. The resuscitation of 'real' rock'n'roll started to seem less like the delusional dream of nostalgic fanzine writers and more like a real prospect.

Except that real rock'n'roll was *already back*, in the form of homages and echoes across the entire span of mainstream pop culture. Nineteen seventy-three was the year of nostalgia movies like *American Graffiti* and *That'll Be the Day* (starring David 'Rock On' Essex). 10cc hit no. 1 with their 'Jailhouse Rock' pastiche 'Rubber Bullets' in June, the same month *The Rocky Horror Show* opened at the Royal Court's Theatre Upstairs and the London production of the musical *Grease* launched. For his smash LP *Goodbye Yellow Brick Road*, Elton John wrote 'Your Sister Can't Twist (But She Can Rock'n'Roll)', a fifties pastiche even more cloying than 1972's monster hit 'Crocodile Rock'. And later in 1973 John Lennon recorded his 'oldies album', *Rock 'n' Roll* (although its release would be delayed to 1975).

Good old rock'n'roll was very much in the air in 1973. But then it had been in the air for most of the decade so far. Pop culture in the first half of the seventies was in large part *defined* by this yearning to return to the fifties. The nostalgia craze spilled beyond music to movies and television. And it carried on into the late seventies and, fitfully, the eighties too. The fifties just kept on coming back, wave after wave of never-ending revivalism.

In truth, the revival began even before the seventies kicked off, as early as 1968. Ironically, this return to rock'n'roll – a reaction against *Sgt Pepper's* and the art-ification of rock – was initiated by The Beatles themselves, with their Chuck Berry pastiche 'Back in the U.S.S.R.'. John Lennon was the driving force, the Beatle who renounced the studio excesses of psychedelia in favour of a studied primitivism. Even as The Stooges bashed out proto-punk anthems like 'No Fun', Lennon was resurrecting the snarling insolence of the Cavern/Hamburg Beatles on solo singles like 1969's 'Cold Turkey'.

The Beatles didn't singlehandedly instigate rock's retreat from 'progression'. Bob Dylan and The Band were hugely influential, while the Stones' *Beggar's Banquet* marked their return to blues-based virility after the foppish psychedelic debacle of *Their Satanic Majesties Request*. Other major groups like The Byrds and The Doors dropped sophisticated arrangements and trippy sleights of production for the rootsy fundamentals of country (with *Sweetheart of the Rodeo*) and blues (*Morrison Hotel*) respectively. Still, The Beatles were the first to sense the exhaustion of

277

a particular phase of rock, perhaps because it was they who'd brought it into existence in the first place.

Writing in *Rolling Stone* in 1969, Lester Bangs argued that 'the back-to-the-roots movement' had been triggered by *The Beatles*, aka *The White Album*, which was released on 22 November 1968. But *The White Album* was not simply an abandonment of studio artifice. Some tracks extended the approaches of *Revolver/Sgt Pepper's*, while the musique concrète soundscape of 'Revolution 9' went further into tape editing than anything The Beatles had done previously. The double album was eclectic in a way that had never been seen in rock before: it didn't simply try out many different styles or reach outside rock and pop for influences (a common enough practice) but cast back across the history of rock itself – all fifteen years of it to date.

In the 1969 book *The Story of Rock*, Carl Belz hailed *The White Album* as a breakthrough precisely for this playful referentiality, the way particular songs were 'openly derived' from The Beach Boys, Chuck Berry, Bob Dylan, even the earlier stages of the Beatles' career. 'Back in the USSR', for instance, combined a witty twist on Berry's 'Back in the USA' with the early Beach Boys sound (before Brian Wilson fell under the influence of The Beatles, in fact) and sealed the deal with a lyrical 'sample' from a Ray Charles song (the line 'Georgia's always on my mind' – the joke being that Georgia was a Soviet republic as well as a Deep South state). Belz was defending *The White Album* from those critics who'd argued that The Beatles had effectively '"dropped out" of the rock evolution', insisting that this move towards rock-reflexive self-consciousness represented an advance of a different kind. At a time when the dominant view was that rock 'was becoming more sophisticated, more electronic, and more like fine art than it was in the past', *The White Album* 'asks, "is it necessarily becoming *better*?"'. The Fab Four's 'return' to older styles amounted to 'a critical disengagement from the concept of rock "progress'" – the very ideology they, more than anyone, had fostered with the astounding surge of artistic growth across *Rubber Soul/Revolver/Sgt Pepper's*. The term 'postmodernism' was not available to Belz in 1969 – it was only just beginning to be formulated in art-theory and architectural-criticism circles – but this was the concept he was reaching towards.

Another example of postmodernist rock *avant la lettre* came from Frank Zappa, whose creative arc had closely mirrored (and at points satirised) the Beatles', especially in terms of his flair for studio experimentation using tape editing. Released a few weeks after *The White Album* at the end of 1968, *Cruising with Ruben & the Jets* was an entire album devoted to doo-wop pastiche, with Zappa and The Mothers of Invention playing the parts of a fictitious fifties vocal group modelled on outfits like Little Caesar & the Romans and The Flamingos. As much as it was a fond exercise in nostalgia for the pop sounds of his youth, *Cruising with Ruben & the Jets* was also, Zappa claimed, a 'scientific' dissection of a period style, cold-bloodedly breaking it down to 'stereotyped motifs' that were then reconstructed into 'careful conglomerates of archetypal clichés'. Pop emotion was exposed as a set of standardised techniques, mechanisms for manipulating the listener's feelings. In true Zappoid style, Frank's affection for this bygone form was mingled with condescension: the sleeve notes referred to the doo-wop era's 'greasy love songs & cretin simplicity', and in a 1969 interview he referred to deliberately writing 'imbecile words' for *Cruising*. Also typical of Zappa was his need for high-cultural validation: he identified a precedent for *Cruising*'s 'experiment in cliché collages' in Stravinsky's neoclassical period of the twenties, when the composer abandoned the rhythmically tempestuous modernism of the *Rite of Spring* and embraced the strictures of eighteenth-century forms such as the concerto grosso and fugue. 'If he could take the forms and clichés of the classical era and pervert them, why not do the same with the rules and regulations applied to Doo-Wop . . .?' Zappa wondered.

The Beatles' own rock'n'roll revival was not couched in irony to anything like the same degree as Zappa's. There was a real urgency to the nostalgia. Lennon especially felt a desperate need to ground himself after a mid-sixties phase of constant LSD intake that left him with a tenuous sense of self. In a 1970 *Rolling Stone* interview, he equated rock'n'roll with 'reality'. Hearing the music of Elvis Presley, Little Richard, Jerry Lee Lewis et al. for the first time when he was fifteen was like being struck by a lightning bolt: 'the only thing to get through to me . . . The thing about rock and roll . . . is that it's real and realism gets through to you despite yourself.' What gave rock'n'roll its true power (and power of truth) was its direct connection to instinct, emotion, sexuality. This cut through both social pretences and artistic pretensions. The surrealism of his work between 'Tomorrow Never Knows' and 'I Am the Walrus' seemed to him, in retrospect, a detour from his core as both an artist and a human being.

Paul McCartney, for his part, wanted to revitalise The Beatles by bringing back the camaraderie and musical focus of their early days as a live band. He proposed a one-off eight-song concert to be recorded live. The *Get Back* project, as it was called, collapsed almost immediately but did produce the rootsy-sounding 'Get Back' single: 'The Beatles as nature intended,' the advert claimed. The band then tried to record an 'honest' album, also titled *Get Back*, with no overdubs or tape trickery. That fell apart too, although it was later salvaged as *Let It Be*. Among the album's contents was 'One After 909', which actually dated back to 1957. One of the first Lennon–McCartney compositions, '909' had been an attempt to write a 'bluesy freight-train song', McCartney recalled. Resurrecting this relic really did briefly transport the estranged friends 'back to where [they] once belonged': the halcyon days when they were teenagers besotted with the rough new sound of rock'n'roll.

In 1968/69, there were plenty of reminders of happier days around. Bill Haley & His Comets toured the UK, filling the Albert Hall on 1 May 1968. So many veterans of the original rock'n'roll era were treading the boards again that *Melody Maker* reported: 'Haley, Perkins, Eddy, Everleys – suddenly in Britain it's rock.' In December of that year, Elvis Presley appeared on television with his *1968 Comeback Special*, an electrifying resurrection of his 'Memphis Flash' self. Presley stripped away the schmaltzy, strings-y pop of his neutered movie-making years for virile rockabilly and sounded happier and more alive than he had for years.

Many of the big new groups sounded like Memphis flashbacks too. The most popular American band of 1969 were Creedence Clearwater Revival, who released three albums that year alone and dominated pop radio with a flurry of hits that Greil Marcus described as 'Elvis's Sun singles, without their innocence'. Creedence were a bit like Flamin' Groovies who actually succeeded. They came from Northern California, where they played the San Francisco ballrooms but – like the Groovies – never went acid rock. Creedence mostly stuck with two-and-a-half-minute songs in the jukebox/AM radio mould. What's striking listening to their music now is how plain its textural palette is in comparison with the paisley colour-swirl of psychedelic rock. It's as if a late-sixties movie-maker had deliberately reverted to black and white in the early-sixties style of *Jailhouse Rock* or *A Taste of Honey*.

What made Creedence's music more than just a recreation of the past was the group's break with two key aspects of fifties rock'n'roll: glamour and sexuality. Dressed in workman-like flannel shirts and projecting an everyman-like anti-image, Creedence had none of the charisma of Presley or Little Richard. For all the rasp of his voice, John Fogerty was incapable of communicating erotic urgency. Instead the group's songs were evenly divided between populist protest and celebrations of rocking and a-rolling.

281

Creedence's 'Up Around the Bend' features a chorus about hitching 'a ride to the end of the highway/ where the neon turns to wood'. The Band tapped into the same end-of-the-sixties vibe of pastoral nostalgia with music that was even more naturalistic-sounding and woodsy. *Music from Big Pink*, their super-influential 1968 debut, and 1970's *The Band* were symphonies in brown. Elektra Records' Jac Holzman hailed *Pink* as 'a homemade record in a sea of highly produced records' that 'brought us back to our roots'. Critic Ian Macdonald praised its aura of 'hand-tooled Shaker furniture simplicity' and argued that the record served as a form of 'cultural detox' after the excesses of *Sgt Pepper's* and *Are You Experienced*. The 'slow and measured pace' of the songs exuded maturity: 'this music was made by men, not youths'.

Like Creedence, The Band were besotted with the South, and like the Californian group, none of them (with one exception) actually came from there. True, they'd paid their dues as backing band for rockabilly also-ran Ronnie Hawkins, playing all across North America to rough crowds in juke joints and roadhouses, a training camp as testing as The Beatles' speed-fuelled all-night-long Hamburg residency. But there was an element of self-conscious artifice to The Band's return to roots, as the roots were never theirs, since nearly all of them were Canadian. This was more striking still with their second album, when Robbie Robertson started writing songs that drew on American history, like 'The Night They Drove Old Dixie Down' (about the defeat of the Confederacy) and 'King Harvest' (about late-nineteenth-century farmers struggling not to go under). They pioneered rock's 'historical turn', influencing British folklore-drenched records like Fairport Convention's *Liege & Lief*. The portrait of the group on *The Band* looks like a daguerreotype of bearded homesteaders or migrant workers in a West Virginia mining town, and the music itself feels, as Greil Marcus put it, as if it would 'sound as right to a gang of 19th century beaver trappers as it does to us'.

According to Marcus, The Band's old-timey sound provided its audience – the rock generation, the counterculture – with a way to reconnect with 'America' culturally at a time (1968–70) when it was most alienated from the US politically, on account of Vietnam, the assassinations of Bobby Kennedy and Martin Luther King, Nixon's election and the shootings of student protesters at Kent State. A similar impulse towards healing and reconciliation motivated a much more frivolous-seeming outfit that would strike an unexpected chord with the Woodstock generation: Sha Na Na.

Formed in early 1969 by students at the Ivy League Columbia University, this fifties-revival group was prompted into existence by the discord that had overrun the college in April 1968, when student anti-Vietnam War protesters occupied university buildings, leading to counter-protests, 'a police riot' and the closure of the campus for the remainder of the term. Sha Na Na's mastermind George Leonard – at the time a twenty-two-year-old cultural-history student, now a college professor – yearned to bridge the divide in the student body between anti-war liberals (many of whom were members of Students for a Democratic Society (SDS)) and patriotic jocks (some of whom were in the Reserve Officers' Training Corps (ROTC)). The solution he came up with was to remind everybody what they had in common: rock'n'roll. It was the music they'd all grown up on, indelibly linked to a happier time – the fifties.

'The Columbia riots had been a ghastly experience,' Leonard recalls. 'Like the Civil War, but on campus. The university authorities dithered for a long time and then they let the cops go in. My brother Rob saw it and said he was crying because the police were beating people with these long flashlights.' Rob Leonard was president of Columbia's a cappella group The Kingsmen, so George persuaded them to transform their glee club into a fifties song-and-dance troupe and to stage a spectacular called *The Glory That Was Grease*. Leonard's pitch – made first to The Kingsmen, then to the student population – was, 'Jocks! Freaks! ROTC! SDS! Let there be a truce! Bury the hatchet (not in each other)! Remember when we were all little greaseballs together.'

In preparation for the show, Leonard left flyers in college dorms and communal areas: 'Hey you hoods, so you're a sophisticated college guy, huh? Bullshit. You know who you are, greaseball. Face it, deep down inside you somewhere there's still the same greasy kid standing on the corner in his continental jeans watching the 8th grade girls . . . singing "Duke of Earl" to himself . . . For one glorious night revert to type. . . . Grease your hair back with KY, roll up the sleeves on your T-shirt.'

Leonard's aim was to evoke what he later called 'the pre-political teenage Eden' of the fifties. But this was a consciously fabricated myth and didn't reflect how people would have felt at the time. Greasers – known in the fifties as hoods, short for hood-lums, or JDs, short for juvenile delinquents – were folk-devil figures. Most likely the majority of the students on campus would have been scared of them as children in the fifties and unlikely to have been from the same social class. 'Everyone remembered clearly that hoods had been rough,' says Leonard. 'They knew what the fifties had been, but they still took the myth. I guess they needed it.' Other aspects of Sha Na Na's performance were equally falsified. The dance routines that Leonard choreographed bore little resemblance to how bands moved or kids danced in the fifties, but instead mish-mashed elements of Busby Berkeley's mass symmetries, the soul moves Leonard had seen at the Apollo Theater in Harlem (just a few blocks north of Columbia University) and bits of ballet (he'd been studying dance). Not only that, but the group's repertoire of rock'n'roll classics was played at 'twice the speed of the originals: I insisted we do the music the way it was remembered instead of the way it was'. Even the word 'greaser' was anachronistic, not part of common parlance in the fifties. Leonard may have been indirectly influenced here by S. E.

Hinton's teenage fiction classic *The Outsiders*, which was published in 1967 and, while set in the present, depicted a fifties-like mid-American town whose youth are bitterly divided between working-class 'greasers' and smartly dressed middle-class 'socs', short for 'socials'. With hardly any archival resources to draw on – no videos or readily accessible movies, just a few faded memories and record sleeves – Leonard was necessarily fictionalising the recent past. 'Did we actually feel nostalgic for the fifties? No. The whole thing was very deliberately made up. Amateur historians write about history, professionals make it up!'

From their borderline ridiculous stage moves to their name – a mangling of the refrain of The Silhouettes' 1957 hit 'Get a Job' – Sha Na Na were camp as hell: closer to a Gay Pride float or scene in one of John Waters's 'cute'-period movies like *Hairspray* than the earnest harking back of Creedence and Lennon. In interviews at the time, Leonard described himself as a fan of Susan Sontag and claimed to be directly inspired by her 'Notes on Camp' essay. Today he downplays her influence – 'Sontag was just summing up, and summing up well, what was already in the air, what we were already living' – and instead pinpoints Andy Warhol ('a huge star to us, just ordinary guys in the dorms') as the real guru of the era.

Performed in the spring of 1969 at Columbia's Wollman Auditorium, *The Glory That Was Grease* was a huge success. It was quickly followed by *The First East Coast Grease Festival: Grease Under the Stars*, staged on the steps of the Low Memorial Library at Columbia and drawing five thousand kids – not just from the campus but from other Ivy League colleges on the East Coast. More Sha Na Na gigs followed, one of which was caught by Jimi Hendrix, who was blown away and wangled them onto the bill at Woodstock. Sha Na Na performed on the final day as the act before Hendrix. The film crew had fallen asleep because it was 5.30 a.m., but they woke up just in time to document Sha Na Na's rendition of the Danny and the Juniors classic 'At the Hop', the

troupe bopping and jiving in their Brylcreemed DAs, with cigarette packets rolled up in their T-shirt sleeves.

Within a few months of Sha Na Na's appearance at Woodstock,
the back-to-the-fifties fad gathered further momentum with a
pair of one-day rock'n'roll revival festivals – unconnected with
each other – that took place in Toronto and New York in the
autumn of 1969. Staged at Madison Square Garden's Felt Forum
on 18 October, the First Rock Revival filled the 4,500-capacity
hall, with thousands more eager to see the line-up (Bill Haley,
Chuck Berry, The Coasters, The Shirelles and, yes, Sha Na Na)
turned away. When Haley stepped onstage there was an eight-
minute ovation. By October 1970, the Rock Revivals had graduated from the Felt Forum to the 20,000-capacity Madison Square
Garden itself. Promoter Richard Nader found himself the mogul
of a rock'n'roll nostalgia industry, staging concerts all over North
America. His concept was widely copied, and he himself branched
out to do Big Band Festivals catering to the pre-rock generation's
nostalgia for the days of Duke Ellington and Guy Lombardo.

Nader became proactive, tracking down groups that had dispersed, such as Dion and the Belmonts and The Five Satins, and
persuading them to reunite. Participating in the revival concerts
was rewarding in terms of income and attention, but it was not
always a joyous experience for those whose careers it resusci-
tated. Fifties heart-throb rocker Ricky Nelson wrote the hit single 'Garden Party' about playing one of Nader's Madison Square
concerts in 1971 and getting booed by the audience. They wanted
to see the teenage idol of their youth. Instead they got the grown-
up Nelson, who'd moved with the times, sported long hair and
bell-bottoms, and whose current group, The Stone Canyon Band,
played country rock in the early-seventies style.

By October 1974, Nader's Rock Revival was the longest-
running concert series at Madison Square Garden. Looking back,
Nader explained that his original concept in 1969 had been to

create something for the generation that had grown up with fifties rock'n'roll but didn't understand or feel at home in the sophisticated rock culture that The Beatles had brought into being: 'The world isn't the one they were brought up in, and they're not quite comfortable with the new thing. But the Revival gives them that womb again, it gives them that security, that escape.' When Ricky Nelson played country-rock versions of songs like the Stones' 'Honky Tonky Woman', that ability to slip through time, back to where they once belonged, was disrupted. So they jeered and cat-called, and eventually Nelson stalked offstage in a rage.

GIMME SOME TRUTH

'Garden Party' contains a line about Yoko Ono bringing 'the Walrus' – John Lennon – with her to that 1971 Madison Square Garden show. Two years earlier, Ono and Lennon had attended the other big back-to-the-fifties festival of autumn 1969: the Toronto Rock and Roll Revival. This one-day, twelve-hour festival took place on 13 September 1969 and drew around 20,000 people to see a bill that mixed current bands like Alice Cooper and The Doors with fifties greats like Bo Diddley, Chuck Berry, Little Richard, Gene Vincent and Jerry Lee Lewis. Lennon was originally invited to host the festival, but at the last minute he decided to perform with a pick-up band that included Eric Clapton and Yoko as 'lead screamer'. As was rapidly becoming the norm in those days, the festival was filmed, eventually reaching movie-theatre screens as *Sweet Toronto*, and the audio track of D. A. Pennebaker's footage of Lennon and his band's performance became the rush-released Plastic Ono Band album *Live Peace in Toronto*. The set started with 'Blue Suede Shoes' and juxtaposed the kind of songs covered by the early Cavern-rocking Beatles ('Money', 'Dizzy Miss Lizzy') with equally raw but recently written originals like 'Cold Turkey' and Ono's avant-shriek pieces like 'Don't Worry Kyoko'.

This was where Lennon's head was at as the sixties drew to a disillusioned end: primal-scream therapy meets back-to-basics rock'n'roll. From now on he was obsessed with stripping music and words back to an authentic core. Expressive urgency demanded speed and directness, no fancy frills. Accordingly, 'Instant Karma' was written, recorded and released within ten days. Lennon recalled producer Phil Spector asking, '"How do you want it?" I said, "You know, 1950's." He said, "Right," and boom, I did it in about three goes or something like that.' Spector put Sun Studios-style echo on Lennon's voice, but the singer wouldn't let him gussy up the production with strings. The song's seemingly naturalistic production did involve artifice, though: Spector instructed drummer Alan White to remove all his cymbals and put a towel over the tom-toms, and in the mix pushed the famously walloping beat and crash-bash fills right to the fore, bolstering the groove with handclaps and extra percussion. This wasn't a straight document of a band performing live but a heightened, exaggerated staging of 'raw': its stomping, clod-hopping beat was closer to Gary Glitter than to the '1950's' that Lennon had requested from Spector.

Lennon's debut solo album, released towards the end of 1970, extended this process of paring back musically and emotionally. Stark in sound, sung with a raw-throated mix of vulnerability and surliness, and featuring his most painfully honest lyrics ever, *John Lennon/Plastic Ono Band* was an extraordinary act of self-exposure and catharsis that reached its peak with the Fats-Domino-meets-Arthur-Janov exorcism of 'Mother'. In a *Rolling Stone* interview around the album, Lennon repeatedly affirmed his belief in 'simple rock and nothing else', declaring, 'the best stuff is primitive enough and has no bullshit . . . the Blues are beautiful because it's simpler and because it's real. It's not perverted or thought about.' He defined his taste as 'sounds like "Wop Bop a Loo Bop"' and claimed that 'no group, be it Beatles,

Dylan or Stones have ever improved on "Whole Lot of Shaking"'. Lennon said the only things in contemporary music he rated at all were Creedence Clearwater ('good rock and roll music') and Dave Edmunds, the Welsh rockabilly purist who'd got to no. 1 in the UK with a cover of Smiley Lewis's 'I Hear You Knocking'. In a striking revisionist take on the sixties, he renounced psychedelia and claimed that the Beatles' best work wasn't even the quickly recorded, high-energy rock'n'roll of 'Help' and 'Twist and Shout' but the stuff they did before they even stepped into a recording studio. 'When we played straight rock . . . there was nobody to touch us in Britain,' he said of the Cavern/Hamburg era. 'Our best work was never recorded.'

Lennon's patter in his chat with *Rolling Stone*'s Jann Wenner is astonishingly in synch with the line only then just beginning to be espoused by Lester Bangs, Greg Shaw and the rest. His warnings that 'rock and roll is going like jazz' (i.e. obsessed with virtuosity and subtlety) and his description of his own rhythm-guitar playing ('I'm not technically good, but I can make it fucking howl and move') look ahead to punk. But as much as Lennon was attuned to the shifting zeitgeist, he was largely impelled by private psychological pressures. In his mind there was a deep-rooted emotional association between rock'n'roll and his mother, run over by a car in 1958 only a few months before Buddy Holly's plane crash. It was Julia Lennon, an Elvis fan, who turned the teenage John onto rock'n'roll and bought him his first guitar. He recalled learning, with his mother's help, to play Holly's 'That'll Be the Day': Julia slowed down the record so that he 'could scribble out the words' and showed 'endless patience' as he worked out the chords.

ROCK AND ROLL WILL NEVER DIE

Fifties nostalgia intensified as the mood of bummed-out, burned-out uncertainty deepened in the first few years of the seventies. 'Been a long time since I rock and rolled . . . oh baby, let me get back . . . where I come from,' sang Robert Plant on 'Rock and Roll', the second track on Led Zeppelin's 1971 ⚭⚭⚭⚭. Unconsciously or accidentally, the line echoed what Elvis said at the start of his *Comeback Special* in 1968: 'Been a long time, baby.' Plant, a doo-wop fanatic, also wove into the lyrics nods to classics like The Monotones' 1958 smash 'The Book of Love'. The Monotones popped up again in 'American Pie', Don McLean's rock'n'roll elegy. Starting with 'the day the music died' (the airplane crash that killed Buddy Holly, Ritchie Valens and the Big Bopper), the symbolism-laden verses work their way through the sixties via allusions to Dylan, Lennon, The Byrds, Janis Joplin and Charlie Manson. Number 1 in the US for four weeks and almost as massive in Britain, the song struck a chord with a generation who had no easy answer to McLean's question, 'Do you believe in rock'n'roll?'

The faithful, those who still believed in rock'n'roll's past if not its present or future, gathered at Wembley Stadium on 5 August 1972, when the UK finally got its own revival festival. Several years in the planning, The London Rock'n'roll Show featured the by now usual suspects from the Golden Age: Haley, Diddley, Berry, Richard, Lewis. The line-up also included some of their British fifties counterparts (like Billy Fury and Screaming Lord Sutch, who came onstage in a coffin) and acts from the UK's burgeoning revivalist scene. The Houseshakers, for instance, did a Gene Vincent act that they'd been touring in tribute to the recently deceased singer, but also served as Diddley's and Berry's backing band. There were also a few non-revivalist but rock'n'roll-in-spirit groups too, like MC5 (whose *Back in the USA* album had been bookended with Chuck Berry and Little Richard covers) and Dr Feelgood (albeit moonlighting anonymously as backing band for minor Brit rocker Heinz). More significant in terms of reflecting the back-to-the-fifties vibe of mainstream UK pop at the time was the presence of such rising stars of glam as Wizzard and Gary Glitter.

John Lennon once declared that 'glam rock is just rock and roll with lipstick on'. Everyone who's written about glam concentrates on the lipstick; hardly anybody addresses the rock'n'roll part, the peculiar way that glitter rock musically harked back to the fifties without replicating it. Between them, Lennon and Sha Na Na actually contributed a hefty chunk of glam's sound and vision. Lennon's stomping bootboy drums on 'Instant Karma' and the other hard-rocking portions of his solo career paved the way for glitter's merger of primitivism and production. Sha Na Na's choreographed caricature of a misremembered fifties anticipated the costumes and moves of Wizzard, Slade, Gary Glitter, Alvin Stardust, Mud and the rest.

The mastermind behind Wizzard was Roy Wood, formerly of psychedelic hit-makers The Move. Wizzard's blare of honking horns, kettle-drum rolls, cellos and kitchen-sink kitsch was obviously modelled on the Phil Spector/Ronettes sound, but the sartorial reference points harked back earlier, to the Teddy Boys. Appearing on *Top of the Pops* with smashes like 'See My Baby Jive' and 'Angel Fingers', the group wore drape jackets in gold lamé and sparkly blue. But Wood's electrocuted hippy hair and garish face paint suggested a fifties flashback filtered through LSD. Wizzard's most successful album, *Introducing Eddy & The Falcons*, used the *Sgt Pepper's/Cruising with Ruben* 'fictional band' idea as the conceptual frame for a series of late-fifties/early-sixties pastiches, with songs blatantly impersonating Duane Eddy, Del Shannon and the like.

T-Rex's sound was rock'n'roll and twelve-bar boogie filtered through flower power: John Lee Hooker meets Gandalf's Garden, Chuck Berry overripe and fruity fit to split. Marc Bolan's most radical hit single, 'Solid Gold Easy Action', resembled a jagged Beefheart rewrite of Buddy Holly's 'Not Fade Away'. But the glam era's most creative reinventions of rock'n'roll came from Gary Glitter. Or rather his producer Mike Leander. 'Rock and Roll (Parts One and Two)', Glitter's breakthrough hit, reads like fairly abject nostalgia if you look at the lyrics (references to 'the juke-box hall', 'blue suede shoes' and 'Little Queenie' bopping 'at the high-school hop'). But the music itself is minimal, closer to the Afro-funk of James Brown: a white English soccer hooligan take on 'Sex Machine', maybe. And it was the even more mechanistic, near-instrumental B-side 'Rock and Roll (Part Two)' that took off in the discotheques and resulted in the single's slow climb to the UK no. 2 spot during the summer of 1972.

When Mike Leander went in the studio for the 'Rock and Roll' session, he hadn't been listening to Elvis or Eddie Cochran but to much more recent, tribal-sounding music: the hoodoo-voodoo-bayou sound of Dr. John, Burundi rhythms, the percussive stampede of 'He's Gonna Step on You Again' by South African rocker John Kongos. Building a drum loop of himself playing a tom-tom-pummelling pattern, Leander worked in ominous guitar chords and Gary Glitter's caveman-like chants, with everything filtered through effects to create a kind of dry echo. 'Rock and Roll' wasn't the zombie-like return of 'the brand-new sound' that the lyric located 'in those far-off days' of the fifties. It was a genuinely *new* sound achieved by communing with the decade's lost spirit.

Glitterbeat's atavistic-futuristic brutalism sounded totally seventies. If the singer had been a little less camp and a lot younger- and scrawnier-looking, songs like 'I'm the Leader of the Gang' could have been a proto-punk sound for early-seventies juvenile delinquents: not the retroactively romanticised hoods of the fifties but their scary modern equivalents, the skinhead 'bovver boys' stomping through Britain's housing estates and football terraces in their steel-capped Doc Martens boots.

This idealised version of the fifties reached movie screens in the summer of 1973 in the form of *American Graffiti*, whose cast of characters included a gang of hoods with hearts of gold called The Pharaohs. George Lucas's film mingled the innocent energy of Sha Na Na with 'American Pie'-like 'loss of innocence' undertones to become a monstrous box-office hit (it grossed $115 million in the US alone). Set in a small town in Northern California, strictly speaking *Graffiti* did not actually take place in the fifties: the poster and trailer slogan was 'Where were you in '62?' But culturally these were the dying days of the fifties, just before Beatlemania hit American shores and rock got serious with Dylan.

Despite its overtly nostalgic intent, *American Graffiti* was formally innovative, weaving multiple intersecting storylines to create a feel of the drift of adolescence – hanging out or aimless cruising in cars. Talking to the *New York Times*, Lucas remembered his own teen years in Modesto, California: 'It all happened to me, but I sort of glamorised it. I went through all that stuff, drove the cars, bought liquor, chased girls.' Lucas used pop songs to soundtrack virtually every scene in the movie, as opposed to commissioning an original score – another innovation that would become widespread in the eighties and for ever after.

The movie starts with 'Rock Around the Clock' and shots of cars drawing up outside a diner at dusk. The imagery chimes with all our received images of the fifties, from the sleek, shiny 'Googie' design of Mel's diner to the lustrous chrome tailfins of the automobiles. Adding to the elegiac glisten of the scene is a glorious pinky-blue sunset, as if it's the sun going down on the last day of the fifties. Bittersweet notes are sounded throughout *American Graffiti*, most of whose characters are confronting the end of childhood, with lines like 'You just can't stay seventeen for ever.' One of the characters, a drag-strip racer who left school a few years earlier but stuck around town *trying* to be seventeen for ever, turns off his car radio in disgust at one point and declares, 'Rock'n'roll has been going downhill since Buddy Holly died.' At the movie's end, the fate of all the characters is described: John Milner the drag-strip racer is killed by a drunk driver a few years later; the Buddy Holly lookalike Terry is missing-in-action in Vietnam; the goody-two-shoes Steve is claimed by adult mediocrity; while Curtis is described as a writer living in Canada (a hint that he was a draft dodger). *American Graffiti*, then, is a snapshot of Sha Na Na's 'pre-political Eden': the movie captures the golden sunset of the fifties, just before the sixties – with all its high hopes and crashing disillusion – kicked off full-steam in 1963.

But Sha Na Na's innocuous rewrite of the fifties really blossomed with the TV series *Happy Days*, which launched in 1974 and was effectively a spin-off of *Graffiti*, with Ron Howard reprising his Steve character in the form of the wholesome Richie Cunningham. *Happy Days* in turn spawned the spin-off fifties retro-comedy hit *Laverne & Shirley*. Also heavily influenced by Sha Na Na was the hit Broadway musical *Grease*, set in a late-fifties high school and soon transformed into a saccharine 1978 movie starring John Travolta and Olivia Newton-John. Sha Na Na got payback in the form of a cameo appearance in the film, performing at the high-school hop. By this point they also had their own mega-successful eponymous TV series.

LET'S DO THE TIME WARP AGAIN

'Innocence' is not the only thing that seventies musicians sought and found in the fifties. As fifties revivalism continued and diversified in the second half of the seventies, two other 'essences' of rock'n'roll came to the fore. Some bands, like The Cramps, focused on rockabilly's febrile sexuality and 'real gone' frenzy, making a fetish of obscure artists, those who'd never made it out of the Deep South. Others homed in on the histrionic excess of rock'n'roll's more poptastic and produced side, figures like Phil Spector, Roy Orbison and Del Shannon.

Far and away the most successful version of the latter was Meatloaf. He was *stupendously* successful: the multiplatinum *Bat Out of Hell* was one of 1978's biggest records, especially in the UK, where Meatloaf had the same kind of over-the-top appeal as Queen. Meatloaf had first come to public attention in *The Rocky Horror Picture Show* (the 1975 movie version of Richard O'Brien's cult musical), in which he played a rock'n'roller called Eddie whose brain has been partially removed. While working on the movie in 1974, Meatloaf also began his *Bat Out of Hell* collaboration with songwriter and 'walking rock encyclopedia' Jim Steinman.

Steinman's approach to rock'n'roll resurrection was completely opposed to the reductionism of Creedence, Lennon and Glitter–Leander. Phil Spector's 'wall of sound' and densely layered 'teenage symphonies' were the model. Something of a rock'n'roll philosopher as well as a songwriter-arranger, Steinman talked eloquently about how the music's core was violence and hysteria. Meatloaf, the Pavarotti of rock, had the only voice majestic enough to do his songs justice, he said. Swollen both in width and length (several *Bat Out of Hell* numbers reached nine or ten minutes), Steinman's music grew as corpulent as Meatloaf's physique. But the result wasn't so much rock opera as rock'n'roll opera: beneath the gassy bloat, the roots of the sound were clearly Chuck Berry and The Ronettes, while the songs dealt with fifties-type scenarios, such as a Harley Davidson death ride or making out in a Chevy and struggling to get the girl to go all the way.

Steinman's manager David Sonenberg described him as having 'the intellect of an Orson Welles . . . yet he's kind of frozen in the emotional body of a 17-year-old'. That nails *Bat Out of Hell* precisely: corny yet grotesque, retarded but overblown, as if rock's artistic and emotional development had arrested circa 1957 but its sonic form kept growing. *Bat Out Of Hell* actually came out of an earlier Steinman project called *Neverland* that was primarily based around Peter Pan. The songwriter hailed J. M. Barrie's story as 'the ultimate rock-and-roll myth – lost boys who don't grow up'. Rock'n'roll, Steinman argued, 'has to do with being a teenager, the energy of adolescence. When it starts to get too adult, I think it begins to lose a little of the power.' He complained that in the early seventies, music 'got real bland, tranquilizing'. It lost touch with the epic quality of songs like Del Shannon's 'Runaway', 'that cross-roads, where romance became violent and violence became romantic'. Singer-songwriters like 'Joni Mitchell, James Taylor and Jackson Browne' were 'the exact opposite of my world', he continued, because they wrote about grown-up stuff like 'meaningful relationships'.

If The Cramps' Lux Interior and Poison Ivy had been paying attention, you can't help thinking they would have nodded their heads approvingly at Steinman's sentiments, if not at the grossly overblown music he created. The Cramps' passion was for the most obscure rockabilly sides by one-hit or no-hit wonders like Charlie Feathers or Billy Lee Riley. Their lost ideal was not Steinman's epic melodrama but rock'n'roll that was barely produced at all: songs that were little more than a ragged holler, some scrabbled guitar chords and a frantic beat, captured on singles that were typically recorded in a single take in makeshift studios. These lo-fi recordings twitched with the 'real-gone' spirit of rock'n'roll at its most untamed. Nick Kent, profiling The Cramps in 1979, defined rockabilly as 'rock primitivism at its most blazingly illogical . . . a . . . shuddering splurge of adrenalin-pumping dementia'.

The roots of The Cramps' version of the fifties can be traced to a subculture of hardcore rock'n'roll collectors that formed in the late sixties. Travelling to the US to forage for rare records, British and European dealers returned and launched reissue labels like Union Pacific and Injun, with some also bootlegging rare seven-inch singles complete with immaculately convincing facsimiles of the original labels. Collector Records, founded by a Dutchman called Cees Klop, was the most significant force in the rare rockabilly market. Klop's compilations, like *Rock'n'Roll, Vol. 1*, introduced a whole new generation of converts to obscure tunes like Hank Mizell's 'Jungle Rock'.

The Collector Records compilations caught the ears of a young couple called Erick Lee Purkhiser and Kristy Marlana Wallace, aka Lux Interior and Poison Ivy, and would supply several of the songs covered early on by The Cramps. Starting out in the junk stores of early-seventies Sacramento, California, Lux and Ivy had been picking up doo-wop and rockabilly singles, gradually developing a fetish for the most arcane and insane-sounding stuff. The couple were touched by the deluded ambition of these renegade rockabillies, 'singing about slopping out the hogs or something and they thought it was gonna be a number one, right up there behind Jerry Lee and Elvis', recalled Lux in a 1980 interview. After a stint in Akron, Ohio, the lovers moved to New York and holed up in an uptown apartment with no windows. Here they formulated the Cramps aesthetic, which they dubbed 'psychotic punkabilly' and later condensed to the snappier 'psychobilly'. It was the fusion of non-mainstream rock'n'roll and pulp fiction (comics books, horror and sci-fi B-movies) into a cult of adolescence as a time of life that no one in their right mind would ever want to leave behind. But it was a particular idea of the teenager: the teen as truant and troublemaker.

Lux and Ivy's stance was anti-intellectual and anti-art in the way that only the secretly intellectual and arty can be. They were trash aesthetes who shunned all things improving and 'progressive'. In one of their earliest interviews, with the *NME* in June 1978, Lux derided the experimental No Wave bands who were The Cramps' contemporaries in New York as 'a bunch of snotty-nosed little art students that don't know or care anything about rock'n'roll . . . We want to be a rock'n'roll band, and I'll do it till

297

past when I'm dead.' Of course, there was hardly a shortage of un-cerebral, hard-rocking music for modern adolescents at that time in America – it's just that it was called heavy metal. The Cramps chose the lumpen music of the fifties to avoid both the lumpen music of the present (stadium metal) and its gentrified alterna-tive (post-punk).

The Cramps' 1978 debut single consisted of two cover versions: 'The Way I Walk', an obscure rockabilly number by Jack Scott, and 'Surfin' Bird', a 1962 surf-rock smash by The Trashmen. Their set at this point was crammed with covers, but even the 'so-called originals' were typically 'reworkings of super-obscure rockabilly records', according to the group's first drummer, Miriam Linna. But The Cramps' sound itself *was* original: this was no immac-ulate reproduction, as with The Stray Cats, but a lopsided hall-of-mirrors version, deficient in some respects (there was no bass guitar) and exaggerated in others (the Sun-style reverb became a crypt-like echo; the tremolo lines were swampy and near psyche-delic). Gashes of pure noise defaced the songs in a manner not far from the art-punk bands that Lux Interior scorned.

The Cramps' major gambit in terms of making rockabilly 'edgy' again was to reinvoke the genre's original threatening sexuality. A flyer for one of their early shows at Max's Kansas City reproduced a vintage fifties pamphlet from the inadvertently hilarious genre of anti-rock'n'roll propaganda: 'Does rock'n'roll breed VD? Filthy lyrics, sexy rhythm, drinking and lonely kids – does it all lead to secret sex and disease?' The caption was juxtaposed with a pho-tograph of a girl and boy bopping dementedly. The Cramps were fixated on the moment when rock'n'roll's jungle rhythm and voodoo frenzy was seen as ungodly and subversive. But how to recreate that effect in a world where rock'n'roll had *won*? Sexual permissiveness permeated mainstream pop culture, from the women's magazines at the supermarket check-out to TV sexolo-gist Dr Ruth. The Cramps' response was to shift on their third

298

album from B-movie ghoulishness to a fixation on smut, sexual grossness and the female bodily interior. Hence 'Smell of Female', 'What's Inside a Girl', the cunnilingus anthem 'You've Got Good Taste', '(Hot Pool of) Womanneed', 'Journey to the Center of a Girl', 'The Hot Pearl Snatch' and 'Can Your Pussy Do the Dog?'. Suddenly it made sense that they'd named the group after the American slang for menstruation pains.

Before the group descended into utter sleaze-schlock, though, Lux Interior talked poignantly about rockabilly as 'the height of modern-day culture, [of] the 20th Century'. 'Rockabilly should have inspired something to happen that was so great, so passionate, so sexual that it should have taken us to another place,' he told the *NME* in 1986. '. . . We love it and we live it and it is who we are, whether we want it to be or not. But we respect it enough that I don't think it's something that can be done again. It's something that was done once; it came from a time and a place. You can't take a goddamned 16-year-old kid and expect him to understand what some goddamned ignorant Southern hillbilly moonshiner cool guy knew back then 30 years ago. Cos what some guy knew back then in Tennessee is *way* beyond what anybody in America could enjoy today.' Here Lux seemed to grasp the futile longing at the core of the time-warp cult impulse. The recordings that survived were holy relics. But their spirit could only walk the land again in undead form: the zombie burlesque of a Cramps show. Like a photocopy being itself repeatedly photocopied, The Cramps' caricature of rockabilly would be further degraded in the eighties by a legion of British psychobilly outfits with names like The Meteors and The Guana Batz.

LET'S GET REAL, REAL GONE

Another way of preserving the Lost Moment is to surround yourself with its remains. Because Cees Klop and his kind scooped up most of the actually released vintage rockabilly back in the seventies, subsequent collector-dealers and reissuers had to hunt down barely released records and, eventually, unreleased music. That's the path followed by original Cramps drummer Miriam Linna and husband Billy Miller. Norton Records, the company they started, is not really a reissue label at all: most of its output consists of recordings that were never issued in the first place, anything from Bobby Fuller home recordings to live radio broadcasts by northwest garage punksters The Sonics. It's an article of faith for Linna and Miller that 'the best is still out there. People who twenty years ago said that everything good has been dug up and put out, they're so wrong.'

Linna and Miller's home and Norton's HQ is an enormous, high-ceilinged space, but virtually every square foot of the walls, from carpet to mouldings, is covered with framed B-movie posters, concert handbills and other rock'n'roll memorabilia. The effect is like stepping inside Lux Interior's brain. Completing the period vibe there are vintage sofas and lamps, while a voluminous loft space ten feet from the floor is crammed with quaint radiograms, jukeboxes and Bakelite tube radios.

Appearances to the contrary, 'retro' is a word that Linna scorns. She is disparaging about rockabilly fans who are just into the image. 'You got people going to shows with their creeped-out vintage clothes. The girls are holding a pose, like, "Is this how Betty Page would stand?" or "I have a bullet bra!" The boys don't want to get their slicked-back hair messed up. You just think, "Loosen up!"' Both The Zantees, the rockabilly band Linna formed with Miller after leaving The Cramps, and the couple's later group The A-Bones were never about the period-precise image of stylists like Robert Gordon or The Stray Cats. Hasil Adkins, whose barely released singles and home recordings were the initial spur for them to found Norton, is the couple's touchstone figure precisely because he didn't care about cool. Adkins was the genuine backwoods article, a modern primitive: the Wildman, as they titled one of his Norton albums. 'Hasil would be having a sandwich and singing into this beat-up old machine covered in moss and crud. There would be cheese dust in those tapes. People like Hasil, they just had this need to record, and they recorded all this crazy stuff.'

Before they started Norton, Miller and Linna's main outlet for proselytizing was the fanzine *KICKS*. Linna had previously done The Flamin' Groovies' fanclub magazine for several years, after an oversubscribed Greg Shaw entrusted it to her. The *Bomp!* connection continued with Shaw releasing The Zantees' debut *Out for Kicks* in 1980. Linna says she had regarded *Bomp!* 'as the Bible' for much of the seventies, but 'after a certain point I wasn't interested in the modern bands they were pushing at all. That's why we started *KICKS* in 1979, because we were getting into older stuff. Old records that were new to us.'

Linna and Miller were prime movers in an all-American intifada against the faux and the foreign. The stuff coming out of England in the early eighties was especially abhorrent: 'WHENEVER YOU BUY A RECORD BY DURAN DURAN YOU ARE SPITTING ON THE GRAVE OF EDDIE COCHRAN!' ranted Miller in the third issue of *KICKS*. But there were enemies closer to home too: No Wave, disco-influenced New Wave groups like Talking Heads, and the bespectacled, geeky sounds of what would soon be called college rock.

And yet Linna was actually once tight with the No Wave people. She was (and still is) good friends with performance-art veteran Robin Crutchfield of DNA, and even shared a squalid Lower East Side apartment with Lydia Lunch and Bradley Field of Teenage Jesus and the Jerks. The apartment, which had no hot water, was also used by various bands as a rehearsal space, among them The Cramps. At this point, New York's avant-garde and retro-garde were almost literally in bed with each other. For years people from both sides of the fence also worked alongside each other at Strand, the legendarily vast second-hand bookstore on Broadway and 12th Street.

It was here that Linna developed her passion for period pulp fiction, which both rivals and complements her ardour for fifties rock'n'roll, and whose heyday ran from approximately 1949 to 1959. Using her Strand employee 50 per cent discount, she started picking up two paperbacks for a quarter, at a time (the late seventies) when the collector's market for this trash literature barely existed. Some of those 12.5-cent acquisitions are now worth hundreds of dollars, while Linna's collection numbers 15,000. She loves most forms of pulp (including the 'lavender' subgenre of gay fiction, books like *Let Me Die a Woman* and *From Studsville to Dudsville*), but her favourite subgenres are the juvenile-delinquency and sleaze genres. The JD novels, she says, were grimly realistic about street life: the only destination for kids-gone-bad was jail or an early grave. 'It's the real deal. They were writing when that stuff was happening and they were trying to give a voice to the kids, but without being namby-pamby or grown up about it.'

These entwined interests in rockabilly's unsung heroes (the singers who didn't make it) and hoodlum youth express a form of fidelity to Linna's working-class roots in Ohio. The daughter of a mine-worker, she grew up in a world divided between rich kids and poor kids, just like the greasers and socs of S. E. Hinton's *The Outsiders*. Social allegiance governs her taste, an act of defiance towards the cultured bourgeoisie who look down on pulp entertainment. 'Maybe it's from the other side of the tracks . . . But it's the *better* side of the tracks!'

I totally get the appeal of this populist stance. What I don't understand is why it's so exclusively fixated on the fifties. After all, if you wanted to side against the squares and the genteel, you could embrace the trashy, lowbrow masscult of today and achieve the same effect. Curiosity makes me ask Linna whether she's into gangsta rap. After all, that's the modern-day equivalent of the juvenile-delinquent and sleaze genres: bad boys with the social odds stacked against them; girls sidelined into skeezy roles as gold-diggers or thong-clad pole-dancers. The self-same 'dirty South' that spawned rockabilly today generates vast quantities of cheaply produced rap on shoestring independent labels, music that's seen by critics and do-gooders as socially destructive and artistically destitute – everything a pulp fan could want! Her look is first uncomprehending, then contemptuous. 'It's really not the same thing. With rappers, it's like – you're bad, get rich. You just didn't get rich when you were a juvenile delinquent in the nineteen fifties. You were as good as dead.'

Class loyalty, for Linna, appears to be bound up with keeping faith with an era. That's partly because she sees the fifties and early sixties as the golden age before 'the squares and the super-squares got hold of' rock'n'roll and made it mature and artistic. But it's connected to her personal history. Born in 1955, with an older brother and sister, 'all of the people I really admired would

---

THE PUNK/ROCKABILLY CONNECTION

During 1977, punk rockers and Teddy Boys fought each other on the streets of London. Delinquent but conservative, the Brylcreemed rock'n'roll revivalists thought punks were pretentious weirdos. Some say the Teds were also jealous that Malcolm McLaren had jilted them for a younger, fashion-forward crowd when he shifted from the vintage-fifties orientation of his early boutiques Let It Rock and Too Fast to Live to the confrontational shock aesthetic of Sex and Seditionaries. Yet rockabilly music and fifties style remained a submerged but crucial component of punk's DNA on both sides of the Atlantic, rising to the surface repeatedly all through the second half of the seventies.

• Ian Dury was a rock'n'roll diehard who hated hippies and never grew his hair long during the late sixties/early seventies, even though everyone else did (including the future Johnny Rotten). Dury's first group, Kilburn and the High Roads, recorded 'Upminster Kid', a recollection of being an East End

303

be considered delinquents. My brother was pretty much a greaser, and seeing his friends coming over – I just really thought those were like the cool people. Sometimes people who grow up in that situation aspire to move away from that situation, but it's never been that way for me.' She also refuses to leave behind the purity of adolescence, which in her case coincided with the adolescence of rock'n'roll. 'People think that's a period in your life that you are supposed to grow out of, but I think they miss the point that that is the perfect age – you're *perfect* at that point in time. Physically, mentally, whatever, you've *got it all*. So maybe it's like living your kid years for years and years to come, when you're *way* into adulthood.'

ROCK'N'ROLL GHOSTS

A strange thing happened to rock'n'roll and 'the 1950s' in the eighties and nineties. The style endured as something that bands

---

rockin' teen with 'sideburns to my chin' and 'a mean and nasty grin'. The song referenced 'Gene Vincent Craddock', the full name of the legendary rocker whose 1971 death actually spurred Dury to form the High Roads, and to whom he paid homage by wearing a single black leather glove. In his next group, The Blockheads, Dury penned the bittersweet requiem 'Sweet Gene Vincent', a rockabilly pastiche that was a highlight of 1977's huge-selling *New Boots and Panties* LP.

• The 101-ers's rockabilly tendencies resurfaced in Joe Strummer's next band, The Clash, with 1979's *London Calling*. It started with a cover of 'Brand New Cadillac' (by Vince Taylor, one of the UK's first rock'n'rollers), and the record sleeve mimicked the typeface and colour scheme used on Elvis Presley's debut album.

• Sid Vicious enjoyed posthumous Top 3 hits in 1979 with not one but two Eddie Cochran covers: 'Something Else' and 'C'mon Everybody'. Allegedly, Sid was a huge Sha Na Na fan.

• The Billy Idol-fronted Generation X referred to 'maximum rockabilly' in

would reactivate periodically, usually as a temporary option: a specific song, like Queen's 'Crazy Little Thing Called Love' or Dire Straits' 'Twisting by the Pool', or perhaps a whole album in that vein, as with the rockabilly and doo-wop records by Robert Plant, Neil Young and Billy Joel. But rock'n'roll seemed no longer capable of being a rebel identity, something that could represent a stand you were taking. When artists came along whose whole persona was based around the fifties – British rockabilly entertainers like Shakin' Stevens, Darts and Matchbox, or American pasticheurs like Marshall Crenshaw, Chris Isaak and The Stray Cats – the impression was of a vague evocativeness, emptied of the various meanings projected onto rock'n'roll by the likes of Lennon, Creedence, Steinman and The Cramps. What the style now signified was . . . style itself. It had become classic, and *classy*: a form of elegance that entered the permanent lexicon of the fashion world, popped up in the pages of *The Face* every few years, and filtered down to TV commercials. Like the Ratpack crooners or

---

'Kiss Me Deadly', while The Nipple Erectors, featuring future Pogue Shane MacGowan, recorded songs like 'King of the Bop' complete with Sun Studio-style echo on the singer's vocal.

• Some English punk bands switched to an outright rockabilly sound, e.g. The Polecats, featuring Boz Boorer, later to become Morrissey's guitarist and songwriting partner.

• Some American punks made the same move. The immaculately quiffed Robert Gordon, formerly of CBGB mainstays Tuff Darts, teamed up with rock'n'roll guitar hero Link Wray for one album. Willy DeVille, leader of Mink DeVille, adored *West Side Story* and named an album *Cabretta* after 'very thin, soft, black leather . . . it's tough but tender'. In Los Angeles, ex-punks like The Gun Club and The Flesh Eaters developed a poetically fevered Southern Gothic take on rockabilly with albums like *Fire of Love* and *A Minute to Pray, A Second to Die*. Down in Memphis, Tav Falco's Panther Burns surpassed everyone in primal-ness with the ultra-primitive *Behind the Magnolia Curtain*.

• Going solo, Alan Vega of proto-punk outfit Suicide kept the Sam Phillips-style

the Motown vocal groups, the sound and the look of rock'n'roll had ascended to the level of perennial cool.

George Michael's 'Faith' is the perfect example. The video starts with a glistening chrome Wurlitzer jukebox, the tone arm slowly moving to drop the needle on the record you're 'about to hear'. Michael wears tight blue jeans, metal-tipped cowboy boots and a black leather jacket. There's a Gene Vincent-style black leather glove on his right hand, the one that strums a Bo Diddley-esque 'dum de dum dum, dum dum' riff on a glistening Gretsch guitar. Every last detail is pitch-perfect, then, but all the style communicates by this point is timelessness, the blank universality of a brand like Levi's or the classic Coke bottle. 'Faith' expressed Michael's desire to break America (an ambition coyly indicated by the letters 'USA' that appeared in white on his leather jacket). The song achieved that goal and then some: 'Faith' became the top-selling US single of 1988 and an MTV/VH1 staple for years to come. And in a further indication of the universal appeal of

---

slapback echo on his voice but shed Suicide's electronic sound for guitar-led minimalist rockabilly. The single 'Jukebox Baby' became a hit in France, where they like their rock stylised.

• Bigger still in France were The Stray Cats, who had slicked-back quiffs and tattoos and a pared-down sound of stand-up double bass, a two-drum kit and a Gretsch 6120 guitar with a glowing maple-orange finish, just like the one Eddie Cochran had. 'Runaway Boy' smashed into the UK charts, and the cartoon-style videos for 'Stray Cat Strut' and 'Rock This Town' broke them on MTV.

What's puzzling in hindsight is how all these hipper-than-thou rockabillies differentiated *in their own heads* what they were doing from the mainstream fifties revival that ran all through this period, from John Lennon's *Rock and Roll* to Queen's 'Crazy Little Thing Called Love', from nostalgia acts like Showaddywaddy, Darts and Matchbox to *Grease* and the hit UK musical *Elvis!*. The latter starred Shakin' Stevens as Presley in his Sun Studio prime and helped propel the Welsh rocker towards becoming one of the biggest UK hit-makers of the eighties.

American (and faux-American) pop, the song reached no. 1 in four other countries besides the US. Ironically, the later video 'Freedom '90' expressed Michael's frustration with the straitjacket of his own stardom by having the leather jacket set on fire and the Gretsch blown to smithereens, while the song bleats, 'I hope you understand/ Sometimes the clothes do not make the man.' Yet the very gulf between the faux-rockabilly 'Faith' and the Soul II Soul pastiche of 'Freedom '90' indicates that for Michael, musical style is just a costume change.

From the early eighties on, rock'n'roll recurred only as a ghostly signifier detached from any real-world referents. Like a spook, it moved through the world without affecting it, lingered as a faintly disquieting trace of what-once-was. This idea of rock'n'roll as a spectral persistence, a present absence, underpinned Jim Jarmusch's 1989 movie *Mystery Train*, which is set in Memphis and features Elvis's ghost. Literally, in the form of a Presley phantom in gold lamé who makes a brief appearance, but also in the form of a character – an ageing sideburned rock'n'roller from England played by Joe Strummer – whose workmates have nicknamed him Elvis. In the hotel where he and his friends end up after a bungled robbery, there's a kitschy painting of Elvis in every room. Strummer's greaser character, who bitterly resents his nickname, responds with exasperation: 'Christ, there he is again – I can't get rid of that fucking guy! Why is he fuckin' everywhere?'

Like *Mystery Train*, Jarmusch's earlier movies *Stranger Than Paradise* and *Down by Law* took place in mythic American music towns: New York and New Orleans respectively. And both shared a curious twilight-zone ambience suggestive of some indefinable era that's neither present nor past. Being shot in black and white contributed to this effect, as did the old-fashioned appliances (radios, small black-and-white TVs, etc.) and non-contemporary clothes worn by the characters (pork-pie hats, braces and jackets). The idea of *Stranger* – although it's left oblique and indistinct, a mood rather than a theme – is America as a mythic wonderland that eludes the grasp even of those born in the US. By the time Jarmusch made *Down by Law*, New Orleans had turned its jazz heritage into a tourist attraction, and he took full advantage of the city's out-of-time atmosphere, the sense of a present oppressively haunted by its past.

Memphis, like New Orleans, is horribly overshadowed by its myths and legends. It draws visitors from all over the world looking for what is no longer there. In *Mystery Train*, these tourists are represented by a teenage Japanese couple who disembark the locomotive and head straight to Sun Studios (where the guide's rehearsed patter is so mechanical and rapid-fire it's incomprehensible, meaningless). The taciturn boyfriend and his talkative girlfriend then wander the seriously run-down city, its streets largely empty of people, weeds poking up through cracks in the sidewalk. From his immaculate Brylcreemed quiff to his Zippo lighter and cigarette tucked behind the ear, the Japanese boy is enthralled by and in thrall to an image of cool from thirty years earlier. He looks like the spitting image of the young Presley, but his face is perfectly expressionless, a death mask of you-can't-reach-me. In a sense, through its deadlock hold on his imagination, rock'n'roll has turned him into a ghost too.

3: 'TOMORROW'

10

GHOSTS OF FUTURES PAST

Sampling, Hauntology and Mash-Ups

Sampling is strange. But what's stranger still is how quickly we got used to it. I don't just mean the way that, within a few years of it becoming widespread in the mid-eighties, it was hard to find a musician who objected on principle to having their music sampled. What's really remarkable is how it just became an every-day part of our listening lives to enjoy – and to accept *as* music – records that were made out of fragments of other records: chunks of performance severed from their original time-and-place.

The strangeness of sampling has worn away after all these years, but it hit me viscerally for the first time in an aeon when I heard 'Caermaen', a track on Belbury Poly's 2005 album *The Willows*. You can tell from the quaint diction and the sample's deterio-rated texture – like yellowed, crumbling paper – that the plain-tive English folk singer had been recorded many, many decades earlier. The misty mysteriousness of the voice beckons the listener closer, but meaning always recedes: strain and squint your ears, yet you can't quite make out a single distinct word. Framed in an arrangement at once electronic and medieval, 'Caermaen' is eerie enough in itself. But when you find out the back story, it becomes genuinely creepy. Belbury Poly's Jim Jupp discovered the vocal – Joseph Taylor singing 'Bold William Taylor' – on a CD of English traditional music. The rendition had been originally captured in 1908 on a cylinder recording made by the folk-song collector Percy Grainger. Sampling the whole tune, Jupp 'changed the speed and pitch and reconstructed it to make a different melody with unintelligible lyrics'. Effectively, he *made a dead man sing a brand-new song*. Someone with a superstitious streak might well have hesitated before taking such a liberty.

'Caermaen' and the story of its making gave me a vivid flashback to the disorientation induced by the first hip-hop records based entirely around sampling, tracks from 1986–7 by producers like Herby Azor and Marly Marl. Inspired by the Azor-produced Salt-N-Pepa album *Hot, Cool & Vicious*, I wrote at the time about the sensual but uncanny friction of the grooves, stitched together out of dismembered portions of funk and soul songs, reanimated Dr Frankenstein-style. Uncanny, because different studio auras and different eras were being placed in 'ghostly adjacence'. Belbury Poly's label, as it happens, is called Ghost Box.

SEANCE FICTION

Recording has always had a spectral undercurrent. As audio-technology scholar Jonathan Sterne points out, recording separated the human voice from a living body for the first time. He sees 'phonographic time' as 'the outgrowth' of a nineteenth-century culture that had recently invented canning and embalming. Phonographs held out the prospect of a kind of immortality, the possibility that our voices would be listened to by 'the not yet born'.

Records have certainly habituated us to living with phantoms, from Caruso to Cobain. In a sense, a record really is a ghost: it's a trace of a musician's body, the after-imprint of breath and exertion. There's a parallel between the phonograph and the photograph: both are reality's death mask. With analogue recording, there's a direct physical relationship with the sound source. Music theorist Nick Katranis uses the analogy of fossilisation to explain the profound difference between analogue (vinyl, tape, film) and digital (CD, MP3). Analogue captures 'the physical imprint of a sound wave, like a creature's body pressed into what becomes a fossil', whereas digital is a 'reading' of the sound wave, 'a pointilised drawing of it'. A supporter of analogue, Katranis asks rhetorically: 'Do you like your ghosts to rub up against you?' Roland Barthes likewise described the photograph as 'the ectoplasm of "what-had-been": neither image nor reality, a new being, really: a reality one can no longer touch'. He compared the emotions stirred by looking at photographs of his adored but dead mother with the uncanny sensation he got when listening to 'the recorded voices of dead singers'.

Like a spectre, a recorded musician is at once present and absent. There is even a specific type of ghost that the musical recording corresponds to, what supernaturalists call 'the residual ghost': unlike the intelligent, responsive spook that can be communicated with and often has a specific message to deliver, the residual phantom is 'usually unaware of change in its surroundings and continues to play the same scene repeatedly'. Edison boasted of how his invention could reproduce sound 'without the presence or consent of the original source, and after the lapse of any period of time'. In other words, records are ghosts you can control. Indeed, Edison originally envisaged the phonograph primarily as a means of preserving the voices of loved ones after death.

Recording is pretty freaky, then, if you think about it. But sampling doubles its inherent supernaturalism. Woven out of looped moments that are each like portals to far-flung times and places, the sample collage creates a musical event that never happened; a mixture of time-travel and seance. Sampling involves using recordings to make new recordings; it's the musical art of ghost

313

co-ordination and ghost arrangement. It's often compared with collage. But the added dimension of time that music inhabits makes sample-based music profoundly different from photo-montage. With recorded music, however much it's doctored and enhanced through studio techniques (multitracking, overdubs et al.), what you hear is a sequence of human actions happening in real time. (I'm talking about played music here, of course, but that is overwhelmingly what gets sampled, rather than music that has programmed rhythms or is made with digital technology.) To take a segment of living time – which is what a sample is – and chain it into a loop isn't just appropriation, it's expropriation. In a certain sense – neither literally true nor utterly metaphorical – sampling is enslavement: involuntary labour that's been alienated from its original environment and put into service in a completely other context, creating profit and prestige for another.

It's curious that almost all the intellectual effort expended on the subject of sampling has been in its defence. When sampling first made waves in the mid-eighties, journalistic discussions nearly always focused on the legal aspect, framing the samplers in punk-like terms (as rebellious, iconoclastic). Academic studies of sampling have likewise generally sided with 'the streets' versus the multinational entertainment companies. This reflects the left-wing bias of academia and a tendency to see the whole area of property rights, including copyright, as intrinsically conservative, aligned with corporations and land-owners, the status quo. Some theorists also argue that ideas of originality and intellectual property are ethnocentric, pointing out that non-Western or pre-capitalist folk cultures often have much looser, more collective notions of authorship. Still, it is surprising how few thinkers have considered the issue from the perspective of the samplee rather than the sampler. A Marxist analysis of sampling might conceivably see it as the purest form of exploiting the labour of others. In a more general sense, you could see it as a form of cultural

314

strip-mining, a ransacking of the rich seams of past musical productivity.

Discussing his invention of the 'readymade', Marcel Duchamp said his intention was to free art from the sphere of the hand-made; a sample is like a sonic readymade, and artists who make music out of samples are freeing music from the sphere of the hand-played. The sampler, wrote Jeremy J. Beadle (a champion of sample-based cut-up music of the JAMMS/KLF/Pop Will Eat Itself sort), shifted 'power to the producer – the producer could construct new artifacts from "real" (i.e. non-synthesised) performances without having to endure the presence of musicians'. This is enormously empowering, in a punky do-it-yourself way, for producers; but by the same token, it's disempowering for both the original musicians who've been divested of their performances and for professional musicians as a class, given that they've invested time and energy in acquiring their skills and now find themselves increasingly unnecessary.

Although it's the obviously sampladelic styles (the many sub-genres of dance and hip hop) that blatantly depend on earlier eras of musical creativity and labour, sampling has a more imperceptible presence in all kinds of rock and pop music, thanks to the routine studio use of sampled drum sounds and instrumental timbres. Programmes like SoundReplacer, a 'plug-in' that's used with the industry-standard digital-audio platform Pro Tools, allow producers to replace every single drum hit in a sub-par drumming performance with stronger-sounding percussive timbres; these can be made by the producer in controlled laboratory conditions, but are more likely to come from a commercially sold 'drum sample library'. Sometimes they come from famous drummers like Led Zeppelin's John Bonham, whose feel and timbre is unique and highly covetable.

'Sound replacement' sounds a bit like hip replacement, and the whole procedure, in its precision and sterility, does recall

315

the state-of-the-art surgery of transplanted organs, artificially grown skin tissue and bionic prosthetics. The result of this kind of studio doctoring is horribly familiar to anyone who's listened to radio in the last ten years or so. With genres that foreground their anti-naturalism (R&B, electronic pop, etc.) this doesn't seem to matter so much. But it is particularly unsatisfying – even vaguely perturbing – when the music offers a simulacrum of live energy (as with most rock productions), but what you hear does not have the integrity of a musical performance, is riddled with non-presence.

This kind of subliminal sampling is different from the blatant aesthetic dis-integration of rap and dance music, where a performance fragment is wrenched from its matrix of musical meaning and applied to different purposes altogether, frequently without consultation or even the knowledge of the original performer. One example out of millions: the bass groove of Massive Attack's trip-hop classic 'Safe from Harm', based on a segment from Billy Cobham's jazz-fusion classic 'Stratus'. Despite being reverent fans of jazz fusion, Massive Attack jettison all the noodly improvisational stuff that really mattered to Cobham and the other players on 'Stratus' (Jan Hammer, Lee Sklar, Tommy Bolin) and focus on the driving bass-and-drums groove. Indeed, they pinpoint the most linear, straightforward portion of the rhythm track, which gets looser and wilder at other points in the song. The revenue stream from such licensed sampling (Cobham gets a song credit on 'Safe from Harm') probably sweetens the deal sufficiently. But with a lot of sampling in underground dance cultures not only is there no compensation but the samples may be deployed in ways that are offensive to the originator. As a raver, I loved the cheeky way that hardcore rave producers hijacked snippets of love songs and turned them into paeans to Ecstasy, but – looking at it from a different perspective – I could see how an artist subjected to this kind of indignity could easily be appalled.

316

There's a parallel here with the online-porn practice of taking images of movie stars and other celebrities and Photoshopping their heads onto nude bodies engaged in hardcore sex acts. That seems to me to be a blatant infringement of an individual's rights in their own image. But it could easily be recast as fan fiction, what theorists like Michel de Certeau and Henry Jenkins call 'textual poaching': the creatively impertinent expression of fantasy using the star as 'raw material'.

A photo collage that transposed Michael Jackson's head and leather jacket from the cover of his album *Bad* onto a naked female body appeared on the front of *Plunderphonic*, the infamous 1989 CD by Canadian composer John Oswald, in which he turned sampling into a form of digital iconoclasm, literally smashing pop idols to smithereens. More conceptual than most sampling practitioners, Oswald concentrated on reworking a single work by a single artist, typically putting a famous song like Bing Crosby's 'White Christmas' through the digital mincer and then surgically reconstructing it into a convulsive and grotesquely misshapen doppelganger of itself. 'Dab', Oswald's unravelling of Jackson's 'Bad', is his masterpiece. Not really a pop fan, Oswald attempted to inject life into what he felt was an inert, smothered-in-the-studio recording by chopping it up into a set of Beefheart-goes-disco seizures. But halfway through, the remake takes off into the cosmos: micro-syllable vocal particles are multitracked as if in some infinite hall of mirrors and a strobing swarm of micro-Jacksons billows back and forth across the stereo field.

Despite scrupulously identifying his sources and circulating *Plunderphonic* on a strictly non-commercial basis, Oswald was hounded by the Canadian Recording Industry Association at the behest of several of their clients. Among them was Michael Jackson, who was reputedly more pissed off by the liberties taken with his image on the cover than the audio defacing of his song. 'Bad' was Jackson's bid to toughen up his image to keep pace with

317

hip hop (hence the leather jacket and all the crotch-grabbing in the video), but *Plunderphonic*'s porno photomontage turned him into a dickless hermaphrodite with a neatly trimmed pubic bush. In the end, Oswald was forced to destroy all remaining copies of the CD that hadn't already been sent out to magazines and other interested parties. *Plunderphonic*'s conceptual audio collage was not actually a new thing, though. Avant-garde composer James Tenney had created a musique concrète deconstruction of Elvis Presley as early as 1961 with 'Collage No. 1 (Blue Suede)'. Bernard Parmegiani, a protégé of musique concrète pioneer Pierre Schaeffer, made several tape-based works based around diced-and-spliced pop culture, including 1969's 'Du Pop à L'Ane', which is like a duet between radios that are dialling randomly across the FM spectrum, mingling chintzy Gallic accordions with lewdly honking Dixieland and recognisable rock tunes by the likes of The Doors. In rock itself, or rather on the fringes of rock, there'd been The Residents' defacements of The Beatles and sixties pop classics on 'Beyond the Valley of a Day in the Life' and *The Third Reich 'N Roll*. Vinyl-vandalist Christian Marclay developed his own scratching techniques from the mid-seventies onwards independently of hip hop, and tended to focus on a single recording at a time rather than cutting between discs, or at least concentrate on a single artist's records – Louis Armstrong, Jimi Hendrix, Maria Callas, Ferrante & Teicher, John Cage – rather than leap across genres.

Oswald himself had started messing with plunderphonic pranks before the sampler existed, in the form of his Mystery Lab cassettes, which involved tape-editing or using a doctored turntable whose revolutions-per-minute range was expanded dramatically at either end of the scale. One of the best *Plunderphonic* pieces is a strictly analogue effort called 'Pretender', which inflicts a sex change on Dolly Parton by taking her voice from only-audible-to-dogs ultra-treble (80 rpm) to a testosterone-thick infra-bass (12 rpm). But again, like the hermaphrodite Jackson image, you could see this as a kind of assault on Parton's sexy-but-wholesome image.

Plunderphonics rather often resembles an audio version of Pop Art, but with Warhol's blank affection for mass culture replaced by a Zappa-esque sneer. *Plexure*, the sort-of-sequel to *Plunderphonic*, cannibalised the entirety of contemporary pop'n'rock circa 1990 in one foul swoop, compositing sonic shrapnel from 5,000 songs into a twenty-minute bombardment of crescendos, choruses, soul-screams, whammy-bar back-blasts and power chords. Here the clear intent was to expose the American radio-scape as a moronic inferno of kitsch and schlock.

After this, the only way to go forward for Oswald was to take the plunderphonic techniques of 'audio-quotes' and 'folding' and use them in a sympathetic, even reverent manner. At the invitation of The Grateful Dead, Oswald entered the band's legendary vaults, where recordings of virtually every performance they ever did are archived. Sifting through a hundred versions of 'Dark Star', the perennial launch pad for the Dead's most cosmically probing improvisations, he extracted around forty hours of material, which he then distilled into two hour-long CDs, *Transitive Axis* and *Mirror Ashes*, later to be combined as *Grayfolded*.

What was disconcerting for those of us familiar with plunderphonics' disrespectful treatments of its sources was how *Grayfolded* stayed true to the spirit of the Dead. The first disc especially resembles a seamless, super-fluent monster jam. Most of the time it actually sounds like a plausible real-time event, even though Oswald has Garcia and the other members of the Dead jamming with their own doppelgangers across a twenty-five-year time span, stitched together using samples that are for the most part shorter than fifteen seconds long and sometimes as brief as a quarter of a second. The goal was to capture, or simulate, the intangible magic of the Dead concert experience. 'So I did things that are unnatural,' Oswald told me. 'Like have a young Jerry Garcia sing with an old Jerry, or have an orchestra of multiple Dead musicians, all in order to pump up the sonic experience so that at certain points you think: "What's happening? Have the drugs kicked in?"'

Oswald said his favourite reaction was 'from a guy on the Internet who wrote that *Grayfolded* makes him cry, because it encapsulates twenty-five years of Garcia, and it's unreal in a way that gave him a very visceral sensation of it being a ghost'. Yet *Grayfolded* also anticipated some unnerving developments in pop culture, such as the highly active afterlife of rival rappers Tupac and Notorious B.I.G. (culminating in their grotesque 'duet' together, 2003's 'Runnin' (Dying to Live)'), or the way that digital techniques would enable the cut-and-pasting of moving images of Audrey Hepburn, Cary Grant and Humphrey Bogart from Hollywood's celluloid archive into brand-new TV commercials (in Hepburn's case, infringing her dignity by making her dance to AC/DC!). As technology develops, it may become possible for computers to completely forge the timbre and vocal mannerisms of deceased stars, allowing their estates to exploit their talents long after death.

THE GROOVE ROBBERS

Plunderphonic's original release coincided with the late-eighties wave of sampling in mainstream pop: American hip-hop artists like Beastie Boys, the UK's 'DJ records' craze of artists like Coldcut and M/A/R/R/S, and an array of punky mischief-makers such as the Justified Ancients of Mu Mu (aka The KLF) and Pop Will Eat Itself. The latter cluster of UK pranksters, while far less avant-garde in effect and technically clumsy compared to Oswald, shared the plunderphonic emphasis on the recognisable 'audio quote'. With collage tracks like the JAMMSs 'All You Need

Is Love' or Pop Will Eat Itself's 'Def Con One', listener enjoyment was largely bound up with reference-spotting. Often, the sampled musician was being subjected to various degrees of insult, satire or travesty. Music itself was being given the finger, its pomposity undercut. Coldcut called one of their early tracks 'Beats + Pieces' to spotlight its thrown-together nature and put the slogan 'Sorry, but this just isn't music' on the cover. This was a boast masquerading as an apology, representatives of the newly empowered class of DJs disavowing their reliance on recordings (and the labour of trained musicians) while asserting their upstart status as auteurs.

But even as this self-consciously confrontational approach to sampling flared up in the mainstream, other approaches to the new machine were stealthily emerging. Sampling technology, through its translation of an analogue musical source into the zeroes and ones of digital code, enabled the user to mangle, distort and otherwise transubstantiate the material. This meant that the sampler didn't need to be a quote machine but could also effectively work as an instrument of pure sound synthesis, something that didn't just decontextualise its sources but abstracted them too. Another approach was to retain the sample's recognisability, in the sense that what you heard at the end of the process sounded like 'proper' music (groovy, melodic, hand-played) and also audibly belonged to a particular genre (usually funk, jazz, soul, etc.), but to stick to sources that would be unfamiliar to 99.8 per cent of listeners. This kind of sampling wasn't a form of citation or particularly postmodern at all, but more akin to practices like beachcombing, architectural salvage and recycling.

From the late eighties onwards, a crate-digger culture gradually emerged: beat prospectors in search of obscure raw material who scavenged thrift stores, yard sales and the basements of mom-and-pop record stores choked with second-hand vinyl that had become virtually valueless now that the general public had shifted to CDs. The skill of the auteur crate-digger – figures like

Prince Paul, Premier, the RZA, DJ Shadow – was not just locating those secret record spots and then putting in the hours of dust-inhaling graft sifting through boxes of used and mostly useless vinyl. It was the acute sensibility that enabled them to spot a potential sample that others wouldn't notice: the briefest wisp of orchestration or miniscule rhythm guitar part that could work as a loop, that incidental moment in a jazz-funk track where the instrumentation dropped away and a scatter of notes became isolated that could be repurposed as the central melodic riff of a new track. The parallel for this new form of phonographic artistry was photography, specifically the techniques of cropping and enlargement. With sampling, the detail that's zoomed in on and 'blown up' is not spatial but temporal. A moment that would otherwise just be lost in the forward flow of music is arrested and stretched by looping, allowing the ear to linger lovingly on it, *in* it.

DJ Shadow pushed underground hip hop's crate-digger ethos right up front with the record cover of *Endtroducing*, his 1996 debut album: a photograph of the miles of aisles in his favourite store, Records, in Sacramento, California. In the hip-hop turntablist documentary *Scratch*, Shadow is interviewed in the store's basement, a chaotic and grubby underworld of used records, and a place that only a select few of the shop's patrons are given access to. While making *Endtroducing*, his solution to creative block was to head on over to Records and disappear into the cellar, 'finding solace down there and buying records that would get me out of the jams . . . Record stores are my muse in a certain respect, and that store certainly was for *Endtroducing*.' In the documentary he meditates, movingly, on how the bargain basement is a cemetery of dead dreams, full of shellac relics of the hope and creativity of countless forgotten or never-known musicians who strove to make it in the business.

Early in his career, with the astonishing releases 'In/Flux' and 'Entropy', DJ Shadow actually went under the name DJ Shadow and the Groove Robbers. The pun was funny but it was also appropriately Gothic, for digging in the crates has a certain resemblance to grave-robbing, with DJ/producers as body-snatchers violating the vinyl cadavers and trafficking in organs. (Once in Records' vault of vinyl Shadow actually found a dead bat under a pile of platters – how's that for Gothic?)

I suggested earlier that in a certain sense a sample is both ghost and slave. Looping transforms these phonographic after-images of human energy and passion – a vocal refrain, a drum lick, a guitar riff – into treadmills of posthumous productivity. Certain widely used, endlessly replicated samples have been cloned into entire slave races. A good example is the 'Amen' breakbeat: a brief percussion-only passage on 'Amen My Brother', a filler instrumental tacked on the end of an LP by the gospel/R&B troupe The Winstons. What happened to the 'Amen' break reminds me of Disney's *The Sorcerer's Apprentice*, in which the wizard's minion Mickey Mouse casts a spell on a broomstick so it does his chores for him. When it gets out of control, he takes an axe to the broom, but each splinter becomes a new broom – an ungodly slave swarm dementedly fetching water and causing a flood. Likewise, the 'Amen' break proliferated into thousands upon thousands of jungle tracks based on that one drum snippet, which producers edited into endless subtly different but instantly recognisable variations on just five seconds in the life of Winstons drummer Gregory Coleman.

Digital-era musics like hip hop and dance are deeply dependent on the analogue era's output of hot licks and cool grooves. Hence the spirit of *reverent exploitation* with which producers like LTJ Bukem (one of the first junglists to use 'Amen') and Madlib approach the seventies, which they see as both a golden age and a gold mine. It's a cultural peak that they honour through recycling, in the process conferring a kind of immortality for the music, if not for its anonymous creators.

323

Unlike peak oil or other natural resources, music can be sampled without being used up. But the cultural use-value of a lick or beat (even one as potent and adaptable as 'Amen') does eventually depreciate with overexposure, which means that the crate-digger vanguard is driven in search of ever rarer grooves. One zone that beckoned was private-press recordings. Similar to vanity publishing, these were records that were never commercially released or sold through retail outlets but instead printed up by individuals or small organisations (clubs, schools, religious associations, and so forth) and either sold directly or given away to members. The pressings, being miniscule (usually in the hundreds, sometimes as low as fifty), guarantee the rarity and obscurity of the music. *The Private Press* is what DJ Shadow titled his second album, released in 2001, but he was unusually hardcore about pursuing obscurity, taking a particular interest in personalised discs in editions of one, the kind of things recorded in the make-your-own-record booths of yore.

The other new frontier for crate-diggers was library music. This was the term for incidental music from the sixties and seventies originally made for use in radio, cinema adverts, industrial films and other non-glamorous contexts which was sold by subscription, not in shops, and issued in uniform sleeves complete with track descriptions ('light relaxed swingalong', 'industrious activity', 'neutral abstract underscore') that helped the purchaser to identify the precise mood tint they needed. Listening, it's easy to picture the scene: a recording studio just off London's Wardour Street circa 1971; a failed composer frantically scribbles an arrangement on a score, like Shakespeare finishing the third act while the players are halfway through Act Two; the session players grumble and puff on Benson & Hedges, resting their violins and horns on their laps.

By the early nineties, library records from the sixties and seventies issued by companies like KPM, Studio G and Boosey &

Hawkes were starting to be highly prized by hip-hop and dance producers: their crisply recorded sound quality and session-musician-calibre playing offered a cornucopia of beats, fanfares and refrains for them to use. And at a time when music publishers and record labels were becoming vigilant about sampling and demanding royalty shares, you stood a better chance of getting away with it if you used a vintage library-record lick. Soon the original library albums started to get pretty expensive.

One of the key figures in library music's rising profile was Jonny Trunk. His label Trunk Records debuted in 1996 with the world's first compilation of library music, *The Super Sounds of Bosworth*. Although far from your archetypal Brit B-boy – he looks more like Eric Morecambe and his real name is Jonathan Benton-Hughes – Trunk had passed through the UK crate-digger scene that emerged in the early to mid-nineties: the milieu that produced trip-hop labels like Mo Wax and Ninjatune, salvage labels like Finders Keepers and Cherrystones, and library-loving DJ/producer types such as Luke Vibert, aka Wagon Christ, and

---

JONNY TRUNK AND TRUNK RECORDS

Jonny Trunk first became obsessed with library music, without knowing what it was, as a teenager intrigued by the weird electronic underscores 'on Open University programmes, like when there was a sequence about microbes'. Years later, someone played him an album on the Bosworth library label. 'I thought, "That's it, the Open University sound!"' Spotting the company's address on the back cover, he 'just walked around the corner' to their central London office and 'knocked on the door', finding inside a 'Hammer House of Horror scene' of decades-old dust and teetering piles of sheet music.

The name Trunk actually comes from friends teasing him about being 'nosy'. 'There's a part of me that wants to be a detective. I like digging about.' His sleuthing tracked down maverick composers like Basil Kirchin and Desmond Leslie. The latter's *Music of the Future* – homespun musique concrète recorded in the late fifties – is one of Trunk's great discoveries. An ex-Spitfire pilot and UFO expert, Leslie was 'a member of the landed gentry, so could afford to throw

Joel Martin, aka Quiet Village. 'The British were very good at it,' Trunk recalls. 'There was something really interesting going on in the centre of London at that time. You had figures like Jerry Dammers and Normski, and weirdo fashion people, all hanging out in funny record shops and exploring odd jazz, film music, hip hop. I used to call them "bag boys", people you'd run into around the middle of London and you'd all be carrying a bag of records. You'd be swapping records and there'd be certain cafes you'd meet at.'

HAUNTED AUDIO

The UK beat-digger scene was deeply influenced by American hip hop: the quest for rare grooves, the use of shards of film scores to

---

rotating fans and buckets of sand into pianos'. As for Kirchin, this jobbing composer recorded droves of library LPs and movie scores, interspersed with the occasional full-blown avant-garde album like *Worlds Within Worlds*. Trunk's obsession culminated with a compendium of library sleeves he pulled together for design publisher Fuel. Encompassing stark modernist grids, surreal photocollages, kitschadelic op art and bizarrely clumsy drawings that exert a macabre compulsion akin to outsider art, the artwork collected in *The Music Library* showed how library covers could be as inadvertently avant-garde as the music they packaged. Both were produced in factory conditions where utilitarian practicality and experimental impulses coexisted on a tight budget.

On Trunk's website there's the slogan: 'Music, sex, and nostalgia'. For as long as he can remember, Trunk has been susceptible to a bittersweet attraction to the bygone. While his childhood friends followed the latest pop fashions, he was into Henry Mancini movie scores. 'I don't feel the new market as much as the old one. I'm drawn to old things.' His soundtrack salvage for Trunk ranges from *The Wicker Man* OST to the incidental music for the seventies kids TV classics like *The Clangers* and *The Tomorrow People*. As for sex, that comes into it through his interest in vintage porn, which Trunk claims is all about the period aesthetics rather than any prurient use-value. 'You can't beat a good *Mayfair*,' he chuckles, before explaining that true connoisseurs hunt for late-sixties periodical *Zeta*, with its stylish, cutting-edge photography (nudes in scrapyards). As with record-

create soundtracks for imaginary movies. But if you contrasted the British stuff with American rap, there was a discernible absence of expressive urgency. It could be richly atmospheric and make for pleasant background listening, but apart from testifying to the refined taste of its creators and their record-collecting skills, it wasn't really saying anything. That was partly due to its literally lacking a voice (in the sense of an MC rapping over the beat). But American hip hop communicates a sense of cultural identity just through its sound, being woven from vintage funk and soul, blaxploitation soundtracks, eighties quiet storm and 'slow jams'. Because the British stuff wasn't drawing anything from its own surroundings or history, it ended up just perpetuating the syndrome of the white British middle-class musician who has immaculate taste in black sounds (think Ken Colyer, Alexis

---

collector culture, there are fashions on the vintage skin-mag scene: 'Nineteen eighties rude mags, that's the new hot zone – all DayGlo knickers and shoulder pads.' Trunk put out *Flexi Sex* (a CD collection of the ultra-lewd spoken-word flexi-singles porn mags once stuck between their soon-to-be-stuck-together pages), the self-explanatory *Mary Millington Talks Dirty* and, in collaboration with Fuel, the book *Dressing for Pleasure*, about the vintage leather- and rubber-fetish magazine *Atomage*. Porn also informed one of Trunk's few non-reissue releases, *Dirty Fan Male*, which involved an actor known as Wisbey reading out filthy letters sent to Trunk's sister, a softcore starlet. *Dirty Fan Male* became a cult favourite, inspiring Trunk to turn it into a stage show, which played at the 2004 Edinburgh Fringe Festival and won the *Guardian*'s Best Concept award. He also released a spin-off single, sung by Wisbey and titled 'The Ladies Bras', which actually reached the UK Top 30 after a campaign by DJ Danny Baker to make it a hit.

Cheesy sleaze and sepia-toned melancholy seem unlikely bedfellows at first glance. But in his 1935 travel book *Journey Without Maps*, Graham Greene put his finger on or near the place where musty and lustful meet. He wrote about how 'seediness has a very deep appeal . . . It seems to satisfy, temporarily, the sense of nostalgia for something lost; it seems to represent a stage further back.' With their aura of wistful reverie and faded decay, the sounds exhumed by Trunk offer a portal into Britain's cultural unconscious.

Korner, John Mayall) but whose creative efforts pale next to the real thing.

For there to be a true British counterpart to hip hop, it might use the same techniques (samples, loops, crate-digging), but it would have to be plugged into uniquely native resources and traditions. Enter hauntology, a term that critic Mark Fisher and I started bandying around in 2005 to describe a loose network of mostly UK artists, central among them the musicians on the Ghost Box label (The Focus Group, Belbury Poly, The Advisory Circle et al.) and their kindred spirits Mordant Music and Moon Wiring Club. All of these groups explore a zone of British nostalgia linked to television programming of the sixties and seventies. Consummate scavengers, the hauntologists trawl through charity shops, street markets and jumble sales for delectable morsels of decaying culture-matter. Their music typically mixes digital and analogue: samples and computer-edited material mingle with antique synthesizer tones and acoustic instruments; motifs inspired by or directly stolen from library music and movie scores (particularly pulp genres like science fiction and horror) are woven together with industrial drones and abstract noise; and there's often a musique concrète/radio-play element of spoken word and found sounds.

'Memoradelia', an alternative term proposed by writer Patrick McNally, captures the sense of a collective unconscious, the ghosts of our life coming back to haunt us, as well as the personal reveries of 'lost time' that this music often conjures like Proust's madeleine cake. But hauntology, a term borrowed from Jacques Derrida's 1994 book *Spectres of Marx*, is the term that's stuck. A pun on 'ontology' (in French '*hantologie*' and 'ontology' sound almost the same because the 'h' isn't pronounced), the concept allowed Derrida to use the philosophically problematic figure of the ghost – neither being nor non-being, both presence and absence simultaneously – to discuss the uncanny persistence of

328

Marx's ideas after the death of communism and 'the end of history' (the supposed triumph of liberal capitalism announced by Francis Fukuyama).

'Hauntology' was a hot concept in academia all through the 2000s, where it was used to frame conferences on memory and ruins. It even cropped up in fashion-theory circles, informing the 2004 Victoria and Albert exhibition *Spectres: When Fashion Turns Back*, whose subject was retro and recycling in couture: the way that, as curator Judith Clark put it, 'uncanny recognitions and unpredictable conjunctions are integral to the fashion machine'. Hauntology also became a buzzword in the art world, where work based around archives, historical memory, lost and decayed futures et al. was in vogue for much of the decade. In the summer of 2010, two separate American exhibitions based around the concept took place concurrently. Berkeley Art Museum's *Hauntology* was co-curated by musician Scott Hewicker but largely consisted of paintings. Meanwhile, over in New York, the Guggenheim's photography and video exhibition *Haunted* divided the work displayed into categories such as 'appropriation and the archive', 'documentation and reiteration', 'landscape, architecture and the passage of time' and 'trauma and the uncanny'. The catalogue text argued that all recordings (photography, film, video, phonograph and tape) are 'ghostly reminders of lost time and the elusiveness of memory' and observed that 'Much contemporary art seems haunted by the apparitions that are reanimated in reproductions . . . By using dated stylistic devices, subject matter and technologies, such art embodies a longing for an otherwise irrecuperable past.'

'Hauntology' mainly appealed to me because it was a cute handle for Ghost Box: the '-ology' suggested solemn laboratory researchers investigating the sonic paranormal. But Derrida's ideas certainly have applications to what Ghost Box and their fellow travellers are doing. Running through a lot of the music, as well as the artwork and conceptual framing of the project, are

329

ideas of a lost utopianism: the post-welfare-state era of benevolent state planning and social engineering. Derrida writes about the spectral nature of the archive; Ghost Box-type music often has a musty-and-dusty aura, like 'a museum come to life', as Mike Powell put it. Hauntological music also typically foregrounds the phantasmagoric aspects of recording. On albums like The Focus Group's *hey let loose your love*, the half-erased or never-quite-attained song forms reminded many listeners of the way that dub producers use reverb and other studio techniques to shroud reggae music in wraith-like after-images. In blog and webzine discussions, hip hop also came up as a reference point: not just for the role of sampling, but because of the similar use in both of the crackles, pops and hiss of vinyl surface noise, drawing attention to the fact that you were listening to a record made out of other records. But the wispy unreality of the music and its mood blend of whimsy and witchy seemed equally to slot Ghost Box and their allies into an English psychedelic tradition of studio sorcery going back to The Beatles' 'Strawberry Fields Forever' and Joe Meek's *I Hear a New World*.

THE PAST INSIDE THE PRESENT

The immediate ancestor for the UK hauntologists was Boards of Canada, who emerged in the late nineties with a darkly enchanting mix of electronica and psychedelia, spoken-word samples and uncanny atmospheres. Released on Warp in 1998, *Music Has the Right to Children* led to the Scottish duo (Marcus Eoin and Michael Sandison, brothers despite the different surnames) being hailed as successors to The Aphex Twin. BoC anticipated Ghost Box et al. with their talk of music's 'almost supernatural' powers ('I think you actually manipulate people with music,' said Eoin in one interview) and their obsession with 'the past inside the present' (a sample on the 2002 track 'Music Is Math').

330

Boards of Canada also pioneered the hauntological approach to creating old-timey and elegiac atmospheres through the use of sound treatments suggestive of decay and wear-and-tear. Our cultural memories are shaped not just by the production qualities of an era (black and white, mono, certain kinds of drum sound or recording ambience, etc.) but by subtle properties of the recording media themselves (photographic or film stock that screams seventies or eighties, for instance). These properties include the medium's specific rate of decay. BoC's artificially faded and discoloured textures stir up the kinds of feelings you get from watching old home movies that are speckled with blotches of colour, or from leafing through a family photo album full of snapshots that are turning an autumnal yellow. It's like you're witnessing the fading of your own memories. Eoin and Sandison achieved these simulated effects of erosion-by-time by avoiding digital processing and using analogue treatments, such as running elements of a track through a defective tape recorder. In one case, they took a melody played on whistles and 'bounced it back and forward between the internal mics of two tape-decks until the sound started disappearing into hell', Sandison told *Pitchfork*. 'Like when you look at an image reflected within two mirrors forever, in the distance it gets darker and greener and murkier.'

It took me a while to fall under the spell of *Music Has a Right to Children*, but when it happened, the record took over my life for a good while. The crumbly smudges of texture, the miasmic melody lines, the tangled threads of wistful and eerie seemed to have an extraordinary capacity to trigger ultra-vivid reveries that felt like childhood memories. I would experience a flood of images that were emotionally neutral yet charged with significance, a mysticism of the commonplace and municipal: playgrounds with fresh rain stippling the swings and slides; canal-side recreation areas, with rows of saplings neatly plotted, wreathed in morning mist; housing estates with identical back gardens and young mums pegging damp wind-flapped sheets on clothing lines as clouds skidded across a cold blue winter sky. I was never sure if these were actual memories from my childhood in the late sixties and early seventies or false ones (dreamed or seen on television).

The intense association with a specific era and time of my life was partly cued by BoC's musical choices: their penchant for particular analogue synth tones that recalled the incidental music in seventies wildlife documentaries or the perky-yet-poignant electronic interludes between mid-morning TV for schools. The group actually took their name from the nature docs produced by Canada's National Film Board that they watched as kids. Beyond these particular nostalgic associations, BoC's detuned and slowly modulated synth tones have a wavering, mottled quality similar to washed-out Super-8 films or a pre-recorded cassette that's been played to death. *Music Has a Right to Children*'s cover fit the atmosphere perfectly: an overexposed holiday snap of a mum and dad and five children posing in front of mountainous grandeur. In a sinister touch, the faces of the family have been bleached out to complete featurelessness.

BoC's fondness for sampling children's voices and voice-overs from nature programmes limns their music with evocations of pastoral serenity. Sometimes, as with songs like 'Roygbiv', the feeling is purely halcyon; more often, there's an ominous tinge creeping around the edges of the idyll. Unlike most hip-hop and dance music, BoC tend to use their 'found voices' as singularities rather than loops. Their approach recalls David Byrne and Brian Eno's *My Life in the Bush of Ghosts*, but where that album used ethnomusicological exotica, Muslim singers and African-American evangelical preachers to create a vibe of ritual and trance, BoC go for British voices plus the occasional white American broadcaster-type voice, creating a quite different atmosphere: innocence, calmness and rationality, pedagogy . . . but always with an undertow of unease. Alongside the samples, another hip-hop aspect of BoC's music is the looped breakbeats that underpin most tracks. But their effect isn't boombastic: the breaks trudge stoically like an elderly shire horse on a canal's towpath pulling a barge behind it.

Another proto-hauntological outfit that emerged in the late nineties, Position Normal – the London-based duo of Chris Bailiff and John Cushway – went further towards creating a singularly British equivalent to hip hop, albeit generally avoiding drum loops or anything resembling a groove. Main man Bailiff's earliest stabs at music-making as a teenager involved a primitive ersatz form of sampling: he used the family's Amstrad music centre to do tape-to-tape multitracking, layering it over beats from a cheapo drum machine. 'I wanted to be like Mantronix,' he told one interviewer. 'It was terrible, but I still use the same process today, only with a big sampler keyboard.' Apart from the occasional ethereal guitar part and trippy vocal from Cushway, Position Normal music is woven almost entirely out of samples which have a musty quality redolent of things stowed away in attics and forgotten for decades. This is B-boy crate-digging adapted to the English landscape of jumble sales and Oxfam. Many of the found voices on the group's 1999 album *Stop Your Nonsense* sound like they come from ancient reel-to-reel tapes or worn-out answer-machine cassettes. This analogue bias was emblazoned in the group's name: 'position normal' indicated that the blank cassettes were standard, non-chrome, mediocre-quality tapes. When the group made their 2009 comeback, it was with a cassette-only release.

Many of the vocal samples had a private hauntological resonance for Bailiff: they were 'ghosts of his life', to misquote the Japan song. His father had been an avid vinyl collector, with a particular bent for spoken-word records, documentaries and nursery-rhyme collections. 'Ultra-well spoken kids reciting stuff like "catch a fox, stick it in a box",' recalled Bailiff in one interview.

333

'That made no sense to me then, doesn't now. It was the absurdity I grew up with.' When he left the family house, he emptied the attic of the records. 'I was really archiving my own history,' Bailiff told *The Wire*. But the fate that befell his father – Alzheimer's, starting at the early age of fifty-eight and turning him into a ghost of his former self – adds a further spectral aura to Position Normal: the music is sourced from records that his dad collected but would no longer be able to recollect. Other raw material included voices from the sixties documentary series *Seven Up!* (which looked at the British class system from the child's point of view) and 'found speech' like the borderline incomprehensible patter of Cockney fruit 'n' veg stallholders at Walthamstow Market (Bailiff hiding his microphone under his giant parka, a surreptitious ethnologist of vanishing English folk ways).

On *Stop Your Nonsense*, Bailiff expertly tiled together all these shards of speech into melodious mosaics. 'Lightbulbs' juxtaposes a chirpy schoolboy praising 'a lovely bit of string' with a hi-fi buff droning on about 'my main gain faders'. 'Nostril and Eyes' could be smithereens of *Under Milk Wood* reassembled into sur-realist sound-poetry: 'Is there any *any*? Rank, dimpled, drooping . . . Smudge, crust, smell: *tasty* lust.' Much of *Stop Your Nonsense* is steeped in a mildly menacing anglo-Dadaist atmosphere that's redolent of the British comedy tradition of cracked whimsy: writer/performers like Spike Milligan, Ivor Cutler, Viv Stanshall, Reeves & Mortimer and Chris Morris. Other tracks bring to mind the cabinet of curiosities, Joseph Cornell's boxes of found objects and Kurt Schwitters's Merz collages and sculptural assemblages made of consumer detritus.

Listening to *Nonsense* obsessively through the summer of 1999 (it ended up as my favourite album of that year), I had ultra-vivid flashbacks similar to those induced by *Music Has a Right to Children*: chalk-dust motes irradiated in the shaft of light streaming from a classroom window . . . a paper bag of boiled sweets from the row of jars behind the counter . . . butcher shops with bloody sawdust on the floor . . . bus conductors with comb-overs . . . all the bygone crapness of an England banished thanks to New Labour's modernising gloss and the twin pressures of Americanisation and Europeanism. Strangely, at the time I never saw the connection between *Nonsense* and *Music Has a Right*, even though both featured children on their covers. Nor did I see the link between the effect they had on me and the fact that I had turned thirty-six and was about to become a father; which is to say, I would soon be bidding farewell to unnaturally prolonged adolescence and tipping decisively into middle age. It was also five years since I'd moved to America, settling into what looked like a permanent exile from my homeland, with a child (Kieran, born September 1999) who would grow up completely American, unaware of nearly everything that makes me who I am. A time of change then. And loss.

SPIRIT OF PRESERVATION

Hauntology is all about memory's power (to linger, pop up unbidden, prey on your mind) and memory's fragility (destined to become distorted, to fade, then finally disappear). Often treated as fellow travellers with the Ghost Box contingent but coming from a more experimental composer tradition, Philip Jeck and William Basinski have made memory the primary subject of their work. Jeck is an avant-garde turntablist who uses similar techniques as Christian Marclay but whose music – from 1993's *Vinyl Requiem*, a performance that deployed 180 Dansette record players plus numerous slide and movie projectors, to his reworking of Gavin Bryars's *The Sinking of the Titanic* – has an elegiac, even funereal cast. Basinski's celebrated series of releases *The Disintegration Loops* came about when in 2001 he embarked on a project of digitally archiving music he'd made in the early eighties based around tape loops and delay systems, in the mini-malist tradition of Steve Reich and Brian Eno. As he listened to these twenty-year-old loops, Basinski became aware that the tapes were being gradually wiped by the process of playing them: 'the iron oxide particles were gradually turning to dust and drop-ping into the tape machine, leaving bare plastic spots on the tape, and silence in these corresponding sections of the new recording'. *The Disintegration Loops* series, along with similar releases like *Melancholia*, documents this process of decay: sound-dust gradu-ally accumulates into a gentle sandstorm, eroding the music's clear lines into craggy amorphousness. Basinski's records draw attention to the foredoomed nature of recording's attempts at cultural embalming: all things will pass, everything must go.

With the UK school of hauntology – the Ghost Box groups, Mordant Music, Moon Wiring Club – this sense of loss is cultur-ally specific. What matters here is not so much the fact of sam-pling (and the way it foregrounds and intensifies the supernatural subtext of recording) but the specific material being used and the associations that it carries. The immediately noticeable thing about all these artists is that they use exclusively British voices: often creaky thespians and plummy poets from spoken-word LPs, or dialogue snippets from vintage mystery and horror pro-grammes. So on Moon Wiring Club albums like *An Audience of Art Deco Eyes*, you hear patrician English voices warning about 'the treacherous elm' or offering mysterious guidance ('keep to *small* . . . avoid large places'), woven into propulsively rhyth-mic tracks that sound like hip hop if its sample palette didn't draw on funk and jazz but the incidental music in *The Prisoner*. Mordant Music trumped everybody, though, by bringing out of retirement the TV announcer Philip Elsmore, whose warm Ovaltine-like tones are recognisable to anyone who grew up in the UK in the seventies because of his 'continuity' work for ITV regional franchises like Tyne Tees and Thames. On the album

Dead Air, Elsmore intones over Mordant's brilliantly idiosyncratic electronic sound (like early-nineties techno gone mouldy) an increasingly unsettling series of utterances, from 'Apologies for the sundry glitches . . . in the meantime, keep your nerve' to 'The following contains graphic scenes of a strobing magpie's wing' and 'Mordant Music will be back once the dust has settled with more vague unpleasantness.'

The speech samples used by the UK hauntologists are both archaic and *classed* (usually posh, occasionally regionally inflected or working-class). These are voices from a different age, redolent of both the image Great Britain liked to present to itself (through public broadcasting) but also of actual social realities (and divisions) that have shifted significantly in the last quarter-century. Accent is relevant because it is a ghostly trace of past generations. A person's accent is intimate yet oddly impersonal: it's an inheritance, something that precedes you, that places you and that gives you away. Beyond class, these voices are bound up with a sense of nationality: that matrix of collective character that involves gesture and intonation, phrase and fable, and an immense array of common reference points that are seldom consciously apprehended (until they start to disappear) – anything from the shape of post boxes to newspaper fonts. There are so many British people with whom I have no common interests or shared values, yet there is a level on which I'm connected to them which I will never have with even my most simpatico American or European friends, people who are very much my cultural and musical compatriots.

Perhaps this music feels ghostly because it is a form of 'memory work', Freud's term for the grieving process. What's being mourned is 'a particular period of time in British history – more or less 1958–78,' says Ghost Box co-founder Jim Jupp, aka Belbury Poly. The UK hauntologists are self-consciously playing with a set of bygone cultural forms that lie outside the post-Elvis/Beatles rock and pop mainstream, stuff that was either

337

pre-rock'n'roll or that *remained outside* rock'n'roll. They conjure a Britain unaffected by Americanisation. The cut-off date of 1978 refers to the last year before the election of Margaret Thatcher, who wanted to make Britain more like the US by freeing up a go-getting entrepreneurial spirit and reducing the role of government. She launched a programme of denationalisation, derided social workers as interfering do-gooders, and blamed bureaucracy for strangling enterprise with red tape.

After twenty years of post-socialism under Thatcher–Major–Blair, the whole idea of the public sector – from the BBC to the library system – no longer seems stuffy and square but oddly cool: a benign system of support and pedagogy whose eclipse is regretted. Ghost Box are obsessed with the spirit of technocratic utopianism that flourished in the period between the birth of the welfare state and the ascent of Thatcher. Optimistic and forward-looking, this was the era of new towns and ambitious urban-redevelopment projects (slums torn down and replaced by the ultimately notorious but initially welcomed high-rise tower blocks and housing estates), the age of polytechnics, the Open University (further education made available for all) and the sixties paperback explosion spearheaded by Penguin Books with their blue-spined drive to expand the horizons of the common man. This lost era of planning and edification represented a paternalism (or perhaps maternalism, given its association with things like free milk for schoolkids or BBC children's fare like *Watch with Mother*) that rock'n'roll in some sense rebelled against by celebrating desire, pleasure, disruptive energy, individualism. But by the early 2000s, these bygone ideals of progress started to acquire the romance, pathos and honour of a lost future. The idea of a 'nanny state' didn't seem so suffocating and oppressively intrusive any more.

Hence the mixed emotions behind The Advisory Circle's debut EP for Ghost Box, *Mind How You Go*. The project was named after an imaginary government (busy)body that issues guidance to the general public on every aspect of behaviour. 'The Advisory Circle: helping you make the right decisions,' a female voice on *Mind How You Go* declares, her faintly sinister tone of solicitousness recalling the telescreen announcers in Truffaut's movie of *Fahrenheit 451*. Jon Brooks, the figure behind Advisory Circle, was inspired by the sound of the old public-information films from children's television in the seventies: short and sometimes bizarrely gruesome films warning of the dangers posed by, say, a seemingly harmless visit to a farm (kid #1 drowns in hogshit after tumbling into a pigpen, kid #2 gets impaled on a pitchfork, and so forth).

The memoradelic imprint left by vintage TV on the child's impressionable grey matter is central to hauntology. The name Ghost Box came from a seventies *Watch with Mother*-type programme called *Picture Box*, but subsequently spiralled outwards in a rich complex of associations. 'TV as a sort of dream machine,' muses the label's co-founder Julian House, who records as The Focus Group. He connects the 'ghost box' idea both to 'our shared memories and collective unconscious' and to 'the spookiness of cathode rays, phosphor, after-images'. Quotes from the scholar of parapsychology and extrasensory perception T. C. Lethbridge adorn various Ghost Box releases: 'The television picture is a man made ghost'; 'Are ghosts "television" pictures carried by forces of resonance from a projecting machine in one mind to a receiving machine in another?'

Strangely, House and Jupp never mention the well-established if relatively esoteric meaning of 'ghost box' as a device for contacting the spirits of the dead, something that Edison allegedly worked on and which is pursued today by supernaturalists investigating 'electronic voice phenomena' (speech submerged but audible within radio transmissions or background noise). For Ghost Box, the term has an exclusively televisual meaning, with a specific slant towards a certain kind of seventies supernatural drama for children, series like *The Stone Tape* (Nigel Kneale's 1972 show about a place that 'records' traumatic events and replays them) or *The Changes*, set in a Luddite near future when people turn against technology. 'I like to think of Belbury Poly as the kind of music that might have existed on TV programmes that were too difficult to schedule, too sexy or scary or odd to be aired,' says Jupp.

Some of the music on these programmes was made by the BBC Radiophonic Workshop, an organisation that occupies a central place in the hauntological pantheon akin to the ancestral stature of James Brown in hip hop. Founded in the late fifties as an adjunct to BBC Radio's drama department, the Workshop's remit was to provide sound effects, atmospheres and musical underscores for radio plays and comedy programmes like *The Goon Show*. Within a few years it was churning out theme tunes, jingles and 'special sound' for television as well as radio, most famously for *Doctor Who*. Not so much state-funded as state-underfunded, the Workshop relied on repurposed technology and the ingenuity of its small staff. Toiling with tape and scissors, they edited together sound collages whose quirky sonic treatments paralleled the musique concrète being made in Europe at that time, but which were miniature in scale and unassuming in function. Unlike the electronic studios in France, Germany and Italy (many of which were associated with state-owned radio stations, for whom they functioned as research units), the Radiophonic Workshop was never designed to pursue experimentalism for its own sake: the vast bulk of the department's output was bespoke sound tailored to an ancillary function in other people's creations (radio dramas, TV series, etc.). But it was this very subordinate, craft-not-art status that enabled the Workshop to infiltrate the consciousness of a mass audience, whereas the European pioneers of electronic music were confined to the high-culture ghetto of concert halls and art spaces.

340

Ghost Box and their peers belong to a generation that was exposed to weird electronic sounds at a formative age thanks to the Workshop's work for children's television: the shuddery impact of those unearthly timbres left a scar, like being molested by aliens. A cult following emerged during the nineties (just as the Workshop itself was winding down, a victim of market-oriented reforms at the BBC). But the music was hard to find, until reissues and excavations of never-before-available work started coming out in the last decade, some of them on Trunk Records.

Part of the appeal goes beyond the nostalgic associations with being spooked as a small child by shows like *Doctor Who* and relates to the institutional aura that clings to the music. In an odd way the Radiophonic Workshop is an extension of Lord Reith's original belief that a state-owned national broadcaster should be in the business of expanding the horizons of the general public. 'The Radiophonic Workshop belongs to a period of British cultural activity which I caught growing up, when strange things existed on their own terms, outside the dictates of marketing,' says Julian House. 'It's now unthinkable that a public body could produce for the masses such avant-garde, forward-thinking, sometimes difficult music. And that it was well received.' There are also particular sonic properties of the early Radiophonic works. 'There's a particular feel that you get from the older stuff where they've used a musique concrète sound source or a sine wave, then endlessly dubbed it onto tape, until what you're listening to, the music itself, is the reverb of a reverb of a reverb,' says House. 'It's like ghost music, made from the traces, memories of an object.'

Along with the Radiophonic Workshop, the other big influence for Ghost Box and the British hauntologists is library music. Through its use in TV and also B-movie thrillers and horror films, library music seeped into the memory fabric of an entire generation (roughly, people born between 1955 and 1975). It was wed

341

to some of these people's most profound early aesthetic experiences of wonderment and trauma. When producers like House or Moon Wiring Club's Ian Hodgson use shards of library music as sample sources – bittersweet, crestfallen orchestrations; bright, childlike, sunshine-beatific guitar chords; the 'yellowy-brown' tones of the ambiguously jazzy yet very British music used in thrillers or detective series to evoke an atmosphere of corruption or psychological malaise – they can play with all the non-specific emotional associations ingrained from a childhood misspent in front of the goggle box. Particular instrumental textures and types of chords set off strange reverberations inside you.

SPECTRAL AMERICANA

If hauntology in the Ghost Box sense is so bound up with the shared cultural memory bank of a particular generation and nationality, this ought to mean that its appeal is rather limited. Actually, this doesn't appear to be the case, not completely

---

THE FOCUS GROUP

The music made by Ghost Box's Julian House under the name The Focus Group is hauntology at its most abstract and unsettling. Released on albums like *Sketches and Spells*, *hey let loose your love* and the collaborative mini-LP *Broadcast and The Focus Group Investigate Witch Cults of the Radio Age*, it often sounds like hip hop if it had been invented in England in the late fifties. House turns library music's 'science of mood' against itself by creating barely classifiable emotions (macabre whimsy, pensive rapture, 'reverie and efficiency') or making atmospheres clash and mingle like colours on a paintwheel going muddy. Sometimes the music is an idyllic flutter, like the slow dance of light that is 'Modern Harp' or the cascade-in-reverse of 'Lifting Away'. Often, it's a crepuscular, cobwebby sound, the sources processed until they resemble ectoplasmic tendrils or a supernatural luminescence out of H. P. Lovecraft. The Focus Group's most uncanny work – ultra-abstract pieces like 'The Leaving' – feel like flickered glimpses into another reality behind the one we inhabit.

A designer by day for the company Intro, House sees direct technical parallels

342

anyway: Ghost Box do have fans outside Britain, and some of them are in their twenties. Nonetheless, it obviously pushes the buttons of a specific age group; in self-critical mode I've occasionally wondered if the peculiarly cosy unease provided by this genre (music that's like 'ghosts you've come to love', to borrow a line from my wife Joy Press) means that it amounts to a sort of menopause muzak catering to a demographic that's British and mostly male (the kind of person who remembers watching *Doctor Who* back when it was *worth* watching). This in turn begs the question: does that mean that every country, and each successive generation within that nationality, will produce its own version of hauntology – a self-conscious, emotionally ambivalent form of nostalgia that sets in play the ghosts of childhood? For instance, what would a properly American equivalent of hauntology look like?

An obvious candidate would be the free-folk (also known as freak folk) movement that came to prominence in the early

---

between his music-making and his graphic work for releases on Ghost Box and for friends and clients such as Broadcast and Stereolab. 'With visual collage there's always a sense that however incongruous the elements and surreal their juxtaposition, they exist in the same space – or at least a space that is defined by their arrangement. Even images with different textures, maybe from different print media, feel they belong together in that space. With the audio collages I try to achieve the sensation that there is a real acoustic space that all the sounds exist in, even if it sounds slightly unreal. So reverb may be added to some samples to make them fit the space if needed. There's also a strange sensation when the reverb reflections of the different sounds bind together. It's a sort of acoustic glue.'

A fan of the inadvertent avant-gardeness of 'bad' or 'clunky' design (as with library-music sleeves or Polish movie posters), House intentionally achieves similar effects through 'bad looping . . . looped samples that change their start and end points'. It's an approach that resists and subverts the CGI-style seamlessness that today's sequencing-and-editing music software at once

2000s, pioneered by the likes of Charalambides and MV & EE, and popularised by Devendra Banhart and Joanna Newsom. These musicians' invocations of 'the old weird America' (Greil Marcus's term, inspired by Harry Smith's 1952 *Anthology of Folk Music*) point to a vanished era of cultural identity that was both national and deeply local, and one that's been vanquished by the rise of a trans-American but rootless culture of consumerism and entertainment, oriented around brands, strip malls, Clear Channel, TicketMaster, multiplex movie theatre chains et al.

Free-folk musicians are just as much crate-diggers as the hip-hoppers and the hauntologists; it's just that instead of library music and spoken-word records, they patch together their 'strange quilt' (as Byron Coley put it) from Folkways-style field recordings of traditional music, outsider minstrels and maverick composers like Robbie Basho and Angus Maclise, obscure acid rock and esoteric improvisation and drone groups. Where the hauntologists eulogise the paternalist state of Britain and all its public works, the free-folkers' guiding fantasy is the unsettled wilderness of early America: a self-reliant existence, outside society and remote from urban centres. Free folk echoes the hippy and Beat movement's own yearning invocations of the American frontier spirit; the beards that almost every man in the freak-folk

---

enables and enforces. 'With visual collage there's a way in which images that are cut out "badly", maybe with bits of their background or surrounding image, make it difficult to discern where one part of the collage begins and another ends. This *trompe l'oeil* effect brings you deeper into the collage, confuses your ability to discern images as surface. In the same way, the shifting loop points of the samples mean that it's difficult to discern which sample is which. Indeed, if you can't identify a definite loop, it's difficult to label it as a sample at all.' This helps to create a disconcerting sense of The Focus Group's music as organic rather than assembled, something heightened by House's attraction to woodwind samples: sibilant curlicues that slither like triffids or sentient ivy, a sound of tendrils and twilight. The Focus Group's music feels 'alive'. Or more accurately, 'undead'.

scene wear simultaneously recall The Band, Allen Ginsberg and the early-nineteenth-century trapper and mountaineer Grizzly Adams. One of the centres of free folk is Brattleboro, Vermont, a long-established hippy getaway that combines the backwoodsy and the countercultural: a sort of Appalachia *sans* rednecks.

Just as I was settling on free folk as the American cousin to British hauntology, though, a better candidate hoved into view: the amorphous genre known variously as chillwave, glo-fi and hypnagogic pop. Under these overlapping terms you find everything from the ecstatically blurry and irradiated lo-fi pop pioneered by Ariel Pink's Haunted Graffiti and including outfits like Neon Indian, Ducktails, Toro Y Moi, Washed Out, Gary War, Nite Jewel, etc., to the New Age and seventies cosmic-synth-rock-inspired likes of Emeralds, Oneohtrix Point Never, Dolphins into the Future and Stellar Om Source, to the tripped-out, tribal exotica of James Ferraro, Spencer Clark, Sun Araw and Pocahaunted. Overall, this is the sound of hip left-field music in late-2000s America, an Internet buzz-fuelled underground where the music sells to a hardcore following in the form of ultra-limited editions of vinyl and cassette, but reaches an unquantifiably larger audience through illegal downloads and artist-sanctioned MP3s and YouTube videos posted on blogs. By 2010, this diffuse, ever-shifting region of contemporary sound had become sufficiently epochal that America's leading alternative-music webzine *Pitchfork* launched a sister site, *Altered Zones*, to keep tabs on it, but they farmed out the site's content (buzz-band profiles, MP3s, mix-tapes, video premieres) to a collective of leading blogs already specialising in this area.

I love the term 'glo-fi' myself, but the most conceptually provocative name is 'hypnagogic pop', the coinage of *The Wire*'s David Keenan, a long-time tracker of currents within the noise/drone/free-folk underground. Keenan noticed that memory-mangled traces of eighties music were starting to flicker through the hallucinatory haze spewed out by all these groups: crisp funk bass and spangly guitar parts redolent of the slickly produced rock 'n soul and 'yacht rock' of that decade (Hall & Oates, Don Henley, Foreigner, Michael McDonald), the taut sequenced rhythms and bright digital synth sounds of eighties Hollywood soundtracks (think Harold Faltermeyer, Jan Hammer, etc.), even the rippling electronic arpeggiations and wind-chime tinkles of New Age.

'Hypnagogic' came from a comment made by James Ferraro, who with Spencer Clark had made up the super-influential noise duo The Skaters but was now producing his own music with torrential frequency using a bewildering array of aliases. Ferraro suggested that all these eighties sounds seeped into the consciousness of today's twenty-something musicians when they were toddlers falling asleep (and thus in the state of semi-consciousness known as 'hypnagogia'). He speculated that their parents played music in the living room and it came through the bedroom walls muffled and indistinct. As creation myths go, this was pretty darn cute. And who knows, as with the impact of the Radiophonic Workshop or library sounds on the hauntologists-to-be, it might conceivably account for the emotional pull of the eighties sound palette on these musicians. Spencer Clark described the memoradelic sensations stirred by eighties pop-production hallmarks as 'a form of time travel', while Ferraro compared it to being 'trapped inside of somebody else's dream'. Yet just like the hauntologists, there is a lot of knowing play with cultural reference points going on too, mostly indexed to TV or the kind of movies watched over and over again on the domestic video player. Ferraro titles like *KFC City 3099: Pt. 1 Toxic Spill* and *Last American Hero/Adrenaline's End* are redolent of Philip K. Dick and David Cronenberg's *Videodrome*: the schizo or drug fiend going *inside* the TV screen, joining the characters in crass action movies, Jane Fonda-style work-out programmes and the Home Shopping Network.

The big difference between the British and American forms of hauntology comes down, appropriately enough, to nationality: Ghost Box and their allies tend to map out their cultural reference points with an Asperger's-like attention to detail that's almost too tight-assed, whereas Ferraro/Clark and all the outfits they've influenced come across more off-hand and space-cadet scrambled. The absurdist mysticism that runs through this scene reminds me of the movie *Slacker*, with its conspiracy theorists and Smurfs-worshippers, and specifically of the character played by Butthole Surfers drummer Teresa Nervosa, who accosts people in the street and tries to sell them what she claims is Madonna's pap smear (complete with actual Ciccone pube).

Underground music culture is propelled forward by a form of cultural economics in which esoteric influences are consciously acquired and then dropped when they become devalued by overuse. Cutting-edge creatives are driven to seek out earlier forms of popular music that have been discarded. There's literally an economic aspect to this subliming of kitsch: whatever can be found cheaply in yard sales and thrift stores. Many of the mainstream eighties influences that hypnagogic popsters draw on were produced in vast quantities that now circulate as unwanted vinyl; few things could be less covetable or collectable than a pre-recorded cassette of New Age music. There's also an element of 'Do I dare?' to plunging into the uncool Hallmark mysticism of New Age culture, with its crystals, positive visualisation, flotation tanks, wind chimes and power spots. At the same time there's a certain aesthetic logic to the interest in New Age, which has historical connections to much more respectable genres, such as ambient music and Krautrock.

New Age's Arcadian pastoralism is one source of the vein of imagery running through a lot of hypnagogic pop to do with summer, beaches, palm trees, tropical vibes, oceans, dolphins et al. The summer break is the ultimate slacker time, a lacuna in the educational cycle and the relentless onward march to adult-hood (which in the late 2000s must have seemed a particularly grim and besieged life stage, given the economic collapse). Both of the godparents of hypnagogic – The Skaters and Ariel Pink – are based in Southern California (San Diego and Los Angeles respectively), the land of endless summer, but also of sun-and-drug-baked beach bums and a certain derangement caused by perpetual blue skies. Like Ferraro with his parents-playing-music-through-the-bedroom-wall scenario, Pink has his own creation myth: he identifies the roots of his pop sensibility in his having watched MTV incessantly from the age of five onwards (i.e. from 1983, only a few years after the channel launched). As a result, on the many recordings he's issued under the name Ariel Pink's Haunted Graffiti, his reverb-saturated psychedelic sound is haunted by the friendly ghosts of Hall & Oates, Men Without Hats, It's Immaterial, Blue Öyster Cult, Rick Springfield – an approach to songwriting and melody he assimilated as an ears-wide-open child for whom 'MTV was my babysitter'.

The instant analogy that springs to most reviewers' and listen-ers' minds on hearing Pink's music is not television, though, but radio: the child listening rapt with cupped ears to a tiny tinny transistor, the station's signal drifting in and out, or interrupted by bursts of interference. The reverb haze that cloaks albums like *The Doldrums* could be a semi-conscious attempt to recreate the blissfully indiscriminate way that children listen to pop music in their pre-teen years, before they learn what's cool or uncool.

Pink actually called one of his albums *Worn Copy*, evoking the elegiac idea of the cassette or vinyl LP whose sound has become ghostified through repeated play. Unlike digital formats, analogue degrades through overuse: each listener kills the sound she loves. Tape, with its lo-fidelity warmth and hiss and its frailty in the face of time, is integral to Ariel Pink's musical means of production. All of his early, most influential releases were recorded at home on an eight-track tape-mixer, with Pink playing all the instrumental parts and crudely overdubbing them, and simulating the drums with his mouth, human beat-box style. James Ferraro goes one step further into analogue lo-fi: he makes his music using cassette boom-boxes, an ultra-primitive substitute for the multi-track home studio. These associations have been picked up on by the musicians who followed in the wake of The Skaters and Ariel Pink – groups with names like Tape Deck Mountain, Memory Tapes, Memory Cassette – and turned into cliché.

Most of the people in the post-Skaters/Pink scene actually put out the bulk of their music as cassettes. This resurgence of the cassette format in underground music scenes in recent years (at the start of the 2000s the music would have been more likely to circulate as CD-Rs or, for the real aesthetes, vinyl) stems from an odd mix of aesthetics, ideology and pragmatism. Part of it relates to the double association cassettes have with the eighties. On the mass level, the pre-recorded cassette was that decade's quintessential format, how most kids would have listened to music (either on boom-boxes in their bedrooms or using Walkman-style portable players). But cassettes were also the preferred means of dissemination for ultra-underground eighties scenes like industrial and noise, the ancestors of today's hypnagogic and drone. Tape was the ultimate in do-it-yourself, because it could be dubbed-on-demand at home, whereas vinyl required a heavier financial outlay and a contractual arrangement with a manufacturer.

Today's post-noise micro-scenes maintain the tape-trade tradition both for the sense of countercultural continuity and for economic reasons. According to Britt Brown, who co-manages the Los Angeles-based label Not Not Fun, 'The bulk of CD manufacturers require the customer to order a minimum of 500 units just to run a job. But tapes can be purchased in boxes of as few as fifty copies. They can be dubbed at home, or professionally dubbed, for an extremely reasonable cost.' He says that contrary to rumours that blank cassettes are no longer being manufactured, they are still very easy to come by because they remain a staple format in the developing world and are still popular among certain communities in America (like fundamentalist Christians, who use them to record and distribute sermons). Another advantage to using cassettes is that the low cost and fast turnaround means that the artists can record frequently and release quickly, which helps explain why artists like Ferraro and Clark have immense, endlessly accruing discographies that seep out into the world like a continuous spoor of semi-conscious creativity.

Cassette-mania also has an aesthetic dimension: tape fans enthuse about the 'warmth' of the sound, a lot like vinyl but much cheaper to achieve. 'Foggier, texture-based music' suits tape, says Brown, whereas 'sparkling Technicolor pop' made in a proper recording studio would obviously come across to its fullest on CD. 'The trancier, drugged, hazy-style psych/drone styles we focus on sound fantastic on cassette.' Cassettes also offer more opportunities for artwork than CD-Rs (elaborate fold-out inlays, boxes, and so forth). Hypnagogic pop has created its own highly defined cassette-cover art style: washed-out, 'photocopy-of-a-photocopy' images that are like fading after-images of a dream that you're struggling to cling onto after waking; and photo collages that montage images cut out of magazines (lots of eyes and mouths) and have an effect that is gauchely grotesque yet oddly powerful, and that above all suits the music.

Cassettes could be considered a hauntological format because, like the scratches and surface noise on vinyl, the hiss of tape noise reminds you constantly that this is a recording. But cassettes are also a ghost medium in the sense that as far as mainstream culture is concerned, they are dead, an embarrassing relic. The cult of the cassette has spread beyond the no-fi underground to become a retro fad, with young hipsters wearing T-shirts adorned with cassettes or belt buckles actually made out of old cassette shells.

During the writing of this book, our twenty-four-year-old baby-sitter turned up with a chic tote bag decorated with the image of a blank cassette; the plastic was writeable, allowing you to person-alise the cassette with the name of a band or the title of an imagi-nary mix-tape. There is a massive cult among the young for dead media and outmoded appliances (the pre-electric typewriter seems particularly popular), although it rarely extends beyond displaying the image to actually *using* the bygone format or device. One exception is the vogue for digital-photography appli-cations like Hipstamatic and Instagram, whose filters simulate the period look of photographs taken by vintage cameras. This creates a pre-faded, ersatz-analogue effect of 'instant nostalgia'.

The fascination with obsolete technology seems related to the nostalgia for just-barely-remembered pop culture of the eighties (and with the latest hypnagogic bands coming through, the early nineties). The kind of kitschy reference points that these hipster bands litter through their records – aerobics, Schwarzenegger films, late-eighties kids cartoons and teen dramas like *Beverly Hills 90210* – are similar to the bygone ephemera that fill up all those *I Love the '70s/'80s/'90s* programmes. Just look at the density of references and the arch tone in this post by the blog Rose Quartz celebrating the 'plastic Spelling-infused hits' made by Axl, a hypnagogic musi-cian who also goes by the moniker Luke Perry: 'A slo-mo Mario bassline crossed with those typical drifting infomercial feelings that come from either really digging back through "yr mom's workout tapes" . . . or watching way too much *Tim and Eric* or maybe just the internet, which has a lot of things on it.' The reference to the Internet is revealing: hypnagogic is bedroom pop, made by young shut-ins whose window on 'the world' is their computer.

If the fetish for dead media like cassettes is on some level an instinctive impulse to put the brakes on technological progress, perhaps there's a similar recalcitrance in the face of the entertain-ment industry's relentless obsolescing of pop culture: a desire

351

to cling on to all this stuff that received so much of our attention and affection, that took up so much of our time. Oneohtrix Point Never's Dan Lopatin says his decelerated, slurry-vocalled 'echo jam' versions of eighties pop songs relate to his interest in 'slow modes of listening in an otherwise fucked up/hypersped society'. An admirer of the way hip-hop producers like the RZA and Premier isolate the peak moments in a movie soundtrack and build a track around it, Lopatin talks of 'the seduction of the loop, and the meditative promise of it, how it hints at infinity'. Loop-based or trance-inducing music like hip hop and hypnagogic pop is a balm for 'the deep melancholy which arises from our inability to stop time just long enough to experience it'.

Of course, hip hop itself – especially in its underground form, the world of magazines like *Wax Poetics* and labels like Stone's Throw – bears an elegiac reverence for the past and the passed. The music of producers like J Dilla and Madlib teems with invocations and evocations from all across black music history. Self-described as 'the loop digga' and recording much of his music under the alias the Beat Kondukta, Madlib – real name Otis Jackson, Jnr – uses phantom identities and collaborates with imaginary bandmates in a manner similar to James Ferraro and Spencer Clark. His Quasimoto project has four members: himself, plus blaxploitation soundtrack composer/film-maker Melvin Van Peebles (present in sampled form), Astro Black (Sun Ra) and token Brit DJ Lord Sutch (apparently the son of rock'n'roll jester Screaming Lord Sutch).

Along with the infinitely rich resources of black music, the late J Dilla – also known as Jaydee and probably the most celebrated and influential hip-hop producer of the last fifteen years – used library music and vintage commercials as his raw material. In a direct parallel with the UK hauntologists, Dilla's sublime 'Lightworks' is based on samples from Bendix's 'The Tomorrow People' advert and from the music for a Baltimore Gas and Electric Co. commercial made by American electronic pioneer Raymond Scott (a sort of one-man Radiophonic Workshop cobbling together primitive synths and rhythm boxes in his basement). There's the same harking back to bygone futurism as Ghost Box et al., but naturally in America this is linked to the corporate sector and commerce rather than the state and public broadcasting.

After his death Dilla himself joined the black-music pantheon, inspiring ancestor worship with tracks like Flying Lotus's 'Fall in Love (J Dilla Tribute)', as well as a FlyLo remix of 'Lightworks'. But the real hauntological dimension to FlyLo's music is personal: the ghost of Steven Ellison's great-aunt Alice Coltrane, a pioneer of spiritual jazz fusion, flits through his music in the form of harp and string orchestrations, while secreted all through *Cosmogramma* are samples of his dying mother's last days, hospital sounds such as her vital-signs monitors and respirator.

Beyond such deeply personal allusions, underground hip hop plays on the heart strings of its core demographic in a similar way to hauntology and hypnagogic. The music is woven out of sources that activate the elegiac sector of the middle-aged African-American brain: rap fans who remember the 1987–91 golden age of hip hop, and in some cases are old enough to remember the seventies funk and soul and fusion it was sampled from. It's not just the music that is evoked but the whole web of life and community that surrounded it. Greg Tate captures beautifully the way that 'the instrumental compositions' of Dilla 'immediately give you the sense of being inside the whole of African American culture looking out – like he's recreated the sweat, smells and skin of the spaces where real human beings once danced, ate, sexed, cried, lied, fried, testified and signified to all that warm and epic soul music he samples . . . He taps into that place where music lives inside of us all – as broken snatches of song and sound that evoke communal memories and personal memoirs.'

Set adrift on memory bliss, Tate feels Dilla's music as the score to the movie of his life. His emphasis on the sensory aspect of this

353

Proustian recall fits the distinction between restorative nostalgia and reflective nostalgia made by Svetlana Boym. Restorative in a hip-hop context would mean black nationalism or the Afrocentric Native Tongues movement: dreams of repatriation, reparations and the repairing of lost sovereignty. Reflective nostalgia is about nationality rather than nationalism: the local and the concrete as opposed to larger-than-life ideals and heroism. Such reveries conjure the life world of customs and quirky differences, the sensuous and sensual realm of taste, smell, sound, touch.

MASH HITS

Some commentators have mounted a critique of hauntology and hypnagogic pop on the grounds that they are merely forms of

---

JAMES KIRBY: V/VM AND THE CARETAKER

'It's very northern British, very working-class,' says James Kirby, about the sample-based music he made in Stockport during the late nineties using the name V/Vm. 'A lot of the material on those albums reminds me of being at a horrific family fortieth birthday party where all of a sudden fights erupt because somebody owes somebody else cash or looked at their girlfriend in the wrong way. V/Vm is heard through drunken lager ears for sure.'

The arc of Kirby's sampladelic career stretches from Plunderphonics/KLF-style vandalising of mainstream pop through to some of the most consummate hauntological music made this side of Ghost Box. Early V/Vm releases like *AuralOffalWaffle* and *The V/Vm Christmas Pudding* seemed driven by a weird ecological recycling impulse, creating 'new' music by digitally mutilating the records that nobody wanted any more: chart-busting but now unsellable crap by middle-of-the-road entertainers like Russ Abbott and Shakin' Stevens. Like John Oswald, Kirby focused on single artists and single tracks, rather than sampling and combining bits and bobs from all over. Technology had advanced by the late nineties to the point where using some cracked software he could feed whole tracks into the machine and subject the song/performer to cruel and unusual punishment. Indeed, Kirby uses the term 'butchering': 'It was all an experiment, to hack up what was considered the offal, the forgotten embarrassing output of the music industry.'

musical postmodernism: 'good retro' rather than 'bad retro'. It's true that hauntology emerged from the same matrix of baseline cultural conditions – the scrambling of pop time, the atrophy of any sense of futurity or forward propulsion – that generated many of the things I've castigated in this book. For instance, Ghost Box's Jim Jupp talks about the notion of 'eternalism and non-existence of time' as being central to the label. In a 2009 interview, he described 'the Ghost Box world' as 'an "all at once" place where all of the popular culture from 1958 to 1978 is somehow happening all at the same time'. That sounds rather close to the kind of ahistorical entropy that produced the shuffle aesthetic of the iPod, the archival maze of YouTube, and so forth. But what makes hauntology different, what gives it an edge, is

---

But there was already a proto-hauntological aspect to V/Vm, later to flower with his alter ego The Caretaker. Kirby was tomb-raiding pop's cemetery, defiling the corpses. He was 'bringing dead pieces of audio back to life' as zombies condemned to some twilight-zone version of the cabaret circuit, where they sang their greatest (s)hit night after night with clumps of pop flesh falling off their bodies. Another pre-echo of Ghost Box et al. was V/Vm's focus on strictly British sources: the kind of massive-in-the-UK novelty singles and M.O.R. that never crossed over to America or Europe. Our unique national crud: the British equivalent to *schlager*, Germany's light-entertainment and variety-show fare.

Eventually, Kirby wearied of spattering the post-rave electronic scene with V/Vm matter and shifted in a more atmospheric, pensive direction. The Caretaker's *Selected Memories from the Haunted Ballroom* (1999) drew inspiration from Stanley Kubrick's *The Shining*, in which Jack Nicholson plays a hotel caretaker who succumbs to the supernatural malaise hanging over the place and ultimately re-enacts the murders committed by an earlier caretaker, who went insane and butchered his family. Specifically, it was the 'ballroom scenes which play out in Jack's head' that inspired the album and track titles like 'Thronged with Ghosts'. 'He is having some kind of emotional breakdown and walks into the empty ballroom and then, right there in his own mind, the empty ballroom is full again and music is playing.' The project's main musical source was as British as V/Vm's raw material, but from a couple of generations earlier: pre-World War II

355

that it contains an ache of longing – for history itself. Most main-stream retro-pop, from The White Stripes to Goldfrapp to Amy Winehouse producer Mark Ronson's eighties-nostalgia album *Record Collection*, offers nostalgia with the 'algia' – the pain and regret – almost completely muted.

The nadir of this sort of numbing nostalgia-without-nostalgia came early in the new millennium with the fad for mash-ups, bootleg remixes that combined two or more pop hits. Based around the same sampling techniques that run through all the music in this chapter, the mash-up phenomenon (also known as 'bastard pop') actually shared some roots with hauntology, in the sample mosaics wrought by such crate-digging, library music-loving British DJ/producers of the nineties as Luke Vibert (aka Wagon Christ), The Chemical Brothers and Bentley Rhythm Ace. A virtuoso at the sampling alchemy of turning stale cheese into

---

British popular song, and specifically the 'tragic figure' of Al Bowlly. 'He was the golden voice of his generation, but he was killed by a parachute mine outside his London home. Bowlly always sang as if haunted; his voice is otherworldly. It's very strange music from this time between the two world wars: optimistic but also very much about loss and longing, ghosts and torment. It seems haunted by the spirits of those who went to the trenches and never returned.'

The 'haunted ballroom' trilogy peaked with *A Stairway to the Stars*, which included the resonantly titled song 'We Cannot Escape the Past'. Kirby then shifted his focus to memory itself, and specifically memory disorders. *Theoretically Pure Anterograde Amnesia* was about the absolute horror of escaping the past altogether. Disorienting in its scale and abstraction, this six-CD work was an attempt to imagine what it would be like to suffer from a rare form of amnesia in which sufferers are incapable of forming short-term memories and exist in a depersonalised void. *Deleted Scenes/Forgotten Dreams* and *Persistent Repetition of Phrases* explored similar zones of queasy amorphousness.

Collective memory was the subject of the *Death of Rave* project, inspired by Kirby's participation in the Manchester club scene of the late eighties and early nineties. 'The energy in clubs at this time was amazing. Nobody knew what to expect next.' But by the middle of the noughties, Kirby felt that when he visited

gold, Vibert talked about *preferring* to sample 'shit records'. But he was outdone by Australian outfit The Avalanches, who combed Sydney's charity shops for a year, then built their wondrous 2001 album *Since I Left You* using 1,000-plus samples from 600 cut-price albums.

Mash-up producers took this kind of sampladelia much further. The goal was to have as little original music added as possible, just enough to glue the two halves together. The mash-up fad took off at almost the same time as the iPod was launched in the autumn of 2001. Coincidence? Yes, but at a deeper level, no. Both were products of the same deeper technological revolution: the compression of musical data in the MP3, the increase of bandwidth allowing for the transmission of music through the Web at consumer-convenient rapidity. Although some mash-ups were pressed up as seven-inch singles or CDs, the vast majority of

---

dance clubs, 'the energy and adventure seemed completely lost. I just wanted to reflect that. I took old rave tracks and stripped them down, removing all their life.' Spectral echoes of familiar rush-inducing riffs and anthemic refrains intermittently flicker through the dense smog of sound, but 'the beat and drive have gone'. Recalling the surge years of rave between 1988–96, Kirby says, 'Everyone thought everything was possible on those long nights. The world was ours. Now I think this generation is very disillusioned. They saw a glimpse of light on the dance floors, but that light has gone out and the future seems grim and predictable.'

Kirby's most recent work is the first music he's released under his own name, James Leyland Kirby. *Sadly, The Future Is Not What It Was* is a three-CD opus mingling his signature style of gaseous decayed sounds with Harold Budd/ Erik Satie-style piano (the first time that his own physical self, as a player of an instrument rather than a programmer, has been present in his music). 'Maybe it was a year 2000 thing,' Kirby mused in one interview. '2000 was always the future for us. We expected something significant from that year. When it came it was just the same as it ever was except we had no 2000 to look forward to anymore. It could be a psychological post-millennial hangover for us all which will take some time to pass for this generation.'

their listeners heard them as MP3s circulated across the Web.

There was another affinity between iPod and mash-up: in a way, a mash-up is an extremely short mix-tape or playlist, so short that the two songs are heard concurrently rather than consecutively. Nearly all the most successful mash-ups worked by contrast and collision. You had the fire-and-ice combinations that Richard X, aka Girls on Top, specialised in: 'We Don't Give a Damn About Our Friends' welded the vocal of Adina Howard's hypersexual R&B hit 'Freak Like Me' onto the glacial, sorrowful synth sweeps of Gary Numan's synth-pop classic 'Are "Friends" Electric?'. You had indie-meets-pop clashes (The Freelance Hellraiser's 'A Stroke of Genius' combined The Strokes' 'Hard to Explain' and Christina Aguilera's 'Genie in a Bottle'). Canonical rock meets hip hop was another favourite: 2 Many DJs crush-collided Salt-N-Pepa and The Stooges, and Dangermouse upped the ante on everybody by meshing together The Beatles' *White Album* with Jay-Z's *The Black Album* (resulting in *The Grey Album*).

Most mash-ups worked through superimposition; for instance, the topline vocal of one song over the groove/arrangement of another. Very occasionally, you got a collage where the slicing was 'vertical': rather than songs bisected across the middle and then joined up chimera-style (head of dog on body of chicken), you had a segue of song segments, each of which was whole and intact. The most famous example of this was Osymyso's remarkable 'Intro Inspection', a twelve-minute piece stitched together out of hundreds of intros to famous pop songs, from 'The Message' to 'Love Cats', Sinatra to Spice Girls. But with either kind of mash-up, the pleasure was totally bound up with pop knowledge and pop knowingness: listen to 'Intro Inspection' and you smile with recognition or surprise as you identify each intro.

The big difference between the mash-up producers and what their immediate predecessors like Luke Vibert or The Avalanches did is that the latter mostly worked with little-known and often denigrated music (bargain-basement finds, library records, obscure jazz fusion like the Neil Ardley samples that pop up deliciously on *Since I Left You*). But mash-ups almost always work with the well-known, things you already love or at least recognise. There is no creation of surplus value, musically: even at their very best they only add up to the sum of their parts. The bonus element is conceptual: the wit of an incongruous juxtaposition, making musicians from entirely different walks of pop life talk to each other. Mash-ups therefore have the shelf life of a wisecrack.

People came up with all kinds of interpretations of the mash-up fad, mostly modelled on punk ideas: pop consumers fight back by seizing the means of production and doing it themselves; or the mash-up as throw-up, a retaliatory regurgitation of all the pop music force-fed down our throats. Ultimately, though, it all seemed more like pseudo-creativity based on a blend of mild irreverence and simple pop fandom: we like these records, let's try to double our pleasure by sticking them together.

The apex of Mash-Up Mk1 came when Kylie Minogue performed a mash-up of her monster hit 'Can't Get You Out of My Head' with 'Blue Monday' by New Order at the 2002 Brit Awards. The fad did spawn a couple of careers: Richard X became a UK hit-maker, and his Girls On Top suturing of Gary Numan to Adina Howard was 'covered' by Sugababes and reached no. 1 in the UK. Dangermouse went on to become a respected producer, working with Beck and Damon Albarn's supergroup The Good, the Bad and the Queen, and scored huge success with his own group Gnarls Barkley. But overall the fad seemed to have petered out by the mid-2000s. Only to come back, like a badly digested dinner, in 2008, with the massive critical hype for Girl Talk, aka DJ Greg Gillis, who brought a new level of crowd-pleasing pandering to mash-ups, combining technical slickness with a kick-ass live show that wowed audiences on America's college circuit.

The praise for Girl Talk had a bizarrely amnesiac quality.

Reviewer Sean Fennessey gurgled about Gillis's hook-crammed tracks, which could each contain as many as twenty highly recognisable tracks: 'It's surprising no one came along with an idea like this sooner.' The precedents were myriad, starting with the early-eighties hip-hop montages of Steinski (whose work was actually reissued by Girl Talk's label Illegal Art) and running through many of the figures in this chapter, from John Oswald to DJ Shadow. Then there was Norman Cook, who a good decade before taking on his riff-pilfering Fatboy Slim alter ego was putting out Steinski-esque cut-ups under the name DJ Mega-Mix while he was still day-jobbing in eighties indie-pop stars The Housemartins, and then did the proto-mash-up Beats International, who hit no. 1 with a song that combined The SOS Band's 'Just Be Good to Me' with The Clash's 'Guns of Brixton'.

What was 'new' about Girl Talk was the sheer number of thefts per minute Gillis pulled off, and the slickness with which all these different grooves and tempos were merged thanks to digital-editing software. A typical sequence might involve Busta Rhymes's 'Woo Hah!! Got You All in Check' going into The Police's 'Everything Little Thing She Does Is Magic', into Ini Kamoze's 'Here Comes the Hotstepper', into Faith No More's 'Epic'. As with Osymyso's 'Intro Inspection', there's the same play of momentary unfamiliarity ('What's that? I know that!') and recognition ('I love that!'). Romping across five decades of rock, rap and R&B, Gillis celebrated the crass, pounding, instant-gratification appeal of pop at its most populist. Mash-ups mash the history of pop like potatoes, into indistinct, digital-data-grey pulp, a blood-sugar blast of empty carbohydrate energy, flava-less and devoid of nutritional value. For all their aura of mischief and cheeky fun, mash-ups exude pathos. This is a barren genre – nothing will come from it. Not even a mash-up. Like the iPod and online music-streaming services, the overall effect is to flatten out all the differences and divisions from music history. There are no ghosts in this machinery.

360

Playfully parodying heritage culture, hauntology explores two ways to, if not resist, then perhaps bypass the 'no future' represented by mash-ups and retro. The first strategy involves the rewriting of history. If the future has gone AWOL on us, those with radical instincts are necessarily forced to go back. Trying to uncover alternate pasts secreted inside the official narrative, remapping history to find paths-not-taken and peculiar but fertile backwaters adjacent to pop's official narrative, they turn the past into a foreign country. The other strategy is to honour and resurrect 'the future inside the past'. In UK hauntology's case, that's the eyes-on-the-horizon optimism of the post-World War II modernists and modernisers; with hypnagogic pop, that means mangled memories and distorted ideas of the eighties. In reference to some hot new hypnagogic act, the blog 20jazzfunkgreats wrote, hopefully, that 'When the past sounds more like the future than the present does, revival becomes progressive.' Ghost Box's Julian House, for his part, talks about 'looking back to looking forwards'. The snappy turn of phrase can't disguise the fact that this is a precarious and paradoxical strategy.

11

OUT OF SPACE:

Nostalgia for Giant Steps and Final Frontiers

Staring out of my window at Manhattan's East Village a few years ago, it struck me suddenly that the street scene below did not differ in any significant way from how it would have looked in 1963, the year I was born. Oh, the design of automobiles had changed a bit, but combustion-engine-propelled ground-level vehicles are still how we get around, as opposed to flying cars. Pedestrians trudge along sidewalks rather than swooshing by on high-speed moving travelators. From the trusty traffic meters and sturdy blue mailboxes to the iconic yellow taxis, twenty-first-century Manhattan looked distressingly non-futuristic.

For a former science-fiction fanatic like me, this is rather disappointing. The cliché landmarks of tomorrow's world – vacations on the moon, robot butlers, 900 miles-per-hour transatlantic trains hurtling through vacuum tunnels – never turned up, obviously. But the absence of futuristic-ness is felt equally in the fabric of daily life, in the way that the experience of cooking an egg or taking a shower hasn't changed in our lifetime.

I'm not the only one feeling a pang for the future that never arrived. The frustration is widely felt and has been mounting for some time, gathering serious speed in the late nineties as the really-ought-to-be-momentous new millennium loomed. This peculiar unrequited emotion – nostalgia for the future, 'neo-stalgia' – has a jokey signifier: the personal jetpack. But despite the campy tone of band names like We Were Promised Jetpacks or book titles like *Where's My Jetpack? A Guide to the Amazing Science Fiction Future That Never Arrived*, underneath the arch there's an ache of genuine longing. When I asked James Leyland Kirby about his *Sadly, The Future Is Not What It Was* album, he talked about wishing he could 'look out of those childlike eyes still and believe that if I want to live on the moon soon then I will be able to, or when I meet a friend I will put on my jetpack and be there in seconds instead of having to walk there'. Kirby suggested that the year 2000 had always possessed a special reverberation. Switching from '19' (the numeric signifier for the twentieth century) to '20' seemed like it should automatically place us on the other side of a great divide, as if we'd made an abrupt leap *into* the future. But of course the new millennium has so far turned out to be barely different from the tail end of the last one.

Written by robotics expert Daniel H. Wilson, *Where's My Jetpack?* reads like a former SF nerd's tantrum of impatience. Beneath the facetiousness, though, lurks a sketch for a more probing work, an archaeology of prematurely abandoned futures, from the US Navy's lapsed Sealab programme for building living environments on the ocean's floor to the 'space elevator' that would carry us from the earth's surface 300 miles up to the threshold of outer space (perfectly feasible but in a literal sense *astronomically* expensive). Wilson also reports on science-fiction dreams that are actually near-future likelihoods, such as the smart home. But this won't be a sentient domicile that anticipates your moods with decor changes and keeps the fridge stocked with your favourite delicacies, as imagined in numerous SF novels; instead, it'll be an extension of the assisted-living facility for senior citizens, apartments kitted out with movement sensors that develop a feeling for their elderly inhabitants' routines and send out alarm signals when, say, that regular hourly visit to the toilet isn't made.

This prosaic reality of something that once seemed fantastically advanced typifies the way that our ideas of the future have been gradually scaled down in the last three decades. Oh, it's there all right – in lots of ways, we're *in* the future – but it infiltrates our lives in a low-key fashion. There have been astounding advances in medicine and surgery, but you don't really *see* them, as they take place in hospitals and their achievement is precisely to enable patients to return to healthy, high-functioning normality. The most remarkable transformations have occurred in the realm of computing and telecommunications, and these have permeated our everyday lives. As technical achievements, the compression of information and the miniaturisation of communications technology are just as mind-blowing as the space stations and battle robots once pictured as the future's everyday scenery. Trouble is, micro *looks* so much less impressive than macro. And look at the kinds of things we're *doing* with all this astounding new telecom tech: documenting our lives obsessively, chatting to our friends, trafficking in digitally encoded entertainment, locating restaurants, gossiping about celebrities and, as discussed in this book, wallowing in the pop-culture nostalgia that we're frenziedly archiving on the Web . . . None of this is particularly new, culturally speaking, and little of it is especially impressive. The future is supposed to be heroic and grand, but the activities (or should that be 'passivities'?) enabled by the new technology are more redolent of the decadent, inward-looking phase of an empire rather than its outward-bound, boldly-going-forth phase.

Sometimes it can feel like progress itself has actually slowed down, with the sixties as the climax of a twentieth-century surge of innovation and the decades that followed a bewildering muddle of stagnation and roll back. The first two thirds of the twentieth century seemed to teem with spectacular feats of centralised planning and public investment: huge dams, gigantic state-administered projects of rural electrification, free-way construction, urban redevelopment and poverty banishment. Science-fiction writers who grew up with this kind of endeavour (including the darker side of 'public works' – the mobilisation of entire populations and economies for war, the Soviet collectivisation of peasant farms that resulted in massive famine, Nazi genocide, and so forth) naturally imagined that change would continue to unfold in a dynamic, grandiose, often hubris-laden fashion. So they foresaw things like the emergence of cities enclosed inside a single giant skyscraper, or grain being harvested by combines the size of small ships voyaging across vast prairies.

It's no coincidence that SF's non-fiction cousin, futurology, aka 'future studies', emerged as a discipline during this era of state intervention. World War II ratcheted up popular belief and trust in the exercise of judiciously applied force by government, and the post-1946 world offered plenty of opportunities for benevolent state power to be flexed, from the challenges of post-war reconstruction to the development of the newly independent developing nations that emerged out of the British Empire. The fifties and sixties were characterised by future-mindedness, an ethos of foresight that attempted not just to identify probable outcomes but to steer reality towards preferred ones. It's no coincidence that those decades were the boom years for both science fiction and for a spirit of neophilia in the culture generally – the stream-lined, shiny aesthetic of Modernity that embraced plastics, man-made fabrics and glistening chrome as the true materials of the New Frontier. This is the era that produced *The Jetsons*, a prime source for many of the futuristic clichés that haunt the collective memory: personal rocket cars parked in the front drive, food pills, videophones, robo-dogs.

Today we seem to have trouble picturing the future, except in cataclysmic terms (*28 Days Later*, *I Am Legend*, *Wall-E*, *The Day After Tomorrow*, *The Road*, *2012*) or as the present gone drastically worse, as with near-future dystopias like *Children of Men*. Science fiction's inability to generate attractive, full-of-promise images of tomorrow's world has been accompanied by the fading prominence of futurology as a form of popular non-fiction. It carries on as an academic discipline, as research and speculation conducted by think tanks and government-funded bodies. But there are no modern equivalents of Buckminster Fuller or Alvin Toffler. The latter, probably still the most famous futurologist in the world, warned in his 1970 best-seller *Future Shock* that change was moving too fast for ordinary citizens' nervous systems and adaptive mechanisms to cope with; 1980's *The Third Wave* sounded a more positive note about the democratic possibilities of technology. But Toffler was just the most visible exponent of a bustling paperback subgenre of 'popular thought'. I recall getting one such fat paperback for my sixteenth birthday in 1979, a book predicting all kinds of marvels, such as the resurgence of lighter-than-air travel, which would fill the skies with giant freight-carrying balloons as well as a new breed of blimps and Zeppelins, the aerial equivalent of ocean cruise liners that would elegantly transport people across continents at a leisurely pace.

True, a good deal of that fifties/sixties confidence in the future had worn off by the seventies. Ecological anxieties manifested themselves in everything from Neil Young's 'After the Gold Rush' (with its 'look at Mother Nature on the run/ in the 1970s' chorus) to the movie *Silent Running*, about a space-station-dwelling botanist conscientiously keeping alive plants and trees that are extinct on a ruined Earth. By the eighties, thinking about the future in non-negative terms seemed to have become much harder. The common *mise en scène* of *Star Trek/2001, A Space Odyssey/The Andromeda Strain/Logan's Run* – a gleaming, sterile environment of plastic interiors and fluorescent lighting – gave way to a shabby squalor of rust and shadows. Even space travel became grotty: *Alien* director Ridley Scott opted for an implausible, if atmospheric, murkiness (hmmm, so they can propel commercial freight-carrying spaceships across the vast void between solar systems, but they can't afford a few extra 100-watt light bulbs?) and the incessant dripping of trapped condensation. Scott would use shadowplay and dampness to similar neo-noir effect in *Blade Runner*. Both movies are set in near futures dominated by ruthless mega-corporations who are busily exploiting the mineral resources of the solar system.

As the popular-culture vision of the future grew ever more unprepossessing, the profile of futurology as a non-fiction genre also waned (can you name anything Toffler wrote after 1980?). The best-sellers in the popular-thought category tended to be conservative backlash-attuned jeremiads and 'Where did we go wrong?' investigations like Neil Postman's *Amusing Ourselves to Death* (1985) and Allan Bloom's *The Closing of the American Mind* (1987). The nineties did see a modest resurgence of futurism, driven by the information-technology boom and theorised by magazines like *Wired* and *Mondo 2000*. While some of the new breed of futurologists were gee-whiz technology types like Kevin Kelly, others were 'zippies' (hippies minus the technophobia and back-to-the-land nostalgia) such as Jaron Lanier and Ray Kurzweil. A millionaire inventor enthralled by the potential of nanotechnology, virtual reality, artificial intelligence and trans-humanism, Kurzweil argued that the exponential curve of progress would hit vertical sooner rather than later. The result would be a rupture in human history, a technological version of the Rapture involving machine sentience, the disembodiment of human intelligence and personality, and immortality.

After the info-tech boom's bust and 9/11, we didn't hear so much from these digi-prophets. (Lanier returned in 2010 with a curmudgeonly, disillusioned book, *You Are Not a Gadget: A Manifesto*, about the betrayed promise of the Internet.) All that Dow Jones-indexed mania sagged to a sour calm. Nowadays, futurology as a popular non-fiction genre has been largely reduced to short-term cool-hunting in the service of marketing people and brand-makers. Take 2006's *Next Now: Trends for the Future*, by Marian Salzman and Ira Matathia. Almost without exception, everything Salzman and Matathia 'prophesy' was already a highly visible and well-established trend: wikis, blogging, celebrity chefs, gastro porn, branding, the privatisation of space, overwork and sleep deprivation, the prolongation of adolescence into the thirties and beyond, online dating, an ageing population . . . The near future, apparently, will just consist of *more of the exact same*.

NOSTALGIA FOR THE FUTURE

'Nostalgia for the future' is a phrase that crops up all over the place yet is hard to source. I've found it attributed to SF legend Isaac Asimov (from his 1986 non-fiction monograph *Future Days* about artist Jean-Marc Côté's 1899 illustrations of life in the year 2000) and to Jean Baudrillard, whose *America* references a specifically European malaise of 'nostalgia for the future', which compares unfavourably to American confidence that the present is already a fully achieved utopia. Transhumanist philosopher F. M. Esfandiary, aka FM-2030, talked about feeling 'deep nostalgia for the future' in his 1970 book *Optimism One*. But equally Richard J. Daley, the conservative mayor of Chicago, once declared that people 'should be nostalgic about the future'.

The phrase and the concept seem to have a particularly strong resonance in the context of music. The first time I noticed it was in a record review by the musician and critic David Toop describing a peculiar poignant yearning that infused nineties electronic music by outfits like The Black Dog and Aphex Twin. Later I came across an earlier quote by Toop's ambient-music peer Brian Eno, who in 1989 described the 'video paintings' (like *Mistaken Memories of Medieval Manhattan*) he'd made earlier in the eighties as stirring 'in me a sense of what could have been . . . a nostalgia for the future'. But then there was also the Buzzcocks' 1978 song 'Nostalgia', on which Pete Shelley sings, 'Sometimes there's a song in my brain/ and I feel that my heart knows the refrain/ I guess it's just the music that brings on nostalgia for an age yet to come.' It could be that Toop, Eno and Shelley all got the idea, directly or indirectly, from critic and composer Ned Rorem. In the text for a 1975 music catalogue, Rorem argued that 'music, in contrast to pictures or words, does not deal in facts – that is, in associations which, by their nature, concern the past. Yet music is associative. Of what? Music is the sole art that evokes nostalgia for the future.' As a music obsessive who privileges that art form above all others, I like the boldness, the *patriotism* of Rorem's claim. I wonder if it's actually true? More to the point, I'm not exactly sure what he means: that music's abstraction expresses all those unclassifiable and contradictory mixed emotions that we can't articulate? That music's truest yearnings are impossible, in revolt against the Real?

It's perfectly likely, even probable, that Rorem came up with the phrase all by himself. As it happens, though, someone else got there first: the Portuguese poet Fernando Pessoa, who scribbled it down at some point in the early decades of the twentieth century in the notebooks that would eventually see publication in 1982 as *The Book of Disquiet*. One of Pessoa's major preoccupations as a writer was boredom, or '*tédio*' in Portuguese. In a passage describing the oppressive ennui that descends upon on him during late afternoons, Pessoa writes of 'a feeling worse than tedium but for which there's no other name. It's a feeling of desolation I'm unable to pinpoint . . . the physical universe is like a corpse that I loved when it was life . . . And yet what nostalgia for the future if I let my ordinary eyes receive the salutation of the declining day! . . . I don't know what I want or don't want . . . I don't know who I am or what I am. Like someone buried under a collapsed wall, I lie under the toppled vacuity of the entire universe.'

As with 'Nostalgia' by the Buzzcocks – a group whose career started with a song entitled 'Boredom' – there's a longing to escape to an absolute elsewhere, the non-place, or utopia, of a desire that can't be defined, because any realisation would always fall short of the ideal. Nostalgia can project the absent ideal into the past or into the future, but mainly it's about not feeling at home in the here-and-now, a sensation of alienation.

In recent decades, nostalgia for the future has gradually lost its vagueness and become tied to a specific *idée fixe*: an archaic and sometimes comically ossified idea of what the future is going to be like. It's become a *retro*-futurist emotion: those sensations of wistfulness, mixed with irony, and amazement, offset by amusement, that are induced by old science-fiction movies, modernist cooking ware and furniture from between the two world wars, and images from the fifties and sixties World's Fairs, with their exhibitions of technological innovations and scientific breakthroughs. Looking at all these bygone projections into the future – which is actually our present – you can still faintly feel, as a kind of after-image, the awe that was stirred by these technological marvels and stark modernist ziggurats. But it is coloured by the hindsight knowledge that very little of this became reality.

Alongside the World's Fairs, probably the most influential source of popular-culture notions of what the future would look like was Disney's Tomorrowland. At the opening ceremony in 1955, Walt Disney described Tomorrowland as an 'opportunity to participate in adventures that are a living blueprint of our future' and hailed today's scientists for 'opening the doors of the Space Age to achievement that will benefit our children and generations to come'. Some of those scientists, including Wernher von Braun, the man responsible for the V2 rockets that bombarded London during the final stages of World War II and later a key figure at NASA, actually worked as technical consultants for the design of Tomorrowland. Alongside Rocket to the Moon, Astro-Jets,

Autopia and a monorail, Tomorrowland featured corporate-sponsored attractions such as the General Electric Carousel of Progress, the TWA Moonliner and the Monsanto House of the Future. The latter was made almost entirely of plastic, the material of the future.

Tomorrowland was rebooted in 1967 as New Tomorrowland, but over the ensuing decades it grew shabby and faded. So in 1998 it was remodelled as 'a classic future environment', in the words of the Disney press release: a *museum* for now kitschy-quaint notions of the future. Reporting on the relaunched Tomorrowland for *Time*, Bruce Handy opened with the quip: 'The future isn't what it used to be.' Attractions included the Astro Orbitor, which P. J. O'Rourke joked was 'built in a style that might be called "Jules Vernacular".' Intriguingly, though, this new ironic Tomorrowland didn't play well with the public, suggesting that retro-futurist irony was still at that point a minority sensibility, appealing to the kind of sophisticates unlikely to visit Disneyland.

In which category you'd probably find me. But I have kids, and on a visit to Los Angeles a few years ago to see my brother and his family we all made the trek out to Anaheim. My consolation for the bad food and the sharp pain in the wallet was that I would get to see what had become of Tomorrowland after it had abandoned both futurism and retro-futurism. Tomorrowland did not disappoint, in the sense that it was even more disappointing than I'd imagined. For the most part it was overrun with movie-franchised attractions, like a Buzz Lightyear ride and a *Star Wars* training session for kids to be junior Jedi Knights jousting with light-sabers. Instead of Monsanto's House of the Future, there was now the The Innoventions Dream Home, a lacklustre and desultory showcase for domestic-entertainment technology that seemed at most a year or two ahead of the Radio Shack mainstream.

After being greeted at the entrance by a vintage-style robot that could have stepped off the set of a fifties sci-fi movie like

371

Forbidden Planet, we reached the first display, an array of alleg-edly futuristic musical instruments made by Yamaha. A bleached blonde went through her strained perky patter for the umpteenth time that day, encouraging children to have a go on a sort of keyboard-guitar that could be made to sound like a koto or a dul-cimer, and to take turns bashing the drum kit, whose pads trig-gered samples like a man's laugh or a lion's roar. That was similar to things I'd seen bands like Disco Inferno do in the mid-nineties. She also demonstrated a microphone that could pitch-shift your voice from mouse-squeaky to slowed-down ultra-baritone: again, no great shakes. Further inside the Dream Home, whose decor of fake wood panels and dingy tones of beige and fawn reminded me of a motel chain or convention centre, there was moving-image wall art in old-fashioned picture frames, a coffee table with inlaid video screen on which you could piece together a virtual jigsaw, and a wall-size movie screen that was really not that much bigger than the flat-screen TV in our Los Angeles hotel. It was all desperately uninspiring and lugubrious. P. J. O'Rourke – a won-derstruck child fan of the original Eisenhower-era Tomorrowland – argued that this new incarnation was not so much 'the fault of the "Disney culture"' as 'the fault of *our culture*. We seem to have entered a deeply unimaginative era.' The problem isn't an inability to innovate; it's an incapacity to come up with visionary goals to aim for. The future promised by the Innoventions Dream Home heralded only slight increments of convenience and vivid-ness to our lives as consumer-spectactors.

BRUTAL AND BRITISH

Retro-futurism has been a current in pop culture since the early eighties. Steely Dan man Donald Fagen's solo debut *The Nightfly* evoked with wry affection the optimism of the late fifties on songs like 'New Frontier' and 'I.G.Y. (International Geophysical Year)', which dreamed of a 'graphite and glitter' age to come. Synth-pop albums like The Buggles' *The Plastic Age*, Thomas Dolby's *The Golden Age of Wireless* and OMD's *Dazzle Ships* harked back further still, to the stirring spirit of modernity that permeated the first half of the twentieth century. William Gibson's story 'The Gernsback Continuum' likewise examined the culturally persistent after-image of yesterday's visions of tomorrow (the title nodded to Hugo Gernsback, who in 1926 founded the SF magazine *Amazing Stories*). Ahead of everybody, though, had been Kraftwerk. From 1974 onwards, even as they invented the eighties with their synths and programmed rhythms, the German group cast backwards for their idea of the future, invoking the Mittel Europa modernism of autobahns and *Metropolis*. On the cover of 1978's *The Man-Machine*, they used the red-and-black colours and stark, slant-wise typography of El Lissitzky, who alongside Malevich had been the great Suprematist graphic designer during that brief heyday of Soviet modernism following the Revolution. This was precocious of Kraftwerk, anticipating the mid-eighties fad for Constructivist chic that ranged from Neville Brody's designs for *The Face* to Swatch watches.

The first decade of the new millennium saw a new boom in both retro-futurism (an eighties synth-pop revival) and retro-modernism. But with the latter, the interest was far less surface-oriented than all those pop bands and record designers who recycled Constructivist and Futurist ideas during the eighties. The focus was not just on the thrilling severity of modernism as style but on the movement's ideas and political idealism. And the focus expanded from the first two or three decades of the twentieth century to look at modernism's phase two: the post-World War II resurgence of abstraction and minimalism in art, interior and commercial design, and above all architecture. The latter, in the form of the Corbusier-influenced school of Brutalism, reshaped the look of large swathes of the urban West.

373

Far more than anything going on in art museums, it was the everyday visibility of these imposing new buildings that provoked the seventies-onward backlash against modernism. The problem wasn't the bricks in the Tate (Carl Andre's *Equivalent VIII* sculpture, made in 1966 but controversial in 1976), it was the bricks, and 'raw' concrete, outside it. By the early 2000s, though, you were starting to get photo blogs with names like I Adore Eyesores, operated by roving 'collectors' documenting their favourite sixties tower blocks, housing estates and shopping centres. I started to notice myself succumbing to this sensibility over the course of the decade. On visits to Ladbroke Grove, I would stare admiringly at Trellick Tower, whereas when I first lived in London in the mid-eighties I'd probably have barely glanced at it, except perhaps to think, 'Glad I don't live there.'

This deliberately contrarian ardour for the kind of buildings Prince Charles abhorred as 'monstrous carbuncles' (there was actually a website called I Heart Carbuncles) emerged around the turn of the millennium with a spate of books about motorways and service stations, most famously Martin Parr's 1999 pictorial anthology *Boring Postcards*, which became a cult success, but also including *Leadville*, Edward Platt's 'biography' of the A40, Pieter Boogaart's *A272 – An Ode to a Road* and David Lawrence's history of motorway service areas *Always a Welcome*. As Michael Bracewell observed, an unlikely period charm had attached itself to things like 'the Fortes restaurant in the bridge across the M6 at the Charnock Richard service station', these peculiar non-places that were at once urban (in the sense of having been imposed inorganically over the English countryside) and between cities. As well as serving as a 'portal to nostalgia' (with 'the Motorchef sugar sachet' taking the place of Proust's Madeleine), these dreary transport interzones also seemed – just like the Brutalist tower blocks and new-town shopping centres – to serve as 'a quasi-ironic metaphor of some lost state of innocence', on account of their association with the modernising spirit of the fifties and sixties. Bracewell mused lyrically about 'the strange poetry of boredom', the way 'these places seem to offer, in their very emptiness, an idea of the future that constantly reinvents itself'.

By the mid-2000s, this new elegiac modernism had an eloquent advocate in the form of blogger-turned-author Owen Hatherley. He is engaged in a paradoxical project of *harking forward* to modernism's utopian spirit: critical, radically democratic, dedicated to the conscious transformation of everyday life, determined to build a better world. *Militant Modernism*, his first book, starts with the declaration, 'We have been cheated out of the future.' Yet 'the future's ruins lie about us, hidden or ostentatiously rotting', and Hatherley proposes sifting through its 'remnants'. That sounds a bit musty, glum, forensic even, and Hatherley immediately wonders aloud, 'Can we, should we, try and excavate utopia?' But the bulk of *Militant Modernism* does essentially consist of an archaeology of lost futures.

There are uncomfortable resemblances between retro-modernism and heritage culture. You have the venerated tradition that must be safeguarded from developers by custodians; you have the monuments to abandoned ideals (Corbusier and Bauhaus-inspired housing projects here replacing mansions, castles and cathedrals); you have a present that uniformly disgusts and dismays; you have the keenly felt sense that History took a wrong turn somewhere. To an unsympathetic eye, this could look a lot like a kind of left-wing fogeyism. Anticipating such critiques, Hatherley points to hip hop and its British counterpart grime as proof that futurism still has genuine appeal to working-class youth, at least when it comes to music. Rather than offering a chance to wallow in nostalgia, Hatherley insists that modernism's past can supply 'spectral blueprints' for the future.

At the exhibition *Cold War Modern: Design 1945–1970*, which opened at the Victoria and Albert Museum in September 2008,

375

you could see an actual blueprint for the tomorrow that never came: House of the Future, a 'prefabricated space-age unit' furnished with labour-saving devices that was originally displayed at the 1956 Ideal Home Exhibition. At the V&A, you only got to see the plans, designed by Alison and Peter Smithson, the leading figures of Brutalism. *Cold War Modern* teemed with images of the impressively stark buildings that Brutalist architects and their allies erected across the world in the decades immediately after the war, from convention centres in the US to congress halls in the USSR. The focus of the exhibition was the competition between the superpowers over which ideology – consumerism or communism – had the strongest claim to the future. When modernism resumed in full force in the fifties and sixties, it was no longer an anti-bourgeois vanguard but was verging on being the official culture of the developed world, the architectural style and design aesthetic favoured by government and corporations alike. Embracing new materials like fibreglass and the ever-expanding array of plastics, it filtered down into ordinary people's lives through sleek radiograms, streamlined kettles and elegantly austere chairs.

There were plenty of retro-futurist frissons to be had at *Cold War Modern*, from Buckminster Fuller's geodesic domes to the television towers (like the Post Office Tower in London) that were the twentieth-century equivalent of medieval cathedrals: the spires of a new telecom theology based around Marshall McLuhan's notion of the global village. But for me the big thrill of the exhibition was the recreation of the *Poème électronique*, aka the Philips Pavilion: a fabulously futuristic looking sonic–visual–architectural collaboration between Le Corbusier, Edgard Varèse and Iannis Xenakis staged at the Brussels World's Fair in 1958 but demolished immediately afterwards.

Well, it would have been a big thrill, but in truth it rather underwhelmed at small-scale. Perhaps sensibly, no attempt was

376

made to simulate the jaggedly geometric surfaces of the interior, inspired by hyperbolic paraboloids and designed by Xenakis (at that point an architect working for Corbusier and only a fledgling composer). Instead you could see the photographic images (Corbusier's primary input, although they were taken by filmmaker Philippe Agostini) projected onto the pavilion's walls: a sequence of sombre black-and-white pictures that told the story of mankind in seven stages, using images of babies, tribal masks, machinery, the Eiffel Tower, Charlie Chaplin, mushroom clouds, and so forth. Cool, but as a fan of post-war electronic music and musique concrète I was disappointed by the downgrading of the sonic aspect of the Philips Pavilion. Varèse's *Poème électronique* and Xenakis's *Concrèt PH* were composed to work as a disorienting surround-sound experience via 325 speakers distributed throughout the pavilion. But at the V&A recreation, these landmarks of sonic futurism were piped through a single muzak-like speaker situated at shin level. At a volume just above inaudible.

Bizarrely, this is not the only restaging of *Poème électronique* I've attended: the other was a few years later at a decommissioned church in downtown Manhattan, as part of a Xenakis festival. The full-on experience, devised by a team at the University of Turin's School of Multimedia and Arts, was a virtual-reality simulation with a headset that enabled people to 'walk' inside a computer-generated Philips Pavilion. But at the New York event, the seated audience of two hundred just got to see images projected onto a movie screen. The music, at least, was awesome: fully immersive and *loud*, Varèse's sculpted blocks of electronics and Xenakis's soundscape built entirely from the noise of smouldering charcoal moved around the auditorium in 360 degrees.

We'll never really know what it was like to experience the *Poème électronique*, one of the pinnacles of twentieth-century modernism. And even if it could be recreated down to every last detail, we'd still never have that same shock of the new that the millions who visited it during the Brussels World's Fair felt. Most were as perplexed as the reporter from the *New York Times* who described it as 'the strangest building at the fair', with sounds equally as 'bizarre as the building'. The pairing of Le Corbusier and Varèse was inspired and apt: both were pre-World War II figures who had their biggest influence after the war. Varèse had been working on the incorporation of noise into music and talking up the urgent necessity for the invention of sound-generating machines for decades before this new frontier actually opened up at the end of the forties, when composers like Pierre Henry and Pierre Schaeffer started to grapple with the possibilities of tape recorders, followed a few years later by the first forays into synthetic sound using primitive oscillators undertaken by Herbert Eimert and Karlheinz Stockhausen. Although Varèse had incorporated pre-war proto-synthesizers like the theremin and *ondes martenot* into his compositions, *Poème électronique* was his first stab at using the new techniques. Indeed, between 1936 and 1953 he'd barely composed anything because the technology didn't exist to achieve his aspirations: 'the possibility of obtaining any differentiation of timbre, of sound-combinations' and 'a sense of sound-projection in space by means of the emission of sound in any part or in many parts of the hall'.

As for Le Corbusier, he'd written *The City of Tomorrow* back in 1924. Believing that rationally designed buildings would instil reason and orderliness into their inhabitants, he dreamed of the emergence of what he called 'the White world' (all clarity and clean lines, stripped of ornament and built using modern materials like concrete and iron) out of 'the Brown world', with its congested muddle of residues from different architectural eras. But his only real successes at building La Ville Radieuse (the Radiant City) came post-war with projects like the Unité d'Habitation in Marseilles. In the post-WWII climate, with the reconstruction of bomb-damaged inner cities and a spirit of hope and renewal

378

impelling efforts at benign social engineering via redevelopment, Corbusier's ideas bore fruit with the Brutalists.

ELECTRONIC PANORAMAS

One irony of the post-war vanguard was that these usually social-ist modernists (Xenakis, for instance, was a communist and had fought in the Greek Resistance against the Nazis) were often funded by capitalist corporations. Philips was an electronics giant based in Holland; the pavilion was intended to showcase the com-pany's latest innovations in tape machines, sound reproduction and light projection. When Philips's artistic director Louis Kalff approached Corbusier, the latter loftily declared: 'I will not make a pavilion for you but an Electronic Poem and a vessel containing the poem; light, color image, rhythm and sound joined together in an organic synthesis.' Because Corbusier was busy building an entire city in India at the time, most of the actual work was done by Xenakis (who found the experience so stressful he didn't do another architectural project for another decade). But Corbusier provided the guidelines and insisted on Varèse's involvement.

Philips had its own record label and was already sponsoring explorations of electronic sound at its research facility Natlab, where composers like Tom Dissevelt, Henk Badings and Dick Raaijmakers (also known as Kid Baltan) worked. In the sixties, the Philips label would also release probably the most famous series of avant-garde electronic recordings, the imprint Prospective 21ème Siècle, also known as The Silver Records on account of their futuristic-looking metallic gloss sleeves with mindblowing abstract geometric patterns. I had one of the series for two decades – Pierre Henry's *Voile D'Orphée I et II*, picked up at a jumble sale in 1983 for just £1 – before I discovered there were another thirty or so records like it, including *meisterwerks* by concrète colossi such as Bernard Parmegiani, François Bayle and Luc Ferrari.

379

By that point (the early 2000s) I was fully immersed in an obsession with the golden age of post-WWII electronic music and musique concrète. It kicked off in 1999, that most science-fiction of years. Looking back, the obsession must have had something to do with the way the forward thrust of contemporary electronic music – the rave scene I'd been so immersed in – was slowing down. The music had pursued various extremes of speed and noise and hit a bunch of brick walls, causing producers and listeners to retreat to slower tempos and pleasanter textures, to the very ideas of musicality and 'warmth' that techno once thrillingly stampeded all over. Another thing that happened in 1999 was the birth of our first child. Sensing that my raving days were now numbered, it was as if I was subconsciously striving to turn the domestic space into terra incognita, to have adventures close to home. Hence the attraction to what historically had been the most alien-sounding and incontrovertibly unprecedented music ever made.

Soon I was picking up electronic and musique concrète records faster than I could listen to them. It had to be the original vinyl, not the CD versions, because part of the music's mystique was the sombre moral seriousness of high modernism exuded by the black-and-white photographs of the composers, who were usually dressed in formal wear of suits and ties and posed next to gigantic banks of synthesizer technology. Adding to the lofty, forbidding aura of these modernist relics were the sleeve notes, with their grave tone and technical descriptions of the complex methodologies that underpinned the music, and the front covers, usually reproductions of abstract expressionist paintings or hallucinatory op-art swirls in the style of Bridget Riley and Vasarely. It's this kind of album, and above all the now hideously expensive Silver Records series, that spurred my humiliating 'time-travelling record collectors' daydream. I wanted to go back to the future, and buy it at yesterday's prices.

I asked Sébastien Morlighem, a French acquaintance, what Prospective 21ème Siècle meant. Apparently '*prospective*' is a philosophical term coined by Gaston Berger to describe the study of possible futures. The word fuses the French words '*perspective*' and '*prospection*' (as in a prospector exploring new territory, searching for gold or indeed silver). That struck me as perfect: here was I, in the early years of the honest-to-goodness *21ème siècle*, obsessed with these records and wondering whether our culture would ever again witness anything with that same Eureka!-like spirit of discovery.

When it comes to music, the post-WWII surge of innovation – technical, conceptual, compositional – is the greatest 'lost future' of them all. Those composers believed that the ideas they developed and machines they invented would form the foundation of all that followed (well, in high culture anyway, as opposed to mass music). These new developments in music commanded attention from the media, garnering respectful coverage in magazines as mainstream as *Time*, and even eliciting a fair amount of curiosity from the general public. From the early seventies onwards, though, modern classical music veered off on a different path: there was a return to the traditional orchestral palette of sounds, the rediscovery of tonality and consonance. In 1983, the critic John Rockwell could recall, bemused, the time only a few years earlier when 'electronic seemed ready to sweep all other music aside. Traditionalists worried nervously about music composed by machines, and predicted a dehumanizing Armageddon. Today, outside a few specialist enclaves, one hears very little about the subject.' Electronic and tape music had indeed become an increasingly rarified specialist field, an academic music ghetto. Nowadays, work in these areas continues quite energetically, but the audience for it has shrunk to not much larger than the community of practitioners itself.

Which raises an intriguing question: why did I, like so many others, fixate on the vintage vanguard, rather than take an interest in the current exponents? The fifties and sixties definitely seem like 'the golden age', in a historically objective sense, but there's something else going on here: I had *zero interest* in the contemporary operators in sound art and computer music. Maybe this isn't so odd: we do privilege the emergent phase of a genre, the seventies dub-reggae producers or sixties psychedelic bands, rather than those who came later and carried on their work; the latter are settlers not pioneers, what the critic Philip Sherburne calls the après-garde. Clearly there's a large element of projection by the historically informed listener, a kind of mental restaging of the moment of bursting through into the unknown. But I really think you can feel the difference. In some near-mystical way, the spirit of the age permeates the music of eras of change and turbulence, imbuing them with a palpable momentousness. When you listen to the fifties and sixties electronic composers, there's a sense of probes being sent into unknown sound worlds.

What also seems heroic is the Herculean effort required to make this music using tape and scissors, the struggle against extreme technical limitations. 'For someone like Herbert Eimert, a two-minute piece took a month of eighteen-hour days to achieve,' says Keith Fullerton Whitman, a contemporary synthesizer experimentalist who has also reissued obscure electronic-music recordings from the 1948–84 period via his Creel Pone label. 'It involved sitting down with a piece of paper and scoring out your sounds, making a chart of all the different combinations. And then actually *doing it*.' It's infinitely easier nowadays to achieve the same results using digital technology, and, perhaps superstitiously, I sense that as a profound difference between the original concrète and its modern-day equivalent.

For me there is also something about knowing that this music was felt and responded to as epoch-defining (Columbia Records named its modern-classical division Music of Our

Time). Newspapers like the *New York Times* covered the concerts and festivals; corporations like Bell Telephone Laboratories funded research into electronic sound and sponsored events like 'Nine Evenings of Art in the Armory', a 1966 series involving luminaries like John Cage and Robert Rauschenberg that showcased the growing interface between art and technology; Charles Wuorinen's electronic *Time's Encomium* won the Pulitzer Prize for Music in 1970, while Morton Subotnik's 1967 *Silver Apples of the Moon* topped the classical charts. Today, composers beaver away in the sound laboratories that most universities across the world still maintain, researching 'granular synthesis' and designing ultra-immersive multispeaker set-ups for sound-art installations. There are concert series and conferences, but it's a backwater of modern culture, not something that makes waves.

So what happened to the brave new world of electronic music that in the fifties and sixties seemed to beckon and loom? Why did the frontier lose its allure? The parallel that comes to mind is the fading profile during the seventies and eighties of the quest to conquer space. The post-WWII electronic and tape pioneers were engaged in the musical equivalent of the space race. Both drives into the unknown peaked at around the same time – 1968–70 – and neither would ever again command the level of public attention they did in their heyday. There are even a few direct links between the two races: for instance, as well as exploring electronic music and sound synthesis, Bell Laboratories was also involved with NASA in its early days. Most developed nations, and even a few developing ones, had their own electronic studio. In Europe, these were usually based out of government-controlled radio: Germany's WDR (Westdeutscher Rundfunk), France's RTF (Radio-diffusion et Télévision Française), Italy's Studio Fonologia Musicale at Radio Italiana. In America, they tended to be linked to academic institutions and sometimes looked to the private sector for funding. The Columbia-Princeton Electronic

Music Center, for instance, was launched with a grant from the Rockefeller Foundation and formed an alliance with the electronics giant RCA (which originally stood for Radio Corporation of America) in order to access the vastly expensive RCA Synthesizer Mk II. The sums of money involved in these early sound-synthesis machines and computers were as massive – half a million dollars in the case of the Mk II – as the technology was physically monstrous. Your typical electronic music centre, with its banks of blinking lights and wires, its intently focused technicians with suits and spectacles, even looked a bit like the Houston Space Center.

But the parallels run much deeper. The concept of 'space' – in all senses: outer, inner, architectural – suggests itself irresistibly when you listen to the music of the post-WWII vanguard. The new technology of tape and synthesis promised to place within the composer's grasp for the first time the ability to control totally every parameter of sound: pitch, timbre, duration, its envelope (its attack, decay, etc.), and above all the placement and movement of musical elements within the sound field. The new music often featured alarming panning effects that exploited the disorienting spatial possibilities of stereophony, so that the composer worked with blocks of timbre that moved through space as they moved in time. Listen to the 'experiences' created by Bernard Parmegiani and it's like you're moving inside a maze built using all four dimensions rather than the usual two. A parallel with op art springs to mind: just as the eyeball is almost physically wrenched by Bridget Riley's disorienting patterns, you can imagine ear strain being induced by Parmegiani's perspectival distortions. Increasingly, composers explored quadraphonic or eight-speaker set-ups: sounds circled around the listener's head, swooped and veered, receded and surged. Stockhausen had a spherical auditorium built to his specifications at the 1970 World Fair in Osaka, Japan, with nests for musicians scattered throughout the

384

audience; the latter sat at 'the equator', on a sound-transparent platform and surrounded by fifty speakers distributed in ten circles (eight above the equator, two below).

Space seemed to be what this new music was *about* in the larger, spiritual sense too. Even before he'd got his hands on the new electronic tools, Varèse was thinking along these lines: his two great unfinished projects of the thirties were *Astronomer* (about communication with the star Sirius) and *Espace* (which he envisioned as a radiophonic piece sung by choirs situated in capital cities like Moscow and New York). Varèse described *Déserts*, an early-fifties piece that combined wind and percussion instruments with electronic tape, as being about 'all physical deserts (of sand, sea, snow, of outer space, of empty streets) . . . that suggest bareness, aloofness, timelessness', but also those desolate regions of inner space that 'no telescope can reach . . . a world of mystery and essential loneliness'.

When the space race actually kicked off with the 1957 Soviet launch of sputnik into orbit, composers jostled to title their works in reference to mankind's new frontier: Philips's sound researchers Tom Dissevelt and Kid Baltan rushed out *Song of the Second Moon* (a reference to the satellite), and Dissevelt reprised the idea with 1963's *Fantasy in Orbit*. Later in the sixties, inspired by cosmonaut Yuri Gagarin's first steps outside the Earth's atmosphere and the landing on the lunar surface of NASA's unmanned Surveyor, came Otto Luening's 'Moonflight', Musica Electronica Viva's 'Spacecraft' and Subotnik's *Silver Apples of the Moon*. On the eve of the first manned landing, John Cage and Lejaren Hiller staged their cacophonous computer-music piece *HPSCHD* (the worst avant-classical purchase I ever made) at the University of Illinois, with sixty-four slide projectors displaying 6,400 slides largely supplied by NASA, plus a showing of Georges Méliès's classic 1902 film *Trip to the Moon*.

The excitement about space wasn't limited to the avant-garde, of course, but pervaded popular culture, from the Joe Meek-produced instrumental hit 'Telstar' to jazz (George Russell and Bill Evans put out the LP *Jazz in the Space Age*). Then there was Sun Ra, né Herman Poole Blount, who from the late fifties onwards started telling people he was from Saturn. The self-professed Ambassador for the Omniverse, Ra and his Arkestra played abstract but swinging pieces with titles like 'Space Is the Place', 'Spiral Galaxy', 'Other Planes of There' and 'Astro Black'. When I interviewed him in 1989, Sun Ra smugly informed me: 'All of what I said has come true. Interplanetary travel is now a reality. But that's what I was saying fifty years ago. Now I'm far in advance. I'm the top innovator on the planet.'

A Teutonic Sun Ra, Stockhausen was obsessed with space even before sputnik pierced the stratosphere. As a young music student he had noticed that Wernher von Braun had been recruited by America as a rocket scientist. He titled one of his first piano pieces 'Star Music', and as early as 1953 was convinced that 'the synthesis of sound and space music would be the most important aspect of the music of our time and of the future'. By 1961, he was proclaiming that in the future every major city in the world would have an auditorium specially designed for the performance of 'space music'. In 1967, shortly after premiering his master-work *Hymnen*, he noted that 'many listeners have projected that strange new music which they experienced . . . into extraterrestrial space . . . Several have commented that my electronic music sounds "like on a different star," or "like in outer space." Many have said that when hearing this music, they have sensations as if flying at an infinitely high speed, and then again, as if immobile in an immense space.'

THE CLOSING OF THE FRONTIER

I vividly recall seeing the 1969 moon landing on a TV in the lounge of a bed-and-breakfast hotel in Swanage. I'd just turned six and didn't quite understand the rapt focus of the adults in the room. In the immediate aftermath of the landing, PanAm airlines started accepting reservations for flights to the moon, while NASA talked of aiming to establish a permanent moon base by the eighties. The Race Into Space seemed intimately bound up with the whole neophiliac dynamic of the sixties, its cult of breakthroughs and breaking-on-through, energy smashing through all constraints and limits. It seems no coincidence that the moon shot – the money shot of an entire era – culminated in the summer of 1969, only a few weeks before Woodstock, itself the climax of the sixties cult of youth and the new/now generation.

Almost inevitably, 1970 could only be a year of deflation and comedown: The Beatles split, and music seemed to stall as rock looked back to its rootsy past. And the turning point for NASA may have occurred as early as those pivotal months at the end of the sixties and the start of the seventies. There had been a frenzy of missions, five between December 1968 and November 1969. But according to Tom Wolfe, who visited the space centre shortly after the moon landing, the lay-offs began at NASA while Armstrong and Aldrin were still on their victory tour. Its annual budget sank from $5 billion in the mid-sixties to $3 billion in the mid-seventies. Wernher von Braun talked up space exploration as a giant evolutionary stride for mankind, equivalent to primitive life leaving the sea. But for the US government the whole thing had been a gigantic dick-waving contest with the USSR, without any real philosophical or spiritual drive behind it. As Wolfe puts it, 'It had been a battle for morale at home and image abroad.' By April 1970, TV coverage of the Apollo 13 mission was being cancelled in favour of *The Doris Day Show*.

Perhaps the public expected an exponential advance – Mars to follow the moon in quick succession. What they got was far less spectacular: 'a series of orbital projects . . . Skylab, the

Apollo–Soyuz joint mission, the International Space Station', or as Wolfe phrases it more sharply, NASA 'killing time for 40 years' in order to 'keep the lights on at the Kennedy Space Center and Houston's Johnson Space Center'. The *Phoenix* landing on Mars and *Voyager 1* heading out of the solar system with recordings of Chuck Berry and Beethoven were stunning achievements, but they didn't capture the public imagination like men on the moon.

In the past couple of decades, the space-shuttle programme has stripped away any vestiges of romance attached to the image of the astronaut. As 2001, the year of Kubrick's *Odyssey*, rolled around without even a lunar base, science-fiction fans like myself have gradually reconciled ourselves to the depressing fact that we aren't going to see vacations on the moon in our lifetimes. Then NASA's profile slipped even lower during the 2000s. George W. Bush proposed a renewed commitment to space exploration, with support for NASA's Constellation programme to return to the moon by 2020, followed by a 'small lunar outpost', and possibly a manned mission to Mars in the third decade of the twenty-first century. But it was empty talk, backed up with no funding. Barack Obama, pressed hard by the mounting deficit, put the programme on hold, realising that the Kennedy-style bridge to the stars could easily become a bridge to nowhere. Eugene Cernan, who in 1972 became the last human to stand on the moon's surface, said, 'I'm quite disappointed . . . I thought we'd have gone back long before now.'

The Soviets never even made it to the moon, and their own space programme seemed to run out of steam even quicker. Commenting on a 1995 piece by cosmonaut-watcher James Oberg, science-fiction author Bruce Sterling used terms like 'institutional senility' and 'deadwood' to describe Russia's rocket-scientist 'gerontocracy' of retirement-age space experts. And he noted that Oberg's photographs of ex-Soviet space centres – ghost town-like to the point of having 'tumbleweeds (an Asian species) roll unimpeded through the launchpads' – uncannily resembled J. G. Ballard's stories about a space race fallen into dereliction.

Dubbed the 'Cape Canaveral' stories by aficionados and later gathered in the 1988 collection *Memories of the Space Age*, these shorts bore titles like 'A Question of Re-entry' and 'The Dead Astronaut' and showed Ballard to be a couple of beats ahead of the culture as usual. 'Myths of the Near Future', for instance, takes place thirty years after NASA has disbanded. The Space Center in Florida has been overgrown by forest canopy. In his Cessna light airplane, the protagonist, Sheppard, flies back and forth 'above the abandoned space grounds . . . with their immense runways leading to no conceivable sky, and the rusting gantries like so many deaths propped up in their tattered coffins. Here at Cape Kennedy a small part of space had died.'

Avant-garde composers, with the exception of the increasingly dotty Stockhausen, may have stopped giving cosmic titles to their work in the seventies (a move that ran in parallel with

---

THE FUTURE IS NOT WHAT IT USED TO BE

The Future Is Not What It Used to Be is the title of a 2002 documentary about Erkki Kurenniemi, a brilliant, eccentric figure – imagine a Finnish hybrid of Stockhausen, Buckminster Fuller and Steve Jobs – who from the sixties onwards was a pioneer in electronic music, computing, industrial robotics, instrument invention and multimedia. Short of presiding over Finland's space programme, he was involved in every aspect of the Future. Rediscovered and championed by the Finnish techno outfit Pan Sonic, Kurenniemi's clangorous bleepscapes such as 'Electronics in the World of Tomorrow' (1964) compare favourably with the avant-classical creations emanating from Paris and Cologne during that time. He was also something of a techno-prophet, talking in the voice-over to 1966's 'Computer Music' about how 'in the 21st century people and computers will begin to merge into hyperpersonas. It will be hard to say where man ends and machine begins.'

The documentary – made by director Mika Taanila, who's carved out a retro-futurist niche with similar films like *Futuro: A New Stance for Tomorrow*, about a Finnish plastic house similar to the efforts of Monsanto and Alison and Peter

the widespread retreat from electronic tonalities – surely no coincidence). But space (and synths) just went low-brow, seeping into rock and pop. Nineteen sixty-eight's *Switched on Bach*, an album of classical music rendered on the Moog synthesizer by Walter (later Wendy) Carlos, became a million-seller and inspired a swathe of copyists. The fad faded but resurged for a second climax in 1977 with Tomita's best-selling electronic interpretation of Holst's *The Planets*. In between, 'space rock', an offshoot of psychedelia oriented largely around synthesizers, took off, with mostly German artists like Tangerine Dream and Klaus Schulze unfurling trance-inducing pulse rhythms and amorphous swirls of texture across long tracks that often took up the entire side of an LP. Stoner music designed to trigger eyelid movies, the genre – nowadays often known as 'analogue synth epics' – fit right into the mass culture of *Omni* magazine, popular-science writers like Carl Sagan, paranormal-ists and UFO-oligists like Erich von Däniken, and the sword-and-sorcery space opera *Star Wars*. This was also the era of holograms and laser shows, and Jean-Michel Jarre, creator of the mega-selling electronic albums *Oxygene* and *Equinoxe*, plunged into full-on audio-visual fantasia mode with

---

Smithson – also looks at what became of Kurenniemi in the twilight of his career. Grey-bearded and careworn, the ageing innovator spends most of his time documenting himself. He takes 20,000 pictures a year, which are carefully touched up and filed on his computer. He inputs 'cassette diaries' he made during the seventies and records new ones detailing the minutiae of his existence, like the good steak he enjoyed courtesy of a friend.

Why? Kurenniemi believes that medical advances will virtually eliminate mortality in the not-too-distant future. 'Mine is probably the last generation of mortals.' Two hundred years from now, when the greater part of humanity lives off-world in the asteroids or orbital zones, while the Earth is 'a museum planet', he believes that the indolent immortals, confronted by '100,000 years of uneventful life' and 'with nothing else to do but study old archives', may be 'genuinely interested in reconstructing the 20th and 21st centuries'. Kurenniemi's 'manic registration' of every trivial detail of his life is intended to provide the 'core

a series of increasingly spectacular extravaganzas watched by millions (and including a mega-concert in Houston to celebrate NASA's twenty-fifth birthday). Jarre also received an honour to make other electronic space rockers green with envy – having an actual heavenly body named after him, the asteroid 4422 Jarre.

The link between synthesizers and outer space faded during the eighties, but it came back strong in the techno-rave nineties. The Orb's *Adventures Beyond the Ultraworld* was laced with Apollo 11 and 17 mission dialogue and musings from various cosmonauts. Astronomical imagery permeated virtually every sector of the electronic dance culture: artist names like Cosmic Baby and Vapourspace, track titles like Acen's 'Trip to the Moon' and The Prodigy's 'Out of Space', clubs with names like Final Frontier, Orbit and even NASA.

In 1993, London pirate radio was playing to death an underground rave anthem (one I've never been able to identify) that took liberties with 'Sleeping Satellite', Tasmin Archer's no. 1 hit of the previous autumn. 'Did we fly to the moon too soon?' Archer sang plaintively. It wasn't a metaphor for something else, like love: Archer really was wondering, with endearing earnestness, if

---

material' for this resurrection project. In the near future, it will be possible to do 'brain back-ups', to download consciousness and personality into a computer. But Kurenniemi can't count on lasting that long. So, he advises, 'We just have to keep every tram ticket and sales slip, and write down or record all our thoughts.' Video would make for a better imprint of his consciousness, a document of the world seen through his eyes, but it's impractical; the still snapshots will at least provide a 'jerky account'. He plans on doubling his current rate of a hundred pictures a day.

Erkki Kurenniemi's journey from future-minded visionary working at the interface of science and art, a fresh-faced young man who pioneered computers and robotics and kept one bright eye always on the stars above, to the haggard and slightly potty sixty-something frantically collating the remains of his days for the benefit of some future race of curators strikes me as a perfect parable for our times.

'Man's greatest adventure' had been premature. Maybe humanity just hadn't been ready. The rave track took the poignant lyrics and turned them into an Ecstasy anthem, describing a different kind of crash landing after reaching the highest heights. In 'Myths of the Near Future', Ballard had speculated poetically that space had been 'a metaphor for Eternity which they' – the astronauts and cosmonauts – 'were wrong to try to grasp'. You could see both the space race and the various electronic-music vanguards of twentieth-century music – including rave – as manifestations of an Icarus complex, projections beyond our natural sphere.

Rave itself fell back to earth. In the late nineties, electronic dance music reached the 'postmodern turn' that seems to be inevitable for, and integral to, every progressive music movement. It double-backed on its own history and prehistory, with revivals of acid house and eighties electropop. By the early to mid-2000s, people were even recycling ideas from the nineties, from jungle or trance; acid house was on its third or fourth resurrection.

Then, around 2006, a kind of battle of the retro-raves took place. Spearheaded by The Klaxons, the 'nu-rave' movement was a gaggle of British indie bands flirting with the 'early-nineties euphoric feeling' of house and techno. Although too young to have participated at the time, an *idea* of rave – blurrily grasped, based on pre-teen memories of outfits like N-Joi and Altern-8 miming on UK television – gripped their imaginations. The Klaxons covered Kicks Like a Mule's 1992 anthem 'The Bouncer' and named another tune 'Golden Skans' after a spectacular light machine once touted on rave flyers. The lyrics to their 'apocalyptic pop songs' were fantastical and garish, depicting 'a fantasy future world made up of jumbled things from our past'. The Klaxons titled their 2007 debut album *Myths of the Near Future*, the name of one of the Ballard 'Cape Canaveral' stories collected in *Memories of the Space Age*. Because the group stuck with the standard indie set-up of guitars, bass and drums, their music could only be an energetic travesty of electronic dance music, and ageing ravers and hip young clubbers alike scorned their efforts. But *Myths* was the surprise winner of the Mercury Prize for Best British Album. By which point The Klaxons were starting to disown 'nu-rave', claiming it was a publicity gimmick to kick-start their career. Yet whatever the group's intentions, the concept had briefly sparked a flurry of underground activity, with indie rock bands and DJ outfits throwing gigs in derelict pubs, and audiences waving glowsticks and miming mentalist behaviour in a half-ironic, half-earnest simulation of happenings fifteen years ago. You could see the appeal: rave circa 1990–3 was the last youth-culture *movement* complete with its own fashion, slang, dance moves, rituals. But techno was also the last time that music felt like it was really *moving forward*, the last blast of full-tilt, irony-free futurism in mainstream pop.

The other rave flashback came courtesy of a single artist, Burial. Like The Klaxons, his music harked back to hardcore and early jungle, but filtered the euphoria through a misty-eyed prism of loss. Although Burial's fidgety, clacking beats mimic the hyper-syncopated bustle of British rave music, the fog-bank synths, yearning slivers of vocal and shroud of sampled rainfall and vinyl hiss makes his music more suited to melancholy private reverie than rave-floor action. This is hauntological dance, music for abandoned nightclubs. True, his music is partly inspired by its urban environment, specifically South London: the isolation and anomie of living in the city. But Burial's own interview comments suggest that even though he never participated in rave first-hand but experienced it vicariously through his older brother's DJ mixtapes and stories, the post-rave comedown is a large part of what his music addresses. The track 'Night Bus', for instance, evokes the loneliness of catching the late-night bus back to the outer zones of London after going to a club. But it is also a post-millennial nocturne for the loss of a collective sense of purpose: it says, 'After the nineties, we're all on the Night Bus now.' Another track on the debut album, 'Gutted', makes a similar point using a sample of Forest Whitaker's voice from Jim Jarmusch's *Ghost Dog: The Way of the Samurai*: 'Me and him, we're from different, ancient tribes . . . now we're both almost extinct . . . sometimes . . . you gotta stick with the ancient ways . . . old-skool ways.'

Burial's label-mate Kode9 pinpointed the mood with the title of his own 2006 album, *Memories of the Future*. In an interview, Burial talked about 'the tunes I loved the most . . . old jungle, rave and hardcore, sounded hopeful'. Elsewhere he claimed, 'All those lost producers . . . I love them, but it's not a retro thing . . . When I listen to an old tune it doesn't make me think "I'm looking back, listening to another era." Some of those tunes are sad because they sounded like the future back then and no one noticed. They still sound future to me.' Burial resolves the contradictions of retro-futurism by imagining that this music still *is* the future, some-how: a bridge to tomorrow that was never finished but just hangs there in space, poised, pointing to something out-of-reach and unattainable.

TO BOLDLY GO

In his 1931 book *Man and Technics* – a sort of precis-cum-sequel to the more famous *The Decline of the West* – Oswald Spengler contrasted the motor principles of various civilisations. He defined the 'Faustian' essence of the West as 'a spiritual reach-ing out into boundless space'. That is the dynamic behind mod-ernism and modernisation, the impulse that propelled both the space race and twentieth-century music's exploration of sonic space through electronics.

In the last couple of decades, that drive into the unknown seems to have collapsed back on itself, imploded. When you look at the culture of the West in the last decade or so – the dominance of fashion and gossip, celebrity and image; a citizenry obsessed with decor and cuisine; the metastasis of irony throughout society – the total picture does look a lot like decadence. Retro culture would then be just another facet of the recline and fall of the West.

That leaves the possibility of the new coming from outside the West, from regions of the globe where culture is less exhausted in both the 'used up' and 'tired' senses. It could emerge from Eastern Europe or East Asia, or from Latin America, Africa or elsewhere in the southern hemisphere. China and India are set to be the economic and demographic powerhouses of this century; paradoxically, these most ancient cultures feel 'younger' than us at the moment. Ironically, that's because, in a sense, they're behind us, still in the mid-twentieth century – the era of rampant industrialisation, of hubris-laden state initiatives like massive dam projects.

It seems significant that both those countries recently launched their own space races. After a very late start, China is overtaking the US and Russia. In 2003, it became the third nation to send a human into space; there have been further missions, manned and robotic, and there are plans for space stations and a Chinese lunar rover. India has sent unmanned missions to the moon, and hopes to get an astronaut into orbit by 2016. Brazil wants to get in on the outer-space action too, and even Iran announced it's going to have a bash at manned space flight by 2021.

But it is China that has really taken on the mantle of the 'spiritual reaching out into boundless space' that was once the West's core drive. The *New York Times'* David Brooks characterised China as 'the nation of futurity', after the Global Innovation Survey revealed that the Chinese are the most optimistic people on the planet. Eighty-six per cent of them believe their country is headed in the right direction, compared with a mere 37 per cent of Americans.

In popular-music terms, this outlook for the next century would suggest that while the Anglo-American pop tradition is all innovated out, it could be that the ball is now in the court of the rest of the globe. The overdriven economic metabolisms of rising mega-nations like China and India will doubtless generate all manner of social rifts and cultural turbulence. Popular energies and desires will be stoked that will come into friction with existing political structures and social norms, producing sparks and possibly conflagrations. You could imagine a sixties-like moment, a neophiliac delirium crashing through the barricades of tradition. Out of this may come some cool music or some other compelling cultural forms. So maybe it's simply time for the West to ... *rest*.

FUTURE FATIGUE

In her 2001 essay 'Science Fiction without the Future', author Judith Berman surveyed the state of her genre, breaking down the contents of recent issues of leading SF magazines and discovering a preponderance of short stories about ageing, nostalgia and fear of the future, with a surprising proportion actually set in the past or having a disconcerting 'retro' flavour. What she considered 'real futures', involving speculative extrapolation from present tendencies, could be found in only a quarter of the stories. In a striking parallel with this book's retrophobic anxieties about music, Berman wondered if science fiction was 'becoming anti-sf ... a closed system where recycling subject matter and theme is all that's possible'.

Two years after Berman's essay, William Gibson published *Pattern Recognition*, his first novel of the new millennium. It was also his first novel not set in the future. All three of the books he's published since that magic year 2000 – *Pattern Recognition*, *Spook Country* and *Zero History* – are set in the present. At a Book

Expo talk he gave in 2010 a few months before *Zero History* came out, Gibson spoke of how 'Future Fatigue' had displaced Toffler's old notion of future shock. He argued that where his generation had made a cult of 'the capital-F Future', the youth of today 'inhabit a sort of endless digital Now, a state of atemporality enabled by our increasingly efficient communal prosthetic memory'. 'Atemporality' is a term that Gibson and his fellow cyberpunk pioneer Bruce Sterling have been bouncing around recently. Sterling characterises 'atemporality' as a byproduct of networked culture and claims that the concept of 'the future' is an old paradigm and that the word itself will go out of use. Amid a shower of *pensées* issued via Twitter, Gibson asserted that 'the most intelligent twenty-first-century fashion strives for a radical atemporality'. He thinks atemporality is a 'very good thing'.

Gibson told the Book Expo audience that his shift to a contemporary setting for his work came about not so much because of his own 'future fatigue' but because he was finding 'the actual 21st century richer, stranger, more multiplex, than any imaginary 21st century could ever have been'. Only science fiction's 'toolkit' could grapple with the 'cognitive dissonance' of everyday life in the 2000s. In a BBC News interview later in 2010, Gibson upped the ante, claiming that things were changing so fast these days that 'the present is the length of a news cycle . . . the present is really of no width whatever'. Science fiction, in the traditional speculative sense, was simply unnecessary: the future had arrived; it was upon us. What we needed was an 'investigation of our alien present', whose most salient features – judging from *Pattern Recognition* and the two novels that followed – are fashion, branding, cool-hunting, graphic design, viral marketing, corporate espionage, and so forth.

Gibson's perspective is so completely other to my own that I'm flabbergasted. When I travel through the urban–suburban landscape of America or Britain, it seems to have changed remarkably

397

little in three decades. When I look or listen to the cultural landscape of the West, there's a similar sense of familiarity. The cognitive dissonance is the *absence* of cognitive dissonance. The shock is the shock of the old.

THE RETROSCAPE (Slight Return)

2010/January: UK release of Ian Dury biopic *Sex & Drugs & Rock & Roll*, with the Blockheads singer played by Andy Serkis, the actor who travestied Martin Hannett in *24 Hour Party People* >>>>>>> 2010/February: Pub-rock retro mini-boom continues with Dr Feelgood rock doc *Oil City Confidential*, the final instalment in Julien Temple's punk-doc trilogy, following *The Filth and the Fury*, about The Sex Pistols, and *The Future Is Unwritten*, about Joe Strummer >>>>>>> 2010/February: VH1 start a 'reissue' programme for their popular and admired rock-doc series *Behind the Music*, calling it *Behind the Music Remastered*. Each band story is updated with new interviews and footage added to fill in what happened to e.g. Metallica after the programme originally aired >>>>>>> 2010/February: Abbey Road studio is given Grade II 'protected status' by the Labour government's Minister of Culture Margaret Hodge, after consultation with English Heritage, in response to the public outcry at the prospect of EMI Records selling the place where The Beatles recorded their albums >>>>>>> 2010/April: Release of *The Runaways*, biopic about the seventies proto-punk all-girl band created by svengali Kim Fowley and featuring future star Joan Jett >>>>>>> 2010/April: John Lennon no. 1 ultra-fan Liam Gallagher of Oasis announces that In 1 Productions, his newly formed film-production company, are developing a rock movie about the chaotic story of The Beatles' Apple Corps company >>>>>>> 2010/April: 'Don't Look Back' celebrates its fifth anniversary with performances of *Raw Power* and Suicide's self-titled debut. Although the original Stooges had ended with guitarist Ron Asheton's death in 2009, the non-original line-up of the band as Iggy and the Stooges (featuring guitarist James Williamson, who played on *Raw Power*) are a going concern, says Iggy Pop, with plans to record new albums >>>>>>> 2010/April: Grime rapper Plan B undergoes Winehouse-style retro-soul makeover with *The Defamation of Strickland Banks*. It goes triple platinum in the UK >>>>>>> 2010/May: Peter Hook commemorates the thirtieth anniversary of Ian Curtis's death by performing the entirety of *Unknown Pleasures* with his new band The Light. There are rival Curtis-related exhibitions in Macclesfield and at Manchester's The Factory Club, and a walking tour of Curtis-related sites in Macclesfield draws Joy Division fans from all corners of the globe >>>>>>> 2010/May: The Rolling Stones re-release 1972's *Exile on Main*

Street in deluxe expanded form, with ten never-before-issued tracks and a documentary about the making of the iconic double album, *Stones in Exile* >>>>>> 2010/May: US publisher Dutton sign up for an oral history of MTV's Golden Age (1981 to 1992, when reality TV took over the channel) due for publication on MTV's thirtieth anniversary in the summer of 2011 >>>>>> 2010/May: The Allman Brothers Museum opens in Macon, Georgia, based in the Big House, where the band and their family and friends lived communally >>>>>> 2010/June: A re-formed Devo release *Something for Everybody*, their first album in two decades >>>>>> 2010/July: In what may be the ultimate retromaniac act, Beck records a cover of Sonic Youth's 1986 album *EVOL* which will be given a cassette-only release as part of a Sonic Youth box set. Whole album covers x cassette fetishism x box set = game set and match to Beck >>>>>> 2010/August: *Banned in the UK – Sex Pistols Exiled to Oslo in 1977*, a photo-book about a single Pistols gig in Norway, is published >>>>>> 2010/August: The Faces re-form, with Mick Hucknall of Simply Red substituting for Rod Stewart and ex-Pistol Glen Matlock on bass, and play a show at the Vintage at Goodwood, a festival 'for people who feel too old at Glastonbury . . . and a celebration of British cool from the 1940s to 1980s'. Also on the bill: Buzzcocks, Heaven 17 >>>>>> 2010/September: Pavement re-form for their first gig in over a decade at Rumsey Playfield in Central Park, New York >>>>>> 2010/September: Almost thirty years after his chart-topping Supremes cover 'You Can't Hurry Love', Phil Collins releases his Motown tribute album *Going Back*. Remaking eighteen sixties classics with help from Motown's original hit squad The Funk Brothers, Collins says his 'intention was to make an "old" record, not a "new" record' >>>>>> 2010/September: Legendary post-punk firebrands The Pop Group play two reunion gigs >>>>>> 2010/September: Goth Revival in full swing with 'witch house' pioneers Salem's debut album *King Night*, a split EP from Zola Jesus and LA Vampires, and a debut EP from the 4AD-influenced dubstep act Raime on the Blackest Ever Black label >>>>>> 2010/September: Cold Wave Revival intensifies with Frank (Just Frank)'s *The Brutal Wave* LP on New York's Wierd Records and split EP from Soviet Soviet and Frank (Just Frank) on Mannequin >>>>>> 2010/September: *SoulBoy*, Shimmy Marcus's movie about Northern Soul, hits screens. Another movie about the early-seventies revival scene, Elaine Constantine's *Northern Soul*, is set for 2011 release >>>>>> 2010/September: Roger Waters launches a global tour of *The Wall*, with 117 concerts across North America and Europe, and more to follow elsewhere in the world, if he hasn't physically collapsed >>>>>> 2010/September–October: Stressing that it's not a Crass reunion, Crass singer Steve Ignorant launches UK tour of The Last Supper: Crass Songs 1977–1982, an expansion of his 2007 performances of Crass's debut LP, *The Feeding of the 5000*, at London's Shepherd's Bush Empire. Crass meanwhile launch *The Crassical Collection*, a series of remastered reissues of the anarcho-punk legends' albums >>>>>> 2010/28 September: The Buggles reunite for one gig only >>>>>> 2010/October: Biopic of John Lennon's fifties adolescence *Nowhere Boy* gets its US release timed for the seventieth anniversary of Lennon's birth >>>>>> 2010/October: The Cars announce that they've reunited and recorded an album, and this time it's the true Cars, not 'The New Cars', with original member Ric Ocasek rejoining despite having demurred earlier in the decade >>>>>> 2010/October: Focusing on the friendship between Alan McGee, the Arthur Negus of indie rock, and Bobby Gillespie, the chief librarian of rock'n'roll, the Creation Records documentary *Upside Down* premieres at the London Film Festival. As do documentaries about Motörhead's Lemmy, the reunion of Mott the Hoople after thirty-five years apart, and Stephen Merritt >>>>>>> 2010/October: It's announced that Sacha Baron Cohen of Ali G and Borat fame is to play the role of Freddie Mercury in an upcoming biopic of the Queen singer's life >>>>>>> 2010/October: Retro-soul producer Mark Ronson of Amy Winehouse fame switches to ransacking the eighties with his new album *Record Collection,* featuring cameo vocals from Simon Le Bon and Boy George >>>>>>> 2010/October: Twenty-seven years after the fact, La Roux's Elly Jackson declares that eighties synth pop is 'so over. It was my thing and I'm bored with it. I don't want to make synth music for the rest of my fucking life. If I see anything more '80s-themed, I'm going to bust.' >>>>>>> 2010/October: Hotly tipped post-dubstep outfit Darkstar release 'Gold', a cover of a Human League B-side from 1982 >>>>>>> 2010/October: Talk of a 'Britpop Revival' gathers momentum with the hotly hyped Brother, whose 'gritpop' harks back to the 'lad band' era of Oasis >>>>>>> 2010/October: Genesis P-Orridge quits the re-formed Throbbing Gristle shortly before a series of performances in Poland, Italy and Portugal. To avoid disappointing the fans, the remaining members offer to play live as X-TG >>>>>>> 2010/November: Mumford and Sons. Just Mumford and Sons >>>>>>> 2010/November: Bruce Springsteen takes the deluxe expanded reissue to the nutty next level with *The Promise*, a three CD + three DVD inflation of his 1978 album *Darkness on the Edge of Town* encompassing a documentary on the record's making, reproductions of the Boss's notebooks, performance footage, a concert film and out-takes galore >>>>>>> 2010/December: Back to the Phuture concerts in Manchester and London feature live performances from electronic legends Gary Numan and John Foxx >>>>>>> 2011/January: Rhino Records announce a sixty-disc box set documenting every single live performance of the Grateful Dead's 1972 European tour. All 7,200 copies of the $450 limited edition sell out in advance in a few hours >>>>>>> 2011/February: Mid-nineties retro intensifies as recently reunited post-rock micro-legend Seefeel release their first LP in fourteen years >>>>>>> 2011/March: Techno futurist Richie Hawtin, aka Plastikman, releases the eleven-CD career retrospective *Arkives Reference 1993–2010* >>>>>>> 2011/March: Debut album from nouveau-Britpop band The Vaccines, anointed 'game-changers' by *Clash Music* for their unprecedented amalgam of (in the band's words) "50s rock 'n' roll, '60s garage and girl groups, '70s punk, '80s American hardcore, C86' >>>>>>> 2011/June: Eighties nostalgia promoters Here and Now celebrate their tenth anniversary with a UK tour featuring Boy George, Jimmy Somerville, Midge Ure, A Flock of Seagulls, Jason Donovan, Jean Baudrillard and Pepsi & Shirlie >>>>>>> 2011/Summer: Dennis Wilson biopic released to coincide with The Beach Boys' fiftieth anniversary >>>>>>> 2011/October: The 'Lost Generation All Stars' tour of UK post-rockers – Disco Inferno, Moonshake, Long Fin Killie, Crescent, Third Eye Foundation – plays seventeen dates across Britain >>>>>>> 2011/November: Facebook campaign to persuade Iggy Pop to keep his shirt on tops 4 million signatures >>>>>>> 2011/December: Julien Temple unexpectedly turns his punkdoc trilogy into a tetralogy with *So What*, a film about The Anti-Nowhere League >>>>>>> 2012/January: *It's Trad, Dad*, Shane Meadows's movie about Britain's revival-jazz scene of the fifties, opens, starring Julian Barratt as Ken Colyer and David Mitchell as George Melly >>>>>>> 2012/30 April: Culture Club re-form to play celebration gig for the thirtieth anniversary of their first single, 'White Boy' >>>>>>> 2012/Summer: A re-formed Stone Roses headline one night of the Glastonbury Festival, with Inspiral Carpets guitarist Graham Lambert subbing for John Squire, who declines to participate >>>>>>>

12
THE SHOCK OF THE OLD

Past, Present and Future in the First Decade of the Twenty-First Century

At the start of this book I posed some questions, most of which have been answered along the way. But here's one I haven't really addressed:

> *Given that I enjoy many aspects of retro, why do I still feel deep down that it is lame and shameful?*

If contemporary pop culture is addicted to its own past, I belong to a minority of future addicts. It's the story of my pop life, really. I was born in 1963, which for various, not completely narcissistic reasons I regard as The Year That Rock Began. (Rock'n'roll in the fifties sense was both rawer and more showbizzy; 1963, the year of The Beatles, Dylan, the Stones, is when the idea of Rock as Art, Rock as Revolution, Rock as Bohemia, Rock as a Self-Consciously Innovative Form, really began.) When I started taking more than a passing interest in pop, as a teenager in the post-punk seventies, I immediately ingested a strong dose of modernism: the belief that art has some kind of evolutionary destiny, a teleology that manifests itself through genius artists and masterpieces that are monuments to the future. It was there already in rock, thanks

403

to The Beatles, psychedelia and progressive rock, but post-punk drastically amped up the belief in constant change and endless innovation. Although by the early eighties modernism was thoroughly eclipsed within art and architecture, and postmodernism was seeping into popular music, this spirit of modernist pop carried on with rave and the experimental fringe of rock. These surges of renewal served as a booster shot for me, reconfirming the modernist credo: art should constantly push forward into new territory, reacting against its own immediate predecessors in violent gestures of severance, jettisoning its superseded stages like a rocket shooting into space.

There is an argument that the linear model of progress is an ideological figment, something that should never have been transposed from science and technology, where it does apply, onto culture. Moreover, our belief in progress itself has been shaken badly recently – by the resurgence of faith-based fundamentalisms, by global warming and toxic catastrophe in the Gulf of Mexico, by evidence that social and racial divisions are deteriorating rather than improving, by the financial crisis. In a destabilised world, ideas of durable tradition and folk memory start to appeal as a counterweight and a drag in the face of capitalism's reckless and wrecking radicalism. In pop terms, this might translate into scepticism about the shock (of the new) doctrine, a suspicion that addiction to innovation might be as much of a problem, a distortion, as dependency on the past. Yet as a died-in-the-wool modernist who grew up during one period of full-tilt innovation (post-punk) and later participated as both a wide-eyed fan and crusading critic of another (rave), I would find it hard to break the habit of a lifetime, to kick 'tomorrow'. Giving it up would feel like giving in, learning to settle for less.

So with these biases in plain view, I now venture to make as objective an assessment of the past decade as possible. I come not to bury the 2000s but to appraise them.

Thinking about the first ten years after the Future arrived (the year 2000), the word that springs to mind is 'flat'. The nineties felt like this long, sustained ascent, what with the Internet and the info-tech boom, techno rave and its associated drugs. But the 2000s turned out to be a plateau. Oh, there was bustle and buzz, a fast turnover of new names and micro-trends. Casting an eye back over the soundscape of the 2000s as the era drew to a close, though, it seemed like nothing *momentous* had happened. Worse, it was a struggle to pinpoint what defined the era as a separate era musically. In his 2010 polemic *You Are Not a Gadget*, Jaron Lanier waspishly threw down the challenge: 'Play me some music that is characteristic of the late 2000s as opposed to the late 1990s.' It's hard to see what anyone could come up with in response. This deficit in newness can be seen across the spectrum, from the semi-popular fringes to the money-pumping heart of the mainstream.

If you monitor the margins – experimental music, underground dance, independent-label rock and all the other musical milieus covered by magazines like *The Wire, Pitchfork, FACT, Urb* et al. – it is rare that you'll come across something that could be honestly described as groundbreaking. Most left-field genres – drone/noise, underground hip hop, extreme metal, improv, etc. – seem to have settled into a steady-state condition, evolving at an incremental rate that is unspectacular at best and often barely perceptible. From glitchy electronics to wispy post-noise, most contemporary operators are trading off the breakthroughs achieved by ancestors long ago. Occasionally this rises to the surface of critical consciousness. Reviewing the 2010 compilation *New Directions in Experimental Music* for *The Wire*, Nick Richardson observed that 'it's not like the directions here are really new . . . The techniques deployed – drones, noise, tape collage – have been stock tokens of avant-gardism for decades.' Then, as if recoiling from the alarming implications of this acutely accurate perception, Richardson rallied with an unconvincing: 'But so what!? Novelty is massively overrated anyway.'

In the mainstream, meanwhile, you get the phenomenon of 'arrested futurism'. Global chart-toppers The Black Eyed Peas fill their music and videos with future-schlock retro kitsch: robot imagery, android voice treatments, glossy plasticised textures (sonic and sartorial). In their admittedly thrilling 2008 smash 'Boom Boom Pow', vocalist Fergie raps, 'I'm so 3008/ you're so 2000-and-late.' But rhythm-wise the song is no further advanced than Missy Elliott's records at the turn of the millennium, and the deployment of Auto-Tune on the vocals, while inventive, can be traced back to Cher's 1999 monster hit 'Believe'. There's an even stronger sensation of frozen future with recent *Billboard*-topping groups like Far East Movement (a sort of Asian-American Black Eyed Peas), whose music is based on eighties electro. From cyborg divas like Lady Gaga to party rappers like Flo Rida and robo-R&B singers like Taio Cruz, the state-of-the-(ch)art is an omnipop that pulls every trick in the book of eighties and nineties club music, meshing together elements from R&B, electro, house, 'Euro' and trance to create a high-fructose sound of brash, blaring excitement. This super-compressed, MP3-ready, almost *pre-degraded* sound is engineered to cut through on iPods, smartphones and computer speakers. This is the way that pop history ends, not with a whimper but a BANG BANG BANG.

Another way of assessing the past decade is to compare it with its predecessors in terms of genre formation: the arrival of new sounds and subcultures of the kind that are accepted as a New Thing even by people who detest the music. The sixties gave us the beat-group explosion (white R&B Brits like The Beatles, Stones, etc.), along with folk rock, psychedelia, soul and the birth of Jamaican pop with ska. Arguably even more fertile, the seventies spawned glam, heavy metal, funk, punk, reggae (and dub production), disco and more. The eighties maintained the pace with

406

rap, synth pop, Goth, house. The nineties saw rave culture and its spiralling profusion of subgenres; the grunge and alternative-rock explosion; reggae turning into dancehall; and hip hop's continued full-tilt evolution, which led in turn to the nu-R&B of Timbaland and all who followed.

How do the 2000s measure up? Even the most generous assessment of pop in the first decade of the new millennium must surely conclude that nearly all the developments were either tweaks to established genres (emo, for instance, is a melodic and melodramatic variant of punk) or archive-raiding styles (freak folk, for instance). Two of the few arguable exceptions were grime and dubstep: exciting sounds, certainly, but so far they have proved to be contained explosions within the UK's post-rave tradition, except for a few watered-down crossovers into chart-pop terrain with acts like Tinchy Stryder and Magnetic Man.

The surge decades of pop history were characterised by the emergence of new subcultures and an overall sense of forward propulsion. What was lacking in the 2000s was movements and movement. One manifestation of the sense of deceleration: 2010 didn't feel that different from 2009, or even 2004. Whereas in the past, the differences between years – between 1967 and 1968, or 1978 and 1979, or 1991 and 1992 – felt immense.

Part of the problem is that the musical landscape has grown cluttered. Most of the styles of music and subcultures that have ever existed are still with us. From Goth to drum'n'bass, metal to trance, house to industrial, these genres are permanent fixtures on the menu, drawing new recruits every year. Nothing seems to wither and die. This hampers the emergence of new things.

It can reach the point where you actually forget that once upon a time totally new things did emerge from out of pop culture. I was forcefully reminded of this when I came across a photo book about the early days of UK hip-hop culture, *Wild Dayz*. What struck me, looking at shots of British B-boys and fly girls DJing,

407

MCing, break-dancing and graffiti-ing, is how quickly and *absolutely* hip hop seized the imagination of black and white youth across urban Britain. They saw something fresher than anything else around, something that looked like the future, and threw themselves into it unreservedly, embracing the clothes and the slang as well as the records. Hip hop's historical roots can be traced back to the mid-seventies Bronx, but at the time of its wider emergence (the early eighties) it seemed to come out of nowhere fast. Rave culture is another case of a movement assembling itself with incredible speed, something so compellingly new and total that people became converts overnight, abandoning what they'd been into before.

Nothing on the game-changing scale of rap or rave came through in the 2000s. Instead we saw a lot of activity still carried on under the name of hip hop or of rave-aligned genres like house and techno. This attachment on the part of young people to genres that have been around for decades mystifies me. Don't they want to push them aside? Especially given that both hip hop and electronic dance music hit the plateau this decade. Rap, after a spurt of vigour and invention that began in the late nineties and carried on into the first few years of the new decade, got stuck on a treadmill of bling and booty. Post-rave culture chugged along, cycling through micro-trends that mostly turned out on close inspection to be rehashes of ideas from the nineties or eighties.

But the problem wasn't just the failure of new movements and mega-genres to emerge, or the sluggishness of the established ones. It was the way that recycling and recursion became structural features of the music scene, substituting novelty (difference from what immediately preceded) for genuine innovation. It seemed like everything that ever was got its chance to come back into circulation at some point during the 2000s. Decades usually have a retro twin: the seventies looked to the fifties; in the eighties you had multiple different versions of the sixties vying for attention; and then seventies music started to get rediscovered in the nineties. True to form, and right on cue, the noughties kicked off with an eighties electropop renaissance and was soon followed by a separate but parallel retro craze for post-punk. But the noughties music scene had countless other retro sectors drawing heavily on the pre-eighties, from the freak folkers to neo-psychedelic bands like Dungen to the garage-punk revival (a re-revival, actually). The pop present was caught in the crossfire of revival simultaneity, with shrapnel from multiple different pasts whizzing past our ears at any given point.

One of the strangest aspects of the 2000s was the way that campy eighties retro battled with earnest sixties revivalism in a war to win the hearts and minds of hip youth. The sixties here mostly figured as the last two years of that decade, 1968–9: the shift away from psychedelia to folk and country, roots and authenticity – music at its least plastic, at its most unlike the synth-pop eighties, in fact. Freak folk and the new Americana restaged the beard-ification that overran rock in the late sixties, when looking like an early American homesteader signified integrity, maturity, disdain for image and distance from pop's superficiality. Figures like Bon Iver, Will Oldham (aka Bonnie 'Prince' Billy), Iron & Wine, Band of Bees, Band of Horses and Blitzen Trapper chucked their Gillette razors in the trash can.

Fleet Foxes were the poster boys for the new bearded bucolicism. Their self-titled debut album featured songs like 'Ragged Wood' and 'Blue Ridge Mountains', while actual livestock appeared in the video for 'He Doesn't Know Why' – goats whose tufty throats accentuated the band's own whiskers. The record was a *succès d'estime* in their American homeland (album of 2008 for the critics of both *Billboard* and *Pitchfork*) and actually made the UK Top 5. Fleet Foxes weren't so much nouveau hippies, though, as simply children of hippies. 'We grew up listening to the music of our parents,' singer Robin Pecknold declared, citing as their inspirations Crosby, Stills & Nash, Joni Mitchell, Fairport Convention, Bob Dylan and 'every other perennial '60s band you'd expect to find in the record collections of baby boomers'.

Another sign of the continued presence of the sixties in the popular imagination was the UK no. 1 success in 2006 of Sandi Thom's 'I Wish I Was a Punk Rocker (With Flowers in My Hair)', a song that purposefully conflated 1967 and 1977 to speak to the vague nostalgia felt by many young people for a lost golden age when music had power and integrity. Or as Thom sang it: 'When music really mattered and when radio was king/ When accountants didn't have control and the media couldn't buy your soul.' The song almost seems like a spoof of generational inferiority complexes. But the singer's own explanations suggest it's a heartfelt plaint from someone 'born too late', as does the single's B-side, a cover of The Stranglers' punk anthem 'No More Heroes', whose chorus wonders, 'Whatever happened to the heroes?'

These were the terms in which 'I Wish I Was' struck a chord with the public, judging by the sentiments of fans on the Web: 'I almost cried the first time I heard this song, I connected with it so much'; 'Would have been nice to be around with all that revolutionary spirit in the air'; and so forth. As one fan put it astutely, 'The yearning for this totally blurred memory of the past is delicious, but the songwriter clearly recognises that there seems to be no going back. "When popstars still remained a myth, and ignorance could still be bliss," is a wonderful line . . . It's as if she's trying to point a way to the resurrection of a music that cares, but doesn't know exactly what the way is.' But because 'I Wish I Was' is just a pretty ditty whose acoustic folksiness is a notch above busking and lacks the fire of sixties rock or punk, the song's ultimate effect is wistful resignation.

The irony of sixties nostalgia is that the very idea that pop music should be challenging and perpetually progressing comes from the sixties. It's because the sixties moved so fast and always looked to the future that we judge today's stasis and retrospection harshly. The decade set the bar impossibly high. And not just in pop: 'Everything happened during the Sixties,' recalled J. G. Ballard in 1982, citing the space race, the assassinations, Vietnam, LSD and what the media in those days called 'the youthquake'. 'It was like a huge amusement park going out of control. And I thought, "Well, there's no point in writing about the future – the future's here. The present has annexed the future onto itself."'

But Ballard's notion that the sixties had annexed the future came true in a way that he didn't envision. In a hideous twist, the sixties became the major generative force behind retro culture. (Its only rival, perhaps – and as per Sandi Thom – is punk.) Through its hold on our imagination, its *charisma* as a period, the decade that constituted the greatest eruption of new-ness in the entire twentieth century turned into its opposite. Hence the endless Beatles/Stones/Dylan covers on magazines like *Mojo* and *Uncut*, the interminable repackaging of baby-boomer music, the steady stream of biopics and rock docs, biographies and memoirs. Hence exhibitions like Tate Britain's *Art & The 60s: This Was Tomorrow*, a play on 1956's *This Is Tomorrow* exhibition (which involved British Pop Artists and the Brutalists Alison and Peter Smithson).

It's like we can't get *past* this past. Neophilia turns into necrophilia.

Pitchfork writer Eric Harvey recently observed that the 2000s may be destined to be 'the first decade of pop music . . . remembered by history for its musical technology rather than the actual music itself'. Napster Soulseek Limewire Gnutella iPod YouTube Last.fm Pandora MySpace Spotify . . . these super-brands took the place of super-bands such as Beatles Stones Who Dylan Zeppelin Bowie Sex Pistols Guns N'Roses Nirvana . . .

It's glaringly obvious that all the astounding, time–space rear-ranging developments in the dissemination, storing and access-ing of audio data have not spawned a single new form of music. McLuhan's axiom about the medium being the message has renewed aptness. The content being mediated is unchanging (it's a mixture of old music and contemporary music that is either 'new old' or that tweaks established forms). What is unprecedented is the way that the content gets distributed through the new net-works and playback devices, which in turn creates the 'message': the distinctive sensations and affects of our time, a mesh of con-nectedness, choice, abundance, speed. That is the 'rush' of the 2000s: a frictionless, near-instantaneous transit *within* networks, archival systems, and so forth, as opposed to the future-rush of the sixties (outward bound, into the unknown).

During the past couple of years, cultural critics have made vari-ous attempts to get a fix on the zeitgeist. Investigating 'the cultural effects of new technologies' and the impact of computerisation on the arts, Alan Kirby coined the term 'digimodernism' to describe the dawning of a new era that has superseded postmodernism. Meanwhile, Britain's leading art magazine *Frieze* developed the concept of 'super-hybridity' to describe the combination of post-modernist bricolage and the time-and-space dissolving effects of the Internet. In a September 2010 round-table discussion between artists and critics organised by *Frieze*, film-maker Hito Steyerl described the super-hybrid aesthetic in terms of 'immer-sion, entanglement . . . sudden rupture and repeated breakdown', and suggested that the crucial question of our era was 'how to be immersed without drowning'. Others were more sceptical about the term and the contemporary artworks it sought to corral: multi-media artist Seth Price, for instance, wondered if super-hybridity wasn't just a 'more and faster' version of postmodernism.

In his editorial for that issue, *Frieze*'s co-editor Jörg Heiser picked an example from modern music as his 'poster boy' for

412

super-hybridity: Gonjasufi, a leading figure in the same Los Angeles post-hip-hop scene as Flying Lotus and The Gaslamp Killer. Heiser made much of Gonjasufi's mixed-race background (Mexican–Ethiopian–American) and the transcultural influences percolating in the music, such as the use of ethnomusicological samples. But what immediately struck me listening to *A Sufi and a Killer*, Gonjasufi's debut for Warp Records, is not that its sonic palette is pan-global, but that it sounds *old*. If you want to put that more nicely (and it is a brilliant album), you could say it sounds 'out of time'. With FlyLo and Gaslamp Killer involved as co-producers, the methodology is hip hop, as is the rhythmic pulse, but it is buried beneath textures that sound like sixties punk and psychedelia, recalling early Captain Beefheart or obscure garage bands like The Hombres. The exotic elements are generally from the past too, like the presence in one track of sixties *rebetiko*, a style of music from Greece that is similar in spirit to the blues.

This mixture of 'advanced tech-iness and the deliberately ante-diluvian', as Heiser puts it, can be found in all kinds of places in the contemporary sonic landscape. Take 'Diplomat's Son', the stand-out track on Vampire Weekend's 2010 album *Contra*. The track gathers its components from all across the globe, but also from all across history too. It welds together rhythms that recall bachata as well as more recent hi-tech Caribbean beats like reggaeton, with crooned vocals that channel Morrissey channelling early-sixties vocalists like John Leyton and harmony backing vocals that almost sound pre-World War II. It also throws in an interpolation of 1969's 'Pressure Drop' by Jamaican reggae legends Toots and the Maytals and a cheeky sample from M.I.A. (one of the 2000s' most controversial pop nomads). 'Diplomat's Son' is real everywhere/everywhen pop. Utterly disparate sources cohere to gorgeously rhapsodic effect. Although the lyric is an oblique gay confessional about a fling with a Washington, D.C. consulate brat, the title 'Diplomat's Son' seems to have extra resonance, evoking the idea of rootless and guiltless cosmopolitanism (dip-lomatic immunity means that you can go to foreign countries and get away with all kinds of mischief).

Vampire Weekend's licence to appropriate doesn't just vali-date expeditions across the wide world of contemporary music; it permits a form of time tourism too. Much has been made of the group's African influences, but in fact they are almost all from seventies and eighties Afro-pop (whereas earlier appropriators like Paul Simon, Talking Heads, Malcolm McLaren et al., were responding to contemporary or relatively recent African sounds). What is striking about Vampire Weekend is the lack of hesitation with which they go about their borrowing, a nonchalance that caused some critics to accuse them of entitlement. Where does it come from?

Prior to the formation of the band, singer Ezra Koenig was involved in a rap group, which suggests that like many of his indie-rock generation, he grew up with hip hop and assimilated its sampling and crate-digging sensibility. Koenig also main-tained a blog called Internet Vibes, whose 2005 mission statement announced: 'My goal is to categorise as many vibes as I can.' In that spirit, the blog's topics included Native American pop, the clothing style of the English land-owning gentry (Barbour jack-ets, etc.), seventies New Age fusion star Paul Winter, Jamaican 'one riddim' albums, Billy Joel, preppy aesthetics, Dominican guitar pop, seventies cookbooks, sixties mod, and much more. In a manifesto-like aside, Koenig wondered aloud: 'What is authen-tic for a guy like me? Fourth-generation Ivy League, deracinated, American Jew . . . raised in [New Jersey] to middle-class post-hippie parents with semi-Anglophilic tendencies . . . The obvi-ous answer is that I, like all of us, should be a truly post-modern consumer, taking the bits and pieces I like from various traditions and cultures, letting my aesthetic instincts be my only guide. In fact, all of my friends (even the children of immigrants) seem to be in the same boat. We are BOTH disconnected from AND connected to EVERYTHING.'

Drawing a provisional conclusion about super-hybridity, Jörg Heiser suggested that while its exponents do not make 'for a clearly distinguishable avant-garde', so long as the approach 'doesn't regress into messy plagiarism trying to pass for magic, this could be its achievement'. Vampire Weekend have managed to weave together an insanely varied array of sources, a testament to their skill and taste, but also their meta-critical sensibility – the ability to see a connection between West African guitar tonalities and Scottish indie pop from the early eighties, for instance.

Here is Rostam Batmanglij – along with Koenig, the principal writer in the group and the producer of their records – providing a breakdown of the constituents of *Contra*'s opening track 'Horchata': 'It opens with a harmonium drone like you might find in Bollywood music, Ezra's voice comes in with a kind of Buddy Holly echo, he's doubled by a Kalimba thumb piano, which is intertwined with his vocal melody . . . then suddenly you get a deep house synth and a mass of our voices: me and Ezra and some women's voices as well. And they're all soaked in this classic 80's reverb.' That's at least three different continents (Africa, Asia, America) and just about every decade from the fifties onwards. But, like 'Diplomat's Son', 'Horchata' doesn't seem like 'messy plagiarism' or even contrived; it feels right, it sounds natural.

'Super-hybridity', like 'digimodernism', is basically an attempt to complete the equation 'postmodernism + Internet = ?' In *Frieze*'s super-hybridity issue, Jennifer Allen argued that the Internet had rendered postmodernism obsolete as an artistic strategy, by assimilating its principles, making them ubiquitous and accessible to everyone, naturalising them so that they make up the fabric of everyday life. A theory had been replaced 'by a technology that did the same job more effectively'. As Seth Price put it elsewhere in the same issue, 'with the Internet, the amount of material at hand approaches infinity, and using aggressively disparate material isn't really a matter of taking things out of context anymore, because that step has already been done for you'.

Behind these concepts there is also a great yearning, an *ache*, to see what lies beyond postmodernism, to identify the next phase of culture. Curator and theorist Nicolas Bourriaud has made the most concerted attempt to formulate a vision of 'what's next' for art and assess the post-geographical and post-historical implications of the Internet.

Coiner of controversial concepts like 'postproduction' and 'altermodernism', Bourriaud argues that creativity today involves 'strategies of mixing and combining products'. He holds up the DJ as the model for contemporary artistic practice. DJs don't engage in quotation, citation or even referencing; they just 'wander' through history and take whatever they need. This method might look like postmodernism, but the mindset is different. Citation implies deference to authority, to the Old Masters and their Masterpieces. Concepts like the anxiety of influence or the pathos of belatedness (as still discernible with appropriation artists like Sherrie Levine) are irrelevant. But equally so is the irony and iconoclasm of sampler-wielding punks like The KLF. The past is just material, to be used.

In his book *Postproduction*, Bourriaud declares that the crucial move today is to 'positivise the remake'. His whole take on contemporary culture is a kind of 'sunny side of the street' view of the same syndromes that *Retromania* critiques. Postproduction artists, he claims, erase the distinction between consuming and producing. Celebrating the flea market as a model for artistic inspiration, Bourriaud aims to rescue eclecticism from the condescension of ageing modernists who see it as incoherent, weak, 'lost in kitsch'. He parries the objections of anti-postmodernists like Yve-Alain Bois who condemn the 'logic of bric-a-brac and

416

the flattening of cultural values in a sort of international style'. Unlike the heroic modernists plunging into the unknown, 'DJs, Web surfers, and postproduction artists' develop navigational skills that enable them to find 'original pathways through signs'.

It's true that Bourriaud's point that 'overproduction is no longer seen as a problem but as a cultural ecosystem' – the more material, the merrier – offers a nice rejoinder to the anxieties voiced by people like me about the glut of influences and images stifling young artists' ability to be original. But much of the work he champions seems to involve a melange of déjà vu ideas from Pop Art, appropriation art, Duchampian readymades, junk art, and so forth. Bourriaud's patter itself often feels like a remix of Brian Eno's line of chat about remixing and curatorship.

Nonetheless, if you subtract the positive spin, a lot of what Bourriaud is saying makes sense. A shift from production to postproduction can be seen on many different levels of Western culture. Fusion cuisine, for instance, does not create new dishes (because those are only hatched within 'young', growing cultures) but instead comes up with cosmopolitan juxtapositions of existing dishes, techniques and tastes. ('Molecular gastronomy' – eerie foams, the use of liquid nitrogen and blow torches – is perhaps the last paroxysmic blast of Western culinary modernism, based on the pure fetishism of technology.)

In pop terms, 'postproduction' would cover all the musical activity that involves the reworking – through pastiche, pick-and-mix and outright photocopy, aka sampling – of material generated during the earlier phases of primary musical productivity. As far as pop music goes, that 'primary productivity' refers largely to black music of the first three decades after World War II (rhythm and blues, soul, funk, reggae, disco, etc.), and to the immediate white responses to those surges of black musical innovation in rhythm, production, vocal style, expression and mood. I say first three decades after WWII because that brings the date up to 1976:

417

the very beginning of hip hop. In both its DJ-oriented early days and in the later phase of sampling and breakbeat loops, hip hop was based on recycling music from earlier phases of black music history. The hip-hop generation extracted 'surplus vibe' from the musical manual labour of preceding black generations.

Even when it is not based on sampling, the pop culture we have today mirrors the way that so much of the economy in the West is no longer based on production. R&B, funk, reggae . . . these major musical forms were created by people whose everyday life was surrounded by the making of things (industry) or growing of produce (agriculture). Think of the connection of Motown to Michigan's auto industry. Much the same applies to country music or to white working-class responses to black music such as heavy metal (born in the West Midlands, the heartland of British motor manufacturing). Today's postproduction pop is far more white-collar. It involves a different skill set (information

---

THE BIRTH AND DEARTH OF DJ CULTURE

The first phase of the postproduction pop era – the emergence of hip hop, the transition from disco to house and early techno-rave – was a remarkably fertile period. Simplifying things drastically, hip hop was the postproduction form of funk; house was the postproduction form of disco. Particularly where sampling was central, the analogue to digital conversion created jagged shapes using physically played music that had been dismembered and then stitched back together Frankenstein-style. All these postmodern dance sounds *felt* modernist in their starkness and inorganic brutalism.

But what happened next is that as digital technology improved from the lo-res crudity of its early days, slick seamlessness and recessive subtlety became the norm in dance music. At the same time, DJ culture's ability to generate the shock of the new faded. From the seventies through the eighties and into the early to mid-nineties, the DJ was midwife to new forms – disco, hip hop, house, techno, jungle – which in turn spawned youth movements. What happened in the noughties is that DJs either perpetuated the existing genres/scenes (house, etc) or championed recombinant subgenres largely based around reshuffling the established building blocks. Furthermore, while there were refinements of

processing, editing, framing, packaging) that breaks with the 'work aesthetic' of earlier black and black-inspired forms. These also involved much more physicality in the hands-on playing of musical instruments, rather than the scroll-and-click work of programming and processing, endless small decisions and obsessive-compulsive tweaking.

These shifts – from musical production/innovation to post-production/recombination – paralleled what was happening to the wider economy: a transition from making money through making stuff to wealth generation achieved through information, services, 'signification' (style, entertainment, media, design, etc.) and, most unrooted of all from the real, the finance sector's manipulations of monetary value. Earlier in the book I drew a parallel between record-collection rock and the financial world with the semi-whimsical notion of a hipster stock market based around trading in pasts, not futures. But the parallels are

---

DJing technique (assisted by software programs like Ableton Live and Traktor Pro), nobody in DJing really advanced conceptually beyond what was already thinkable and achievable (albeit often with great difficulty) in the eighties and nineties: the long mix, turntablism, screwing (drastic slowing down of tracks), etc. The remix lost its novelty and event status. There was even a kind of retro version of remixing, the 're-edit': a return to the eighties approach, where remixes actually bore a resemblance to the original tracks and were largely composed out of it, as opposed to the obliterative reworkings of the nineties that increasingly consisted of all-new music.

Here is where the reliance on the DJ model (and related concepts like the remix, the DJ set as journey) by Bourriaud, and by other critics heralding a post-postmodern new dawn, becomes a major liability. In the noughties, the DJ's cultural profile waned: superstar DJs became passé, guitars began to outsell turntables again after having been eclipsed during the nineties. Worse than this, DJs seemed to lose their culturally generative power. By the end of the decade, it was becoming clear that there was a vital distinction between production and DJing that dance culture had blurred (because so many DJs also produced music, using their knowledge of what the crowd were responding to

actually rather striking. The world economy was brought down by derivatives and bad debt; music has been depleted of meaning through derivativeness and indebtedness. The imbalance in Western economies towards financial and real-estate speculation meant that too much of the wealth generated was meta-money: not cotton money or steel money, but money money. Similarly, the profusion of hyper-referential bands and micro-genres whose stylistic involutions are understood only by hipsterati and bloggerati resembles the 'complex financial instruments' that only a handful of people in Wall Street and the City of London comprehend.

Speculation led to a spectralisation of the economy: money that has only the most tenuous, remote relation to the material world. In his essay 'Culture and Finance Capital', Fredric Jameson writes about 'spectres of value . . . vying against each other in a vast world-wide disembodied phantasmagoria'. That sounds a lot like modern music in the post-sampling/post-Internet era. (A recent example: M.I.A. 'riding' the ghost of Suicide into the charts with her track 'Born Free', almost entirely based on that band's 1977 classic 'Ghost Rider'.) Culture, as the superstructure to the economy's base, reflects the gaseous quality of our existence. The insubstantiality of the economy revealed itself, horribly, a few

---

that season to make high-functioning tracks). But the two activities are different, even when one individual engages in both of them. The skill set is not the same; you can be a great DJ without having any musical talent whatsoever, while some of the greatest dance producers are useless on the decks. DJing really is postproduction in the Bourriaudian sense: selecting, sequencing, framing, editing – all forms of working with the readymade. Production is making the material in the first place for DJs to use. In hip hop, the distinction has become much clearer, to the DJ's disadvantage. For a long while now, rap records have been made by producers who are almost never DJs. The traditional hip-hop DJ is retained for live performances as a vestigial nod to the music's distant past, embellishing the pre-recorded beats with scratching that is largely superfluous.

years ago. We are still waiting for the music-about-music bubble to burst.

Is this mirroring between meta-money and meta-music simply coincidental? Or are they really connected at some fundamental level? Jameson, the great theorist of postmodernism and its relationship to late capitalism, would say yes. He argues that late capitalism is partly defined by the effects of information technology on time and space, enabling lightning-fast transfers of capital back and forth across the globe. But although his 1991 treatise *Postmodernism, or The Cultural Logic of Late Capitalism* contains numerous references to 'the nostalgia mode' and various manifestations of retro (not a word he actually uses), Jameson never quite pinpoints, in that book or his copious later writings on the subject, the actual mechanics of the link between an economy dominated by financial speculation and a culture oriented around recycling.

Fashion is the nexus between late capitalism and culture, where they intermesh. Popular music gradually assimilated fashion's artificially accelerated metabolic rate, its rapid cycles of engineered obsolescence. In fashion, the future cannot be invented fast enough, while the recent past piles up in mounds of symbolically depreciated commodities. Following the trails capitalism blazed, fashion first spread across space, appropriating stylistic ideas, fabrics, etc. from traditional cultures around the world. Then, in an innovation all of its own, fashion moved to colonise time, asset-stripping the historical past.

Talking about 'Movement', his bitterly satirical song about hipster culture, LCD Soundsystem's James Murphy told me the song was specifically a reaction to talk of guitar rock making a comeback, 'all the inanity that gets bandied about as rock journalism. It's a complete rip off of fashion journalism – "the high-waisted pant is BACK". Like that's supposed to mean something. I mean, I hope you don't go around hearing, "Abstract expressionism is

BACK! And HOTTER than EVER!" in art mags.' Well, actually, James, you do. Fashion – a machinery for creating cultural capital and then, with incredible speed, stripping it of value and dumping the stock – permeates everything.

But 'fashion-isation' can't totally explain the rise of retro rock. The reasons relate to the internal lifecycles of genres and art movements. It is a process that is analogous to the syndrome that economists call 'overaccumulation' (when a surplus of capital builds up that can't find profitable outlets for investment, because the consumer market is saturated, causing capitalists to move into financial speculation to stave off a collapse). Like a boom-time economy, the more fertile and dynamic a genre is, the more it sets itself up for the musical–cultural equivalent of recession: retro. In its young, hyper-productive phase it burns through stages of development that could have been stretched out for longer, and lays down an immense stockpile of ideas that then exert a black-hole-like pull on later waves of artists. That is why dance music in the 2000s got stuck on a recombinant plateau: precisely because in the preceding decade it had moved so fast, stretched so far and wide in such a short space of time. But you could say much the same about pop music in general: the sheer creativity of its surge years (the sixties, seventies and parts of the eighties) inevitably made it increasingly irresistible to be re-creative.

Just like the Western economy's bumpy but implacable shift away from industry, the shift from production to postproduction in music did not occur in a neat, clear transition but in fits and starts. Renewed surges of primary production (like the New Wave/post-punk era or nineties rave) staved off the onset of retro. But it is now pretty clear that pop is living on borrowed time and stolen energy, the deposits laid down in its generative prime. If you look closely at the language used by contemporary critics and fans, or at the rationalisations of the music's creators, you will find a lattice of references to predecessor artists and earlier genres,

422

intricate breakdowns of historical sources and components. With rock, you started to get this kind of densely referential writing in indie fanzines from the mid-eighties onwards; in dance music, it has been the dominant style of criticism all through this past decade. In contrast, the telltale sign of genuinely modernist music is the pressure it puts on writers to come up with new language and new concepts.

I would love to nominate hauntology as the alternative to the curatorial model of art proposed by Bourriaud. But in lots of ways figures like Ghost Box, Oneohtrix Point Never et al., are postproduction artists too, rummaging through the flea market of history and piecing together the audio equivalent of a junk-art installation. Oneohtrix's Daniel Lopatin actually studied library science with a view to becoming a full-time archivist. He speculates about music having shifted from 'its Renaissance period of recording' (i.e. the last hundred years) and entering a period of 'evaluation' and reprocessing. 'If music is recessing into some kind of archival period, I don't think it's bad. It's just natural.'

Even Ariel Pink, who hardly ever uses 'readymades' (samples), is dependent on readymade styles. The production hallmarks his work plays with were all forged during the grand period of primary pop productivity in the sixties, seventies and eighties. (Pink actually told me he believes the nineties will never become a significant source for recycling, will never generate future 'retroliciousness'.) The seventies and eighties especially were the grand era of record-business profligacy, when the industry was awash with cash. Major labels operated in a manner similar to the studio system during Hollywood's golden era: big-budget investment in potential blockbusters, resulting in expensive-sounding records made using crème de la crème session musicians and top-dollar studios. On his early albums like *The Doldrums* and *Worn Copy*, Pink recreated these sounds on a shoestring, not sampling but painstakingly copying 'by hand', like an artist sculpting a replica of a Coke bottle out of clay. *Before Today* completed a strange circle, being his first record made with a proper producer in a proper studio using a proper band of real musicians. The reverb-laden, lo-fi wooze that swathed his earlier music disappeared and what emerged, glistening and majestic like a yacht through fog, sounds like chart material. The only catch is that these would be radio smashes in 1986 or 1978, or whichever year a particular song refers to stylistically. Nothing on the record would make the tiniest dent on today's radioscape.

This leads to a tricky question for me, as an Ariel Pink fan and champion of the hauntological in general: what exactly is this music's *contribution*? Is it laying down anything that future equivalents of Ariel Pink could rework? The question could be applied to all postproduction art: isn't it sterile? (W. David Marx and Nick Sylvester describe Kanye West's 2007 hit 'Stronger', which is heavily based on the 2001 Daft Punk song 'Harder, Better, Faster, Stronger', as a 'cultural vasectomy'! What's more, doubling this recession of creativity into the past, the songwriting credits on 'Stronger' feature not just the two members of Daft Punk but Edwin Birdsong, whose 1979 funk tune 'Cola Bottle Baby' the duo sampled for 'Harder, Better'.) In fact, what in today's musical landscape is rich enough, nourishing enough – which is to say, sufficiently non-derivative – to sustain future forms of revivalism and retro? Surely, at a certain point, recycling will just degrade the material beyond the point that further use-value can be extracted.

Without necessarily striking an alarmist or disapproving tone, Paul Morley recently wrote about the 'directionless direction' of modern music. 'Direction', applied to culture, suggests the existence of a linear path forward. This way of thinking about music is becoming less and less tenable. Movement within culture now has more in common with the way a scroll-wheel on an iPod

424

functions. At best, things can be 'forward' in the way that people in the fashion world talk of being 'fashion forward': change is differential, a break with what immediately preceded it, but not an advance as such.

Because music history is splayed out as an atemporal smorgasbord, with sounds from every different era of history equally available as current music, the presence of the past in the present is massively increased. But this spatialisation of time causes historical depth to drop out; the original context or meaning of the music becomes irrelevant and harder to recover. Music becomes material, to use as you choose, as a listener or as an artist. Losing its remoteness, the past inevitably loses much of its mystery and magic.

In these circumstances, revivalism becomes something completely different to what it was for fanatical movements like Northern Soul or garage punk. Revivalism once involved a mixture of anguish and reverence: the true believers really thought music was better back then; they genuinely wished they could go back in time. Equally, this was a response to the present, a pointed rejection of specific aspects of the modern world. It's become a truism to say that music revivals are less to do with the past they reference than they are about the present. But what if nowadays music revivals not only don't tell you much about the past, they also don't say anything much about the present either? For this is what's striking about music in the past decade: the way that so many artists revisit past styles without much apparent affect, least of all nostalgia.

Just as the past has lost its lost-ness through digiculture's total access, similarly the future (and futurism, futuristic-ness) no longer has the charge it once did. My own extremely unscientific survey – canvassing my eleven-year-old son and my daughter's twenty-year-old babysitter – confirms William Gibson's take on the young generation: they're not the least bit interested in the capital 'f' Future, barely ever think about it. The urge to escape the here-and-now, the bland suburban everyday, is as strong as ever, but it's satisfied through fantasy (the tremendous popularity of novels and movies based around magic, vampires, wizardry, the supernatural) or digital technology. Why should my son give a fig about what the world will be like in 2082, when right now, despite our having recently moved to California, he can hang out with his New York friends in cyberspace?

There was another question I asked back at the start, which remains unanswered:

Is retromania here to stay or will it prove to be a historical phase?

This is the quandary that has produced theories like super-hybridity and postproduction, wishful attempts to see a New Era on the horizon that aren't fully convincing. That said, the emergence of these concepts does suggest that we are quite deep into a phase of anything-goes, guiltless appropriation, a free-for-all of asset-stripping that ranges all over the globe and all across the span of human history. The sheer recombinant density of the music produced in these conditions seems profoundly different from the slowly spawned mutations and mongrels of earlier pop history – reggae emerging out of mis-copied New Orleans R&B, for instance, or rock'n'roll as the 'baby' of blues and country.

Along with the speed and complexity of these new hybrids, the difference seems to correspond to the analogue versus digital divide. Turning sound into code enables producers to combine incompatible-seeming sources much more seamlessly, sealing over the cracks. (Which is why so much contemporary music has a CGI-like sheen and slickness.) The combination of digital techniques and the Internet enables artists to harvest influences and raw materials from far and wide, but also from far back in time. The results aren't particularly retro (in the sense of explicitly

426

referring to a period or citing an artistic ancestor) but nor are they New in the old-fashioned modernist sense. The best work created under these conditions – 'Diplomat's Son', *Before Today*, *A Sufi and a Killer* – has the same quality that William Gibson detected in cutting-edge fashion, 'a radical atemporality'. The doubt remains, though: what, if anything, does that 'radical' actually mean?

During the writing of this book I came up with my own glass-half-empty concept to describe the conditions that others gesture at with buzzed-up words like 'atemporality' or 'postproduction'. The term is *hyper-stasis*. It popped into my head after too many encounters with hotly touted records by new artists that induced a frustrating mix of emotions: feeling impressed by the restless intelligence at work in the music, but missing that sensation of absolute newness, the sorely craved 'never heard anything like *this* before'. Hyper-stasis can apply to particular works by individual artists, but also to entire fields of music. It describes situations in which potent musical intellects engage in a restless shuttling back and forth within a grid-space of influences and sources, striving frenetically to locate exit routes to the beyond. Bruce Sterling compares this aesthetic quality of anxious unrest to games players trying to get to the next level – and of course the phrase 'This is some next-level shit' is a cliché of music fandom.

In the analogue era, everyday life moved slowly (you had to wait for the news, and for new releases) but the culture as a whole felt like it was surging forward. In the digital present, everyday life consists of hyper-acceleration and near-instantaneity (downloading, web pages constantly being refreshed, the impatient skimming of text on screens), but on the macro-cultural level things feel static and stalled. We have this paradoxical combination of speed and standstill.

'Entropy' is not the right word for today's music scene. What we are witnessing is not ever-decreasing circles but ever-accelerating circles. On a good day, this doesn't seem such a dismal predicament. At other times, the centrifugal churn of quasi-new microgenres resembles the 'febrile sterility' that, for Alain Badiou, characterises contemporary culture. That feverishness is digiculture's hallmark: rapid movement within a network of knowledge, as opposed to the outward-bound drive that propelled an entire system into the unknown.

In pop history, the surge decades of the sixties and nineties were each followed by a period of going-in-circles (the seventies and 2000s respectively). During these directionless phases, it's easy to convince yourself that originality is overrated, that artists have always recycled, that there's 'nothing new under the sun'. It can become a real struggle to recall that pop hasn't always repeated itself and that in the not-so-distant past it has produced, repeatedly, something new under the sun.

I remember the future-rush. Just a handful of examples from my own lifetime as an alert listener: 'I Feel Love', *Computer World*, 'More Bounce to the Ounce', 'Ashes to Ashes', *Remain in Light*, 'Love Action', 'Ghosts', *Into Battle with the Art of Noise*, 'Hip Hop Be Bop', 'Needle to the Groove', 'This Brutal House', 'Acid Trax', 'Energy Flash', 'Terminator', 'We Have Arrived', 'Renegade Snares', 'Who Am I (Sim Simma)', 'Are You That Somebody?', 'Frontline' . . .

The future-rush is different from the thrill of encountering a true original (the charisma-glow of a unique personality, the style of an utterly individual voice and way with words – a Morrissey, Björk, Jay-Z, Dizzee Rascal). This sensation is electric but impersonal; it's about new forms, not new faces; it's a much purer, harder hit. It's the same scary–euphoric rush that the best science fiction gives: the vertigo of limitlessness.

I still believe the future is out there.

ACKNOWLEDGEMENTS

Thanks to my wife Joy Press, this book's first reader and most merciless editor. Gratitude also to Joy and our children Kieran and Tasmin for their patience during what has been yet another protracted 'pregnancy'.

Thanks to my editors Lee Brackstone and Mitzi Angel for their support throughout the process and their invaluable suggestions, which contributed greatly to the finished result. Thanks also to Denise Oswald, who originally signed the book in America.

Thanks to my agents Tony Peake and Ira Silverberg for getting this project airborne.

Thanks to my assistant Judy Berman for her crucial contributions at the book's research stage.

Thanks to everyone involved in the production and promotion process at Faber UK, especially Ian Bahrami, Anna Pallai, Lucie Ewin, Ruth Atkins. Thanks also to Michele Piumini for his input.

Many people have been helpful in terms of providing useful material or pointing me in interesting directions. I would especially like to thank for their generosity Hilary Moore, W. David Marx, Ed Christman and Bob Bhamra. Thanks also to Bethan Cole, Joe Kroll, Kristen Haring, Sébastien Morlighem, Andrej Chudý, Graham Eng-Wilmot, Glenn Drexhage, Sean Pemberton, Thomas Huthmayr, Nadav Appel.

Thanks to the interviewees for sharing their stories and insights:

Harold Bronson, Britt Brown, Billy Childish, Mark Cooper, Peter Doggett, Jasen Emmons, Iain Forsyth and Jane Pollard, Gareth Goddard, Jeff Gold, Jim Henke, Jim Hobermann, Brian Hodgson, Barry Hogan, Julian House, Matthew Ingram, Jim Jupp, James Kirby, Johan Kugelberg, George Leonard, Ian Levine, Miriam Linna and Billy Miller, Daniel Lopatin, Mary McCarthy, W. David Marx, Dick Mills, Jo Mitchell, Baron Mordant, Nico Muhly, James Murphy, David Peace, Kevin Pearce, Ariel Pink, Ken Shipley, Patti Smith, Paul Smith, Valerie Steele, Jonny Trunk, Tim Warren, Keith Fullerton Whitman, Lynn Yaeger.

A book like this does not emerge out of a vacuum. Ideas have been catalysed and thinking sharpened through countless conversations over the years, which have taken place through print and blog back-and-forth, via email and in face-to-face discussion (and in some cases go back to long before I ever considered writing a book on this subject). Big up to Mark Fisher, Matthew Ingram, Carl Neville, Dan Fox, Paul Barnes, Michaelangelo Matos, Anwyn Crawford, Sam Davies, Nicholas Katranis, Paul Kennedy, Owen Hatherley, Mike Powell, Tim Finney, Julian House, Jim Jupp, Ian Hodgson, Seb Roberts, Robin Carmody, Geeta Dayal, Patrick McNally, Andy Battaglia, Adam Harper, Alex Williams, Peter Gunn, John Darnielle and doubtless others I am forgetting.

BIBLIOGRAPHY

Anderson, Chris, 'The Long Tail', *Wired*, October 2004, issue 12.10.

Anderson, Perry, *The Origins of Postmodernity* (London: Verso, 1998).

Arns, Inke, 'History Will Repeat Itself: Strategies of Re-enactment in Contemporary (Media) Art and Performance' (curator's text for the exhibition at KW Institute for Contemporary Art in Berlin, 18.11.2007–13.01.2008). Online at http://www.agora8.org/reader/Arns_History_Will_Repeat.html.

Attali, Jacques, *Noise: The Political Economy of Music*. Originally published in French in 1977, trans. Brian Massumi (Manchester: Manchester University Press, 1985).

Auslander, Philip, 'Looking at Records', in *TDR: The Drama Review*, Vol. 45, No. 1 (T 169), Spring 2001.

Ballard, J. G., 'Myths of the Near Future' and 'The Dead Astronaut', in *Memories of the Space Age* (Sauk City, Wisconsin: Arkham House, 1988). And also in *The Complete Stories of J. G. Ballard* (New York: W. W. Norton & Co., 2009).

———— *Quotes*, selected by V. Vale and Mike Ryan (San Francisco: RE/Search Publications, 2004).

Bangs, Lester, *Psychotic Reactions and Carburetor Dung* (New York: Alfred A. Knopf, 1987).

———— 'Rages to Come: Creem's Predictions of Rock's Future', in *Rock Revolution: From Elvis to Elton – The Story of Rock and Roll* (New York: Popular Library, 1976).

Barnes, Ken, 'Democratic Radio', in Dave Marsh (Ed.), *The First Rock & Roll Confidential Report* (New York: Pantheon, 1985).

Barthes, Roland, *The Fashion System*, first published 1967, trans. Matthew Ward and Richard Howard (Berkeley and Los Angeles: University of California Press, 1990).

———— *Camera Lucida: Reflections on Photography*, trans. Richard Howard (New York: Hill and Wang, 1981).

———— *Empire of Signs*, trans. Richard Howard (New York: Hill and Wang, 1982).

Baudrillard, Jean, 'The System of Collecting', in *The Cultures of Collecting (Critical Views)* (London: Reaktion Books, March 1994).

———— 'The Ecstasy of Communication', in Hal Foster (Ed.), *Postmodern Culture* (London: Pluto Press, 1985).

Beadle, Jeremy J., *Will Pop Eat Itself? Pop Music in the Soundbite Era* (London: Faber and Faber, 1993).

Beezer, *Wild Dayz: Photos by Beezer* (Bristol: Tangent Books, 2009).

Belz, Carl, 'Rock and Fine Art' (The Beatles' White Album). Originally from Belz, Carl, *The Story of Rock* (1969). Reprinted in Mike Evans (Ed.), *The Beatles: Literary Anthology* (London: Plexus, 2004).

Benjamin, Walter, 'The Work of Art in the Age of Mechanical Reproduction', 'Unpacking My Library: A Talk About Book Collecting', 'Theses on the Philosophy of History', in *Illuminations: Essays and Reflections*, trans. Harry Zohn, edited and with an introduction by Hannah Arendt (New York: Harcourt Brace Jovanovich, Inc. 1968).

Berman, Deborah Baiano, 'Deadheads as a Moral Community', dissertation, 2002, Department of Sociology and Anthropology, Northeastern University.

Berman, Judith, 'Science Fiction without the Future', originally published in the *New York Review of Science Fiction*, May 2001. Reprinted in James Gunn, and Matthew Candelaria, *Speculations on Speculation: Theories of Science Fiction* (Lanham, Maryland: 2005).

Blackson, Robert, 'One More . . . With Feeling: Reenactment in Contemporary Art and Culture', *Art Journal*, Spring 2007.

Blanning, Lisa, Madlib profile, *The Wire*, issue no. 306, August 2009.

Blom, Philipp, *To Have and to Hold: An Intimate History of Collectors and Collecting* (New York: The Overlook Press, 2003).

Bloom, Harold, *The Anxiety of Influence: A Theory of Poetry* (New York: Oxford University Press, 1973).

———— *A Map of Misreading* (New York: Oxford University Press, 1975).

Booker, Christopher, *The Neophiliacs: A Study of the Revolution in English Life in the Fifties and Sixties* (London: Wm. Collins, 1969).

Bourriaud, Nicolas, *Postproduction: Culture As Screenplay: How Art Reprograms the World* (second edn) (New York: Lucas & Sternberg, 2005).

———— Interview by Bennett Simpson, *ArtForum*, April 2001.

Boym, Svetlana, *The Future of Nostalgia* (New York: Basic Books, 2002).

Bracewell, Michael, 'Road to Nowhere', *Frieze*, issue 54, September–October 2000.

Bromberg, Craig, *The Wicked Ways of Malcolm McLaren* (New York: Harper & Row, 1989).

Brooks, David, 'The Nation of Futurity', *New York Times*, 16 November 2009.

Brown, Stephen, *Marketing – The Retro Revolution* (Thousand Oaks, CA: Sage Publications, 2001).

———— and John F. Sherry Jr (Eds), *Time, Space and the Market: Retroscapes Rising* (Armonk, New York: M. E. Sharpe, Inc., 2003).

Burchill, Julie, 'Rock's Rich Tapestry', singles reviews column, *New Musical Express*, 25 October 1980.

Burton, Johanna, 'Repeat Performance: Marina Abramovic's Seven Easy Pieces', *ArtForum*, January 2006.

Carr, Nicholas, *The Shallows: What the Internet Is Doing to Our Brains* (New York: W. W. Norton & Company, 2010).

Cohn, Nik, *Awopbopaloobop Alopbamboom: Pop from the Beginning* (London: Weidenfeld & Nicolson Ltd., 1969).

Cope, Julian, *Krautrocksampler: One Head's Guide to the Great Kosmische Musik – 1968 Onwards* (London: Head Heritage, 1995).

———— *Japrocksampler: How the Post-War Japanese Blew Their Minds on Rock 'n' Roll* (London: Bloomsbury, 2007).

Crowley, David, and Jane Pavitt (Eds), *Cold War Modern: Design 1945–1970* (London: V&A Publishing, 2008).

Davis, Fred, *Yearning for Yesterday: A Sociology of Nostalgia* (New York: Free Press, 1979).

Derrida, Jacques, *Specters of Marx: The State of the Debt, the Work of Mourning, and the New International* (New York: Routledge, 1994).

———— *Archive Fever: A Freudian Impression*, trans. Eric Prenowitz (Chicago: The University of Chicago Press, 1995).

Dettmar, Kevin J. H., *Is Rock Dead?* (New York: Routledge, 2005).

De Walley, Chas, 'Power Pop Part 1: Suddenly, Everything Is Power Pop!' *Sounds*, 11 February 1978.

Dibbell, Julian, 'Unpacking Our Hard Drives: Discophilia in the Age of Digital Reproduction', in Eric Weisbard (Ed.), *This Is Pop: In Search of the Elusive at Experience Music Project* (Cambridge, MA: Harvard University Press, 2004).

Dick, Philip K., *The Man in the High Castle*, originally published in 1962.

Reprinted in Philip K. Dick, *Four Novels of the 1960s* (The Library of America, 2007).

Drummond, Bill, 'Silence Is Golden – Or for at Least One Day of the Year It Is'/No Music Day manifesto, *Observer*, 15 October 2006.

Eisenberg, Evan, *The Recording Angel: Music, Records and Culture from Aristotle to Zappa*, originally published in 1987 (second edn: New Haven: Yale University Press, 2005).

Eklund, Douglas, *The Pictures Generation, 1974–1984* (New York: Metropolitan Museum of Art, 2009).

Elsner, John, and Roger Cardinal (Eds), *The Cultures of Collecting (Critical Views)* (London: Reaktion Books, March 1994).

Eno, Brian, Review of Jay David Bolter's Writing Space, *Artforum International*, Vol. 30, November 1991.

——— Interviewed by Kevin Kelly, *Wired* 3.05, May 1995.

Evans, David, *Appropriation* (Cambridge, MA: MIT Press, 2009).

Fellows, Will, *A Passion to Preserve: Gay Men as Keepers of Culture* (Madison, WI: University of Wisconsin Press, 2004).

Finney, Tim, Review of Kompakt compilation *Total 7*, *Pitchfork*, 15 September 2006.

Fisher, Mark, *Capitalist Realism: Is There No Alternative?* (Winchester: 0 Books, 2009).

——— (writing as K-punk), Belbury Poly/Jim Jupp interview. *FACT* magazine, 4 February 2009. Online at http://www.factmag.com/2009/02/04/interview-belbury-poly/.

Foreman, Richard, 'The Pancake People, or, "The Gods Are Pounding My Head"', published online 3 August 2005: http://www.edge.org/3rd_culture.

Fukuyama, Francis, 'The End of History?' *The National Interest*, summer 1989.

Gibson, William, 'The Gernsback Continuum', originally published in *Universe* 11, 1981. Collected in *Burning Chrome* (*New York: Arbor House, 1986*).

——— *Pattern Recognition* (New York: G. P. Putnam, 2003).

——— Book Expo America Luncheon talk. Online at http://blog.williamgibsonbooks.com/2010/05/31/book-expo-american-luncheon-talk.

——— Interview by BBC News. 12 October 2010. Online at http://www.bbc.co.uk/news/technology-11502715.

Goldman, Vivien, 'The Road to Wigan Casino: Northern Soul', *New Musical Express*, 11 October 1975. Reprinted in *The Sound and the Fury: 40 Years of Classic Rock Journalism* (Ed. Barney Hoskyns) (London: Bloomsbury,

2003).

Greene, Jo-Anne, 'Long-Lost Punk and Folk Resurface', *Goldmine*, 21 September 2008.

Gregson, Nicky, Kate Brooks and Louise Crewe, 'Bjorn Again? Rethinking 70s Revivalism Through the Reappropriation of 70s Clothing', in *Fashion Theory: The Journal of Dress, Body & Culture*, Vol. 5, No. 1, February 2001, pp. 3–27 (25).

Guffey, Elizabeth, *Retro: The Culture of Revival* (London: Reaktion Books, 2006).

Hatherley, Owen, *Militant Modernism* (Winchester: 0 Books, 2008).

Heiser, Jörg, 'Pick & Mix: What Is "super-hybridity"?' *Frieze* magazine, September 2010.

———— with Ronald Jones, Nina Powers, Seth Price, Sukhdev Sandhu and Hito Steyerl, 'Analyze This' (a round-table discussion on super-hybridity), *Frieze* magazine, September 2010.

Hilderbrand, Lucas, *Inherent Vice: Bootleg Histories of Videotape and Copyright* (Durham, NC: Duke University Press, 2009).

Hobsbawm, Eric, and Terence Ranger (Eds), *The Invention of Tradition* (Cambridge: Cambridge University Press, 1992).

Hogan, Marc, 'This Is Not a Mixtape' (article on the cassette resurgence), *Pitchfork*, 22 February 2010.

Hughes, Robert, *The Shock of the New* (New York: Alfred A. Knopf, 1982).

Huyssen, Andreas, 'Present Pasts: Media, Politics, Amnesia', in *Public Culture*, Vol. 12, No. 1, winter 2000.

———— 'Monumental Seduction', in Mieke Bal, Jonathan Crewe and Leo Spitzer (Eds), *Acts of Memory: Cultural Recall in the Present* (Darmouth: Dartmouth College Press, 1998).

Jameson, Fredric, *Postmodernism, or, The Cultural Logic of Late Capitalism* (London: Verso, 1991).

———— 'Culture and Finance Capital', in *The Cultural Turn: Selected Writings on the Postmodern, 1983-1998* (London: Verso, 1998).

———— *A Singular Modernity: Essay on the Ontology of the Present* (London: Verso, 2002).

———— *Archaeologies of the Future: The Desire Called Utopian and Other Science Fictions* (London: Verso, 2005).

———— 'Periodizing the 60s', in *The 60s Without Apology* (Eds Sonya Sayres, Anders Stephenson, Stanley Aronowitz and Fredric Jameson), pp. 208–9 (Minneapolis, MN: University of Minnesota Press, 1984).

Jamieson, Mark, 'The Place of Counterfeits in Regimes of Value: An Anthropological Approach' (Northern Soul and rock'n'roll revivalism), in *Journal of the Royal Anthropological Institute*, Vol. 5, 1999.

Jenss, Heike, 'Dressed in History: Retro Styles and the Construction of Authenticity in Youth Culture', in *Fashion Theory: The Journal of Dress, Body & Culture*, Vol. 8, No. 4, December 2004, pp. 387–403 (17).

Jones, Dylan, *iPod, Therefore I Am* (New York: Bloomsbury USA, 2005).

Jones, Max, 'A New Jazz Age', *Picture Post*, 12 November 1949. Reprinted in *The Faber Book of Pop* (Eds Jon Savage and Hanif Kureishi) (London: Faber & Faber, 1995).

Keenan, David, 'Hypnagogic Pop', *The Wire*, issue no. 306, August 2009.

Kelly, Kevin, 'Scan This Book!', *New York Times Magazine*, 14 May 2006.

Kent, Nick, *Apathy for the Devil: A '70s Memoir* (London: Faber and Faber, 2010).

———— 'The Cramps and Rockabilly', *New Musical Express*, 23 June 1979.

Kirby, Alan, *Digimodernism: How New Technologies Dismantle the Postmodern and Reconfigure Our Culture* (London and New York: Continuum, 2009).

———— 'The Death of Postmodernism, and Beyond', in *Philosophy Now*, November/December 2006. Available online at http://www.philosophynow.org/issue58/58kirby.htm.

Kugelberg, Johan, *Vintage Rock T-Shirts*, (New York: Universe/Pizzoli International Publications, 2007).

———— 'Interview with Johan Kugelberg' (by Sean Bidder), in *Various, Old Rare New: The Independent Record Shop* (London: Black Dog Publishing, 2008).

Landau, Jon, 'I Saw Rock & Roll Future and Its Name Is Bruce Springsteen', in *The Real Paper*, May 1974. Reprinted in Clinton Heylin (Ed.), *The Penguin Book of Rock & Roll Writing* (New York: Viking, 1992).

Lanier, Jaron, *You Are Not a Gadget: A Manifesto* (New York: Knopf, 2010).

Levine, Sherrie, 'First Statement', 1981. Preserved at http://www.afterwalkerevans.com/. Also reprinted in David Evans. *Appropriation* (Cambridge, MA: MIT Press, 2009).

Levy, Steven, *The Perfect Thing: How the iPod Shuffles Commerce, Culture and Coolness* (New York: Simon & Schuster, 2006).

Lewandowski, Joseph D., 'Unpacking: Walter Benjamin and his Library', *Libraries & Culture*, 34.2 (1999), pp. 151–7..

Livingston, Tamara E., 'Music Revivals: Towards a General Theory', in

Ethnomusicology, Vol. 43, No. 1 (winter 1999).

Lowenthal, David, *The Past Is a Foreign Country* (Cambridge: Cambridge University Press, 1985).

MacDonald, Ian, *Revolution in the Head: The Beatles' Records and the Sixties* (London: Fourth Estate, 1994).

———— 'The Band Music from Big Pink', in *The People's Music* (London: Pimlico, 2003).

McDowell, Colin, *Fashion Today* (London: Phaidon Press Ltd., 2003).

McEwan, Ian, 'Solid Geometry', first published 1975, collected in *First Love, Last Rites* (New York: Vintage, 1998).

McKay, George, '"Unsafe Things Like Youth and Jazz": Beaulieu Jazz Festivals (1956–61), and the Origins of Pop Festival Culture in Britain', in Andy Bennett (Ed.), *Remembering Woodstock* (Aldershot and Burlington: Ashgate, 2004).

McLaren, Malcolm, 'Dirty Pretty Things' (New York Dolls), *Guardian*, Friday 28 May 2004.

McNeil, Legs, and Gillian McCain, *Please Kill Me: The Uncensored Oral History of Punk* (New York: Penguin, 1997).

McRobbie, Angela, 'Secondhand Dresses and the Role of the Ragmarket', in Angela McRobbie (Ed.), *Zoot Suits and Second-Hand Dresses: An Anthology of Fashion and Music* (London: Macmillan, 1989).

Marcus, Greil, 'The Band: Pilgrim's Progress', in *Mystery Train: Images of America in Rock 'n' Roll Music* (London: Penguin, 1975).

Marinetti, F. T., *Critical Writings*, trans. Doug Thompson, edited by Gunter Berghaus (New York: Farrar, Straus and Giroux, 2006).

Melly, George, *Revolt into Style: The Pop Arts* (London: Allen Lane/Penguin, 1970).

Merewether, Charles (Ed.), *The Archive* (Cambridge, MA: MIT Press, 2006).

Moore, Hilary, *Inside British Jazz: Crossing Borders of Race, Nation and Class* (Farnham, Surrey: Ashgate, 2007).

Morley, Paul, *Words and Music: A History of Pop in the Shape of a City* (London: Bloomsbury, 2003).

O'Neill, Alistair, *London – After a Fashion* (London: Reaktion Books, 2007).

Orlean, Susan, 'Orchid Fever', *The* New Yorker, 23 January 1995.

O'Rourke, P. J., 'Future Schlock', *The Atlantic*, December 2008.

Parr, Martin, *Boring Postcards* (London: Phaidon Press, 1999).

Pessoa, Fernando, *The Book of Disquiet* (originally published 1982; London: Penguin Classics, 2002).

Petrusich, Amanda, *It Still Moves; Lost Songs, Lost Highways, and the Search for the Next American Music* (New York: Faber and Faber, 2008).

Powell, Mike, 'Through the Cracks #5: Ghost Box', *Pitchfork*, 20 May 2008.

Reel, Penny, Mod reminiscence, in special Mod issue of *New Musical Express*, 14 April 1979.

Rockwell, John, 'Electronic & Computer Music & the Humanist Reaction', in *All American Music: Composition in the Late Twentieth Century* (New York: Vintage, 1984).

Rombes, Nicholas, *A Cultural Dictionary of Punk 1974–1982* (New York: Continuum, 2009).

Rorem, Ned, 'Is New Music New?', in *Music from Inside Out* (New York: George Braziller, Inc., 1967).

———— *Critical Affairs: A Composer's Journal* (New York: George Braziller, 1970).

Rothenbuhler, Eric W., and John Durham Peters, 'Defining Phonography: An Experiment in Theory', Musical Quarterly 81.2 (1997).

Rushton, Neil, 'Out on the Floor: A Northern Soul Primer', in *The Face*, September 1982. Reprinted in *Night Fever: Club Writing in the Face 1980–1997* (London: Boxtree, 1997).

Salzman, Marian, and Ira Matathia, *Next Now: Trends for the Future* (New York: Palgrave Macmillan, 2007).

Samuel, Raphael, *Theatres of Memory: Past and Present in Contemporary Culture* (London: Verso, 1994).

Shaw, Suzy, and Mick Farren, *Bomp!: Saving the World One Record at a Time* (Los Angeles: Ammo Books, 2007).

Showalter, Elaine, 'Fade to Greige' (review of multiple fashion books), *London Review of Books*, Vol. 23, No. 1, 4 January 2001.

Spengler, Oswald, *The Decline of the West* (New York: Alfred A. Knopf, 1926/ One Volume Edition, 1932).

———— *Man & Technics – A Contribution to a Philosophy of Life* (New York: Alfred A. Knopf, 1932).

Sprinker, Michael (Ed.), *Ghostly Demarcations: A Symposium on Jacques Derrida's Specters of Marx* (New York: Verso, 1999).

Starr, Karla, 'When Every Song Ever Recorded Fits on Your MP3 Player, Will You Listen to Any of Them?', *Phoenix New Times*, 5 June 2008.

Sterling, Bruce, 'Memories of the Space Age', 'Catscan' column in *Science Fiction Eye* journal, date unknown. Online at http://w2.eff.org/Misc/ Publications/Bruce_Sterling/Catscan_columns/.

Sterne, Jonathan, *The Audible Past: Cultural Origins of Sound Reproduction*

(Durham, NC: Duke University Press, 2003).

—— 'The MP3 as Cultural Artifact', in *New Media and Society*, Vol. 8, No. 5 (November 2006).

Stewart, Susan, *On Longing: Narratives of the Miniature, the Gigantic, the Souvenir, the Collection* (Durham, NC: Duke University Press, 1993).

Stone, Linda, 'Beyond Simple Multi-Tasking: Continuous Partial Attention', http://lindastone.net/2009/11/30/ beyond-simple-multi-tasking-continuous-partial-attention/.

Straw, Will, 'Sizing up Record Collections; Gender and Connoiseurship in Rock Music Culture', in Sheila Whiteley (Ed.), *Sexing the Groove: Popular Music and Gender* (New York: Routledge, 1997).

—— 'Exhausted Commodities: The Material Culture of Music', in *Canadian Journal of Communication*, Vol. 25, No. 1 (winter 2000).

Stubbs, David, Interview with Position Normal/Chris Bailiff, *The Wire*, issue no. 311, January 2010.

Sylvester, Nick, and W. David Marx, 'Theoretically Unpublished Piece about Girl Talk, for a Theoretical New York Magazine Kind of Audience, Give or Take an Ox on Suicide Watch', Riffmarket blog, 22 December 2008.

Tate, Greg (writing as 'avantgroidd'), Comments section of Simon Reynolds's column 'The Cult of Dilla', *Guardian*, 16 June 2009, at http://www.guardian. co.uk/music/musicblog/2009/jun/16/cult-j-dilla.

Thorne, Christian, 'The Revolutionary Energy of the Outmoded', *October*, http://www.mitpressjournals.org/toc/octo/-/No. 104, Spring 2003.

Trunk, Jonny, *The Music Library: Graphic Art and Sound* (London: Fuel, 2005).

Turner, Bryan S., 'A Note on Nostalgia', in *Theory, Culture & Society*, February 1987.

Vermorel, Fred, *Vivienne Westwood: Fashion, Perversity and the Sixties Laid Bare* (Woodstock, NY: The Overlook Press, 1996).

Walcott, James, 'A Conservative Impulse in the New Rock Underground' (report on CBGB festival), *Village Voice*, 18 August 1975.

Walters, Idris, 'Is Northern Soul Dying on Its Feet?' *Street Life*, 15–28 November 1975. Reprinted in *The Faber Book of Pop* (Eds Jon Savage and Hanif Kureishi) (London: Faber & Faber, 1995).

Wenner, Jann S., *Lennon Remembers: The Full Rolling Stone Interviews from 1970* (New York: Verso Publishing, 2000).

Willis, Ellen, 'Creedence Clearwater Revival', in Anthony DeCurtis and James Henke with Holly George-Warren (Eds), *The Rolling Stone Illustrated History of Rock & Roll* (New York: Random House, 1992).

Wilson, Daniel H., *Where's My Jetpack? A Guide to the Amazing Science Fiction Future That Never Arrived* (New York: Bloomsbury, 2007).

Wolfe, Tom, 'One Giant Leap to Nowhere', *New York Times*, 18 July 2009.

Wright, Patrick, *On Living in an Old Country* (London: Verso, 1986).

Wurtzel, Elizabeth, 'Get a Life, Girls', *Guardian*, 10 August 1998.

Yaeger, Lynn, 'Sui Generis? Anna Sui, Others Sue Forever 21: How Original Are You?', *Village Voice*, 18 September 2007.

York, Peter, *Style Wars* (London: Sidgwick & Jackson, 1980).

INDEX

A-Bones, The, 300
Abbey Road recording studios, xxi, 25, 399
Abbott, Russ, 354
ABC, xvi, 185
Abramović, Marina, 48
Acconci, Vito, 48, 144
Ace label, 154, 160
acid house, 239
Acid Mothers Temple, 137, 163
Acker, Kathy, 148–9
Action, The, 204
Actress *see* Cunningham, Darren
Adele, xix
Adkins, Hasil, 300–1
Adorno, Theodor, 11, 196
Adult., 174
Advisory Circle, The, 328, 338–9
Agostini, Philippe, 377
Aguilera, Christina, 358
Ainley, Mark, 159
Alaia, Azzedine, xvii
Albarn, Damon, 359
Alien (movie), 366–7
All Tomorrow's Parties (ATP), xx, 32–3, 35–6,
    144
Allen, Dave, 41; *see also* Gang of Four
Allen, Jennifer, 416
Allen, Paul, ix, 14, 15
Allen, Woody, 207
Allman Brothers Museum, 400
Alpert, Herb, 104
Altered Zones (website), 345
Amazon, 65, 66
'Amen' breakbeat, 323
American Graffiti (movie), 292–4

Anderson, Chris, 65–8
Andre, Carl, 374
Andrews, Bob, 247
Angry Brigade, 188–9
Animal Collective, 179
Ant, Adam, 185, 244
antiques, 23–4
Antonioni, Michelangelo, 186
Anvil! The Story of Anvil (documentary), 29, 30
Aphex Twin, The, 330, 368
Apple, 113
Apple Corps, xxii, 399
appropriation art, *see* Pictures Generation
Archer, Tasmin, 391–2
architecture: modernism, 373–9
Archive Fever, 26–8
archives, 26–31; on the Internet, 56–63
Ariel Pink's Haunted Graffiti, 345, 348–9; *see
    also* Pink, Ariel
Armstrong, Roger, 250
ArtCore (exhibition/sale), xix, 20–1
Ashley, Laura, 189
Asimov, Isaac, 368
Atomage (magazine), 327
Attali, Jacques, 95–6, 122
Avalanches, The, 357, 358–9
Aykroyd, Dan, 199
Azor, Herby, 312

back catalogue, 63–8, 151–61
Back from the Grave (compilation series), 264,
    266–7
Badings, Henk, 379
Badiou, Alain, 54, 428
Baiano-Berman, Deborah J., 231–2

441

Bailiff, Chris, 333–5
Baker, Danny, 327
Baker, Stuart, 156
Ball, David, 222
Ball, Kenny, and His Jazzmen, 211
Ballard, J. G., 389, 392, 411
Baltan, Kid *see* Raaijmakers, Dick
Band, The, 133, 277, 282–3, 345
Bangles, The, 146, 260
Bangs, Lester, 241, 251, 254–5, 278
Banhart, Devendra, xxxiv, 344
Barber, Chris, 209, 211
Bargeld, Blixa, 51, 146; *see also* Einstürzende Neubaten
Barnes, Julian, 24
Barnes, Ken, 195
Barratt, Julian, 174, 401
Barrett, Syd, 142, 271, 272
Barrie, Dennis, 14
Barrow, Steve, 155
Barthes, Roland, 162, 191, 313
Basinski, William, 335–6
Batmanglij, Rostam, 415
Battaglia, Andy, 124
Battiste, Rose, 223
Baudrillard, Jean, 91, 92–3, 95, 149, 368, 401
BBC Radiophonic Workshop, 340–1
Beach Boys, The, xi, 132, 133, 146, 278, 401
Beadle, Jeremy J., 315
Bear Family label, 160
Beastie Boys, 320
Beat Kondukta, 352
Beatles, The: and Abbey Road, xxi, 25, 399; and The Clash, 10; cover versions, 132, 134, 135, 136, 146, 198; Dylan Jones on, 118; and fifties revivalism, 277–9, 280; film about Apple Corps, 399; Hamburg live album, 269; *A Hard Day's Night* premiere, 5; influence, 151, 177–8, 257; *Let It Be*, 280; *Let It Be . . . Naked*, x–xi; *Love* show and album, xiii, xiv; mashed-up, 358; memorabilia, 19–20; quoted musically, 268; remastered albums, xxii; sampled, 318; *Sgt Pepper's*, 131–2, 251, 259, 266, 277; skiffle origins, 209; 'Strawberry Fields Forever', 330; tribute songs, 135; USA first trip, xxxvi; video-game, xxii; and vintage clothing, 193; *The White Album*, 278–9; *Yellow Submarine* adaptation, xxii; *see also* Harrison, George; Lennon, John; McCartney, Paul; Starr, Ringo
Beats International, 360
Beaulieu Jazz Festival (1961), 212
bebop, 208
Beck, 359, 400
Beethoven, Ludwig van, 58, 388

Behind the Music Remastered (TV series), 399
Belbury Poly, 311–12, 328, 337, 340
Bell Telephone Laboratories, 383
Belushi, John, 199
Belz, Carl, 278–9
Benjamin, Walter, 87, 88–9, 94–5
Bentley Rhythm Ace, 356
Berger, Gaston, 381
Berman, Judith, 396
Berry, Chuck: cover versions, 224, 250; influence, 245, 246, 247, 278; at revival concerts, 286, 287, 290; and *Voyager 1*, 388
Biba, 187–9
Biff Bang Pow!, 272
Bilk, Acker, and His Paramount Jazz Band, 211–12
Birdsong, Edwin, 424
Birthday Party, The, 32, 131; *see also* Cave, Nick
Björk, 179, 428
Black, Jack, 53
Black Dog, The, 368
Black-Eyed Peas, The, 406
Black Flag, 137, 146
Black Sabbath, 99
Black Sheep, 143; *see also* Cope, Julian
Blackpool Mecca (club), 218, 219, 220
Black to the Future (TV series), xix
Blade Runner (movie), 367
Blake, Norman, xxxii–xxxiii
Blast First label, 37
Blind Faith, 34
Blockheads, The, 304
blogs, 62–3; whole album/sharity, 104–11
Blom, Philipp, 96, 100
Blondie, xiii, 260
Blood and Fire label, 155
Bloom, Allan, 367
Bloom, Harold, 175, 177
Blowup (movie), 186
Blue Cheer, 164
blues, xxv, 17, 28, 37, 42, 132, 133, 158, 170, 206, 207, 208, 209, 210, 269, 277, 288, 413, 426
Blues Brothers, The (movie), 199
Blur, 20, 31
Boards of Canada, 330–3
Bogart, Humphrey, 133, 320
Bois, Yve-Alain, 416–17
Bolan, Marc, 291
Bomp! (magazine) *see Who Put the Bomp!*
Bomp! label, 243, 260
Bonham, John, 315
Bonnie 'Prince' Billie *see* Oldham, Will
Boogaart, Pieter, 374
Booker, Christopher, 184, 186
Boon, Clint, xvii

Boorer, Boz, 305
Boosey & Hawkes, 324–5
bootlegs, 60, 99–100
Borders book store, 65
boredom, changing nature of, 74–5
Boredoms, The, 163
Boris, 139, 163
Born in the Bronx (exhibition and book), 17, 20
Bosworth label, 325
Bourdieu, Pierre, 141
Bourriaud, Nicolas, 416–17, 419
Bowery, Leigh, 176
Bowie, David: and British Music Experience, 5; equipment stolen after concert, 276; influence, 185; and Lady Gaga, 176; *The Man Who Fell to Earth*, 75; originality, 176; *Pin Ups*, 133; restaging of farewell Ziggy concert, 45–6, 52
Bowlly, Al, 356
box sets, 159–61
Boym, Svetlana, xxvii–xxviii, 354
Bracewell, Michael, 374–5
Bradley, Slater, 48
Brainfeeder label, 76
Bramlett, Bonnie, 7
Brand, Russell, xv
Brando, Marlon, 245
Brattleboro, Vermont, 345
Braun, Wernher von, 370, 386, 387
Bremner, Tony, 217
Brian Jonestown Massacre, 137
Brilleaux, Lee, 248, 249; *see also* Dr Feelgood
Brinsley Schwarz, 247
Brit Art, 274
British Library ethnographic music archive, 62
British Library Sound Archive, 30
British Music Experience (museum), xx, 3–8
Britpop, 200, 401
Broadcast, 344
Brody, Neville, 373
Bronson, Harold, 160
Brooks, David, 395
Brooks, Kate, 194
Brother, 401
Brown, Alan, 27
Brown, Britt, 349–50
Brown, James, 136, 199, 214, 215
Browne, Jackson, 296
Brussels World's Fair (1958), 376–8
Brutalism, 373–9
Bryars, Gavin, 335
Buckler, Rick, xvi
Buckley, Tim, 57, 135, 136
Buggles, The, 373, 400
Bukem, LTJ, 323
Bunyan, Vashti, xxxiv

Burchill, Julie, 6–7
Burial, 393–4
Burnham, Hugo, 39; *see also* Gang of Four
Burroughs, William S., 144
Bush, George W., 388
Bush, Kate, 176
Butthole Surfers, 279, 347
Buzzcocks, The, 37, 369, 370, 400
Byrds, The, 135, 136, 272–3, 277, 290
Byrne, David, 332

C86 (cutie), 286
Cage, John, 146, 149, 318, 383, 385
Cairns, Dave, 226
Cameron, Donald, xxxi–xxxii
Campaign for Nuclear Disarmament, 211
Can, 77, 137
capitalism: Fukuyama on, 329; and Gang of Four, 40; and obsolescence, 83; financial crisis of late 2000s, 419–21; and popular culture, 197; late capitalism, 127–8; *see also* consumerism
Captain Beefheart, 131, 149, 291, 317, 413
Cardin, Pierre, 183, 184
Caretaker, The, 355–6
Carlos, Walter (Wendy), 390
Carpenter, Karen, 146
Carr, Nicholas, 72–3, 77
Carroll, Ted, 250
Cars, The, xiii, 400
Carstairs, The, 220
Carthy, Eliza, xxxiii, xxxiv
Carthy, Martin, xxxiii
cassettes, 232–3, 349–51
Cave, Nick, xx, 32, 131, 132
Cavern Club, 262
CBGB, 13–14, 41, 250, 255, 276
CDs, 71, 125
Celtic Frost, 166
Cernan, Eugene, 388
Certeau, Michel de, 317
Cervantes, Miguel de, 148
Changes, The (TV series), 326, 340
Charalambides, 344
Charles I, King, xxvi–xxvii
Charles, Prince, 374
Charles, Ray, 199, 278
Charley label, 154
chavs, 24, 194–5
Cheap Trick, 34
Checker, Chubby, 212
Chemical Brothers, The, 32, 356
Cher, 406
Cherrystones label, 88, 153, 325
Chesterfield Kings, The, 262

Childish, Billy, 267–75
chillwave *see* hypnagogic pop
Chilton, Alex, 135
China, 395
Chiswick label, 250
Chords, The, 226, 228
Christie's auction house, 17, 19–20
Christman, Ed, 63–5
Chung, Mark, 50; *see also* Einstürzende Neubaten
Ciccone Youth, 146–7
cinema: remakes, xv–xvi, 53; UbuWeb, 62
Cirque du Soleil, xiii
Clangers, The (TV series), 326
Clapton, Eric, 287
Clark, Judith, 329
Clark, Spencer, 345, 346, 347, 350
Clash, The, 8–10, 258, 304, 360; *see also* Strummer, Joe
class, and taste for vintage, 195–6
Clinic, The (club), 271
clothes *see* fashion
Clowes, Daniel, 206
Cobain, Kurt, 48
Cobham, Billy, 316
Cochran, Eddie, 244, 304, 306
Cocteau, Jean, 196
Cohen, Sacha Baron, 400–1
Cohen, Sheila, 186
Cohn, Nik, 3
Coil, 132
Cold Wave, 400
Coldcut, 320, 321
Coldplay, xii
Cole, Bethan, 191
Cole, Matthew, 73
Coleman, Gregory, 323
Coley, Byron, xxxiv–xxxv, 344
Collector Records, 297
collectors and collecting: file sharing and sharity, 103–14, 121–8; and gender, 101–2; Internet's influence, 96–7; and iPods, 114–21; least collectable records, 103–6; overview, 15–21, 86–128; reasons to cut down, 122–8; theories of collecting, 94–6
Collins, Phil, 198–9, 400
Colly, Joe, 77
Coltrane, Alice, 353
Coltrane, John, 136
Columbia-Princeton Electronic Music Center, 383–4
Columbia Records, 382–3
Columbia University, 283–4
Colyer, Ken, 209–10, 211, 327, 401
Commitments, The, xvi

communism, 109, 113, 188, 329, 376
Comus, xxxiv
concentration, negative effects on caused by the Internet, 71–5
Concerto for Voice and Machinery (performance), xiv–xv, 49–52
Constanten, Tom, 231; *see also* The Grateful Dead
Constantine, Elaine, 400
consumerism, 86, 109, 110, 120, 138, 170; *see also* capitalism
Conte, Ivan, 159
Control (movie), xvi
Conzo, Joe, Jr, 17
Cook, Norman, 360
Cook, Paul, 276
Cool Kids, The, xv
Cooper, Mark, 28–31
Cope, Julian, 141–3, 164
Corbijn, Anton, xvi
Cornelius, 166, 169
Cornell, Joseph, 334
Cornwell, Hugh, xvi, 43
Corso, Gregory, 144
Costello, Elvis, 7, 34, 134, 249
Coté, Jean-Marc, 368
County, Wayne, 246
Courrèges, André, 183–4
covers albums, 132–7
Cramps, The, x, 46–7, 166–7, 294, 296–9, 301
Crash, Darby, 144
Crass, 400
crate-diggers, 321–6
Crawdaddys, The, 261
Crawford, Anwyn, 32
Cream, xii, 251
Creation, The, 204, 224, 229, 272
Creation Records, 272, 400
Creedence Clearwater Revival, 145, 281–2, 288
Creel Pone label, 382
CREEM (magazine), 241–2
Crenshaw, Marshall, 305
Crewe, Louise, 194
Crosby, Bing, 317
Crumb, Robert, 206
Crutchfield, Robert, 301; *see also* DNA
Cruz, Taio, 406
Crypt Records, 264–5
Cult, The, 199
Culturcide, 59, 136
Culture Club, 198, 401
Cunningham, Darren (Actress), 178, 246
curators, 129–61; etymology, 130–1; Japanese curatorship, 166–73
Curtis, Ian, xvi, 25, 399

Cushway, John, 333–5
Czukay, Holger, 77

D Double E & Footsie, 8
Daft Punk, 174–5, 424
Daley, Richard J., 368
Dammers, Jerry, xx, 326
Dangermouse, 358, 359
Däniken, Erich von, 390
Danny and the Juniors, 285–6
Darkness, The, 140
Darkstar, 401
Darts, 305, 306
Davies, Dai, 248
Davies, Ray, xxviii
Davis, Fred, xxix, 30, 207
DB, 237–8
De Burgh, Chris, 80, 174
Dead Weather, The, xxi
Deadheads, 229–33
Deleuze, Gilles, 126, 148
Deller, Jeremy, 48
Densmore, John, xi
Derrida, Jacques, 26–8, 328–9, 329–30
DeVille, Willy, 305
Devo, xi, 400
Devoto, Howard, 132
Dexys Midnight Runners, 174, 226
DFA label, 172
Dibbell, Julian, 109–10
Dick, Philip K., 162–3
Dickinson, Rod, 48, 52
Dictators, The, 256
Diddley, Bo, 245, 249, 287, 290
digimodernism, 412
Dilla, J, 352–4
Dinosaur Jr, xii, 31, 146, 273
Dion, Mark, 179
Dire Straits, 305
Dirty Fan Male (recording and show), 327
Dirty Projectors, The, 136–7, 171
Disco Inferno, 401
Disney, xxii, 323, 370–2
Dissevelt, Tom, 379, 385
DJ culture, 418–20
DJ Screw, 81
DJ Shadow, 322–3, 324
DJ Twist, 237
DNA, 263, 301
Doctor, The (DJ), 271
Doctor and the Medics, 271
Dr Feelgood, xxi, 29, 248–9, 290, 399
Dr John, 292
documentaries (rock docs), 28–31
Doggett, Peter, 19

Dolby, Thomas, 373
Donegan, Lonnie, 208–9
'Don't Look Back' concerts, xii, 35, 399
Doors, The: *Morrison Hotel*, 277; influence, 253, 271; interviews, 241; mashed-up, xiii; reunion tours, xi; sampled, 318; at Toronto Rock and Roll Revival, 287; *see also* Morrison, Jim
Doors of the 21st Century, The, xi
Dopplereffekt, 174
Downliners Sect, The, 261
Down by Law (movie), 307, 308
downloading *see* file sharing
Dream Syndicate, The, 273
Dreweatts auction house, 20
Drummond, Bill, 122–3, 140
dub (dub reggae), 154, 330, 382, 406
Dubale, Yeshimebet, 84–5
dubstep, 179, 236, 238, 400, 401, 407
Duchamp, Marcel, 315
Ducks Deluxe, 247, 248
Duffy, xvii, xix
Dukes of Stratosphear, The, 272
Dungen, 409
Duran Duran, 301; *see also* Le Bon, Simon
Dury, Ian, 249, 303–4, 399
Dust to Digital label, 158–9
Dylan, Bob: and *American Pie*, 290; cover versions, 134; documentaries, xi–xii; *John Wesley Harding*, 277; and Fleet Foxes, 410; influence on Beatles, 132; live reworkings, 99; memoirs, xi; motorcycle accident, 252; and Patti Smith, 252, 253; U2 collaboration, 198; and *The White Album*, 278

Ebert, Roger, 19
Echo and the Bunnymen, xviii–xix, 271
echo jams, 80–3
Ecorse studio, 157
Edison, Thomas, 313, 339
Edmunds, Dave, 243, 289
Edsel label, 154
8-Eyed Spy, 263
eighties: art world and postmodernist sensibility, 179; emergence of new genres, 406–7; fashion revived, 191; heritage culture's rise, 23, 25; museum exhibit, 7; music industry changes, 114; nostalgia for, ix, xii, xv, xxix, 172, 345–6, 349, 351, 356, 361, 401; postmodernist pop, 185; revivals of, xii, xix, 173–6, 345–6, 349, 351, 356, 373, 392, 401, 409; retrorock's rise, 199; Sixties revivalism during, 271–3, 409; style culture, 115
Eimert, Herbert, 378, 382
Einstürzende Neubaten, xiv–xv, 49–52, 146; *see also* Bargeld, Blixa

Electric Lady studio, 252
Electric Light Orchestra (ELO), 174, 177–8
electro, 175–6
electroclash, 173–6
electronic music, 379–86, 389–94; national
    electronic studios, 340–1, 383–4
Elliott, Missy, 406
Ellison, Steven *see* Flying Lotus
Elsmore, Philip, 336–7
Emin, Tracey, 274
Emmons, Jasen, 15
emo, 407
English Civil War (1642–51), xxvi–xxvii
English Heritage, 23
Eno, Brian, 130, 172–3, 332, 336, 368–9
Eoin, Marcus, 330–3
Erickson, Roky, 142
Ersatz Audio label, 174
Esfandiary, F. M., 368
Espers, xxxiv
Essex, David, 276
Estrus label, 271
Evans, Bill, 386
Evans, Walker, 147
Experience Music Project, ix, 14–15

Face, The, 73
Faces, The, 42–3, 400; *see also* The Small Faces
Fagen, Donald, 372–3
Fahey, John, xxxv, 144
Fahrenheit 451 (movie), 339
Fairport Convention, 282, 410
Falco, Tav, 305
Fall, The, 132
Faltermeyer, Harold, 346
Fantazia rave promoters, 236
Far East Family Band, 164
Far East Movement, 406
Farley, Chris, 55
Farren, Mick, 242, 249
fashion: arbitrariness of change, 191–2, 195;
    Northern Soul aficionados, 216–17; retro,
    xvii, 184–92, 421–2; in the sixties, 183–7; V&A
    Spectres exhibition, 329; vintage, 192–6
Faust, 57
Fellows, Will, 139
Fenêtre sur cour (movie), 53
Fennessey, Sean, 360
Fergie, 406
Ferraro, James, 345, 346, 347, 349, 350
Ferry, Bryan, 133–4
Field, Bradley, 301
Fielding, Noel, 174
fifties revivalism, 276–308
file sharing, 103–14; cons, 110–11, 121, 122–8

File Under Sacred Music (re-enactment), x,
    46–7
Filth and the Fury, The (documentary), ix
financial crisis, current, 419–21
Finders Keepers label, 325
Finney, Tim, x
Fischerspooner, 175, 176
Fisher, Mark, 132, 133, 328
Flamin' Groovies, The, 242–3, 260–1, 301
Flaming Lips, The, xxiii
Flanagan, Bill, 114
Fleet Foxes, 409–10
Fleetwood Mac, xi, xiii
Flesh Eaters, The, 305
Fleshtones, The, 262
Flipper's Guitar, 166–7, 168
Flo Rida, 406
Flower Travellin' Band, 164
Flying Lotus (Steven Ellison), 76–8, 353, 413
Focus Group, The, 328, 330, 339, 342–4
Fogerty, John, 281; *see also* Creedence
    Clearwater Revival
folk music, xxxiii–xxxv, 105–6, 206, 343–5
Folkways label, 132
Fonarow, Wendy, 164
Foos, Richard, 160
Foreman, Richard, 73–4
Forsyth, Iain, x, xx, 44–8, 52
4AD Records, 135
Fowley, Kim, 399
Foxton, Bruce, xvi
France, Anatole, 87
Franklin, Aretha, 198, 199
Fraunhofer, 69
free-folk movement, xxxiii–xxxv, 343–5
Freed, Alan, 12
Freelance Hellraiser, The, 358
Freud, Sigmund, 27–8, 95, 337
Friedman, Bruce, 72
Frieze (magazine), 412–13, 415–16
Fuel (publisher), 326, 327
Fujiya & Miyagi, 171
Fukuyama, Francis, 329
Fuller, Bobby, 300
Fuller, Buckminster, 376
Funk Brothers, The, 400
Fury, Billy, 244, 290
Future, the: contemporary equivalents for
    interest in, 425–6; nostalgia for the future
    concept, 368–72; possible sources of innova-
    tion, 394–6
Future Is Not What It Used to Be, The (docu-
    mentary), 389–91
Futurism, 21–2
futurology, 362–8

Gabler, Milt, 153–4
Gabriel, Peter, 176, 198
Gagarin, Yuri, 385
Gaisberg, Fred, 159
Gallagher, Liam, 399
gaming: retro video games, xvii
Gane, Tim, 150
Gang of Four, xii, xx, 39–41
gangsta rap, 303
garage punk, ix, xix, 142, 151, 152, 224, 240, 241, 242, 250, 251–2, 260–73, 300, 409, 413, 425
Garcia, Jerry, 230, 232, 319–20; *see also* The Grateful Dead
Gardner, Don, 220
Gaskin, Vivienne, 44, 45, 49
Gaslamp Killer, The, 76, 413
Gaultier, Jean-Paul, 189
Gehry, Frank, 14
Generation X, 259, 304–5
Genet, Jean, 148
genres, retroactively invented, 151–3
Germs, The, 144
Gernsback, Hugo, 373
Gershwin, George, 136
Ghost Box label, 312, 328, 329–30, 335, 336–44, 347, 353, 355, 361, 423
Ghost Dog: The Way of the Samurai (movie), 394
Ghost World (movie), 206
Gibson, William, 373, 396–7, 425–6, 427
Gilbert, Bruce, 37–8; *see also* Wire
Gill, Andy, 39, 41; *see also* Gang of Four
Gillespie, Bobby, 135–6, 161, 400
Gillis, Greg, 359–60
Girl Talk, 359–60
Girls on Top *see* Richard X
glam rock, 5, 30, 106, 133, 151, 153, 170, 176, 185, 187, 190, 197, 244, 248, 291–2, 406
Glass, Philip, 78
Glitter, Gary, 134, 291, 292
glo-fi *see* hypnagogic pop
Glory Boys, the, 226
Glory That Was Grease, The (show), 283–4, 285
Go-Gos, The, 260
Go! Team, The, 171
Goddard, Gareth, 88, 157
Godin, Dave, 217
Gold, Jeff, 15–16, 17–19
Goldfrapp, Alison, 177, 191
Goldstein, Jack, 144
Gong, 202
Gonjasufi, 76, 413
Good, the Bad and the Queen, The, 359
Google, 114
Gordon, Kim, 145, 146; *see also* Sonic Youth

Gordon, Robert, 300, 305
Gossip Girl (TV series), xviii, xxiii
Goth, xii, 106, 160, 168, 176, 400, 407
Gothic Revival, xiii, xxx
Graham, Bill (Wolfgang Grajonca), 12, 18
Grainger, Percy, 312
Granny Takes a Trip (boutique), 186–7
Grant, Cary, 320
Grateful Dead, The, 99, 229–33, 241, 273, 319–20
Gray, Dobie, 217
Grease (musical), xii, 277, 294
greasers, 284–5
Greenbaum, Norman, 271
Greene, Graham, 327
Greene, Jo-Anne, 99
Gregson, Nicky, 194
grime, 8, 375, 407
Groenenboom, Roland, 144
Groening, Matt, 32
Groundhogs, The, 143
grunge, xxii, 31, 200, 407
Guana Batz, The, 166, 299
Guattari, Felix, 126, 148
Guffey, Elizabeth, xxxi, 262
Gun Club, The, 305
Gunn, Peter, 153, 154
Guns N' Roses, 135

Hacienda, the, x
Haddon, Alfred Cort, 62
Haden, Petra, 136
Haircut 100, 168
Haley, Bill, & His Comets, 281, 286, 290
Hall & Oates, 198, 346, 348
Hammer, Jan, 316, 346
Handy, Bruce, 371
Hannett, Martin, x
Hanoi Rocks, 138
Happy Days (TV series), 294
Happy Mondays, x, xvi
Hard Rock chain, 11
Harris, Bob, 246, 248
Harrison, George, xix; *see also* The Beatles
Harvey, Eric, 411
Hatfield and the North, 248
Hatherley, Owen, 132, 375
Haunted exhibition (Guggenheim), 329
hauntology, 328–56, 361, 423–4
Hauntology exhibition (Berkeley Art Museum), 329
Hawkins, Justin, 140
Hawthorne, Nathaniel, 148
Haynes, Todd, 144
Head Heritage, 142–3
Hearst, William Randolph, 96

Heaven (club), 220
Heaven 17, ix, 400
heavy metal *see* metal
Heinz, 290
Heiser, Jörg, 412–13, 415
Hell, Richard, xxi–xxii
Hendrix, Jimi: and British Music Experience,
    15; cover versions, 198; influence, 237, 252,
    253; record collection, 18; sampled, 318; and
    Sha Na Na, 285; at Woodstock, xxxvi
Henke, Jim, 12, 13, 15
Henry, Pierre, 378, 379
Hepburn, Audrey, 320
Here and Now (revue), ix, 401
heritage, 23–6, 32, 51, 53, 142–3, 155, 155, 159, 197,
    210, 361, 375
Hewicker, Scott, 329
High Llamas, The, 171
Hilderbrand, Lucas, 59, 61
Hiller, Lejaren, 385
Hince, Jamie, xxi
Hi-NRG, 220
Hinton, S. E., 284–5, 302
hip hop: and DJs, 420; and futurism, 375; Born
    in the Bronx exhibition, 16–17; sampling
    aspect, 312, 326–8; emergence of genre,
    407–8; underground, 405; use of the past,
    352–4, 418
hippies, 202–3
hipsters (hipsterdom, hipsterland), xix, xxxii,
    75, 169–76, 350, 419–21
Hirst, Damien, 274, 275
historicity, 15, 16-8, 162–3
Hitchcock, Robyn, 272
Hives, The, xix, 267, 272
Hodgson, Ian, 342; *see also* Moon Wiring Club
Hofer, Johannes, xxv
Hoffs, Susanna, 146
Hogan, Barry, 32–3, 35–6
Holland, Charles, 25
Holly, Buddy, 289, 290
Holst, Gustav, 390
Holstrom, John, 256
Holzman, Jac, 251, 282
Honest Jon's label, 159
Hook, Peter, 399
Hornby, Nick, 100
Horrors, The, 171
House, Julian, 339, 341, 342–4, 361; *see also* The
    Focus Group
house music (house, acid house, deep house),
    21, 136, 210, 215, 216, 222, 234, 239, 392, 406,
    407, 408, 415, 418
House of Love, The, 135
Houseshakers, The, 290

Howard, Adina, x, 358, 359
Howard, Roland S., 32, 131
Howard, Ron, 294
Hucknall, Mick, 155, 400
Hulanicki, Barbara, 187–9
Human League, The, xvi, 134, 178, 185, 401
Hüsker Dü, 134–5
Huyghe, Pierre, 53
Huyssen, Andreas, 22–3, 26, 56
hyper-stasis concept, 427
hypnagogic pop (chillwave; glo-fi), 345–51, 361

I Love the [Decade] (TV series), xii, xxx, 27–8
ICA, 44–5, 46, 48, 49–50
Idol, Billy, 304–5
I-f, 174
Ignorant, Steve, 400
Illegal Art label, 360
improv, 405
Incredible String Band, The, xxxiv, 202
India, 395
Ingram, Matthew, 111, 119
Inspiral Carpets, xvii, 401
Interior, Lux, 296, 297–9; *see also* The Cramps
Internet: archive materials on, 65; cognitive
    effects of using, 71–5; file sharing and shar-
    ity, 103–14, 121–8; influence on collecting,
    96–7; influence on creativity, 77–85
Interpol, 177
Intro design company, 342
iPods, xiii, 95–6, 113, 114–21, 357–8; shuffle,
    120–1
Isaak, Chris, 179, 305
It's Trad, Dad (movie), 212, 401
Iver, Bon, 409

Jackson, Elly, 401
Jackson, Michael, 317–18
Jacobs, Marc, xvii, 191
Jagger, Mick, xiii, 10, 226; *see also* The Rolling
    Stones
Jam, The, xvi, 224–6
Jameson, Fredric, 128, 420, 421
Japan: influence, 171–3; reissues, music fan-
    dom, collecting and retro, 162–71, 177
Japancakes, 136
Jarmusch, Jim, 32, 307–8, 394
Jarre, Jean-Michel, 390–1
Jay-Z, 35, 358
jazz, 5, 17, 28, 34, 174, 210, 217, 263, 289, 326, 342,
    386; bebop jazz, 207; cool jazz, 207; free jazz,
    150, 156; jazz fusion, 76, 77, 153–4, 316, 353,
    359; jazz funk, 210, 229, 322; jazz-rock, 162,
    197, 241; New Orleans jazz, also known as
    hot jazz, early jazz, 154, 163, 206–14, 229, 308;

trad jazz, also known as revival jazz, 206–14, 233, 401
Jeck, Philip, 335
Jefferson Airplane, 19
Jenkins, Henry, 317
Jesus and Mary Chain, The, 133–4, 136–8, 167, 176, 178, 272
Jetsons, The, 365
Jobs, Steve, 113
Joel, Billy, 305, 414
Johansen, David, 42, 43, 245; *see also* The New York Dolls
John, Elton, xiii–xiv, 7, 277
John's Children, 204
Johnson, Bunk, 209–10
Johnson, Wilko, xxi, 248, 249; *see also* Dr Feelgood
Jones, Brian, 135, 253
Jones, Dylan, 115–18
Jones, Jim, 48
Jones, Max, 213
Jones, Mick, 8–10; *see also* The Clash
Jones, Steve, 11, 246, 276; *see also* The Sex Pistols
Jonestown Re-enactment, The, 48
Jordan, Cyril, 261; *see also* The Flamin' Groovies
Joy Division, x, xvi; *see also* Curtis, Ian
Juno, Andrea, 151
Jupp, Jim, 311–12, 337, 339, 340, 355
Jurassic 5, 235
Justified Ancients of Mu Mu, The *see* The KLF

Kano, 8
Katranis, Nick, 313
Kaye, Lenny, 251–2, 276
Keeler, Christine, 205
Keenan, David, 345–6
Kek-W, 104
Kelly, Kevin, 113–14, 367
Kent, Nick, 244, 296
KICKS (fanzine), 301
Kicks Like a Mule, 238, 392
Kidd, Johnny, 5
Kilburn and the High Roads, 303–4
Kills, The, xxi
King, Eric, 19
King, Jon, 39, 40, 41; *see also* Gang of Four
Kingsley, Gershon, 150
Kingsmen, The, 283
Kinks, The, xxviii, 269, 270
Kirby, Alan, 412
Kirby, James Leyland, 354–7, 363
Kirchin, Basil, 325, 326
Klaxons, The, 171, 392–3

Klein, Yves, 145
KLF, The (aka the Justified Ancients of Mu Mu, aka JAMMS), 59, 123, 140, 320–1, 416
Klop, Cees, 297
Knack, The, 260
Kneale, Nigel, 340
Kode9, 394
Koenig, Ezra, 414–15
Kongos, John, 292
Korner, Alexis, 327–8
KPM, 324–5
Kraftwerk, xii, xxii–xxiii, 172, 373
Kravitz, Lenny, 177, 237
Kubrick, Stanley, 355
Kugelberg, Johan, 15, 16–17, 20, 53, 110
Kurenniemi, Erkki, 389–91
Kurzweil, Ray, 367

La Roux, xix, 176, 401
Lady Gaga, xix, 80, 176, 406
Lagerfeld, Karl, 184, 190
Laibach, 136
Lambrettas, The, 226
Lance, Major, 215
Landau, Jon, 254
Lanier, Jaron, 367, 405
Laroche, John, 92
La's, The, 178
Lauren, Ralph, 189
Laverne & Shirley (TV series), 294
LCD Soundsystem, 172–3, 421–2
Le Corbusier, 376–9
Leander, Mike, 292
Led Zeppelin, xi, 19, 103, 290, 315; *see also* Plant, Robert
Lee, Ang, xxi
Left Banke, The, 151
Lennon, John: childhood home opened to public, x; clothes in museum, 13; favourite Beatles era, 269; and fifties revivalism, 276, 277, 280, 285, 286, 288–9, 290; film about adolescence, 400; and glam rock, 291; influence, 237, 253; memorabilia, 14; solo work, 288; at Toronto Rock and Roll Revival, 287; *see also* The Beatles
Lennon, Julia, 289
Leon, Craig, 257
Leonard, George, 283–7
Leonard, Rob, 283
Leslie, Desmond, 325–6
Lester, Richard, 212
Let It Rock (boutique), 243–4, 245, 303
Lethbridge, T. C., 339
Levi commercials, 198
Levine, Ian, 219–21

Levine, Sherrie, 147–8, 164, 416
Levy, Steven, 113, 115, 116
Lewis, Jeffrey, 136
Lewis, Jerry Lee, 280, 287, 289, 290
library music, 105, 324–6, 341–3, 352, 356
Lindsay, Arto, 263
Linna, Miriam, 298, 300–4
Lissitsky, El, 373
Litter, The, 264
Little Boots, xix, 176
Little Richard, 224, 280, 287, 290
Livingston, Tamara E., 206, 211
London Rock 'n' Roll Show (1972), 290–1
Long Tail theory, 66–8
Longstreth, Dave, 136–7
Lopatin, Daniel, 79–83, 84, 352, 423; see also
    Oneohtrix Point Never
Lounge Lizards, The, 263
Love, 134, 136, 271
Love (album), xiv
Love (show), xiii
Low End Theory (club), 76
Lowe, Justin, 14
Lowe, Nick, 249, 260
Lübbe, Hermann, 23
Lucas, George, 293
Luening, Oscar, 385
Lumbleau, Eric, 107, 152
Lunch, Lydia, 263, 301
Lydon, John, xxiii
Lyman, Arthur, 97
Lyres, The, 266
Lyttleton, Humphrey, 208, 213

McCarthy, Mary, 20
McCarthy, Tom, 48, 54
McCartney, Paul, xv, 55, 151, 257, 280; see also
    The Beatles
Macdonald, Ian, 282
McDonald, Michael, 346
McDowell, Colin, 190
McEwan, Ian, 98
McGee, Alan, 272, 400
MacGowan, Shane, 305
McKay, George, 212
McKean, Colin, 76
McLaren, Malcolm: and African music, 414;
    background, 243–5, 303; and The New York
    Dolls, 245, 247; and The Sex Pistols, xxi, 247,
    258, 276
McLaren, Norman, 62
McLean, Don, 290
Maclise, Angus, 344
McLuhan, Marshall, 376, 412
McNally, Patrick, 328

McNeil, Legs, 256
McPhatter, Clyde, 12
McRobbie, Angela, 193
Madlib, 323, 352
Madonna, 20, 146, 176, 347
Magazine, 132
Magnetic Fields, The, 139
Magnetic Man, 407
Man Who Fell to Earth, The (movie), 75
Manson, Charles, 145, 290
Manton, Robert, 228
Manzarek, Ray, xi
Marclay, Christian, 318
Marcus, Greil, 281, 282–3, 344
Marinetti, F. T., 22
Marl, Marly, 312
Marley, Bob, 13
Marsh, Dave, 251
Martin, George, xiv, 204
Martin, Giles, xiv
Martyn, John, xxxiv, 248
Marx, Karl, 329
Marx, W. David, 164, 165, 167–9, 170–1, 177, 424
Mascis, J., 273; see also Dinosaur Jr
mash-ups, x, xiii, 356–60
Massive Attack, 316
Mastodon, 140
Matador label, 169
Matathia, Ira, 368
Matchbox, 305, 306
Matlock, Glen, 400; see also The Sex Pistols
Matos, Michaelangelo, 124–5
Mavers, Lee, 178
Max's Kansas City, 250
Mayall, John, 210, 328
MC5, The, 134, 143, 252, 290
Meatloaf, 295
Meek, Joe, 330, 386
Méliès, Georges, 385
Melly, George, 209, 212, 213, 401
Melody Maker magazine, 6, 190, 209, 248, 281
Melvins, The, 139
memorabilia, 15–21, 98–9
Memphis Rock 'n' Soul Museum, ix
Mercury, Freddie, xi, 400–1
Merritt, Stephen, 139, 400
metal: extreme metal, 405; hair metal xii, xvi,
    104, 137; heavy metal, 7, 29, 139–40, 242, 298,
    406, 407, 418
Metallica, 30
\m/etal\m/inx, 108
Meteors, The, 166, 299
Meyer, Russ, 19
M.I.A., 413, 420
Micalef, Steve, 97–8

Michael, George, 198, 306–7
Mighty Boosh, The (TV series), 174–6
Miles, Buddy, 146
Milgram, Dr Stanley, 48
Milkshakes, Thee, 267, 269–70
Miller, Billy, 300–1
Miller, Daniel, 38
Miller, James, 26
minimal synth, 152
Mink DeVille, 305
Minogue, Kylie, 112–13, 359
Miss Kittin, 175, 176
Mission, The, xvii
Mission of Burma, 35
Mitchell, Jo, xiv–xv, 49–52
Mitchell, Joni, 296, 410
Mizell, Hank, 297
Moby, 238
modernism, 183–7, 229, 373–9, 394, 403–4
mods, 203–4, 216–17; Mod Revival, 223–9
Mohawke, Hudson, 76
Mojo Navigator Rock and Roll News (magazine), 241
Momus, 33–4
Monkees, The, 160
Monoman, 266
Monotones, The, 290
Monterey Pop Festival, 19
Mood Six, 271
Moody Blues, The, 5, 164
Moon, Keith, 225; *see also* The Who
moon landing (1969), 386–7
Moon Wiring Club, 328, 336, 342
Mooney Suzuki, The, 137
Moore, Hilary, 209, 213
Moore, Thurston, 36, 144; *see also* Sonic Youth
Mordant Music, 328, 336–7
Morley, Paul, 112–13, 424
Morlighem, Sébastien, 381
Morrison, Jim, xi, 142, 252, 253
Morrison, Van, xix–xx, 35, 252
Morrissey: and Boz Boorer, 305; fans, 44; influences on, 413; and The New York Dolls, 246; originality, 428; and reflective nostalgia, xxviii; reissues, xii; on synthesizers, 174; *see also* The Smiths
Morton, Shadow, 245
Mosshart, Alison, xxi
Motown *see* Tamla Motown
MP3s, xxi, 35, 61, 68–71, 103, 113, 114, 121–4, 128, 357–8, 406
MTV, xiii, 348, 400
MTV Cribs, 194
Mud, 103, 291
Mudcrutch, xvii–xviii, 33

Mudhoney, 35
Muhly, Nico, 78–9, 83
Murphy, James, 172–3, 421–2
museums, 3–15
Musica Electronica Viva, 385
musique concrète (tape music, concrete), 278, 318, 325, 328, 340, 341, 376, 380–4
Mutant Sounds (blog), 107
Mute Records label, 38
MV & EE, xxxiv, 344
My Bloody Valentine: cover versions, 136; reunion tours, xviii, 31, 33, 36, 39
Myles, Trevor, 243
Mystery Train (movie), 307, 308

Nader, Richard, 286–7
Napa State Mental Institute, x, 47
Napier-Bell, Simon, 204
NASA, 387–8, 391
NASA (club), 237–8
NASA Rewind (reunion rave), 237–8
National Film Board of Canada, 62
National Trust, 23
Naughty Rhythms (package tour), 249
Nauman, Bruce, 48
Negativland, 59, 136
Nelson, Ricky, 286, 287
Neon Indian, 345
Nervosa, Teresa, 347
Neville, Richard, 203
New Age, 345, 346, 347
New Order, 359
New Orleans, 308
New Psychedelia, 271
New Wave, 259–60
New York Dolls, The, 41–3, 188, 245–7, 276
Newsom, Joanna, xxxiii–xxxiv, 344
Newton-John, Olivia, 294
Nichols, Roger, & the Small Circle of Friends, 168
Nicholson, Jack, 355
Nico, 38
Nine Evenings of Art in the Armory (event), 383
nineties: new genres, 407
Ninjatune label, 325
Nipple Erectors, The, 305
Nirvana, 200
Nite Jewel, 345
NME (*New Musical Express*) magazine, xxviii, 6, 131, 132, 142, 171, 190, 225, 244, 249, 297, 299
No Direction Home: Bob Dylan (documentary), xi–xii
No Music Day campaign, 122–3
No Wave, 144, 149, 258, 263, 297, 301

Noise Fest (1981), 144
NOISE/ART (exhibition), 144
Nolan, Jerry, 246; *see also* New York Dolls
North, Adrian, 121
Northern Soul, 152, 214–23, 229–31, 400; origins of term, 217
Northern Soul (movie), 400
Norton Records, 300–1
nostalgia: eighties nostalgia, 172, 173–7, 356, 409; and fashion, 187, 191, 197, 200–1; fifties nostalgia, 276–309; and hauntology, 326–7, 328, 343; history of the concept, xxv–xxix; nineties nostalgia, 31; nostalgia mode, 421; nostalgia-oriented TV shows, 27–8; and pop culture, xiv, xxiii, xxix–xxx, 239, 364; punk nostalgia, 11, 30, 410; rave nostalgia, 234–9; reflective vs restorative, xxvii–xxviii, 354; sixties nostalgia, xxix, 271–3, 409–10; technostalgia, 83, 350–1; twenties nostalgia, 207
nostalgia for the future concept, 363, 368–72
Not Not Fun label, 349
Notorious B.I.G., 320
Nuggets (compilation), 251, 253, 263, 273
Numan, Gary, x, 174, 358, 359, 401
Numero Group label, 156–8
Nuttall, Jeff, 208

Oasis, 20, 177, 178, 399
Obama, Barack, 388
Oberg, James, 388–9
O'Brien, Richard, 295
Ocasek, Ric, xiii, 400
Oid City Confidential (documentary), 399
Old Grey Whistle Test, The (TV programme), 246
old skool (old skool hip hop, old skool rave), 233–9
Oldham, Will (Bonnie 'Prince' Billy), 409
OMD *see* Orchestral Manoeuvres in the Dark
100 Club, 222
101ers, The, 250, 304
O'Neill, Alistair, 185–6
Oneohtrix Point Never, 80, 82–3, 345, 351–2, 423
Ono, Yoko, x, 13, 150, 287
Opie, Robert, 93
Orange Juice, 167, 185
Orb, The, 32, 391
Orbison, Roy, 34, 294
Orbital, 32
Orchestral Manoeuvres in the Dark (OMD), 373
Orgreave, Battle of (1984), 48
Orlean, Susan, 92
O'Rourke, P. J., 371, 372
Osaka World's Fair (1970), 384–5

Osbourne, Ozzy, 99
Oswald, John, 317–20
Osymyso, 358
Oursler, Tony, 144
Oyamada, Keigo (Cornelius), 166–7
Ozawa, Kenji, 166, 167

Page, Ian, 226
Paisley Underground, The, 273
Palmer, Robert, 146, 147
Pan Sonic, 389
Panther Burns, 305
Parmegiani, Bernard, 318, 379, 384
Parr, Martin, 374
Parton, Dolly, 318–19
Pavement, 31, 400
Peace, David, 165–8
Pearce, Kevin, 153, 227, 229
Pearce, Susan M., 101
Pebbles (compilations series), 263–4
Pecknold, Robin, 410
Peel, John, 74, 248
Penguin Books, 330
Pennebaker, D. A., 45–6, 287
Penny Arcade, 253
Performance (movie), 226
performance art, 38, 47, 48, 54, 274
Perrey, Jean-Jacques, 150
Pessoa, Fernando, 369
Peterson, Gilles, 155, 156
Petrusich, Amanda, xxxiv
Petty, Tom, xvii–xviii, 33; *see also* Mudcrutch
Phair, Liz, 35
Philips electronics company, 379
Philips label, 379–81, 385
Philips Pavilion *see Poème électronique*
Pictures Generation movement (appropriation art), 147–8
Pierce, Jason, 136; *see also* Spacemen 3
Pink, Ariel (Ariel Pink's Haunted Graffiti): on own music, xxiii; and recording, xxxv, 348–9; on the sixties, xxxvi; style and methods, 84–5, 348–9, 423–4
Pink Floyd, xx, xxiii, 7, 186
Pirate Bay, 104
Pitchfork (web-zine), x, 77, 331, 345, 405, 409, 411
Pitchfork Music Festival, 35
Pitney, Gene, 132
Pivovarova, Sasha, xix
Pixies, The, xi, xxii, 31, 33
Pizzicato Five, 169
Plant, Robert, 290, 305; *see also* Led Zeppelin
Plastic Ono Band, 287; *see also* Lennon, John; Ono, Yoko

Platinum Weird, xiii

Platt, Edward, 374

plunderphonics, 317–20

Poe, Edgar Allan, 132

Poème électronique (Philips Pavilion), 376–8

Pogues, The, xvi, 199, 305

Poison, Ivy, *see* Rorschach, Poison Ivy

Pokémon, 90–2

Polecats, The, 305

Police, The, xi, xvi, 33, 176, 360

Pollard, Jane, x, xx, 44–8, 52

Pop, Iggy, 146, 276, 399, 401

Pop Rivets, The, 268

Pop Will Eat Itself, 320, 321

P-Orridge, Genesis, 38, 49, 401; *see also* Throbbing Gristle

Position Normal, 333–5

Postcard label, 168

posters (vintage and collectable posters), 18–19

Postman, Neil, 367

Postmodernism (postmodern, postmodernist, postmodernity), 23, 59, 130, 138, 140, 146, 148, 179, 185, 197–9, 279, 321, 355, 392, 404, 412, 414–6, 418-9, 421

postproduction concept, 416–24, 426, 427

Powell, Mike, 330

power pop, 259–60

Premier, 322, 352

Presley, Elvis: 1968 *Comeback Special*, 281, 290; and The Clash, 304; cover versions, 132, 133; *Ed Sullivan* appearance, xxxvi; *Elvis!* musical, 306; as ghost in Jarmusch's *Mystery Train*, 307, 308; influence, 5, 198; Lennon on, 280; memorabilia, 19; reissues, 154; sampled, 318

Press, Joy, 343

Pretty Things, The, 133, 261

Price, Seth, 412, 415–16

Primal Scream, 134, 135–8, 167, 176, 272

Prince, 178

Prince, Richard, 144, 147, 148

Prisoner, The (TV series), 336

Prog Britannia (documentary), 29

Prospective 21ème Siècle (The Silver Records), 379–81

Protest Records label, 143–4

psychedelia (psychedelic, psych), 196, 230–1, 233, 237, 242, 266, 277, 281–2, 382, 404, 406, 413; Ariel Pink, 348; drugs, 231; English baroque late psychedelia, 151; fashion, 185–6; hauntology as descendant, 330; Lennon's renunciation, 289; neo-psychedelia and Julian Cope, 141–3; psychedelic folk, 106; retreat from, 277–9, 280, 281–2, 289, 409; revivalism, 199, 262, 271–3, 409; San Francisco posters, 18–19; space rock, 390

Psychic TV, 135

Psycho (movie), 53

psychobilly, 46, 47, 166, 167, 296–9

pub rock, 247–50, 276

Public Enemy, xviii, 35

Public Image Ltd, xxiii, 202

public-information films, 339

punk, xxii, xxix, 4, 5–7, 8, 10, 16, 29, 30, 41–3, 53, 115, 134, 198, 200, 202, 224, 228, 229, 240–75, 276, 289, 359, 407, 410–11; aftermath, 259–63; antecedents and origins, 240–57; assimilation into mainstream, 6–7; documentaries, ix, 29, 399, 401; garage punk, 151, 263–73; Japanese retro-punk, 165; memorabilia, 17, 19, 31; museum-ification, 5–7, 8, 13–14, 17, 21, 39, 46–7, 53; non-sonic aspects, 258; relationship with music press, 6; and rockabilly, 303–6

Punk (magazine), 256

Purple Hearts, The, 226, 228, 229

Pussy Galore, 146, 148

Quadrophenia (movie), 226

Quant, Mary, 183, 184–5

Quasimoto, 352

Queen, xi, 136, 305, 306; *see also* Mercury, Freddie

Queens of the Stone Age, 140

Raaijmakers, Dick (Kid Baltan), 379, 385

Rabanne, Paco, 183, 184

Radiohead, 179

Rage Against the Machine, xv, 31

Rain Parade, The, 273

Rallizes Denudes, Les, 164

Ramones, The, 250, 256–7

rap, 8, 170, 194–5, 316, 320, 327, 360, 406, 407, 408, 414, 420; gangsta rap, 81, 303; retro-rap and old skoolist rap, xv, 235, 352–3

Rapp, Tom, 135

Rascal, Dizzee, 8

Raspberries, The, 259

Ratliff, Ben, 34

Ratpack, 236

Rauschenberg, Robert, 383

rave (rave culture, rave scene, ravers), x, xix, xxi, xxii, xxviii, 20–1, 32, 118, 172, 179, 199–200, 216, 233–4, 316, 354, 356–7, 380, 391–4, 404, 405, 406, 408, 418, 422; nu-rave, 175, 392–4; old skool hardcore, 233–9; term for trad jazz fans, 212

Ray-Ban, 192

RCA label, 384

Reagan, Ronald, 273

rebetiko, 413

453

recording: analogue vs digital, 68–9, 313; effect on experience of music, 122; modern purpose, 124; Ariel Pink's method, xxxv, 348–9; private-press, 324; quality of MP3s, 61, 69–71; retro methods, 270; spectral quality, 312–13
Reed, Lou, xiv, 172
Reel, Penny, 225
re-enactments, 44–54
reggae, 117, 138, 155, 170, 210, 258, 330, 382, 406–7, 413, 417, 418, 426
Reich, Steve, 149, 336
reissues, 57, 151–61
Reith, Lord, 341
R.E.M., 272
Replacements, The, 135
Residents, The, 135–6, 318
retro: definitions, xii–xiii, xxx; negative connotations, xxxi–xxxii; origins of the term, xxxi; preconditions, xxxv–xxxvi, 213
retro-futurism, 368–73, 389, 394
retro-modernism, 373
reunions, 10, 31–43, 164, 220–1, 237
Revenant label, xxxv, 158–9
revivals (revivalism, revivalists), xi, xii, xxix, xxxi, 23, 172–5, 189, 194, 201, 202–39, 242, 261, 261, 266, 270–3, 277, 361, 392, 400–1, 409, 424; changing nature of, 425–6; cycles, 197–201
reworkings, 47–8
Reynolds, Kieran, 89–91, 335
Rhino Records label, 160–1
Richard X (Girls on Top), x, 358, 359
Richards, Keith, 10, 15, 225, 253
Richardson, Nick, 405–6
Riley, Bridget, 384
Rinocerose, 112
Riviera, Jake, 249
Robertson, Robbie, 282; see also The Band
rock 'n' roll: first major concert, 12; origins of term, 12; revivals of during seventies and eighties, 276–306
Rock and Roll Hall of Fame and Museum, xix, 10–14, 15
Rock 'n' Roll Public Library, 8–10
Rock 'n' Roll Suicide, A (re-enactment), 45–6, 52
Rock of Ages (musical), xii
Rock On (store and stalls), 250
Rock Revival festivals, 286–7
rockabilly, 296–304
Rocker, The (movie), 53
Rockers, 245
Rocket (club), 221
Rockwell, John, 381
Rocky Horror Show, The, 276–7, 295

Rodgers, Paul, xi
Roeg, Nicolas, 75
Rolling Stone, 241
Rolling Stones, The: cover versions, 134, 135, 136, 146; Exile on Main Street reissue, 399–400; and fifties revivalism, 277; influence, 261; memorabilia, 19; mods' attitude to, 224–5; origins, 210; tribute songs, 135; see also Jagger, Mick; Jones, Brian; Richards, Keith
Rollins, Henry, 146; see also Black Flag
Rombes, Nick, 257
Ronettes, The, 257
Ronson, Mark, 401
Rorem, Ned, 369
Rorschach, Poison Ivy, 296, 297–9; see also The Cramps
Rose Quartz blog, 351
Rotten, Johnny, 7, 8, 240, 250, 258, 303; see also The Sex Pistols
Rowland, Kevin, 174
Roxy Music, 133, 185
Runaways, The (movie), 399
Rundgren, Todd, xiii, 42, 132, 246
Rushton, Neil, 222
Russell, George, 386
Rustie, 76
RZA, 322, 352

Sabin, Roger, 99
Sadier, Laetitia, 149, 150
Sagan, Carl, 78, 390
Saint Etienne, 138–9, 151; see also Stanley, Bob
Saint Laurent, Yves, 189
Salem, 400
Salt-N-Pepa, 312, 358
Saltzman, Marian, 368
sampling, 146, 148, 167, 311–61; hauntology, 328–56, 361, 423–4; and hip hop, 352–4; hypnagogic pop, 345–51, 361; mash-ups, x, xiii, 356–60; types, 321
Samuel, Raphael, xxx, xxxi, 25
Sandison, Michael, 330–3
Santana, Carlos, 174
Savage, Jon, 138, 256
Scandal (movie), 205
Schaeffer, Pierre, 378
School Disco, ix, x
School of Rock (movie), 53
Schulze, Klaus, 390
Schwartz, Barry, 121
Schwitters, Kurt, 334
science fiction, 362–8, 396–8
Science Fiction Museum and Hall of Fame, 15
Scissor Sisters, The, 140
Scorsese, Martin, xii

Scott, Raymond, 352–3
Scott, Ridley, 366–7
Scott 4, 137
Secret Affair, 226
Seeds, The, 43, 251, 271
Serkis, Andy, 399
Seven Easy Pieces (re-enactment), 48
seventies, x, xviii, xxiii, xxix, xxxi, 19, 29, 30, 31,
    57, 179, 189, 194, 197, 199, 200, 229, 240, 245,
    257, 273, 276, 331, 366, 406, 408–9, 418, 422,
    423, 428; new genres, 406
Sevigny, Laura, 34
SEX (boutique), 245, 303
Sex & Drugs & Rock & Roll (movie), 399
Sex Pistols, The, 7, 165, 240, 400; Bill Grundy
    show appearance, xxxvi; documentaries, ix,
    29; memorabilia, 20; origins, 276; reunions,
    xiv, 11; and Rock and Roll Hall of Fame,
    10–11; Strummer on, 250; style inspiration,
    xxi; *Who Killed Bambi?*, 19; *see also* Jones,
    Steve; Rotten, Johnny
Sha Na Na, 283–7, 291, 294, 304
Shakin' Stevens, 305, 306, 354
Shangri-Las, The, 245
Shannon, Del, 291, 294, 296
sharity blogs, 104–11
Sharp, Cecil, xxxiii
Shaw, Greg, 241–2, 243, 259–60, 261–2, 265, 301
Shear, Alex, 93
Shelley, Pete, 6, 369; *see also* The Buzzcocks
Sherborne, Philip, 382
Sherman, Cindy, 148
Shernoff, Andy, 256
Shibuya-kei, 166–71, 177; influence, 171–3
Shining, The (movie), 355
Shipley, Ken, 156–8
Shoom (club), 20, 215
Showaddywaddy, 306
Showalter, Elaine, 193–4
Sickness Abounds (blog), 108
Silent Running (movie), 366
Silhouettes, The, 285
Silver Records, The *see* Prospective 21ème
    Siècle
Silverman, Kaja, 193
Simon, David, 163
Simon, Paul, 414
Simply Red *see* Hucknall, Mick
Simpson, Joe, 66
Sinclair, John, 143
Singleton, Shelby, 154
Siouxsie and the Banshees, 135
Situationism, xxvii, 203, 258
sixties, x, xxii, xxix, xxxi, xxxvi, 5, 8, 19, 30–1,
    134, 150, 177, 184, 193, 197, 198–9, 202–5,
    294, 364–5, 366, 387, 396, 412, 422, 423, 428;
    fashion, 183–7; revivalists and sixties cult-
    ists, 202–5, 214, 223–5, 230–1, 233, 252–3,
    271–3; rate of emergence of new genres, 406;
    nostalgia for, 409–11; reasons for countless
    revivals, xxix, 30–1, 410–11
Skaters, The, 346, 348
skiffle, 208–9
Skinner, Mike, 428
Skrewdriver, 166
Skydog label, 243
Slacker (movie), 347
Slade, 291
Slim, Fatboy, 360
Slow Listening Movement, 124–5
Small Faces, The, 186, 224, 228; *see also* The
    Faces
SmiLE, xi
Smiling Through My Teeth (compilation), 58
Smith, Fred 'Sonic', 252
Smith, Harry, 344
Smith, Mark E., 132, 146
Smith, Patti: Bangs on, 255; influence, xxi, 257,
    258, 276; overview, 250–4; and Sonic Youth,
    144, 146
Smith, Paul, 37–9
Smiths, The, xvi, xvii, 44–5, 132–3, 174; *see also*
    Morrissey
Smithson, Alison, 376
Smithson, Peter, 376
Sniffin' Glue (fanzine), 97
Soft Boys, The, 272
Soft Cell, 152, 222
Some Kind of Monster (Metallica), 30
Sonenberg, David, 295
Sonic Youth: and ATP, 32, 36, 144; cover ver-
    sions, 400; curatorial sensibility, 144–7;
    Daydream Nation performances, xvi–xvii,
    36–7; and tribute albums, 149; TV appear-
    ances, xxiii
Sonics, The, 300
Sontag, Susan, 285
Sorcerer's Apprentice, The (movie), 323
Sorted (club), 237
Soul Jazz label, 155–6
sound replacement, 315–16
space race, 383–92, 395
space rock, 390
Spacemen 3, 134–5, 136–8, 176
Sparks, xviii, 35
Specials, The, xx, 185
Spector, Phil, 257, 288, 294, 295
Speed, Glue & Shinki, 164
Spengler, Oswald, 170, 394
Springsteen, Bruce, 13, 34, 254, 401

Stalin, The, 165
Stanley, Bob, 138–9, 151, 158; *see also* Saint
    Etienne
Star Trek (movie), xv–xvi
Star Wars (movie series), 390
Starr, Karla, 121
Starr, Ringo, xiii, 118, 204; *see also* The Beatles
Stax, Mike, 261
Steele, Valerie, 190–1
Steely Dan, 372–3
Steinman, Jim, 295–6
Steinski, 360
Stephens, John, 186
Stereolab, 149–50, 344
Sterling, Bruce, 388–9, 397, 427
Sterne, Jonathan, 69, 70–1, 312
Stevens, Sufjan, xv
Stewart, Dave, xiii
Stewart, Susan, 90, 91
Steyerl, Hito, 412
Stiff Records label, 249–50
Still Ills, The, 44–5
Stills, Stephen, 7
Stockhausen, Karlheinz, 132, 378, 384–5, 386,
    389
Stone, Linda, 74
Stone Canyon Band, The, 286
Stone Roses, xvii, 178, 401
Stone Tape, The (TV series), 340
Stone's Throw label, 352
Stooges, The: future plans, 399; influence, 134,
    135, 138; mashed-up, 358; musical allusions,
    145; as punk precursors, 246, 276, 277; reun-
    ions, xiii; whole-album performances, xii, 35
Stranger Than Paradise (movie), 307–8
Stranglers, The, xvi, 6, 43, 410
Strasbaugh, John, 33
Stravinsky, Igor, 279
Straw, Will, 101–2, 104–5, 106
Stray Cats, The, 298, 300, 305, 306
Strokes, The, 171, 272, 358
Strummer, Joe, 29, 250, 304, 307; *see also* The
    Clash
Stuckism, 273–5
Studio G, 324–5
Style Council, The, 198
Subotnik, Morton, 383, 385
Sugababes, x, 359
Sui, Anna, xvii, 190
Suicide, 37, 134, 305–6, 399, 420
Sun Records label, 154
Sun Ra, 146, 352, 386
Sunsetcorp, 80
super-hybridity concept, 412–13, 415–16
Supremes, The, 198

Sutch, Lord, 352
Sutch, Screaming Lord, 290
Sweet Toronto (movie), 287
Sylvain, Syl, 42, 43; *see also* The New York Dolls
Sylvester, Nick, 424
Sympathy for the Record Industry label, 271
synthesizers, early, 378, 383–4

T-Rex, 291
T-shirts, vintage, 16–17
Taanila, Mike, 389–90
Taj Mahal Travellers, 164
Taking Woodstock (film), xxi
Talking Heads, 301, 414
Tamla Motown, 214, 218, 400, 418
Tangerine Dream, 390
tape trading, 232–3
Tate, Greg, 353–4
Tate museum, 38–9
Taylor, James, 7, 241, 296
Taylor, Joseph, 311–12
Taylor, Vince, 304
Teardrop Explodes, The, 141, 271; *see also* Cope,
    Julian
techno, 21, 199–200
technology: fascination with obsolete, 350–1;
    futurology, 362–8; recent technology's effect
    on music, 411–12, 426–7; *see also* recording
Teddy Boys, 243–5, 303
Teenage Fanclub, xx, xxxii–xxxiii
Teenage Jesus and the Jerks, 263, 301
television: influence on hauntologists, 339–41;
    retromania, xvi–xvii, 27–31; watching
    repeats, 57–8
Television, 251
Television Personalities, The, 271–2
Temperance Seven, The, 211
Temple, Julien, ix, 29, 399, 401
10cc, 174, 276
Tenney, James, 318
That'll Be the Day (movie), 276
Thatcher, Margaret, 273, 338
theatre revivals, xvi
Them, 252
This Mortal Coil, 135
Thom, Sandy, 410
Thompson, Richard, xxxiv
Thomson, Charles, 273–5
Thorley, David, 217–18
Thorne, Christian, 127–8
Throbbing Gristle, xi, 37, 38–9, 132, 401; *see also*
    P-Orridge, Genesis
Thunders, Johnny, 246; *see also* The New York
    Dolls
Timbaland, 179

Time Has Told Me (blog), 105–6
Times, The, 272
Times Square label, 153
Toerag studio, 272
Toffler, Alvin, 366
Tomita, 390
Tomorrow People, The (TV series), 326
Tomorrowland (Disneyland exhibition), 370–2
Too Fast to Live, Too Young to Die (boutique), 245, 276, 303
Toop, David, 368, 369
Top of the World (club), 222
Torch, the (club), 218, 222
torrents, 104
tours, nostalgia, 31–43
Townshend, Pete, 225, 255–6, 260; *see also* The Who
trad (trad jazz, revival jazz), 206–14
Travolta, John, 294
Tremé (drama series), 163
Trip to the Moon (movie), 385
Truffaut, François, 339
Trunk, Johnny, 325–7
Trunk Records, 325–7, 341
Tubby, King, 155
Tuff Darts, 305
Tupac, 320
Turner, J. M. W., 275
24 Hour Party People (movie), x, 399
Twiggy, 133
Twisted Wheel (club), 217, 222, 223
2 Many DJs, 358
2000s: music assessed, 404–28; rate of emergence of new genres, 407; parallels between music and financial world, 419–21; post-production concept, 416–24; the retro decade, ix–xi, xiv–xv, xix–xxi
2-Tone, 134, 173

U2, 136, 198
UbuWeb, 62
Ugly Things (fanzine), 261
UHCA label, 153–4
Underworld, 32
Union Pacific label, 296
Urge Overkill, 139
utopia and utopianism: and capitalism, 81; and modernism, 375; nostalgia for lost, 149–50, 262, 330, 338, 370; plenty leading to satedness, 127–8; the present as utopia, 368; and sharity, 109; technocratic, 338

V/Vm, 354–5
Valens, Ritchie, 160, 290
Vampire Weekend, 171, 413–15

Van Peebles, Melvin, 352
Van Sant, Gus, 53, 144
Vanguard label, 150
Varèse, Edgar, 376–8, 379, 385
Varvatos, John, 41
Vault, the, 11
Vega, Alan, 305–6; *see also* Suicide
Velvet Underground, The, 134, 136, 138, 272, 273
Vermorel, Fred, 99
Vermorel, Judy, 99
VH1, xiii, xix, 27, 399
Vibert, Luke (Wagon Christ), 325, 356–7, 358–9
Vibrators, 99
Vicious, Sid, 244, 246, 304; *see also* The Sex Pistols
Victoria and Albert Museum: *Cold War Modern: Design 1945–1970* exhibition, 375–7; fashion exhibitions, 183–5, 329
Vietnam War, 283
Vincent, Gene, 244, 287, 290, 304
Vines, The, xix, 272
Vogue Fashion Rocks supplement, xix
Vogueing, 176
Votel, Andy, 153
Voxx label, 261

Waco siege, 48
Wagner, Ty, & the Scotchmen, 266
Wagon Christ *see* Vibert, Luke
Waits, Tom, 34, 146
Walker, Scott, 137
Walley, Chris de, 260
Warhol, Andy, 133, 285
Warren, Tim, 264–7
Waterson, Norma, xxxiii
Watts-Russell, Ivo, 135
Wax Poetics (magazine), 352
We the People, 264
Wedding Present, The, xvi
Weller, Paul, xvi, 224–6
Wenner, Jann, 289
West, Kanye, 424
West Side Story (musical), 305
Westwood, Tim, 8
Westwood, Vivienne, 190, 191, 243–4, 245
Wet Wet Wet, 198
Wet Willie, 255
Wham!, 198
Whitaker, Forest, 394
White, Alan, 288
White, Jack, xxi, 272–3; *see also* The White Stripes
White Stripes, The, ix, 177, 178, 267, 272–3
Whitman, Keith Fullerton, 382
Who, The: cover versions, 250, 252; and the

Mod Revival, 224, 225, 228; *Quadrophenia* movie, 226; and tribute through desecration, 136; *see also* Townshend, Pete
Who Killed Bambi? (movie), 19
Who Put the Bomp! (magazine), 241–2, 261, 301
whole-album blogs, 104–11
whole-album performances, 34–6
Wicker Man, The (movie), 326
Wigan Casino, 221–2
Wild Ones, The (movie), 245
Wilde, Gary, 218
Wilde, Kim, ix
Wilde, Oscar, 132
Williams, Felton, 157
Williams, Hank, 136
Williams, Robbie, 140
Williamson, James, 399
Wilson, Brian, xi, 136, 278
Wilson, Daniel H., 363
Wilson, Tony, x
Winehouse, Amy, xix
Winner, Langdon, 255
Winstons, The, 323
Wire, xx, 37–8
Wisbey, 327
Wizzard, 291
Wolcott, James, 255–6
Wolf, Jamie, 191
Wolfe, Burton H., 230
Wolfe, Tom, 387, 388
Wolff, Christian, 149
Wolfgang's Vault, 11–12
Wolk, Douglas, 149
Womack, Bobby, 215

Wood, Roy, 291
Wooden Wand, xxxiv
World's Fairs: Brussels (1958), 376–8; Osaka (1970), 384–5
Wray, Link, 305
Wuorinen, Charles, 383
Wurtzel, Elizabeth, 101

Xenakis, Iannis, 376–8, 379
XTC, 260, 272
X, xx
xx, The, 178–9

Yaeger, Lynn, 190
Yardbirds, The, 133, 210
Yazoo label, 158, 159
Yellow Submarine (movie), xxii
Young, La Monte, 273
Young, Neil, xx–xxi, 149, 305, 366
Young, Paul, ix, 104
Young MC, 195
YouTube, 56–62, 63, 78–82, 84–5

Zander, Robin, 34
Zantees, The, 300, 301
Zappa, Frank, 279–80
Zermati, Marc, 243
Ziggy Stardust and the Spiders from Mars (documentary), 45–6
Zodiac Mindwarp, 139, 199
Zombies, The, 151
Zwigoff, Terry, 206
ZZ Top, 43